SHAKESPEARE AND HIS CONTEMPORARIES IN PERFORMANCE

*This volume is for Nige;
thank you my friend*

Shakespeare and his Contemporaries in Performance

Edited by **Edward J. Esche**

LONDON AND NEW YORK

First published 2000 by Ashgate Publishing

2 Park Square, Milton Park, Abingdon, Oxon OX14 4RN
711 Third Avenue, New York, NY 10017, USA

Routledge is an imprint of the Taylor & Francis Group, an informa business

First issued in paperback 2016

Copyright © Edward J. Esche, 2000

The editor has asserted his moral right under the Copyright, Designs and Patents Act, 1988, to be identified as the editor of this work.

All rights reserved. No part of this book may be reprinted or reproduced or utilised in any form or by any electronic, mechanical, or other means, now known or hereafter invented, including photocopying and recording, or in any information storage or retrieval system, without permission in writing from the publishers.

Notice:
Product or corporate names may be trademarks or registered trademarks, and are used only for identification and explanation without intent to infringe.

British Library Cataloguing-in-Publication Data
Shakespeare and his Contemporaries in Performance
  1.Shakespeare, William, 1564–1616 – Dramatic production – History and criticism 2.Theatre – England – History –16th century 3.English drama – Early modern and Elizabethan, 1500–1600
  I.Esche, Edward J.
  792.9'0941'09031

Library of Congress Control Number: 00-108814

ISBN 13: 978-0-7546-0046-6 (hbk)
ISBN 13: 978-1-138-26332-1 (pbk)

Contents

Illustrations	vii
Acknowledgements	viii
List of Contributors	ix
Editor's Preface	x
Edward J. Esche	
INTRODUCTION	1
Shakespeare and Cultural Tourism	3
Dennis Kennedy	
SHAKESPEARE ON FILM	21
1 The Recent Films	23
H.R. Coursen	
2 (En)Gendering Desire in Performance: *King Lear*, Akira Kurosawa's *Ran*, Tadashi Suzuki's *The Tale of Lear*	35
Yoko Takakuwa	
NINETEENTH- AND TWENTIETH-CENTURY CONTEXTS	51
3 Touring in Asia: The Miln Company's Shakespearean Productions in Japan	53
Kaori Kobayashi	
4 Interculturalism or Indigenization: Modes of Exchange, Shakespeare East and West	73
Poonam Trivedi	
5 Berlin–Zürich–Düsseldorf: Aspects of German Theatre During the Nazi Period and After	89
Wilhelm Hortmann	
6 Gentlemen You Are Welcome to Elsinore: *Hamlet* in Performance at Kronborg Castle, Elsinore	109
Niels B. Hansen	
7 Culture Clustering, Gender Crossing: *Hamlet* Meets Globalization in Robert Lepage's Elsinore	121
Nigel Wheale	
8 'The Homestead of History': Shakespearean Medievalism on the Mid-Victorian Stage	137
Richard W. Schoch	

RENAISSANCE CONTEXTS — 147

9 Falstaff's Page as Early Modern Youth at Risk — 149
   Mark H. Lawhorn

10 Fashion, Nation and Theatre in Late Sixteenth-Century London — 161
   Janette Dillon

11 The Italian Job: The Poetics of Graced Performance in the Commedia dell'Arte and in Jonson's Humour Plays — 177
   Rocco Coronato

12 The True Physiognomy of a Man: Richard Tarlton and His Legend — 191
   Peter Thomson

13 ''Tis a pageant / To keep us in false gaze': *Othello*, Virtual History and the Jacobean Audience's Turkish Expectations — 211
   Mark Hutchings

FROM TEXT TO PERFORMANCE — 239

14 Don Pedro, Don John and Don … who? – Noting a Stranger in *Much Adoodle-do* — 241
   Pamela Mason

15 'The Silent Griefs Which Cut the Heart Strings': John Ford's *The Broken Heart* in Performance — 261
   Kristin Crouch

16 Cunning with Pistols: Observations on Gale Edwards's 1996–7 RSC Production of John Webster's *The White Devil* — 275
   Nick Tippler

17 The Nineteenth-Century Productions of *A Yorkshire Tragedy* (1608) — 293
   Barry Gaines

18 *The Magnetick Lady*: Is the Unperformed Performable? — 305
   Peter Happé

FEMALE ROLES — 319

19 'A Woman's generall: what should we feare?': Queen Margaret Thatcherized in Recent Productions of *3 Henry VI* — 321
   Randall Martin

20 The Disappearing Queen: Looking for Isabel in *Henry V* — 339
   Diana E. Henderson

Index — 357

Illustrations

Chapter 6	Gentlemen You Are Welcome to Elsinore: *Hamlet* in Performance at Kronborg Castle, Elsinore *Niels B. Hansen*	
1	Kronborg, 1937 production, dir. Tyrone Guthrie, Laurence Olivier as Hamlet	118
2	Kronborg, 1939 production, dir. John Gielgud, John Gielgud as Hamlet	118
3	Kronborg, 1950 production, dir. Hugh Hunt, Michael Redgrave played Hamlet	119
4	Kronborg, 1954 production, dir. Michael Benthall, Richard Burton as Hamlet	119

Chapter 15	'The Silent Griefs Which Cut the Heart Strings': John Ford's *The Broken Heart* in Performance *Kristin Crouch*	
1	Perfect feast	272
2	Wasted table	272
3	Penthea in perfect stoic reserve	273
4	Emotional release allowed only in 'madness'	273
5	Orgilus and the veiled Penthea	274
6	Orgilus/Aplotes and the re-appearance of the veiled Penthea	274

Chapter 16	Cunning with Pistols: Observations on Gale Edwards's 1996–7 RSC Production of John Webster's *The White Devil* *Nick Tippler*	
1	*The Last Judgement*, Herman Tom Ring (1555)	289
2	Frontispiece from *Swetnam the Woman Hater*: the Red Bull Stage	289
3	Isabella: 'Henceforth I'll never lie with you, by this wedding ring' (2.1.254–5)	290
4	Vittoria's arraignment	291
5	Vittoria and Flamineo: 'Strike thunder, and strike loud to my farewell' (5.5.276)	291

Acknowledgements

Acknowledgements are due to the following: Johns Hopkins University Press for Dennis Kennedy's 'Shakespeare and Cultural Tourism'; *Shakespeare Bulletin* for a condensed version of H.R. Coursen's 'The Recent Films'; *Australian Drama Studies* for Kaori Kobayashi's 'Touring in Asia: The Miln Company's Shakespearean Productions in Japan'; Cambridge University Press for Wilhelm Hortmann's 'Berlin–Zürich–Düsseldorf: Aspects of German Theatre During the Nazi Period and After', parts of which appear in *Shakespeare on the German Stage: The Twentieth Century* (Cambridge, 1998); *Theatre Annual* for Richard W. Schoch's '"The Homestead of History": Medievalism on the Mid-Victorian Stage'; Cambridge University Press for Janette Dillon's 'Fashion, Nation and Theatre in Late Sixteenth-Century London', parts of which overlap with material printed in Chapters 3 and 4 *of Theatre, Court and City* (Cambridge, 1999); *Parergon* for Peter Thomson's 'The True Physiognomy of a Man: Richard Tarlton and His Legend'.

I personally owe the deepest debts of gratitude to all of the contributors for their initial work to make the conference such a success and for their patience during a long editing process. I must thank my employer Anglia Polytechnic University, and particularly the Department of English for support in terms of time, money and encouragement. Thanks also to Chris Coward and Carol Everett for their help with initial computing problems, and to Avalon Associates of Chelmsford for final checking, formatting and preparation of camera-ready copy. My family, as always, had to put up with the loss of shared time, and so my apologies to Rosalind, Ben and, especially, Nick.

List of Contributors

Rocco Coronato, University of Florence
H.R. Coursen, University of Maine (Augusta)
Kristin Crouch, University of Glasgow
Janette Dillon, University of Nottingham
Edward J. Esche, Anglia Polytechnic University
Barry Gaines, University of New Mexico
Niels B. Hansen, University of Copenhagen
Peter Happé, University of Southampton
Diana E. Henderson, Massachusetts Institute of Technology
Wilhelm Hortmann, University of Duisburg
Mark Hutchings, King's College, Aberdeen
Dennis Kennedy, Samuel Beckett Centre, Trinity College
Kaori Kobayashi, University of Warwick
Mark H. Lawhorn, University of Hawaii at Manoa
Pamela Mason, The Shakespeare Institute, University of Birmingham
Randall Martin, University of New Brunswick
Richard W. Schoch, Queen Mary and Westfield College
Yoko Takakuwa, Chuo University, Tokyo
Peter Thomson, University of Exeter
Nick Tippler, Anglia Polytechnic University
Poonam Trivedi, University of New Delhi
Nigel Wheale, Anglia Polytechnic University

Editor's Preface

Edward J. Esche

This volume presents a selection of papers from 'Scæna: Shakespeare and His Contemporaries in Performance', an International Conference held at St John's College, Cambridge in August of 1997. The aim of the conference was to bring together English Renaissance drama scholars for the discussion, exploration and practice of performance criticism, and to address Shakespeare within the context of his fellow dramatists. The degree to which we achieved our aim is for others to judge, but we certainly received a wide range of contributions from leading scholars and postgraduate students in the field. Dennis Kennedy presented the keynote address, which we print here as our Introduction, a perfectly judged thought-provoking paper that places the new Globe Theatre in the context of Shakespearean cultural tourism. Although the growing study of Shakespeare in the cinema is mentioned throughout, two scholars address the area directly: H.R. Coursen offers a highly personal view of recent films and Yoko Takakuwa discusses three distinct versions of the Lear story (Shakespeare's original and two Japanese adaptations) from the point of view of gendered subjectivity in performance.

The next section addresses the stage history of Shakespeare's plays, particularly during the nineteenth and twentieth centuries. Here Kaori Kobayashi traces the influence of the Miln Company's Shakespearean productions on Japanese intellectuals, and in particular on Shoyo Tsubouchi. Poonam Trivedi discusses Shakespeare in India, where performances indigenized the playwright; she focuses on two specific productions: *Barnum Vana* (*Macbeth*) 1979 and *Othello* in Kathakali (1996). Wilhelm Hortmann offers a necessarily limited study in the very wide field of German theatre during the Nazi period by concentrating on three areas: 'Theaterstadt Berlin', the 'Zürcher Schauspielhaus' and 'Die Stunde Null'. Niels B. Hansen discusses four English versions of *Hamlet* performed in the grounds of Kronborg Castle, Elsinore between 1937 and 1954. Nigel Wheale writes a searching analysis of Robert Lepage's *Elsinore*, one of the most creative and challenging adaptations of *Hamlet* to date. Richard W. Schoch discusses Charles Kean's productions, particularly *Richard II*, as a socially inclusive articulation of mid-Victorian English national identity.

The next section addresses Renaissance contexts, and here the contributors look at not only Shakespeare, but at his contemporaries as well. Mark H. Lawhorn is clearly aware of children on stage as he examines Falstaff's page through a close reading of *1 Henry IV*, *2 Henry IV* and *Henry V* in the light of sixteenth-century poor laws and vagrancy. Janette Dillon observes that the War of the Theatre plays 'manifest an obsessive interest in linguistic decorums, fashions and excesses' and uses the notions of the *flâneur* to reclaim performability for plays usually considered to be unperformable. She also brilliantly discusses how the theatre itself colludes with its market and adapts its forms to re-validate itself. Rocco Coronato focuses on the Commedia dell'Arte and its influence upon Ben Jonson's ridicule of acting styles in *Every Man in His Humour* and *Every Man Out of His Humour*. Peter Thomson is the only contributor to consider one of Shakespeare's contemporary actors, Richard Tarlton, who was the ancestor of both the Shakespearean clown and the Shakespearean fool. Thomson discusses the Tarlton's 'career', his special relationship with his audience, and very interestingly, his 'jiz'. Mark Hutchings ends this section with an essay that places *Othello* within the historical relationship between Elizabeth's Turkish policy and 'England's apprehension of Catholic Europe in general and Spain in particular'.

The contributors to the next section deal with performance as text that moves directly from the page to the stage. Pamela Mason examines the editorial history of *Much Ado About Nothing* and produces fresh interpretations of masculine behaviour, in part by re-examining the original text and questioning the given editorial tradition. Kristin Crouch offers a reading of a recent production of John Ford's *The Broken Heart* and Nick Tippler does the same for John Webster's *The White Devil*; both supply very helpful photographic materials. Barry Gaines rediscovers the nineteenth-century stage history of *A Yorkshire Tragedy* by reclaiming the records of two performances, one in Boston, Massachusetts, United States of America and one in St Petersburg, Russia. Peter Happé makes a compelling case for the performability of Jonson's *The Magnetic Lady*, a play that he sees as at the heart of Jonson's poetic art. It is worth mentioning in passing that the performance study in the majority of this section, that is, of Renaissance playwrights other than Shakespeare, is a high priority for Scæna, because it directly addresses one of our aims – to help to provide materials that might allow Shakespeare to be considered within a context of Renaissance drama and dramatists. This is an area of study that we hope to enlarge in future conferences. The final section of the volume addresses female roles in Shakespeare and contains two of the most accomplished essays in the collection. Randall Martin closely analyses performance cuts in Queen Margaret's role in four recent productions of *3 Henry VI* to argue persuasively that each is, in his finely coined phrase, 'underachieved Shakespeare'. Diana Henderson looks for Isabel in *Henry V* and, after considering the historical Isabeau, notes that Shakespeare's character is a domesticated version of her original, but that she can be read in two ways: either as a threatening woman or as a tamed version of women's place in history.

These then are the essays on offer. They demonstrate the variability and academic rigour of performance criticism as well as the interest that is worldwide, an interest that we know will continue at the next Scæna conference scheduled for the summer of 2001, again at St John's College, Cambridge.

INTRODUCTION

Shakespeare and Cultural Tourism

Dennis Kennedy

Festive Stages

Tourism, the world's largest industry, despite derision and sleaze, is ever more important in global cultural life. All of us are tourists now and then, reluctantly or eagerly visiting the exotic, consuming the foreign, watching the great universal show. The past is particularly important for tourism: jet travel since about 1960 has become a form of time travel, allowing us glimpses of lost worlds, making us into historians of heritage and connoisseurs of the alien. Though tourists buy physical objects like souvenirs and clothing and great quantities of food and drink, as they once converted wild beasts into travel trophies, what they are actually after is immaterial. Tourists are modernity's paradoxical consumers who seek not merchandise but experience; the attractions of the world draw them with promises of sensation or renewal, inspiration or plain diversion. Experience is hard to commodify. Visits can be structured as in safaris and cruises, but the touristic site is only the occasion for the adventure: seeing the Acropolis, touching its stones, is ultimately a prompt for an event that occurs in the mind of the visitor, as the meaning of a performance occurs in the mind of spectator.

This is why, as sociologist Erik Cohen notes, 'tourism is a fuzzy concept'; his best definition emphasizes that tourists are people who travel 'in the expectation of pleasure from the novelty and change experienced' while away from the everyday rule of their lives.[1] Touristic experience takes many forms, from the purely spectatorial or voyeuristic to hard work like shovelling manure on a dude ranch, but is usually characterized by its extraordinary dimension, temporal limitation and the absence of responsibility – in other words, by the carnivalesque. To be a tourist is above all to be a willing stranger. It's an alienation we rush after. The World Tourist Organization calculates that between 1950 and 1990 tourist arrivals rose from 25 million to 456 million per annum, an eighteen-fold increase, and the number is expected to double again by the year 2010 to 937 million arrivals[2] – about one-sixth of the world's population touring every year.

Cultural tourism, a form of recreation in which travellers spend significant leisure time and money on cultural activity, became important in modern Europe with the rise of the Grand Tour at the end of the seventeenth century.[3] Despite its widening to the bourgeoisie in the nineteenth, the Grand Tour was the property of an elite, like most high culture. A few astute entrepreneurs conceived dramatic festivals with high art appeal that demanded travel, as the master showman Max Reinhardt did with the Salzburg Festival in 1917. The model for modern cultural festivals was established as early as 1876 in a small town in Bavaria by the great tourist agent Richard Wagner, who with the help of the king of that small state created the Bayreuth Festspeilhaus as the first theatre in the world dedicated to the work of a single artist, who happened to be himself, and invited us to drop in for a visit. Like the restored Olympics at the turn of the century, the arts festivals laid claim to a connection with the quasi-religious festivals of ancient Greece, which for the theatre were idealized as arenas of political, social and spiritual integration. Two issues were crucial. First, performances in twentieth-century festivals tended to be placed in unusually designed or round spaces modelled on the circle that encouraged a sense of togetherness among spectators. Many modernist theatre directors believed that a renovated approach to performance could be achieved by returning to the ancient festival ideal of an enveloping audience, and Shakespeare was central to this movement from Jocza Savits in Munich to William Poel and Granville Barker in London to Tyrone Guthrie in Ontario.

Second, the location of the festivals and their calendar limitations meant that a large portion of the audiences had to travel to reach them, encouraging a sense of pilgrimage to a sacred locale. This had been true at Bayreuth since its founding, but the great expansion of arts festivals did not occur until after the Second World War. In a Europe absorbed with social and material reconstruction, the postwar festivals often identified spiritual recovery as essential to their foundation and demanded pilgrimage as a necessary part of the experience. The first examples, the Edinburgh International Festival and the Avignon Festival, set out in the summer of 1947 to revive a fading European memory and used Shakespeare to return to the cultural high ground; remarkably both festivals started with productions of *Richard II*.[4] Especially in Avignon, where the performance took place outdoors in the courtyard of the fourteenth-century Papal Palace, a building dating from the same era as the historical Richard, the attempt to connect with a recovered past was unmistakable. Festival Shakespeare productions followed in the late forties and early fifties among antique ruins or in remodelled Roman theatres across Europe, and all presented themselves as worthwhile arenas for summer holiday travellers.

The major English-speaking Shakespeare festivals fit the same pattern. The town of Stratford had been dependent on pilgrims since Garrick's Jubilee in 1769, though the Shakespeare Memorial Theatre (SMT), built about a century later, just three years after Wagner's theatre, had an early life that was notably banal. When William Bridges-Adams arrived in 1919 as its first permanent director, he realized quickly that the self-satisfied local attitude had to change; 'my choice lay, so to speak', he wrote, 'between Ye Olde Oake Shakespeare Bunne Shoppe and Bayreuth'.[5] Despite his innovations, the SMT lapsed back into a comfortable provincialism and no lasting changes occurred until that pivotal year of 1947, again in a postwar spirit of recovery, when Barry Jackson, Peter Brook and Paul Scofield arrived to make new claims for Shakespeare's postwar centrality, a notion developed in the following two decades by Anthony Quayle and Peter Hall. Stratford grew enormously in cultural importance in the 1960s because of the founding of the Royal Shakespeare Company (RSC), but the town, difficult to reach by rail, could not have supported the greatly expanded seasons of the RSC without the growth in private car ownership and in coach tours from London. Between 1965 and 1985 passenger mileage in Britain grew by 60 per cent.[6]

Similar points can be made about the Festival of Britain in 1951, Guthrie's Stratford Shakespearian Festival in 1953 in Ontario, and the stages constructed under Guthrie's influence in the 1960s from Los Angeles to Sheffield.[7] The New York Shakespeare Festival, established in 1954, and the one in Stratford, Connecticut, that opened the next year, were followed by a number of festivals in North America that yoked Shakespeare with touristic affairs. Indeed the theatres in San Diego and Ashland, Oregon, were built in 1935 as tourist sites, well before Guthrie had begun to think about the open stage. In their buildings these festivals invoked some form of Elizabethanism and clearly marked themselves as separate from the regular commercial theatre by virtue of their locations, their financing, and their repertory.

The Shakespeare of the postwar festivals was a modernist Shakespeare. While it's impossible to define what that means precisely, in general terms the festivals saw Shakespeare as an acknowledged universal monument and attempted in production to realize his greatness. As the restored Olympics appealed to the transcendent spirituality of sport, so the festivals continued Enlightenment claims for the transcendence of high art: Shakespeare as inspiration, as political or moral force and – particularly in Britain and North America – as public heritage. Class was a central issue at many of the venues, usually in a progressive way; Shakespeare festivals wished to widen their spectator base for both political and practical reasons. The most interesting case is that of the RSC under Peter Hall and

Trevor Nunn in the period from 1962 to 1975 or so, when leftist leanings propelled the company to widen its audience to students and the regions of Britain to the north of Stratford. Low-cost student tickets, group rates for schools, adult education endeavours, widespread touring, more contemporary styles like David Warner's déclassé Hamlet, a broadening of the repertory to include new plays and the creation of a permanent RSC venue in London:[8] most of these would now be called 'outreach' programmes meant to democratize the theatre. While some of them, especially those connected to education, eventually played into the hands of the Thatcherite heritage mongers of the 1980s, they initially succeeded in raising the cultural capital of people traditionally indifferent to Shakespeare and the theatre.

But attendance at the flagship house in Stratford still depended upon excursion; the barriers presented by the cost of the tickets, travel, meals and accommodation remained, as well as the unchanged notion in working-class culture that Shakespeare is high-falutin' and boring. The apparent democratization of Shakespeare performance in the first fifteen years of the RSC, whatever widening of the British audience pool it may have achieved, did so by the usual method in the capitalist West, by *embourgeoisement*. In this process the 'new intellectuals', as Pierre Bourdieu calls them, moved up to become the new petite bourgeoisie.[9] Much more significant than any enlargement of the class base was the growth in audiences to Stratford brought by international travel.

History as Theme Park

Richard Sennett holds that in the nineteenth century the nature of human exchange in expanding urban environments was significantly altered: no longer a verbally-charged space of interaction between citizens, the members of the industrialized population became spectacle for one another. The individual, superseding the social group as the centre of human agency, 'fell silent in the city', he writes. 'The street, the café, the department store, the railroad, bus, and underground became places of gaze rather than scenes of discourse'; in the pub or café, a patron could construct the passing crowd into 'a theatre of one's private thoughts'. In a similar vein Robert Hughes notes that rapid train travel made for its riders a new theatre out of the passing landscape, and that the Eiffel Tower created a theatre out of the city. When that monument to industry opened in 1889 almost one million people took its lifts to see the view from the top; for the first time Paris became 'a map of itself'.[10]

Modernity and tourism are intertwined: as the technology of travel increased so more and more of the world became objectified as sights to wonder over or visit for private refreshment. A vast increase in domestic and international tourism occurred after 1960, fostered by paid holidays for workers, a more or less continuously expanding economy and the ease of jet transport. Postmodernity has continued the trend with a vengeance; in keeping with economic globalization, an all-embracing tourism shapes much of social circulation. James Clifford's recent book *Routes* argues that travel and the state of being between cultures most characterized the late twentieth century and its anthropological study.[11] Concomitant with the expansion of tourism has been a substantial elevation of history and heritage. There is considerable controversy surrounding this movement, especially in Britain, with the opponents effectively divided into socialist and conservative views of the past. The end of history has prompted a greater concern for history; *post-histoire* we are all the more obsessed with it. Conservation, as Raphael Samuel wrote a few years before he died, 'whatever the doubts about the notion of "heritage", is one of the major aesthetic and social movements of our time'. If tourism can make the voyager into a minor historian, the expansion of the matter suitable for writing history consistently creates new sites for touristic display. We live, Samuel noted, 'in an expanding historical culture, in which the work of inquiry and retrieval is being progressively extended in all kinds of spheres that would have been thought unworthy of notice in the past'.[12]

But one might take a gloomier approach to the growth market in history. Robert Hewison's *The Heritage Industry* saw the movement as a sign of Britain's decline under Thatcherite policies: 'instead of manufacturing goods, we are manufacturing *heritage*, a commodity which nobody seems able to define, but which everybody is eager to sell'. Industrial age museums, themed historical parks, local history centres, the list goes on. In England alone more than a thousand new sightseeing attractions of various types have opened since 1979, one-third of all those in existence, and Hewison notes that in the mid-1980s in Britain new museums opened at the rate of about one a day.[13] Jean Baudrillard ascribes apocalyptic overtones to this drift in international cultural affairs. We are eminently busy, he says,

> reviewing everything, rewriting everything, restoring everything, face-lifting everything, to produce, as it seems, in a burst of paranoia a perfect set of accounts at the end of the century ... Museums, jubilees, festivals, complete works, the publication of the tiniest of unpublished fragments – all this shows we are entering an active age of *ressentiment* and repentance.[14]

It's easy to apply Baudrillard's notion to both popular and high culture, especially as the traditional distinctions between them continue to break down. Retro-fashion, cannibalizing itself with ever greater frequency; the intercultural culinary fads of the West, exploring Third World diets for new sensations and the healthy-chic; intercultural art forms, pillaging the cultural storehouses of Asia and Africa; Hollywood movies of classic novels and remakes of classic films; the so-called defeat of Communism, reprising in new areas the consumerist victories of a plutocratic planet; and of course historical and heritage theme parks: these tendencies at the turn of the millennium create what looks like a world made out of a recycled objects and ideas, an impotent present, a mannerist savouring of residues. The past becomes a universal Disneyland.

But Disneyland is not just a convenient scapegoat; whether you like it or not, Disneyland is the most logical model of how to present a culture of pastness in a global economy. Despite their extreme merchandising of culture, theme parks are popularly successful because they provide an accessible and diverting thoroughfare to an imagined history or mythical world. Like outdoor heritage museums, they are 'exercises in nostalgia, presenting a sanitised view of culture',[15] but a view that clearly appeals to huge numbers of tourists having fun with commodity experience.

And what about the complexities of art? Many people assume that high art activities, visits to the National Gallery or to Shakespeare plays, are more virtuous, yet corporations have also learned how to respond to the growing market in cultural leisure. The Disney Institute in Orlando hosts conferences in any field and holiday-makers who want to use their time profitably can enrol in a range of classes from cooking to film-making. Visits from celebrities add lustre – including actors from the Royal Shakespeare Company. Disney executives call this 'edutainment' and also have a scientific word for the study of consumer behaviour in theme parks: 'guestology'.[16] It's hard to avoid an ironic tone when pronouncing these terms, but I hasten to point out that they are simply reception theory gone retail.

You might want to escape commercialized environments on your holiday, and you might want me to distinguish between, say, Shakespeare as art and the commodity art in Orlando, but anything can be merchandised if there is a market for it and, as Robert van Kemper has said, 'everything is a potential heritage experience'.[17] It's harder and harder to find an unmediated other, genuine or not. So where can we turn to recover the excitement of the alien? Some look for UFOs and a sci-fi future. More solidly, and more commercially feasible, we turn to the past which always remains unapproachable but which tempts us with the illusion of the knowable. In a world of simulations we seek certified sites, verified objects, confirmed auras: this is Bach's clavier, this is Marlowe's grave, this Agamemnon's bath. In the depths of a sceptical age we long for the absolute, historic, recorded, veritable thing.

In a search for the unfeigned object on your travels you might wish to peer at the distant past and visit the caves at Lascaux to see with your own eyes some of the oldest records of human culture. Sorry, you can't visit the caves at Lascaux, since they were closed in 1963 to prevent further deterioration of the wall paintings. Instead you will enter an enormous concrete bunker built twenty years later that copies in concrete every natural detail of the cave walls; a guidebook says, 'on this background painters have reproduced the figures and symbols as exactly as possible, using the same materials as the Magdalenians'. The replica 'gives visitors more detailed information and is more accessible than anything they could have gleaned by visiting the real cave at Lascaux'.[18] The copy, in other words, is better than the original. The original, under lock and key, will decay and disappear, but the copy is a preservationist paradise.

Exit this way, please, through the gift shop.

Authentic Me

Shakespeare is many things in contemporary culture. He lives on splendidly in a number of contested sites, and even a few remaining uncontested ones. But whatever he is – even if he is the seventeenth Earl of Oxford – there can be no doubt that he is star-quality edutainment. And in the edutainment trade, the International Shakespeare Globe Centre is the most obvious example of commodified heritage, predicated upon concepts of cultural tourism analogous to those of the Lascaux copy or Disney World. There has been considerable disagreement about the value and purpose of the new Globe, centred mostly on the authenticity of the structure or of the playing. I propose a different set of concerns based on the nature of the spectator's experience. Whether audience at a performance or general sojourners to the Globe site, spectators are consumers of cultural product, visitors to another realm. At the Globe they will define that realm in various ways – as art, heritage, history, education, recreation, amusement, frolic – but whatever meanings they ascribe, these visitors are in the most straightforward sense cultural tourists.

Theatre historians and theorists have not paid much attention to this side of the spectator's condition, but a number of sociologists and social anthropologists have. We can begin with Dean MacCannell's foundational book from 1976 called *The Tourist: A New Theory of the Leisure Class*. MacCannell asserts that tourism is a search for the 'absolute other';

recreational travel is prompted by a desire to experience that which is not us. But the starting point for modernity is the alienation of the individual; lacking a sense of wholeness in their own lives, tourists therefore seek to find it in a primitive or pristine or at least alternative elsewhere. But the elsewhere, MacCannell asserts, is most likely a perversion of the real, relying upon 'staged authenticity'.[19] His term is useful to describe much of what goes on in the excursionary domain, from backstage tours of restaurant kitchens to reconstructions of Civil War battles, and should help us to get beyond a difficulty which has plagued discourse about the Globe project, the ontological mousetrap of material authenticity. Is the oak joining accurate to Elizabethan methods, is the plaster made from the correct hair and lime, should the diameter of the walls be 80 or 100 feet?: these questions, no matter how vexed or interesting to specialists, become much less significant when we focus on the spectators rather than the builders. Since the basis of the new Globe is a form of staged authenticity, it really wouldn't matter if the structure were a Tudor prefab manufactured in California. That's an exaggeration, but it wouldn't matter as much as the Globe Centre seems to think now; in 1973 Sam Wanamaker's goal was to build a modern design that contained only the external features of the original.[20]

But MacCannell's hypothesis that all tourists are in search of an authentic other is troubling, since he does not sufficiently investigate what authenticity means. Especially challenging are the numerous cases like the Disneylands where 'blatantly inauthentic attractions do, in fact, attract many tourists'.[21] Even with a genuine site the tourist tends to engage in a complex semiotic, seeing not the authenticity but rather the site as signifier. Whatever its interest or distinction as a building Westminster Abbey fascinates not in itself but because it points to a sedimented history and culture, a connected otherness. Following this line of thinking, some more recent sociological studies, taking a post-structuralist view of tourism, have been critical of MacCannell's assumptions. Drawing on Lionel Trilling and Peter Berger, the Israeli sociologist Erik Cohen is particularly helpful when he suggests that authenticity is not a fixed state but 'a socially constructed concept' whose significance is not given; 'the manner of the negotiation of its meaning', Cohen says, should become 'a major topic in the sociological and anthropological study of tourism'.[22]

If authenticity is not fixed, commodification does not in itself destroy the meaning of cultural products or represent fraud; in fact authenticity may gradually emerge, even in situations that are eminently counterfeit. We can witness the shifting ground of authentication in how the Disneylands, 'once seen as the supreme example of contrived popular entertainment, became over time a vital component of contemporary

American culture'. They will in the future likely 'be perceived even by historians and ethnographers as an "authentic" American tradition'.[23] The bogus nature of much tourist activity, therefore, need not destroy the pleasure of leisure travel. Maxine Feifer goes so far as to call some contemporary visitors 'post-tourists': people who revel in the inauthenticity of routine excursionary activities, taking fun in touristic games.[24]

The movement to recreate the Elizabethan stage is an exercise in nostalgia operating as an 'invented tradition', to use the term of Eric Hobsbawm.[25] It has historical justification, of course, and valuable discoveries in the performance of Shakespeare and other early modern dramatists have been made through its influence. But philosophically speaking Elizabethanism has always solicited a set of material and performative circumstances that are unverifiable. The new Globe is Sam Wanamaker's dream but more importantly it is William Poel's dream, a Victorian progressive dream of reaching through wood and plaster to the land of the dead. In this appeal the Globe seeks to become a touristic obligation, a must-see, based on a promoted connection to a constant called Shakespeare. And it has achieved that status as witnessed by the crowds since its opening. In December 1996 'an organisation of travel journalists voted it the top tourist attraction in Europe',[26] and its 1999 season operated at a profit without public subsidy. If it is willy-nilly in the edutainment business, what is its guestology?

Playing Bacon

Whether or not you accept the analogy with Disneyland, it's undeniable that the Globe is a created heritage structure. Achieving sanctified status for an invented sight is a tricky matter: the producers must first convince the public of its value and then guide them through markers that signal its distinctiveness. Since it is not the original like the Shakespeare Birthplace, nor located next to the surviving original like the Lascaux simulation, nor even built afresh on the very spot of the original like the new wooden horse in the ruins of Troy, the makers of the Globe have assumed that its credibility is tied to accuracy of construction. The Globe cannot just 'be' like Chartres Cathedral or the Tower of London, since its meaning is bound up with a recalled past (a historiography), is hidden in the work of reconstruction, and ultimately a matter for mediation in performance. The Tower of London is also a heavily mediated touristic site, but its Norman stones are incontestable – at least some of them are – whereas the Globe can mean only through the intervention of its managers.

Thus the worry that the Globe might be just another theme park has infected it from the start. When Wanamaker announced the project in 1973, his goals were carefully worded so that the first priority was 'to reclaim Southwark's Thames bank' and then to redevelop the area for 'culture, education and entertainment'. Rebuilding the Globe was ranked third on his list.[27] No doubt he intended these social and civic concerns to give the scheme gravitas; in reality they brought him even closer to Walt Disney, who also saw his parks as models for urban planning and even as experiments for the future, like the EPCOT Center in Orlando – EPCOT stands for 'Experimental Prototype Community of Tomorrow'.[28] They also set Wanamaker on a long and expensive legal battle with Southwark Council that, despite his own leftist credentials, put him in bed with entrepreneurial property developers.

The Bankside anxiety over the serious and civic purpose of the Globe has not gone away. At the time of the prologue season in summer 1996 London newspapers carried a flurry of articles emphasizing that the Globe is not a Disneyland, that its Artistic Director, the actor Mark Rylance, is a serious artist and will not let it become one, that 35,000 people have enrolled in various classes and workshops through the education department. Meanwhile Michael Holden, the Executive Director of the Globe Centre, emphasized that a certain level of seriousness was required on the part of spectators as well: 'if anyone turns up in Elizabethan costume – as they have done in our workshop programme – we eject them from the premises'. The Globe wants to engage with Renaissance drama, he said, 'in the present tense, on stage and off'.[29] This seems a contradiction to the building, which itself is in fancy dress, and I wonder why spectators shouldn't be allowed to play the same game, but the real point here is the continued concern that the Globe will be seen as a tourist trap.

Perhaps the solution to this problem can be found in another commentator on tourism, who has remarked that 'any authenticity claimed for a heritage structure' is a social construction of its creators 'rather than the intrinsic property of the object'.[30] Thus the crucial issue for the visitor, to return to Cohen's phrase, is not the structure itself but 'the manner of the negotiation of its meaning'. If true for a legitimate heritage structure, how much more true must it be for an invented one. The energies that have gone into the Globe – not to mention most of the money – have been centred on the integrity of the edifice. But despite the delays, controversies and historical research, in the most important sense the building was the easy part. How the visitors to the site and the spectators at performances will relate to the enterprise, how its meaning will be negotiated, is much more difficult and problematic.

In this sense Wanamaker was a structuralist like Dean MacCannell: he believed that an appropriate way of playing Shakespeare is inscribed in the texts, and that an authentic building with no scenery would create an environment for studying these methods. Under the pressure of finance and the need for immediate success, however, there has been something of a rupture with the founder's ideas and the meaning of the enterprise is not fully negotiated with its spectators. While the new director believes that Shakespeare's work is mystical and magical, and the task of his enterprise is still to rediscover authentic performance modes, on stage he has attempted few experiments with recovery. Some of those he has tried have been eccentric to say the least, like using reconstructed Elizabethan undergarments in the 1997 *Henry V*, or playing Cleopatra himself in 1999 on the foot of a theory that Shakespeare may have used mature men for older female roles. Even the Elizabethanist productions have relied on modernist concepts of performance that can be seen in any number of Shakespeare productions elsewhere, and have used styles of acting, gesture and body posture notably contemporary in manner.

Andrew Gurr, the leading historian of Elizabethan theatre design, has been for some years the chief advisor to the Globe on architectural matters. Despite the rigours of Gurr's scholarship, Rylance's general approach seems heavily influenced by postmodern eclecticism and contingency. The Globe, for example, is marketing itself based on a playful attitude to its own postulates: in 1996 Rylance undertook a press campaign inviting spectators to throw tomatoes at the actors if they did not like the performance. Thoroughly ahistorical (there were no tomatoes in sixteenth-century England) the solicitation stands as an epitome of the Globe's frisky notions of its purpose. A few years ago the Victoria and Albert Museum authorized an unusual poster: 'ACE CAFF / Quite a nice museum attached'. Like the deliberate irony of that poster, the Globe appeals simultaneously to heritage chic and the bistro trade. The chief production in 1996, *The Two Gentlemen of Verona*, was not chosen for historic reasons – it was not written for the original Globe Theatre and was never performed there – but 'because Rylance's wife dreamed about it'. And most astoundingly for the director of an enterprise named for Shakespeare, Rylance thinks Shakespeare did not write the plays. His choice is Francis Bacon.[31]

Global Capitalism, at Last

Most of these objections are not very important and the Globe will no doubt find a surer path in the future through experience. It is eminently clear already that spectators are going to take charge in a way they cannot or by convention do not in more regular theatres. The open enjoyment the groundlings take might parallel that of their Elizabethan predecessors, but surely no one can argue for long that the detailed and precise architecture of the building has much to do with it. The standees are having fun in the way they are accustomed to have fun at a football match or a rock concert or a panto, talking, drinking, eating, wandering around, shouting back at the actors. They laugh in the 'wrong' places in *The Maid's Tragedy*, or so the review in the *TLS* insists.[32] They regularly hiss the villain without apparent prompting. In 1997 the villains were the French in *Henry V* and the hisses began on their every entrance, while in 1996 the fact that one villain was Mark Rylance made the game all the more enjoyable. Queuing for tickets as at a cinema and paying cinema prices, standing close to the actors under the sky, subject to the vagaries of sunlight and weather, watching an informal performance mode and encouraged to throw vegetables: the effect of the mix breaks down the rigid and solemn attitude that plagues so much Shakespeare performance.

But spectators can have many of these things without a £30 million reconstruction. People are visiting the Globe in great numbers because it is more than a revived Elizabethan venue for Shakespeare. It has museum displays, gives tours, is interesting, diverting, educational, artistic, looks authentic, has a restaurant and a great view, is close to the site of the original Globe, and allows a certain amount of spectator play. Like the postmodern or interactive museum, it invites an audience to join in the fun and gives them tales to tell about the experience when they get home.

Nonetheless the visitor is in a curious social position. The historical reference of the building and its project of producing Shakespeare suggest a high art appeal with all the attendant class implications. The issues of material and performative authenticity underline that status. Yet in the Globe's institutional practice, history, Shakespeare and authenticity are wrapped up in a user-friendly, consumerist package that implies the abolition of class. Different types of touristic activity vary considerably in the amount of cultural capital they require; the romantic gaze upon a historical and authentic site like Stonehenge demands much more legitimate knowledge than the collective gaze upon a modern and inauthentic site like Disneyland.[33] Ancient sites are mediated through intellectual effort and imply that the visitor is obligated; theme parks build in whatever is needed and construct the visitor as already knowing. Even carefully manufactured historical parks like Plimouth Plantation in Massachusetts and Williamsburg in Virginia operate by subversion of knowledge, undermining or evading the large cultural capital that a historical site would otherwise require.

The Globe's exceptional nature is apparent here. Do the performances imply a prior knowledge, an educated eye and mind, as Shakespeare and his contemporaries traditionally do? Yes and no. The Globe is both historical and modern: it looks like a late-Elizabethan structure; yet we know from the start that it's a copy from the late age of second Elizabeth. It is both authentic and inauthentic: it is carefully built using reconstructed Tudor oak carpentry and hair-and-lime plaster; yet it is as counterfeit and synthetic as any theme park.

And it's part of a rapidly developing tourist district. Restaurants and small businesses are moving in, an Underground station is planned on the Jubilee Line extension, the walkway along the river is filled with life. The new Tate Gallery in Bankside Power Station is expected to bring three million people a year to the area, the Globe a half-million more.[34] After a quarter century of Wanamaker's struggle to create the thing, a struggle that recapitulates the plucky postwar festival spirit and that more than once seemed lost for reasons of finance or politics, a great irony has become part of its fruition. The Globe is gloriously successful because it has become the very thing Wanamaker said it was not. Though it arose through his modernist pledge to transmit humanist values, it can operate only inside a touristic postmodernity. It is not alone among Shakespeare producers in this. A strong case can be made that the RSC moved out of the modernist mode about the time that Adrian Noble took charge, and that Stratford in Ontario did the same when Richard Monette became its director, in both cases driven less by the leader than by market forces. Neither of those companies has been very good at pomo Shakespeare, partly because they continue to maintain a modernist credo while regularly violating it in practice. The Globe operates in another mode: by default, its lack of artistic policy is its policy.

Many visitors to the Globe, I suspect, are recreational tourists, perfectly aware that the enterprise is not strictly genuine but willing to comport themselves as if it were. They might well exercise a playful attitude to the building, closely allied to that of a theatre audience who are willing to give a part of themselves up to the performance. Since they will in many cases be playful theatre spectators as well as playful tourists, their interest in the project should increase. Like most contemporary cultural product, theatre in the West is more and more subject to the conditions of trade. This is in key with one of the chief characteristics of post-Fordist or service-based capitalism, a commodification of almost all aspects of life, including charity.[35] Like the Olympics, which have been transformed from a nationalist celebration of amateurism into a globalized commodification of body spectacle, theatres in the West have more or less abandoned the modernist testament. The heavily packaged megamusicals produced by

Cameron Macintosh or Garth Drabinsky, which are cloned around the world in search of new audiences, demonstrate how live performance can be McDonaldized.

'Shakespeare rocks', proclaimed the cover of *Newsweek* at Christmas 1996, 'A Bard for the '90s: Why He's Hot Now'. Shakespeare has made the big time, as Michael Bristol shows, and he's big-time merchandise. *Newsweek* made it plain: 'He's gone Hollywood. He's on the Web. He's got theme parks and teenage fans'.[36] It might also have mentioned *Karaoke Shakespeare*, a CD-ROM that allows the user to read the part of Macbeth or his wife while actors take the other roles on screen. Or Barry Kraft's 'After-Dinner Shakespeare: One hundred parlor cards with questions and answers to stimulate the mind and provoke lively conversation'. Or 'The Walk: A two-hour walk around the Stratford streets that "brings Shakespeare back to life" ... Tickets £5'. Or the enormous tourist success of the Shakespeare Birthplace Trust in Stratford, which will show you the Bard's birth bed (not the authentic original, by the way) and, as you exit through the gift shop, will sell you Shakespeare T-shirts, earrings, spoons, mugs, ties, samplers, pictures, cards, books, videos, teapots, models of Tudor houses and a box called 'Playing Shakespeare – the game of Shakespeare where every man must play a part'.

Whatever high art ideals, social agendas, or traces of residual humanism we might entertain for the Globe, to the providers in the tourist trade it is simply a welcome addition to the universal cultural safari. The Shakespeare boom is another example of the marketplace grabbing 'any pre-tested public domain property with instant name recognition',[37] what we could call the Bardification of culture. It may even be seen as the latest capitulation in cultural affairs to the unstoppable march of a consumerist economy.[38] As I sat near an open window at the unfinished Globe in 1996, I could clearly hear the amplified narrative coming from tour boats on the Thames, describing the rising building as a fully accurate reconstruction of Shakespeare's theatre where a fully accurate reconstruction of performance was now taking place. Cultural tourism had completed its circle: as a tourist in the Globe I had become, for those tourists on river, a touristic site myself.

But for the tourist the division between self and other cannot be absolute. We may seek the other but all too often we find that it has become us, and meanwhile without knowing we have become like the other. Tourism is an exchange that thrives on difference becoming familiar, the distance of the foreign or the unapproachability of the past transformed into a package tour. Like William Poel, Sam Wanamaker sought for Shakespeare's plays a reformed performance style in a radical architecture, a fundamentalist restoration to their pristine Elizabethan state. There are enormous flaws in the idea, but it does have the virtue of highlighting Shakespeare's otherness, of chronicling the distance the texts have travelled across time and culture. Despite his commodification and ideological appropriation by conservative forces, we continue to admire Shakespeare because he is at the heart of Western culture and yet somehow remains mysterious, enigmatic, finally undecodable.

The paradox of the Globe enterprise, however, is that it has turned Shakespeare's distance and strangeness into one of the most familiar of touristic commodities, the easy delights of the heritage museum and historical theme park. Like Baz Luhrmann's film of *Romeo and Juliet* or Richard Loncraine's of *Richard III* with Ian McKellen, the Globe presents a Shakespeare that has crossed over from high art representation to the realm of commodified icon and image available to all consumers. The manufactured authenticity of the building sets the Globe firmly within the heritage industry – even its educational programmes have a postmodern or theme park veneer – and suggests that a spectator's cultural capital can be comfortably left outside the door. The groundlings are pretty middle class and socially the audience is much less mixed than in 1599, but when watching a play from the yard there is a strong illusion that we're all in this together and class doesn't matter. It's fun, it's evocative, it's a jolly kind of New Age Shakespeare, Bard Lite. The Globe has effectively broken down the distinction between and the modernist ideal of the committed spectator and the pomo uncommitted tourist. Far from disdaining its reliance on cultural tourists, as modernist projects regularly did, the Globe actually welcomes them as central to its enterprise.

In a world where the individual is valued mainly as shopper and where difference is simply another market obstacle for Coca-Cola to overcome, could we expect anything else? As Baudrillard says, the world has become 'a triumph for Walt Disney, that inspired precursor of a universe where all past or present forms meet in a playful promiscuity, where all cultures recur in a mosaic'.[39] The Globe may look like Shakespeare's house but the risk continues that too much difference will be collapsed there, too much of the unknown glossed over, making Shakespeare into a heritage property that justifies a self-satisfied and self-serving present, a present always already determined by late monopoly capitalism. If the Globe Centre wishes to be more than Disney it must strive – in the midst of its touristic success – to show that Shakespeare is not us, he is a strangely surviving other in a world of the same, and our fascination with him is a fascination with something that we can never fully assimilate.

Notes

1. Erik Cohen, 'Who Is a Tourist? A Conceptional Clarification', *The Sociological Review*, NS 22 (1974), 547, 533. Also see Donald Redfoot, 'Touristic Authenticity, Touristic Angst, and Modern Reality', *Qualitative Sociology* 7.4 (1984), 291–309.
2. Robert W. McIntosh, Charles R. Goelden and J.R. Brent Ritchie, *Tourism: Principles, Practices, Philosophies*, 7th edn (New York: Wiley, 1995), 4–5.
3. See Maxine Feifer, *Going Places: The Ways of the Tourist from Imperial Rome to the Present Day* (London: Macmillan, 1985).
4. Dennis Kennedy, 'The Language of the Spectator', *Shakespeare Survey* 50 (1997), 29–40.
5. W. Bridges-Adams, *A Bridges-Adams Letter Book*, ed. Robert Speaight (London: Society for Theatre Research, 1971), 29.
6. John Urry, *The Tourist Gaze: Leisure and Travel in Contemporary Societies* (London: Sage, 1990), 6.
7. I discuss this issue in *Looking at Shakespeare: A Visual History of Twentieth-Century Performance* (Cambridge: Cambridge University Press, 1993), 152–64.
8. Sally Beauman, *The Royal Shakespeare Company: A History of Ten Decades* (Oxford: Oxford University Press, 1982), chapters 10–12.
9. See Pierre Bourdieu, *Distinction: A Social Critique of the Judgement of Taste*, trans. Richard Nice (London: Routledge and Kegan Paul, 1984).
10. Richard Sennett, *Flesh and Stone: The Body and the City in Western Civilization* (London: Faber, 1994), 358, 346; Robert Hughes, *The Shock of the New: Art and the Century of Change*, 2nd edn (London: BBC Books, 1991), 12, 14.
11. James Clifford, *Routes: Travel and Translation in the Late Twentieth Century* (Cambridge: Harvard University Press, 1997).
12. Raphael Samuel, *Theatres of Memory* (London: Verso, 1994), 25. See also David Lowenthal, *The Past Is a Foreign Country* (Cambridge, Mass.: Cambridge University Press, 1985).
13. Robert Hewison, *The Heritage Industry: Britain in a Climate of Decline* (London: Methuen, 1987), 9. David T. Herbert, 'Heritage Places, Leisure and Tourism' in Herbert, ed., *Heritage, Tourism and Society* (London: Mansell, 1995), 8.
14. Jean Baudrillard, *The Illusion of the End*, trans. Chris Turner (Cambridge: Polity Press, 1994), 12, 22.

15 Myra Shackley, 'When is the Past? Authenticity and the Commoditization of Heritage', a conference report, *Tourism Management* 15.5 (1994), 396–7.
16 Turgut Var, conference report, *Annals of Tourism Research* 20.2 (1993), 376.
17 Quoted in Shackley, 396.
18 Brigitte and Gilles Delluc, *Discovering Lascaux*, trans. Angela Mazon, photos Ray Delvert (Bordeaux: Éditions Sud-Ouest, 1990), 62. Parallel issues are treated by Barbara Kirshenblatt-Gimblett in 'Afterlives', *Performance Research* 2.2 (Summer 1997), 1–8, and more fully in her *Destination Culture: Tourism, Museums, and Heritage* (Berkeley: University of California Press, 1998).
19 Dean MacCannell, *The Tourist: A New Theory of the Leisure Class* (London: Macmillan, 1976), 102. A revised edition with a new introduction appeared in 1989 (New York: Random House). MacCannell's more recent work on the subject is in *Empty Meeting Grounds: The Tourist Papers* (London: Routledge, 1992).
20 *Bankside Globe*, a promotional newsletter from the International Shakespeare Globe Centre, London (Spring 1973). Copy seen in the Birmingham Shakespeare Library.
21 Erik Cohen, 'Tourism as Play', *Religion* 15 (1985), 292.
22 Erik Cohen, 'Authenticity and Commoditization in Tourism', *Annals of Tourism Research* 15 (1988), 371–86.
23 Ibid., 380.
24 Feifer, *Going Places*, 259–68. See Urry, *Tourist Gaze*, 11.
25 Eric Hobsbawm and Terence Ranger, eds, *The Invention of Tradition* (Cambridge: Cambridge University Press, 1983).
26 David Gates, 'The Bard Is Hot', *Newsweek* 128.26 (European edn, 23 December 1996), 40–48.
27 *Bankside Globe*, 1973 issue.
28 See Margaret J. King, 'Disneyland and Walt Disney World: Traditional Values in Futuristic Form', *Journal of Popular Culture* 15.1 (1981), 116–40.
29 Michael Coveny, 'Shakespeare Incorporated', *The Observer* (25 August 1996).
30 Adolf Ehrentrant, 'Heritage Authenticity and Domestic Tourism in Japan', *Annals of Tourism Research* 20.2 (1993), 270.
31 James Christopher, 'No Holds Bard', *Sunday Express* (11 August 1996).
32 John Mullan, 'Virtue's Humours', *Times Literary Supplement* No. 4927 (5 September 1997), 19.

[33] See John Urry, *Tourist Gaze,* 104. W.B. Worthen's excellent essay 'Reconstructing the Globe, Constructing Ourselves', *Shakespeare Survey* 52 (1999), 33–45, takes a modified view of this issue.
[34] Katy Weitz, 'New Globe Leads Bankside's Revival', *Independent on Sunday* (18 August 1996).
[35] See Fredric Jameson, *Postmodernism, or, The Cultural Logic of Late Capitalism* (Durham: Duke University Press, 1990).
[36] Michael Bristol, *Big-time Shakespeare* (London: Routledge, 1996). Gates, 'The Bard Is Hot', 40–48.
[37] Geoffrey O'Brien, 'The Ghost at the Feast', *New York Review of Books* 44.2 (6 February 1997), 11–16.
[38] See Dennis Kennedy, 'Shakespeare and the Global Spectator', *Shakespeare Jahrbuch* 131 (1995), 50–64.
[39] Baudrillard, *Illusion of the End,* 118.

SHAKESPEARE ON FILM

CHAPTER 1

The Recent Films

H.R. Coursen

One would like to think that the reason for all the Shakespeare films in the 1990s is that at last stage and film are communicating with each other, and there is some truth in that. Branagh did a *Henry V* on stage in 1984 before he made his film and a 'complete' *Hamlet* for Adrian Noble before that film. Branagh's *A Midwinter's Tale* is about a production of Hamlet in a provincial English town full of empty churches, empty pockets, and full pubs. Stoppard's brilliant film of *Rosencrantz and Guildenstern are Dead* is, of course, based on his play, but very different, not just as film is different from stage, but as script. Loncraine's *Richard III* is a very specific, 'historicized' version of the Richard Eyre production at the National in 1990, which sketched in its fascist background against our suspension of disbelief. Noble's *Midsummer Night's Dream* is based on his stage version.

Although Branagh had played Benedick in a *Much Ado* directed for the Renaissance Theatre by Judi Dench, his film version had him engaging in slapstick sight gags with lawn chairs. Furthermore, the sentimentalizing of the Beatrice and Benedick story – that slithery background music that Branagh cannot seem to avoid – undercut Emma Thompson's vulnerable and moving Beatrice. *Prospero's Books* features a great stage actor, of course, and a very conventional reading of *The Tempest*, but it is far from any sense of the stage. Indeed, it introduces high definition television to the mix for a seemingly interminable version of 'The Home Shopping Network' as a bunch of actors so out-of-work that they have pawned their very clothes to present gifts to Ferdinand and Miranda. The Parker *Othello* has no stage production behind it and is so heavily edited toward the imagery of film that it omits the words in the script that show why Othello is doomed, regardless of Iago's malign working. Pacino's *Looking for Richard* is a documentary about making a film of *Richard III* in a city innocent of any knowledge of Shakespeare. Trevor Nunn, director of *Twelfth Night*, has never directed the play on stage. Nunn brought three of his stage productions very successfully to television – *Antony and Cleopatra*, *Macbeth*, and *Othello*. The Luhrmann *Romeo and Juliet* is aggressively a film. One doubts that any of its participants have ever spoken in a theatre, except perhaps to create a disturbance in the fourth row.

The new films insist that we consider the question of what is Shakespeare on film. The successful Shakespeare film captures an archetype that is also in the script and that predates the script, as Shakespeare picks it up and treats it within his conventions and language. Archetypes are plastic energies and not immovable icons. It is not the conventions and language that make Shakespeare continually relevant, but the archetype, which reshapes itself within new historical circumstances suddenly discerned in the Shakespeare script. This is not surprising, of course, because, as Montrose says, Shakespeare 'generates action by combining conflicts grounded in such fundamental cultural categories as ethnicity, lineage, generation, gender, political faction and social rank'.[1] Add to that the dynamics that must exist in any culture of tension between father and son, father and daughter, man and woman, man and power, woman and power, the fact of love and the fact of death and one finds archetypes working beneath the specifics of the Shakespearean script. The script imitates an action fundamental to mankind, regardless of the variations that different cultures inscribe on the action. The Shakespeare film succeeds when it communicates these depth structures. That sounds easy enough, but it is surprising how often the camera gets in the way, that is, how often directors simply erase what is potentially there in favour of their own conception, their own reshaping of the materials to conform with whatever their vision may be. In saying that, I do not deny the need for interpretation of a given script. Any evaluation of the recent films must be very subjective, subject to my own sense of what the archetypes may be and my own sense of the clarity of the mimetic transparency which the film creates as it mediates between script and viewer. But such a stance merely admits the postmodernist tenet of multiple signification, which has always been an aspect of Shakespearean production – Aristotle's fourth cause, which is final cause, the effect of the work on the spectator.

Luhrmann's *Romeo and Juliet* does not attempt to explain the origins of the feud. It simply *is*, like a poisonous plant with a deep network of unseen roots. The film is not set in Belfast or Bosnia, but in a city which serves, like the feud, as a background for the aimless ebb and flow of teenage activity.

The film's major metaphor, though, is religion and its irrelevance. The originating script suggests this hollowing out of Christian symbols and ceding of power to those crossing stars of which the Chorus warns. In a radically condensed shooting text, Luhrmann leaves in lines about 'Some consequence hanging in the stars', and Romeo's 'I am fortune's fool', and 'I defy you stars', and his line about 'shak[ing] the yoke of inauspicious stars'. The pistol with which Romeo kills Tybalt has an ivory portrait of the Madonna on its stock. The church has a huge Madonna on top with outstretched arms, her head ringed with the traditional twelve stars of the Apostles – a Maria of the City – who looks down on Romeo's murder of Tybalt. Romeo holds his arms out as he shouts about being fortune's fool. The statue itself is under repair beneath its own widespread arms. It is a decaying monument in a world of mere bad luck. Tybalt, his own arms spread out, bleeds into the pool at the base of the stony Virgin, who is there in the hour of his death, but only as an absence. The pool is the fatal analogue of the one in the Capulet gardens, where Romeo and Juliet bubble their love in silence. Tybalt, standing in front of a Grunewald crucifixion, sees Romeo and vows vengeance. The Friar has a huge cross tattooed upon his back. He gives good advice about 'violent delights hav[ing] violent ends', but cannot follow it himself. He drinks, smokes pot and betrays a liking for little boys. He fantasizes headlines of reconciliation. His imagery is that of this society, of a tabloid existence. The apothecary's door is adorned with pictures of the Virgin and Child torn from magazines. The bandage on Romeo's wounded left arm is stained with a red cross. A red cross rests later against a funeral wreath. Red crosses are painted on the Friar's medicine cabinet and on the irrelevant ambulances that come to pick up the bodies of the lovers. The Montague's stretch limo sports a bronze cross behind the back seat. As Laurence says, 'My lady stirs!' – anticipating Juliet's awakening – the camera shows a quartz Virgin and Child. Christ has become a clock. Deity is now a commercialized subject of time, not the point at which time ceases and eternity begins.

Against these obscene images is a compensatory softness of sheets, curtains, the clothes on statuary in the Capulet garden, the gauze on Juliet's bier. The god Pan stands near the Capulet pool, a pagan god surviving into this overly-Christianized culture representing energies that have no outlet where religion has lost its mystery and has surrendered to the conventions of a meaningless feud. The lovers first see each other through a fish bowl. It is a vision through the unconscious of desired completion, the archetype of the self mirrored as a beloved alter ego. Romeo and Juliet enjoy their moment in the swirling roil of the pool, in the grotto of the dawn of their wedding morning, and reach the sequel in the tomb. All of that is almost wordless here, a silence earned against the tumult of the vortex of meaningless noise around them.

The film shows them yearning unconsciously for the silence they find, the silence of death. The strength of their love for each other and its fragility were vivified by the environment the film provided for it. The film illustrates the impulse of teenagers in America at least toward death, as Peter Blos says it must be in his classic study on adolescence. Historical circumstances suddenly make sense of the Shakespeare script – or it makes sense of them – as surely as Zeffirelli's version explored the generational conflict that is in the script and that pervaded American society as a result of its government's misguided activity in South East Asia.

Among the sillier of recent films is Greenaway's *Prospero's Books*. Greenaway substitutes crawling, squirming insides of books – as if they were rocks that had been lifted up – for whatever the script may be saying. He imposes television upon film, a blatant reduction of scale and artistic premises. Within this misconception, Greenaway can do nothing with Caliban, giving us instead a standard new critical version of the play. Suppose he had pursued Caliban's suggestion that Prospero's books must be seized, that they are a source of power, and depicted in his film a contest for the control of the media? – seize his books – and his television station! That might have been interesting. As it is, even Miranda and the possibility of her bringing forth brave brood is hardly an issue here since the isle is full of naked people presumably prepared to give delight and hurt not. The Loncraine *Richard III*, fixed as it is in an explicit 1930s London, cannot reach for the script's deeper suggestions. Richard as scripted triggers a response from within him, the *a priori* principles at which he has sneered and will sneer at again once he dismisses conscience as a word that cowards use. The film can only move towards a satire that it has not announced, as a smirking Richmond watches a happy Richard drop into a fiery zone inhabited by the late Al Jolson, suddenly warbling in 1927. While 'I'm Sitting On Top of the World' is intended to remind us of James Cagney in a 1940s film, the song is an optimistic hymn to the booming 1920s. The archetypal 30s song is 'Brother, Can You Spare a Dime', as rendered by Bing Crosby. Now that would have been genuinely funny, as Richard plunges away with his hand held out. Unable to go where the script goes, the film settles for inanity and trusts that postmodernism's ample mantle covers that category as well.

The film's best moment, the royals viewing the newsreel of their own elevation to power, is isolated. It reminds us that the Nazis used film as part of their propaganda. We know Nazi Germany *by* film. Goebbels was desperately completing his film about Frederick the Great, pulling troops from the front as extras in the spring of 1945, even as Zhukov drove from the Vistula to the Oder, only forty miles from Berlin. The Nazis used film, and here we might have seen Buckingham deploying an edited film of the population's less than enthusiastic *collaudatio* for Richard, *à la* the beginning of 'Triumph of the Will' to convince others. Films about films can be exciting. But this script was imported into a moment in history that obscured whatever may be going on in the play.

A more successful example of a script moved into a modern political environment is David Thacker's television production of *Measure for Measure*. Thacker's placement of the script in a contemporary police state diminishes the religious conventions that function so strongly in the play, and other problems weaken the production (a Duke who proposes to Isabella, for example, out of sheer ennui). Its setting and background, however – including the use of television as a central element of politics – strike me as very effective. Branagh's *A Midwinter's Tale* (also known as *In the Bleak Midwinter*) does trade on clichés – the director who threatens suicide in front of his company (and almost has to go through with it, since the counter-thesis is a long time in announcing itself), the actor who cannot remember his lines, the cynical older actor who has never played Shakespeare, the ingenue who says that this ragtag group is her 'family', the designer whose concept is 'space' and then 'smoke', the agent who would pull her client out of the opening night for a three-film Hollywood contract, the Ophelia who actually slaps Hamlet during a performance, etc. Add to the stereotypes that the actor who cannot recall his lines also drinks to forget the rest of his life (he drinks so much that he is likely to affect the next harvest, as one of his colleagues warns), that the ingenue is virtually blind, but will not wear glasses and thus conducts limb-threatening crashes as entrances, and that the director will spend precious moments patiently trying to get Francisco to recall a time when he was terrified, so that 'Who's there?' will carry conviction (his subtext is changing a tyre on a busy motorway, which he mimes before Bernardo appears) and you have unpromising material indeed. Then consider that the production – which finally does occur – brings a son to his father, a mother to her son, a father to his daughter, two lovers (Hamlet and Ophelia, of course) together, Hollywood contracts to a very minor actor and a helpless designer, and Christmas bells to a village named Hope, a town of empty churches, empty pockets and full pubs – and you cry 'Oh no!'

But out of this comes a very funny and moving film which transforms the bleak midwinter into a Christmas card. The film is 'caviare to the general', almost all subtext, some of it having to do with the recent history of British theatre, some to do with the play *Hamlet* itself. The film is superbly edited and *timed*, insisting in a Capotesque way that we overhear the lines as one brief sequence dissolves to the next. Nicholas Farrell develops a subtextual foxiness for his Reynaldo. Gerald Horan delivers Polonius's 'And let him ply his music' as if he were Coriolanus haranguing the Roman mob. The church in which the production is to take place also serves as 'digs'. Two actors sleep in the crypt, 'cryptic actors', as one of them says. A cardboard Shakespeare watches the performance and a cutout American Indian also observes, stonily absorbing the political incorrectness that Judy and Mickey are perpetrating in their backyard extravaganza. But what begins as murder in the cathedral ends as a community of the spirit, so that the setting gradually exchanges its ironies for its sacramental qualities.

Stoppard's *Rosencrantz and Guildenstern are Dead* is likely to get lost in the flood, but it is brilliant. The camera moves in and out of various planes of reality. At *The Murder Gonzago*, puppets are observed by a masked King and Queen. The real king (Donald Sumpter) rises, looks back on masked players, as a flash of recognition washes back and erases levels of fiction. The masks come off the players as Hamlet believes Claudius has also been unmasked. Perhaps he has, but Rosencrantz interprets the King's reaction in aesthetic terms: 'It wasn't *that* bad', he says as he and Guildenstern exit through the wreckage.

As Hamlet and Claudius vie to assert their contradictory interpretations on Elsinore, the film addresses the question of art itself and its relationship to other modes of representation, even that of nature itself, as Rosencrantz brilliantly but fruitlessly experiments with it. His discoveries include gravity, the principle of harmonics, the law of acceleration, hydraulics, the aerodynamic application of Bernoulli's Principle, steam power, the laws of equal and opposite reaction and of conservation of energy and aspects of vector theory and convection. In addition, he sets a 'new record' of 42 seconds for keeping a paper plane in the air, shattering the old Guinness World Record of 18.8 held by Ken Blackburn. Rosencrantz is finding meanings a century before Newton, but is a mute, inglorious Newton, because, as Elizabeth Wheeler says, 'perception both on an individual and a societal level is necessary for awareness of significance'.[2] Since no cultural perception occurs, there is no 'reality' to what Rosencrantz discovers. Furthermore, as Bohr and Heisenberg have shown us, observation changes what is observed, physically and in translation into language and replicable modes. Here what is observed become alms for an oblivion to be reclaimed much later into a new physics. In a sense nature is like the Shakespeare script – the 'meanings' are there but the circumstances required for their formulation have not yet occurred. Rosencrantz, even as he demolishes Aristotelian paradigms, cannot bring his insights to completion. His discoveries prove that probability *is* functioning within this world, but it emerges from a model yet to be defined.

Rosencrantz's disquisition on being alive or dead in a box comes half-true. Neither state is reached, since their existential bodies have been hanged, but their roles as characters remain inside the Players' wagon on the stage that can be lowered at a moment's notice. They are alive *and* dead. They are inside the play, potentially inside another performance in which they will not recognize the play *this* time either. They are doomed to an endless repetition of the same questions without answers, to the same ending. They are in that script chest, their parts 'written', as the Player says, as if the play were a book of fate. They are not dead exactly, but they can come alive only in the radically estranging world known as *Hamlet*. Guildenstern recognizes *The Murder of Gonzago*, but not that it is a play-within-a-play or that he is within a play, both Shakespeare's and Stoppard's. They can come out of the script box – 'Hey you, what's your name, come out of there' – but it is a movement from stasis, suspended animation, into an unfree, scripted world, where, as Guildenstern says, 'There's something they're not telling us'. When Hamlet escapes to the pirate ship, Guildenstern complains, 'We need Hamlet for our release'. What he means is that they 'need *Hamlet* for their release'. They will not get Hamlet to England, but *Hamlet* will get them to England and provide sudden closure. That closure, though, will occur only in one production. They are trapped in the repetition of the script – that is, unless a Laurence Olivier erases them altogether. There never was a moment when they could have said 'No', nor will there be. They will never understand the play in which they are involuntary participants. Nor will we, of course. The existential point rides out, making us much more like them than like Hamlet, who at least motivates much of what it turns out he does not understand either.

 Twelfth Night has to be a difficult script out of which to craft a film – we cannot believe that the others believe that that is a boy. The play has seldom if ever worked in a realistic medium – I recall Joan Plowright's ludicrous attempt to double as Viola and Cesario in a television production of the late 1960s. But Nunn goes right at the gender issue and Imogen Stubbs in a brilliant comic role reminiscent of Harold Lloyd shows how hard it is to be even a stereotypic male. And it is of course – so much energy goes into the role and it does finally demand an escape into the feminine, the anima. The film splendidly depicts the psychology of gender issues – Stubbs chafes from riding a horse, turns green from smoking a cigar, turns a scratch into a great pool shot and at the same time gets Orsino to fall for her androgynous self so that her transformation into woman which lies just beyond the film's ending is a natural further step in a process the film has depicted.

 The film occurs in early autumn, the time of Keats's 'mist and mellow fruitfulness'. Malvolio's deciphering of Maria's letter is accomplished with the help of a cold pastoral that he imagines warm and pulsing in its nakedness. Mist washes the empty choirs of the oak, and apples await their baskets in Olivia's orchards. It is not a cherry orchard, we notice. Olivia's potentially destructive sexuality will be socially absorbed. Bonham Carter's snapping eyes suggest that she would like to free herself of her mourning. Malvolio reads her correctly, but mistakes in reading himself as the object of the release of her repression. Orsino's castle is on an island, open along a causeway only at low tide. It is a dream castle, often viewed from a distance, an outcropping of consciousness scarcely rising above the surface. There Orsino reclines while his officers stand and wait for orders. This Orsino is a version of Meredith's Willoughby Patterne in *The Egoist*. Olivia, for all of her assumed melancholy, lives above a vast kitchen over which Malvolio presides, duke of the downstairs. Appetite is underneath, we are being told, and that applies to Olivia as well as those we find down there. Upstairs the curtains are drawn against the watery autumn light, but the velvet hangings, painted Italian wallpaper and absorbing Persian rugs suggest, as Anthony Lane says, a 'sumptuous relish in [Olivia's] mourning'.[3] Hers is a Thackerayan world in which the widow's weeds must be carefully cut, the roast for the mourners rarely done and the port so fine that the connoisseur will beg a bottle now that the owner is cold. Between these sites is a fishing village, patrolled by Orsino's ominous police force. At one point, while they are chasing Antonio, the soldiers upset a cart and slither around a corner on a carpet of hake and seaweed, an image which links the ocean's primal energy with the festive tables of the rich. The piano at which Sebastian and Viola had sat aboard the ship becomes a tinkling set of keys on the tossing sea. They are ultimately washed to silence on the shore, to be replaced by the several pianos and many songs of Illyria, a peninsula full of harmonies waiting to be heard.

Nunn distributes the script to various locations, so that, as with many films of Shakespeare, knowledge of the script is not an advantage. Viola's soliloquy after Malvolio delivers the ring to her occurs in segments at different moments. The technique shows, however, how a relationship can grow by increments over time and suggests, as film can do better than stage, that lives continue in spaces that the camera visits only occasionally. It is not that Shakespeare's stage cannot achieve a montage effect by shifting from place to place, which we identify by being told where the characters are or by who the characters are. Once Shakespeare gets his characters out on stage, though, he usually likes to keep them there for a while. And, often in Shakespeare's scenes, we are told a lot that a quick camera can show us more economically.

Pacino's technique in *Looking for Richard* is to keep building areas of activity that can then become points of reference. Few films are so self-allusive as this. Pacino cuts back and forth from Richard's opening soliloquy to a discussion of what it means. He shows us rehearsals and establishes the performance itself, a costumed drama amid the Romanesque arches of The Cloisters, the medieval wing of the Metropolitan Museum. He and his director walk the streets around Times Square, interrogating the sidewalkers and panhandlers of New York. The effort to make the film also incorporates a seeking after an elusive 'Shakespeare'. Who is he, or it, to the people amid the horns and police whistles? Will the film be made? One Italian man, claiming ignorance of Shakespeare, leaves Pacino at a 'Walk' sign, saying 'To be or not to be, that is the question!'. For one of the first times in at least a century, the line suddenly absorbs meaning from its context. When a panhandler talks about Shakespeare and *feeling*, we suddenly pick up on Pacino's leaving in so many lines from the play about 'a giving vein' and about begging: 'impotent and snail-pac'd beggary', 'the famish'd beggars, weary of their bones'. 'Spare some change?' the real beggar asks.

Once Pacino's system is established and once we have been educated to it, all the worlds of the film became available as points of reference. Two Richards – one an actor in rehearsal on the floor of The Cloisters and another sweating in the dawn before death of life and soul, in a close up and in a side shot as if lying in state – can alternate in reading the lines. This is a brilliant way of suggesting the split that the character perceives within himself, monarch versus truth-speaking jester, the debate between body and soul, as well as the technique that goes into making a character who runs into the ranks of an inalterable law oblivious to his consummate skills. Richard's dream looks ahead to his battle, as the film incorporates brief glimpses of its own future in creating the shattered imagery of nightmare. The soliloquy is turned into a dramatic film. The film has used different moments as points of reference. Suddenly, the film takes upon itself the power of prediction.

The Branagh *Hamlet* suffers from special effects that make the Ghost laughable, from the most remarked-upon Marcellus in the history of Hamlet-in-performance, from myriad tracking shots required to get all that language in, from a candle-lit world in which the real lighting is palpable but just out of sight, from an excruciating Ophelia and from an intrusive musical score that slithers in irrelevantly to undercut some often excellent verse speaking. One of the few beneficiaries of all the anti-cinematic verbiage is Derek Jacobi, whose Claudius becomes fully dimensional in this film.

I did not like Noble's *A Midsummer Night's Dream* on stage in 1994. I found it full of the ideas of other directors. If a criterion of the Shakespeare film is that it somehow reveals an archetype lurking in the script, this one fails. It never even gets to its genre. It uses the doors of the stage production to little or no effect. Doors are the stuff of farce, of *The Comedy of Errors* or 'I Love Lucy'. On stage and in the film, they open from nowhere to nowhere. They are gimmicks trying to disguise their relevance to anything in the script. The lightbulbs often get in the way in the film, as they did on stage. The film uses the stage's red umbrella, which in the film sails off a sea of dew, so, to Mary Poppins, Traveller's Insurance, 'Pennies from Heaven', Up a Chimney Down and other allusions, I add Winkin, Blinkin and Nod. Noble borrows Mamilius from his *Winter's Tale* of 1992 to make the film a little boy's nightmare, thus overlaying a story on a script already complicated by many narratives. At the end the little boy is integrated into the world of his nightmare, apparently never regaining consciousness. His mother, we assume, finds him dead in bed in the morning. While one must edit for film, Noble's televisual approach might have allowed more language to enter his shooting script. Hermia's plea for patience, immediately and amusingly countered by Lysander's plan for escape, is gone, as is Titania's powerful description of the vicarious pregnancy she has experienced through her vot'ress, as is Hermia's hilarious rationalization that Helena has 'urged her height', as is Bottom's splendid parody of First Corinthians 2:9, as is Hippolyta's besting of Theseus in their debate about 'the story of the night'. Thus, much of the dramatic give-and-take of the inherited script is simply erased. The film does nothing with the lovers. It eradicates the superb role of Helena. The film does not establish any pace or rhythm. Instead, we get confusing cuts to the boy who is by turns observing, manipulating, hiding, dreaming, and calling for his mother. The film seldom gets away from its premises as staged play. Why this production was chosen to become a film remains a mystery to me. In the film, the occasional metaphor of theatre – the toy stage that becomes the real stage for *Pyramus and Thisbe* – suffers a mid-air collision with the metaphor of dream. The effort to fuse the two – the little boy as puppeteer – forces me to ask, what is going on here? And to answer – nothing that I want to spend any more time on.

We can pause now to evaluate the films individually and to assess their impact on our classrooms and our culture, to ask, if we want to, what the Shakespeare film *is*. Who would have predicted, even after the success of Branagh's *Henry V*, that we would have this opportunity? That so many of the films are worth our attention and analysis is itself a cause for celebration.

Notes

1. Louis Montrose, *The Purpose of Playing: Shakespeare and the Cultural Politics of the Elizabethan Theatre* (Chicago: University of Chicago Press, 1996), 33.
2. Elizabeth Wheeler, 'Light It Up and Move It Around', *Shakespeare on Film Newsletter* (December 1991), 5.
3. Anthony Lane, 'Tights, Camera, Action!' *The New Yorker* (25 November 1996), 74.

CHAPTER 2

(En)Gendering Desire in Performance: *King Lear*, Akira Kurosawa's *Ran*, Tadashi Suzuki's *The Tale of Lear*

Yoko Takakuwa

What happens when a seventeenth-century English text is rewritten as a play for twentieth-century Japan? What changes when a play written for the stage is reconceived as a film? What, in other words, are the cultural implications of transposing a text from one culture to another, from one historical moment to another, from one medium to another? In its own day, Shakespeare's *King Lear* was popular entertainment; it was only later that, as it became archaic, it entered Western high culture. In Suzuki's *The Tale of Lear* it reappears as a twentieth-century theatrical text; in Kurosawa's *Ran* it re-enters the popular mainstream, but as a film. How can we read such texts? What reading strategies are appropriate? In this paper I shall read these three distinct versions of the Lear story from the point of view of their treatment of gender and inquire into the question of gendered subjectivity in performance.

Referring to gender identity parodied by drag and cross-dressing, Judith Butler has argued that gender parody as performance destabilizes 'the naturalized categories of identity and desire' in *Gender Trouble: Feminism and the Subversion of Identity*.[1] Butler says that gender is 'an identity' produced through 'the stylized repetition of acts' (gestures, movements), 'a norm' and 'an "act"' as 'the effects of a subtle and politically enforced performativity'.[2] In *Bodies That Matter: On the Discursive Limits of 'Sex'*, Butler reformulates her notion of performativity, not as 'a singular "act"', but as 'a reiteration of a norm or set of norms'; 'to the extent that it [performativity] acquires an act-like status in the present, it conceals or dissimulates the conventions of which it is a repetition'.[3] Butler seems to draw on the Derridian notion of citationality or iterability. When Butler maintains that 'gender performativity cannot be theorized apart from the forcible and reiterative practice of regulatory sexual regimes', however, her notion of gender performativity as 'dissimulated citationality' tends to reaffirm the 'constituting effect of regulatory power as reiterated and reiterable' to a large extent.[4] Butler owes her methodological framework to Foucauldian genealogy and aims 'to expose the foundational categories of sex, gender, and desire as effects of a specific formation of power', as a consequence of which she tends to put too much emphasis primarily on the relation between power and gender identity.[5]

Concerning the citationality of gendered subjectivity, what counts for much in Jacques Derrida's discussion of citationality seems to me an *arbitrary* aspect of the iterability of the sign, contingent on the context, which radically undermines intentionality or 'the "original" desire-to-say-what-one-means [*vouloir-dire*]' – the subject's desire to be self-present as the origin of meaning.[6] The meaning of masculinity or femininity is repeated and performed *with* differences, regardless of the subject-player's authorial intention to be (impersonate) *properly* a 'man' or a 'woman'. Contexts matter in this world theatre, in order for speaking subjects to succeed in impersonating either 'man' or 'woman'.

The fact that Lear's three daughters were played by boy actors in the English Renaissance theatre complicated the question of gendered identity. In *The Tale of Lear*, male actors also perform Lear's three daughters. But their ways of impersonating women are different, not only from those of boy actors whose female clothes and effeminacy were censured in the puritan anti-theatrical tracts, but also from those of the Noh player who symbolizes 'the woman' with a mask, or of the *onnagata* who masquerades femininity with the help of make-up, female costume and gestures. Suzuki elsewhere defines the *onnagata*'s art as the stylization of woman's gestures produced by male actors for men's gaze, and says that the *onnagata*'s 'feminine' sexual appeal is nothing but man's 'seeming likeness', in that it draws attention to the theatricality of the feminine.[7] I think, in addition, that the 'real' woman's sexual appeal or femininity is also nothing more than the 'seeming likeness' or masquerade of (the meaning of) womanliness. In *The Tale of Lear*, Lear's daughters are played by bearded actors by adopting 'feminine' words and gestures – without masks, make-up, 'feminine' costume or appearance.[8] Certainly Suzuki calls into question the meaning of 'beauty' conventionally regarded as the attribute of 'woman' as object of the gaze.[9] The 'feminine' gestures *mimed* and overstated (over-cited) by the bearded, 'masculine' Goneril and Regan (toward Edmund) constitute a pastiche or caricature of femininity, which denaturalizes the meaning of the feminine taken for granted in the everyday signifying system.

Besides such body language as 'feminine' gestures, it is the linguistic structure of Japanese that enables the actors to impersonate the women without 'feminine' appearance or mask. In Japanese, the grammatical subject and verb endings differ, according to gender, age, the social status and the region in which the speaker lives. Unlike English which has only the one genderless subject 'I', Japanese is a gendered language, especially in dialogue. Therefore, not only the changes of clothes or manners of the heroine or hero, but also the very language tells the audience of gender difference. The language is another signpost of gender difference and identity for the Japanese audience, to the extent that the 'masculine' or 'feminine' expressions function as the meaningful indicators of a speaker's gender in conversational speech. In other words, the Japanese have to *learn* how to speak appropriately according to gender, age or social status to fulfil cultural, social, sexual identification.

Suzuki's Fool is played by either a male or female actor in a nurse's white uniform dress and cap.[10] While a nurse-Fool is reading the *original* text, *King Lear*, to a moribund old man (the Lear figure) who was abandoned alone in the hospital, the old man's memory of his disintegrated family merges with the story of Lear's solitude and madness. 'It is his memories and his fantasies which provide a framework within which Shakespeare's *King Lear* is performed', Suzuki writes in his 'Director's Notes' and adds that 'this "Chinese Boxes" concept' is to point to 'the truth of human weakness which has universal significance beyond the differences in historical or racial customs'.[11] Suzuki's 'universal truth' is one possible reading of *King Lear*. Suzuki regards the world as a mental hospital where we all, men and women, are patients, and where we have neither doctors or nurses nor hopes for recovery. The bearded Goneril and Regan and the apathetic nurse-Fool take the roles of 'woman' or 'nurse' perfunctorily without 'feeling' or alleged internal truth of the 'character'. They look like the misplaced signifiers without the presumed signified, as we the audience witness, deformed and monsterized on the boundary of the representations and the meanings of the masculine and the feminine. *The Tale of Lear* is one of Suzuki's attempts as 'the contemporary artist-creator' 'to make clear in what sort of spiritual illness a human being is trapped'.[12] Possibly, either 'male' or 'female' identity might be our 'spiritual illness' or another form of madness as obsessed by the (internalized) 'truth' of what it means to be a man or a woman, alienating ourselves from our alternative possible selves in order to play culturally defined gender-roles on the stage of this world theatre.

Kurosawa's *Ran* raises the question of gender in a different way. Lear's three daughters are made into sons in *Ran*, because daughters did not have the right to succeed to the headship of the family in the primogeniture system of sixteenth-century Japan. At first glance *Ran* seems to feature a homosocial society of men-warriors in power, in which Kaede, the Lear-figure Hidetora's daughter-in-law, manipulates Hidetora's sons to revolt against their father, in revenge for his ruin of her family, and brings to ruin the Ichimonji family. Her feminine masquerade (performance) as a sexy temptress or a loving woman mimes, parodies and appropriates female stereotypes and the conventional idea of female seduction. At the same time, her 'seduction' ironically demonstrates not only her 'demonic' power over men but also her 'unwomanliness' as a more active and stronger woman than men, and disrupts the hierarchical system of sexual difference and identity.

Kurosawa adopts the representation of the female demon in the Noh plays to describe Kaede. Kaede is demonized as an evil she-fox who dupes men. Likewise, the 'she-foxes' Goneril and Regan disregard the *proper* female roles of 'wife' or 'daughter' and avow their desire for the bastard Edmund. Calling Goneril a devil in female disguise, Albany criticizes her as not being *properly* a 'woman' – for her failure to perform the prescriptions of gendered identity. Cornwall's men are disgusted by Regan's 'unwomanly' (monster-like) cruelty to Gloucester. Goneril and Regan are both demonized, 'masculine' women.

Deciphering the textual inscriptions of Goneril and Regan and Kaede, I shall suggest how the women, who disregard the *proper* meaning and place of 'woman' and transgress the line of demarcating sexual difference, are monsterized and demonized. I shall attempt a close reading of *Ran*, focusing on Kaede and giving Western readers details of the film rewritten by Kurosawa in a Japanese context. Referring to the witches, Lady Macbeth or Cleopatra, Catherine Belsey points out the contradictory implications of the 'demonization of women who subvert the meaning of femininity': it places the women 'beyond meaning, beyond the limits of what is intelligible' but, at the same time, endows them with 'a (supernatural) power which it is precisely the project of patriarchy to deny'.[13] The questions of female desire, eloquence and transgression bring to light the fictionality of the gendered identity of 'man' or 'woman' performed on the confines of the meaning of femininity and masculinity.

Ran means 'chaos' (the English title) or 'war', 'rebellion', and further implies the world as 'infinite hell' where human folly has been endlessly repeated. Kurosawa finds many similarities between the English and the Japanese sixteenth century as periods of civil war and considers 'themes and events from Shakespeare' to be 'very suitable for covering this period'.[14] Both *Ran* and *King Lear* dramatize the rebellion of the *discontented* 'children of this degraded age of strife', as the Cordelia-figure

Saburo puts it,[15] against their fathers, and a deep pessimism about 'chaos' in the world, the symbolic order or civilization.

King Lear can be read in terms of his daughters' 'rebellion' against Lear as the king-father-man, and the 'chaos' caused by the violation of the hierarchical differences which uphold the cultural order between man/woman, father/daughter, husband/wife, legitimate/illegitimate or human/animal.[16]

Goneril and Regan, who behave like men and adopt masculine ways, are 'unnatural hags' (2.2.467), neglecting the *proper* roles of 'woman' as 'wife' or 'daughter'. With his abdication, Lear loses sovereign-paternal power over his subjects-children, which enables Goneril to stop *playing* the role of 'daughter'. As the Fool says to Lear, 'thou mad'st thy / daughters thy mothers' when 'thou gav'st them / The rod and putt'st down thine own breeches' (1.4.163–5). In their role reversals, Lear asks, 'Who is it that can tell me who I am?' and the Fool answers, 'Lear's shadow' (1.4.221–2). His loss of the paternal, male power infantilizes and feminizes Lear, inasmuch as women, like babies and children, do not have power within the male-oriented power structures of a patriarchal society.[17] Goneril and Regan's 'unnatural' refusal to perform the *proper* female roles overthrows Lear's paternal-authorial intention to reproduce and circulate the *proper* meaning of 'father' or 'daughter' and brings to a crisis his identities as 'father' and 'man'.

Despising Albany for his effeminacy, Goneril mockingly proposes to exchange the *proper* roles of 'husband' and 'wife': 'I must change arms at home, and give the distaff / Into my husband's hands' (4.2.17–18). Far from a virtuous, submissive wife, Goneril cuckolds Albany. Similarly Regan desires and woos Edmund soon after Cornwall's death. Goneril regards herself as 'the prisoner' of the marriage bond-bed, a 'gaol', outspokenly expresses her contempt for her effeminate husband and desires Edmund as a 'man':

> Oh! the difference of man and man.
> To thee a woman's services are due:
> A fool usurps my bed.   (4.2.26–8)

The moment ironically proves the sexual 'reality', taken for granted by patriarchal values, that even the 'masculine' Goneril can be a loving 'woman', who offers 'a woman's services' to her man-master, affirming the hierarchical order of the sexes. More ironically, however, the 'female' desire which makes Goneril 'feminine', is the illicit, adulterous desire of a wife, which patriarchy cannot approve. The unwomanly Goneril's 'female' desire curiously endorses the patriarchal/misogynist definitions of the 'woman' in love/lust on the one hand, but on the other hand, discloses the inner contradictions within its narrative order.

Another '*Ran*', another 'rebellion' of the sons and daughter-in-law against the father, takes place in the 'degraded age of strife' of the late sixteenth century in Japan. The Lear-figure Hidetora has destroyed his neighbouring warlords, including the family of his two daughters-in-law, Kaede and Sué, extended his realm and come into power as the Great Lord. At the beginning of the film, the senile Hidetora is upset by his dream of being alone in a wilderness and reveals his fear of solitude and thus desire for family solidarity fortified by filial love and piety. He announces that his eldest son Taro is to succeed him as head of the House of Ichimonji and repudiates Saburo, who bluntly points out the frailty of his 'senile' and 'mad' illusion about family solidarity in 'a world where men's evil, cruel instincts are exposed' (16). Saburo's straightforward speech, which dismisses the idealization of the family-bond as 'senile nonsense' or *fiction*, contrasts with Cordelia's resistance by saying 'Nothing' against the forced articulation of the ideological meaning of filial love and piety as defined by patriarchy. Nevertheless they both bring into relief the fictionality of the family-bond as contract (re)produced in and by language and the very vulnerability of the paternal power founded on the presumed performative effects of language, which solely guarantees the stability and continuity of the family-bond-contract.

In *Ran* we find more tactful but powerful female manipulation of the power in another patriarchal society. Political (military) power belonged to the samurai in late sixteenth-century Japan. Kaede has no direct power as a woman allocated to the ideologically excluded place on the margin of the paternal, male power, but she works through her relations to the men in power, first to her husband, Taro, and then to his brother, Jiro. Her 'female seduction' is a means for her to gain the mastery of power, by which she takes her revenge on Hidetora.

After Hidetora's abdication, Kaede motivates and constitutes Taro's will to power as head of the family. She tells Taro that he does not have the standard as the symbol of headship and that he is just a shadow without the forms. Kaede's rhetoric makes a point, to the extent that power neither self-presently nor substantially exists, but is invested and reproduced relatively in 'the forms', for example, the standard, the crown, the throne, the order of seats, the written or spoken pledge, the number of retainers, the kingdom. In other words, it is the theatrical demonstration of 'the power' – the process of citing and summoning its meaning – that represents and reproduces (the desire for) power. The royal 'audience' is an instance of the dependence of sovereignty on the theatrical performance of 'the power'. Taro displays his power by way of letting his father take a lower seat than his. This reversal of the hierarchical order of seats in the family materializes, in spite of Hidetora's first (authorial) intention to 'keep the title and the forms of the Great Lord' (28), his loss of the *proper* place and identity of the Great Lord.

Taro further denounces Hidetora's rude retainers (like Goneril) and demands to sign the pledge of the transference of headship and seal it with his blood. The headship is conferred and confirmed by the form of contract as *promise* given in and by language and through the theatrical ritual of the blood seal. Goneril sarcastically defines Lear's power invested by a hundred knights not as sovereign power but as a mere means to demonstrate his senile, capricious self-will: 'on every dream, / Each buzz, each fancy, each complaint, dislike, / He may enguard his dotage with their powers' (1.4.317–19). To be a king is not 'an immediate natural property of the person of a king', as Slavoj Zizek explains the symbolic function of a king in Marx, but 'a "determination-of-reflection"'.[18] Without the material forms of kingdom, throne or knights, onto which (the meaning of) his sovereign-paternal power is invested by (the gaze of) his subjects-children, Lear is only his 'shadow', as the Fool says. Goneril and Taro, or rather Kaede, bring to light the vulnerability of the sovereign-paternal power, by disclosing their dependence on material 'forms' and theatrical performance.

After Taro's death, the widow Kaede's 'seduction' process is that of her mastery of Jiro's power of headship. On occasion she masquerades as a sexy temptress or a loving woman dependent on man, appropriating female stereotypes. At the same time, her 'female seduction' ironically displays her 'unwomanly' activity and strength and Jiro's 'unmanly' passivity and frailty.

Kaede comes to see Jiro under the pretext of congratulating him on his succession to head of the family. She then attacks Jiro off guard, unsheathes his sword and thrusts it to his throat. Her activity is conventionally defined as 'masculine' to affirm 'male strength'. She accuses him of murdering his brother and stealing the realm and cuts his skin with the tip of the sword. Jiro is compelled to confess that his retainer killed Taro. 'You mean you ordered your retainer to do it but cannot take the responsibility? What a general!' (69). Holding the dagger in one hand and the long sword in the other, Kaede disdains Jiro's cowardly weakness. Her unsheathing of Jiro's swords suggests that the power of the man-warrior and the head of the family symbolized by the phallic image of sword is now moved from Jiro's hand into Kaede's. Jiro is emasculated and virtually castrated by Kaede. She laughs Jiro to scorn: 'You give in so easily. You are undependable'. The power relation between man and woman is 'so easily' overturned.

Besides her 'masculine' strength and activity, Kaede further transgresses the meaning of femininity by her eloquence, refusing 'the place of silent subjection allotted to women'.[19] She takes off her 'feminine' *mask* of a loving, faithful wife and repudiates the ethics of female virtue, which requires her to sacrifice herself to her (dead) husband and live the rest of her life self-effacingly:

> Now I must speak my mind straightforwardly, Lord Jiro. I could not care less about my husband's death. But I am worried about what is going to become of me. I do not want to live as a widow, with my hair cut, nor as a nun with my head shaved bald! (69)

Kaede's straightforward speech and the strength in her voice and expression overwhelm Jiro. But what overcomes him most is perhaps her unexpected defiance of female virtue or female identity itself. Women's speech displaces the *proper* place of silent subjection from another focus in the patriarchal system of signification and disorders the totalizing narrative on 'woman'.

Within the power structures of patriarchy, eloquence is the effective means of resistance for women to the paternal, male power, either to manipulate it or attack it. Goneril and Regan's 'glib and oily art' of speech (1.1.226), appropriating patriarchal ideological clichés, pleases Lear and enables them to manipulate the paternal power on the one hand. On the other hand, Goneril struck Lear 'upon the very heart' with her 'Most serpent-like' tongue (2.2.349–50). As the serpent depraved the garden of Eden, woman's 'serpent-like tongue' *tempts* man to 'sin' in pursuit of her/his? (unconscious) desire. Nonetheless, the garden of Eden as the blessed, seemingly homogeneous place of innocence comprises, from the start, the heterogeneity of the other than man: not only woman and the serpent, but also the (unconscious) other in man himself. These others manifest the disquieting possibility of other voices from the other scene and the impossibility of the homology of patriarchal discourse as well as of the identity of the self-same.

It is Lear who chooses Goneril's and Regan's rhetorical performance of filial love before Cordelia's 'Nothing', driven by the (phallogocentric) desire to make the meaning-identity of 'father' represented in and by his daughter's words. Lear believes in the performative effects of language which calls into existence (the meaning of) the family, power or love. It is ironic that after an excess of his poisonous pleasure of women's 'serpent-like tongue', he comes to count for much Cordelia's 'soft, gentle and low' voice as 'an excellent thing in woman' (5.3.270–71). We find here the inner contradictions in patriarchy: the symbolic identity of 'father' or 'man' and the meaning of patriarchal power must be conferred and confirmed by 'woman', whose voice is 'soft, gentle and low' enough to efface the heterogeneity of her otherness and secure the homogeneity of culture. At the same time, however, its hom(m)ology of meaning and truth may well be disturbed by the different voices of women, whose radical otherness patriarchy cannot anticipate or control.

Kaede attacks Jiro's clandestine desire *and* fear by her 'serpent-like tongue'. She persuasively but menacingly proposes to Jiro that she will not tell his 'immoral acts of treason', stealing the castle and the realm, or his 'cowardly words so unworthy of a master', accusing his vassal in order to save his own life (69). She restates the meaning of what the samurai or the lord ought to be and causes Jiro the fear of losing face. Jiro is inevitably caught up in the trap of symbolic identity as the samurai or 'man'. Throwing the dagger away, Kaede embraces Jiro, 'aghast' and 'trembling', kisses him and then presses her lips on the wound in his throat and sucks his blood. This image of a female vampire identifies Kaede as a demon lover. She wooed Jiro with her sword and won his 'love' doing him injuries. The gender-roles are reversed here. Kaede is more active, powerful and 'manly' than Jiro.

After they make love, Kaede tells Jiro that she should be his wife. 'In her expression, unseen by Jiro, is a snakelike tenacity that her voice completely belies' (70).[20] The snake or serpent is often associated with the vindictive woman or the evil female demon as temptress in Noh and Kabuki drama. Is the serpent the 'universal' signifier of female temptation and carnality? Jiro promises her to divorce Sué, but Kaede insists that she cannot tolerate any woman who slept with him. Performing a weeping woman in love, who is jealous of her rival, Kaede entices Jiro into promising to kill Sué with 'a snakelike tenacity'. While playing the role of the loving woman in tears, Kaede coolly crushes a tiny moth with her kimono sleeve. As in the traditional Japanese idiom 'to appear not to kill even an insect', it suggests the theatricality and fictionality of her performance of a 'woman', who looks – as if she could not even hurt an insect – innocent and gentle. English also has a similar expression, 'she would not harm a fly', which implies gentleness, inoffensiveness or incapability of violence conventionally understood as the attribute of femininity. It is not girls but 'wanton boys' that Gloucester likens to the Gods who kill flies (human beings) 'for their sport' (4.1.38–9). Serpent, snake, fly or insect – the meaning of masculinity or femininity is incessantly constituted but also displaced in the play of metonymical displacement of the signifiers – as *fiction*.

'Good leadership decides who wins' (79): Kaede further dramatically stages Jiro's will to power and lures him into fighting with Saboro. She seduces him by both his desire to be the great ruler *and* his fear of being attacked (punished) by Saburo in alliance with his father. 'As leader of the House of Ichimonji, you should have that ambition': Jiro assimilates the desire of 'leader of the House of Ichimonji', of the Great Lord, of/for the Other, which Kaede seductively represents as *his*. Above all he must prove himself to be a Samurai in order to fulfil *his* identity as 'man'.

When Kaede seduces Jiro into the battle – into death – and, when she shows her 'real' face of the 'treacherous woman' in the last scene, she wears a (triangle) scale-patterned kimono like a reptile, which signifies the identity of the evil demon. In Noh and Kabuki drama, when the (usually beautiful) women reveal themselves as the evil demons, they appear in scale-patterned costumes on stage.

The Noh mask called *hannya* mask also represents the demonized women. Lady Rokujo's living spirit of jealousy and hatred in *Aoi-no-ue*, the spurned girl-serpent of fury in *Dôjôji* and the old woman as ferocious ogress in *Kurozuka* also appear wearing the scale-pattered costume and the *hannya* mask, when they throw off their 'women's' faces.[21] These three evil demons with the *hannya* mask are all female, while the mask, which has two horns on the forehead, knits its brows, goggles its golden-painted eyes and shows its fangs in the wide-open mouth, itself looks neither masculine nor feminine but rather neuter. The *hannya* mask represents the demon (believed to be) *hidden* in women's mind – *behind* the feminine masquerade.

'A Bodhisattva without, a demon inside'. In Buddhist theory, every woman keeps a demon *inside* under her beautiful, merciful woman's face. This Buddhist doctrine 'universally' (from men's viewpoint) coincides with Lear's, Albany's and Edgar's distrust in the feminine masquerade, which *conceals* 'female' desire. The cuckold Albany is disgusted at the 'gilded serpent' Goneril (5.3.85). Even before Albany discovers Goneril's adultery, he denounces the hypocrisy of Goneril's 'woman's shape', which covers up the monstrosity of her 'unnatural' mind *inappropriate* to 'woman':

> Albany. See thyself, devil!
> Proper deformity shows not in the fiend
> So horrid as in woman.
> Goneril. O vain fool!

> Albany. Thou changed and self-cover'd thing, for shame,
> Be-monster not thy feature. Were't my fitness
> To let these hands obey my blood,
> They are apt enough to dislocate and tear
> Thy flesh and bones; howe'er thou art a fiend,
> A woman's shape doth shield thee.
> Goneril. Marry, your manhood – mew! (4.2.60–69)

Albany and Goneril criticize each other as not *properly* a 'man' or a 'woman' – on the grounds of their failure to fulfil the prescriptions of gendered identity. 'When Albany calls Goneril a "devil" and a "fiend"', Steven Greenblatt writes that 'he is not identifying her as a supernatural being'.[22] Albany, however, witnesses 'the denizen of hell' in Goneril's 'female disguise' – in her 'feminine' appearance, which so 'unnaturally' subverts the *proper* meaning of femininity and female virtue.

Likewise, the mad Lear discovers 'hell', 'darkness' and 'the sulphurous pit' behind the woman's chaste masquerade, or more precisely, 'Down from the waist', beneath her girdle (4.6.116–25). Lear monsterizes women as 'Centaurs', though contradictorily Centaurs, half human and half animals, are usually understood to be 'masculine' and embody the uncontrollable sexual drive of 'man'. The image of the 'simp'ring' dame's mask of chastity stresses the artificiality or theatricality of the feminine masquerade to disguise *her* 'riotous appetite'.

Lear and Albany, the men more sinned against than sinning, locate the hellish labyrinth of sin in the locus of 'woman'. Edgar also appallingly finds the 'indistinguish'd space of woman's will' (4.6.266). The identification of the fathomless abyss *in* 'woman' with 'hell', 'darkness' and 'the sulphurous pit' indicates the impossibility of men seeing and knowing the *internal* truth of 'woman' (even by anatomizing her 'hard' heart). Their knowledge of 'woman'-as-monster is constituted only in and by the metaphors of the imaginary topos of 'negative' alterity. It is this *imaginary* abyss *in* 'woman', unseeable and thus unknowable, that dizzies and disquiets 'man' as the subject of (the desire for) knowledge.

As what men imagine they *see* behind the 'deceiving' woman's mask makes them shocked and disgusted, it is men that invest the meaning of the super-*natural* (or unnatural) female power in the signifier 'woman' as unknown and unknowable other. Kaede did not have power, as the marginal other ideologically excluded from the patriarchal system of signification, although it is men who authorize her (super)natural power by succumbing to her seduction or, more specifically, to their unconscious desire and fear (of/for the Other). By demonizing her as evil demon vixen, men acknowledge her *demonic* power over them. The demonization of the women who subvert the meaning of femininity contradictorily endows the women with (super)natural powers which patriarchy tries to repress or exorcize.

Does the demonization of women herald the return of the repressed? Julia Kristeva argues that 'woman' is exiled from the symbolic order, from a patriarchal system of signification – as the 'fragmentation prior to name or to meaning which one calls the Dæmon' – as 'the fragmentation, the drive, the unnamable'.[23] Is the *hannya* mask the dramatization and acculturation of the *demonic* drives of the unnameable other repressed in the symbolic?[24]

The First Castle in *Ran*, the symbol of (patriarchal) power, collapses with the death of the men driven by the desire for power. In the falling castle in flames, Kaede seems to *enjoy* the moment of destruction and death induced by her power and mastery of men – with 'a cold smile' (106). The image of the demonic woman is precisely condensed in Kaede, whom ironically Jiro's retainers first regarded as the 'perfect' object of desire for him.[25] In this sense, does the *fatal* woman Kaede in the scale-patterned costume symbolize the return of the repressed in the symbolic economy of a patriarchal culture: the unconscious desire (of/for the Other), *jouissance*, the uncontrollable drives or death? All these meanings are repressed to be *properly* 'a man' in the symbolic, but they always already subsist in the human psyche. Her subversive power of the marginal reveals dehiscences in the meaning-and-identity of 'man', 'woman', 'wife', 'father', 'son' or 'samurai', and manifests the impossibility of the 'essential purity' of the symbolic identity from *other* scenes/stages.

Nevertheless, this very impossibility of the subject's identity-with-itself – this impediment within the subject which prevents or resists completely realized identity – perhaps opens up the possibility of the differentiating 'I', as performed on the confines of the meaning of femininity and masculinity in this world theatre, where desire is ceaselessly (en)genderd and yet never satisfied.

Notes

[1] Judith Butler, *Gender Trouble: Feminism and the Subversion of Identity* (New York: Routledge, 1990), 139.
[2] Butler, *Gender Trouble*, 140–41, 146.
[3] Judith Butler, *Bodies That Matter: On the Discursive Limits of 'Sex'* (New York: Routledge, 1993), 12, 2.
[4] Butler, *Bodies That Matter*, 15, 13, 22.

⁵ Butler, *Gender Trouble*, viii. Of course, I am amply aware of the political significance of Butler's work in re-signifying and legitimating what she calls abject homosexuality, constructed through the exclusion and repression of the regulatory norms of heterosexuality. At the same time, although Butler seems to take for granted a difference between heterosexuality and homosexuality, but considering that we cannot distinguish conscious from unconscious desire, I wonder whether it is possible to draw a clear line of demarcation between heterosexual and homosexual desire.

⁶ Jacques Derrida, 'Signature Event Context', trans. Samuel Weber and Jeffrey Melman, ed. Gerald Graff (Evanston, IL: Northwestern University Press, 1988), 12. It is the iterability of a sign that makes the proper name or signature performative but also ironically suspends its own and proper identity as present to itself: (the) repetition (compulsion) does not guarantee the identity of the self-same. For example, the name 'Earl of Gloucester' is the symbol of paternal authority and power as headship of the family. This proper name is not yet proper to Gloucester himself or even his property but an iterable sign to be cited, transferred and appropriated from the father to the bastard Edmund, and from the illegitimate to the legitimate Edgar, regardless of paternal-authorial intentions. The iterability of a sign undermines the notion of 'the proper' circulated in the restricted economy.

⁷ Tadashi Suzuki, *Enshutsuka no Hasso* (Tokyo: Ohta Shuppan, 1994), 133.

⁸ The Suzuki Company of Toga has performed *The Tale of Lear* since 1984, recently from 9–12 November 1994 at the Barbican Theatre during the Everybody's Shakespeare International Festival.

⁹ According to Sigmund Freud, the 'love of beauty' is derived from 'the field of sexual feeling', and 'beauty' and 'attraction' [or 'charm'; the German *Reiz* also means 'stimulus'] are 'originally attributes of the sexual object' (*Civilisation and its Discontents, Civilisation, Society and Religion*, ed. Albert Dickson, trans. James Strachey, Penguin Freud Library, vol. 12 (Harmondsworth: Penguin, 1991), 271.).

¹⁰ The Fool has ambiguously the 'feminine' element. Lear calls Cordelia 'my poor fool' (5.3.304). Commenting on this line, Perret considers the two characters of Cordelia and the Fool to be one as 'the representative of utter truthfulness' (Kenneth Muir, ed., *King Lear* (London: Methuen, 1972), 205n). In *Ran* the fool-figure Kyoami is played by Peter, the Japanese transvestite actor and singer. All references to *King Lear* are to the Arden Shakespeare, 3rd series, ed.

R.A. Foakes (Walton-on-Thames, Surrey: Thomas Nelson and Sons Ltd, 1997).

11   Tadashi Suzuki, 'Director's Notes', *Everybody's Shakespeare International Festival Programme*, (1994), 21.

12   Suzuki, 'Director's Notes', 21.

13   Catherine Belsey, *The Subject of Tragedy: Identity and Difference in Renaissance Drama* (London: Methuen, 1985), 185.

14   Nigel Matheson, 'Interviews', *City Limits* (14–20 March 1986), 80, quoted in Ann Thompson, 'Kurosawa's *Ran*: Reception and Interpretation', *East West Film Journal* 3.2 (1989), 5.

15   Akira Kurosawa, *Ran*, illustrations, Akira Kurosawa, screenplay, Akira Kurosawa, Hideo Oguni and Masato Ide, trans. Tadashi Shishido (Boston: Shambhala, 1986), 16. Subsequent page references are given in the text. As for the differences between the screenplay and the film, I adopted the film version as Kurosawa's 'final' text.

16   'Is man no more than this?' Lear finds 'the thing itself' in Edgar, defining 'unaccommodated man' as 'a poor, bare, forked animal' (3.4.101–106). Likewise Gloucester likens man to 'worm' or 'flies' (4.1.35, 38). Also the 'dog-hearted' (4.3.46) Goneril and Regan are called 'pelican' (3.4.74), 'she-foxes' (3.6.22) and 'Tigers' (4.2.41), and Goneril is a 'Detested kite' (1.4.254) and 'vulture' (2.2.324).

17   Refusing 'To bear it tamely' like a woman (2.2.456), Lear distinguishes 'noble anger' as 'masculine' direct resistance on the one hand from weeping as 'feminine' powerless submission on the other. He wishes not to let 'women's weapons, water-drops, / Stain my man's cheeks!' (2.2.466–7) and tries to be *properly* a 'man'. Coppélia Kahn has argued that the men's reluctance to admit their vulnerability like the crying infant (cf. 4.6.174–6, 178–9) reaffirms 'a masculine identity crisis in a culture that dichotomized power as masculine and feeling as feminine' ('The Absent Mother in "King Lear"', *Rewriting the Renaissance: The Discourses of Sexual Difference in Early Modern Europe*, eds Margret W. Ferguson, Maureen Quilligan and Nancy J. Vickers (Chicago: University of Chicago Press, 1986, 33–49), 47.).

18   Slavoj Zizek, *For They Know Not What They Do: Enjoyment as a Political Factor* (London: Verso, 1991), 254.

19   Belsey, *The Subject of Tragedy*, 184.

20   Mieko Harada, cast as Kaede, says that Kurosawa told her to speak as if a snake wriggles along (*Kurosawa Akira Shûsei*, ed. Cinema Jumpô (Tokyo: Cinema Jumpô, 1989), 197).

21   In his sketches, Kurosawa often depicts Kaede with the whites of her eyes painted gold. The Noh mask called *dei-gan* is the mask of the

beautiful woman with the gold-shaded eyes, who is possessed by the extremity of rancour or jealousy. For example, in the first half of *Aoi-no-ue*, the Noh play adapted from *The Tale of the Genji*, Lady Rokujo's living spirit, who is jealous of Genji's wife Aoi and has a grudge against her arrogant insult, appears with the *dei-gan* mask conjured up by the exorcist's prayer, and then in the second half, she reveals her 'real' identity as the evil demon, putting on the *hannya* mask. The evil female demon symbolized by the *hannya* mask is always already *hidden* behind the beautiful, 'feminine' *dei-gan* mask.

22 Steven Greeblatt, 'Shakespeare and the Exorcists', *Shakespeare and the Question of Theory*, eds Patricia Parker and Geoffrey Hartman (New York and London: Methuen, 1985), 180.

23 Julia Kristeva, 'A New Type of Intellectual: The Dissident', *The Kristeva Reader*, ed. Toril Moi (Oxford: Basil Blackwell, 1986), 296.

24 At the end of Noh drama, the three evil 'female' demons with the *hannya* mask are all subdued by the Buddhist priest's prayers. The 'female' *demonic* powers must be controlled by *holy* male powers – if it were possible. In the Noh play *Aoi-no-ue*, for example, the 'evil' spirit of Lady Rokujo is overcome, swears not to come again and finds salvation by the saint's powerful intonation. Conversely, in the *original* text of *The Tale of Genji*, Lady Rokujo's 'malign' spirit repeatedly returns before Genji in 'revenge' for him, in spite of frequent rituals of exorcism. Even after her death, she returns to *talk to* him (from the other scene), although the 'chosen' hero Genji is reluctant to listen to the voices of the other both marginalized in his psychical 'reality' and excluded from patriarchal discourse. At the same time, Genji finds that *she* still loves/hates him and 'knows' his (unconscious) desire *and* fear (as the subject presumed to know) in their 'transferential' relation.

25 After Hidetora's abdication, Jiro's retainers hint that Jiro is more fit to rule the Ichimonji domain than Taro. Jiro answers, 'My brother is no problem. But his wife, Lady Kaede, is'. His 'right-hand' Kurogane agrees, 'That is true. She should be perfect for you. Why not steal her from him?' (30). Kaede appears the 'perfect' object of desire, who might be 'a problem', but who, enigmatic 'woman' as radical other, seduces men all the more.

NINETEENTH- AND TWENTIETH-CENTURY CONTEXTS

CHAPTER 3

Touring in Asia: The Miln Company's Shakespearean Productions in Japan

Kaori Kobayashi

From the late nineteenth century, a number of acting companies began to tour the British Empire. In 1882 the critic of the *Theatre* noted that the 'theatrical life of the present day might be described as a round of glorified strolling. The "circuits" of Bristol, Norwich, and York of the last century are now replaced by those of the United States, South Africa, India, and Australia, and a modern actor thinks as little of a season in Melbourne or New York as his grandfather did of a week's "starring" in Edinburgh'.[1] George Crichton Miln was the actor-manager of such a touring company, which strolled all over the States, Australia and the Far East. In 1891 the company visited Japan with a repertoire of several Shakespearean plays. They were the first Shakespearean productions performed in complete texts on the Japanese stage. This essay is an enquiry into the influence of these productions on Japanese intellectuals, in particular Shoyo Tsubouchi, with an investigation into the itinerary of the Miln Company's tour around the Empire and Japan.

Touring Companies at the Turn of the Century

Most touring companies from Britain went to the United States,[2] because it was only a week's voyage and quite often the tour brought some financial success. For example, Henry Irving with the Lyceum company crossed the Atlantic to North America eight times between 1882 and 1903. These tours brought Irving large profits, which financially supported him in his later years at the Lyceum Theatre. However, apart from the big theatrical market in the United States it was the British Empire that made touring both possible and desirable for English companies. They went to the major Canadian cities of Toronto and Montreal, to Australia, New Zealand, India, South Africa, as well as to Far Eastern countries.[3] Such travelling companies had a repertoire of Shakespeare, comedy, melodrama and the latest West End hits. A tour could be entirely Shakespearean like the Miln

Company's repertory in Japan, or entirely modern, as was the Holloway Company's repertory of West End favourites on their tour of South Africa.[4]

By the 1890s the conventional routes for travelling companies in the Empire were well established. A number of companies toured North America and Eastern Canada, and some of them went westward to San Francisco and either re-crossed America to the East Coast or sailed across the Pacific to New Zealand and Australia. It was a lot simpler to sail directly to Australia from England. After a stay of several months in Australia they usually went to New Zealand, either returning home the same way or continuing to San Francisco via Honolulu and then touring North America. Several other companies sailed from England to the West Indies, going on to the United States or returning home. They also travelled to South Africa and some of them proceeded to India, and then travelled to Australia and New Zealand incorporating brief visits to the Far Eastern colonial outposts, as well as to the settlements of foreign nationals in Shanghai and Beijing. Occasionally they visited the small but growing group of British and American traders in port cities such as Yokohama, Kobe and Nagasaki in Japan. Mrs Brown-Potter and Kyrle Bellew, for example, went to America, Australia, India, the Far East and South Africa in the 1890s; and Russell Craufurd visited Calcutta, Rangoon, Penang, Singapore and Hong Kong. They planned to go on to San Francisco by way of Shanghai, Yokohama and Honolulu, but that part of the tour was cancelled because of an outbreak of plague in Hong Kong.[5]

These journeys were very tiring and lasted for several months; they could sometimes be for one or two years.[6] Touring actors suffered from bad weather conditions and illness. Wilson Barrett, touring in Johannesburg in 1902, wrote to his family: 'We are all upset by colds and influenza, the changes are startling, hot all day, bitter cold at sundown, and the dust is very harmful to nose, throat and lungs'.[7] However, in spite of such adverse circumstances, a number of companies went on tour in the British provinces and in the Empire with the expectation of success in a market far larger and potentially far more profitable than in London.[8] Of course, it was impossible to have such a journey without the transport network within the Empire. As the spread of the railway system had enabled companies to tour around Britain, the replacement of sail by steam as a means of global transport gave the star and his company the opportunity of much expanded touring in the Empire. Moreover, cultural expansionism in the late Victorian era was closely related to this kind of touring in the Empire. As Michael Booth points out, such an expansion of theatrical horizons to encompass the whole globe can be regarded as a remarkable and significant phenomenon of late Victorian cultural imperialism.[9]

Touring Companies in the Far East

Those touring companies which went to Far Eastern countries, and eventually to Japan, often sailed from London via the Suez Canal (opened in 1869). They landed in Bombay, making their way to Calcutta, then to Madras, Colombo, Rangoon (Yangon), Singapore, Manila, Hong Kong, Shanghai, Beijing, Tientsin, Hankow and finally Japan. Some companies travelled to Japan after touring in Australia or South Africa. Such routes were gradually established from the 1860s and the number of companies which followed these routes reached its height around 1912–14.[10]

It is known that around 1862–3 touring companies began to visit Japan. In 1858, five years after the unprecedented visit of the American Commodore Matthew G. Perry to Uraga, the Tokugawa government was forced to conclude a trade treaty with the United States. This was virtually the end to the national isolation policy (*Sakoku*) in Japan, which had lasted for no less than two hundred years.[11] The American diplomat Townsend Harris demanded the opening of major ports such as Edo (now called Tokyo), Osaka and Kobe and extraterritorial rights for all Westerners in Japan. These rights required that, in all legal matters, Westerners would be subjected not to Japanese laws but to their own. In addition, Japan had to agree to fixed tariffs – fixed so as to permit the cheap and easy importation of Western goods.[12] As a consequence a number of foreign traders and civil servants came to the newly opened markets in Japan such as Yokohama, Kobe, and Nagasaki, where they built small foreign settlements. Travelling companies normally visited such foreign communities. As the number of foreigners, most of whom were British, increased, they began to establish their own theatres in the foreign settlements.[13] Three theatres were established in the early 1870s: the Gaiety Theatre in Yokohama (December 1870), the Gymnasium Theatre in Kobe (December 1870), and the Nagasaki Public Hall and Theatre (November 1875). All these theatres offered entertainment not for a Japanese audience but for foreign residents, and the management was undertaken entirely by foreigners. Yet there were several Japanese intellectuals who went to these theatres in order to imbibe Western culture. Among these three theatres, the Yokohama Gaiety Theatre, which was geographically close to Tokyo, exerted the greatest influence on Japanese intellectuals.

The Yokohama Gaiety Theatre

Although the Gaiety Theatre in Yokohama was established by a Dutch merchant called M.J.B. Noordhoek Hegt, it was initially a theatre occupied by British amateur companies in the settlements.[14] It was presumably named after the Gaiety Theatre in London, which had been famous mainly for entertainment such as burlesques and musical comedies since its establishment in 1868.[15] As a matter of fact the name 'Gaiety Theatre' in London had been taken from Théâtre de la Gaité in Paris.[16] As the Gaiety Theatre in London became famous, many theatres called 'Gaiety Theatre' were founded not only in Britain but also in the Empire. The most famous of these was the Gaiety Theatre in Manchester built in 1884, which became well known after the new repertory system introduced by A.E.F. Horniman in 1908.[17] There were also many Gaiety Theatres in Ireland, the United States, Bombay, Sydney, Johannesburg, Hankow and Shanghai.[18] Like these theatres in Britain and in other parts of the Empire, the Yokohama Gaiety Theatre, built in 1870, provided the community with cultural events and entertainment. From its opening it presented a number of amateur stage productions such as classical concerts, burlesques and musical comedies. Moreover, it was visited by various touring companies. The Janet Waldorf Company presented several scenes from Shakespeare in 1899. The Bandmann Company and the Bandmann Opera Company, founded by Maurice E. Bandmann, theatre manager in Calcutta, brought musical comedies and popular West End hits to Yokohama almost every year between 1906 and 1921.[19] Allan Wilkie, with his wife Frediswyde Hunter-Watts, presented several Shakespearean productions and popular plays such as *The Second Mrs. Tanqueray, Salome* and *Candida* at the Yokohama Gaiety Theatre in 1912 during their tour through Asian cities such as Calcutta, Canton, Peking and Manila.[20]

On the one hand the theatre played the role of a public hall for foreigners, and on the other, it provided quite a few Japanese intellectuals with opportunities to encounter 'real' Western culture. In particular, productions of Shakespeare and Ibsen at the Gaiety Theatre had a significant influence on stage practitioners such as Shoyo Tsubouchi (1859–1935) and Kaoru Osanai (1881–1928). After the long closure of the country for more than two hundred years, it was inevitable that the Japanese would modernize the state through Westernization. For such intellectuals as Tsubouchi and Osanai, it was necessary to establish a modern Japanese theatre which was different from traditional theatre, especially Kabuki. Shoyo Tsubouchi was a teacher of English and drama at Tokyo Senmon Gakko,[21] and subsequently translated the complete works of Shakespeare for the first time into Japanese.[22] He was also a stage practitioner who attempted to provide Shakespearean texts for actors to perform on stage. Both Tsubouchi and Osanai established their own companies with a hope of transforming the traditional Japanese theatre scene: Tsubouchi established Bungei Kyokai (Literary Arts Association) with his students in 1906,[23] and Kaoru Osanai, together with Sadanji

Ichikawa, a progressive Kabuki actor, founded Jiyu Gekijo (Free Theatre) in 1909. Tsubouchi, like other intellectuals, insisted that Japan should have a new theatre in order to become a modern nation state. In 1911, he told his students that 'art should reflect the essence of the ideals of its age, but theatre in Japan does not'.[24]

These leading practitioners were preoccupied with Western plays in order to modernize the old-style and actor-centred Japanese theatre. While Tsubouchi presented several Shakespearean productions, Osanai with Jiyu Gekijo produced naturalistic plays written by Ibsen, Chekhov, Wedekind and Gorki. The Bungei Kyokai presented their first production of *Hamlet* in 1907. Then in 1911 they produced *Hamlet* at the Imperial Theatre which was founded in the same year as an institution that symbolized modernization through Westernization.[25] It was consciously modelled on the Comédie Française and the architectural style was Renaissance and French.[26] It was apparent that the Japanese imitated Western architecture in an attempt to imitate Western culture and civilization.

The Yokohama Gaiety Theatre was one of the few places where Japanese intellectuals could see Western plays actually performed by foreign actors. Tsubouchi visited the Gaiety from time to time in order to acquire information on the directing of Western drama. Such information was greatly helpful to him when he directed *Hamlet* and *The Merchant of Venice* in subsequent years.[27] Kaoru Osanai saw productions such as *Salome* and *The Importance of Being Earnest* at the Yokohama Gaiety Theatre, which were valuable references when he directed these plays in later years.

In fact, for a Japanese in those days, visiting the Yokohama Gaiety Theatre was an experience similar to going abroad. When Osanai went to the theatre for the first time, he felt as if he had been in a foreign country and 'sat at the left end of the seats, watching the play humbly'.[28] The Yokohama Gaiety Theatre provided Tsubouchi and Osanai not only with an experience of practical ways of directing Western drama on the stage, but also the atmosphere of Western society, which the Japanese regarded as the model for modernizing their own country.

The Miln Company

Stage productions at the Gaiety Theatre in its first years were mainly melodrama and musicals, in parallel with the repertoires of theatres in provincial cities in Britain. There were also several Shakespeare productions. Most of them had, however, been either amateur productions or merely extracts from Shakespeare plays, before the first and complete

Shakespeare productions by the Miln Company in May 1891.²⁹ They presented *Hamlet, The Merchant of Venice, Romeo and Juliet, Macbeth, Othello, Julius Caesar* and *Richard III* during their two weeks' repertoire in Yokohama. These productions are significant as the first Shakespeare productions staged in complete texts in Japan. In particular for Tsubouchi, the founder of modern Japanese theatre, these productions were his first encounters with Shakespeare plays actually performed on the stage.

George Crichton Miln, the actor-manager of the company, was born in London in 1851. After experience as an accounting clerk, a farm hand and a journalist, he became a Unitarian preacher in Brooklyn, New York. In 1882, he quit holy orders and became an actor-manager in Chicago. His first venture from October 1882 lasted two months, during which he produced 70 performances of three Shakespeare plays (*Hamlet, Macbeth* and *Othello*) in nearly 40 cities in the north-west part of the States.³⁰ The *Chicago Tribune* reviewed Miln's Hamlet in Chicago (17 October 1882) as having 'youth, talent, quickness of intellectual perception, an admirable voice, good elocution'. But the reviewer criticized his lack of inspiration and repose and concluded that 'there is nothing sympathetic in Mr. Miln ... nothing electric in his acting'.³¹

Nearly one year later, Miln presented the first full season tour. It started in Wisconsin, went through Illinois and finished in Michigan City.³² On the way to New Haven from Pennsylvania, the Miln Company produced several plays including *Hamlet* and *Macbeth* at the Academy of Music in New York.³³ The *New York Mirror* reported that Miln 'made a marked impression', while observing that his Hamlet 'talks loudly and declaims with emphasis. There is considerable tendency to rant'.³⁴

Miln's background as a preacher presumably gave him a polished elocutionary style and an active intelligence.³⁵ However, as Alan Woods comments, Miln's productions of Shakespearean plays were in an outdated style, which had been popular in the first half of the century:

> Miln and his fellows existed away from major population centres for the most part, relying instead on less sophisticated cities where old-fashioned oratorical styles still pleased audiences.³⁶

The actor-manager almost completely ignored the current theatrical tradition and paid attention mainly to entertaining people in provincial towns. He seems to have relied rather too strongly on his oratorical skills, which sometimes turned out to be sheer 'ranting'. G.C.D. Odell refers to Miln as 'a good elocutionist but not a very good actor'.³⁷ Marion Moore Coleman, who saw Miln's production of *Hamlet* in Kansas City in 1887 comments that he was 'trying hard to make a place for himself as a legitimate actor, but he had so far to go that he never really made it'.[38] Miln's Shakespeare productions in the States may remind us of the low artistic standard that was inherent in productions of provincial touring companies in England at that time.

In 1888 Miln took his productions all over Australia. His first production was *Hamlet* at Her Majesty's in Sydney on 6 October. It was enthusiastically received by the audience, and several press reviews supported that enthusiasm. Miln's production of *Hamlet* had several changes which apparently gave 'novel' ideas of Shakespearean plays to the Australian audience. For example, the farewell admonition of Polonius to his son was omitted altogether, as was the King's repentant prayer and Hamlet's diverted purpose.[39] Above all, a sudden flash across the stage in the closet scene as a substitute for the visible entrance of the Ghost was the most striking feature in Miln's production. Such innovations were ardently welcomed by the audience. The reviewer of the *Sydney Morning Herald* remarked that Miln's *Hamlet* was staged 'as it has never before been staged in the colonies'. Referring to its popularity in Sydney he wrote, 'If Saturday night may be taken as an indication of how Sydney intends to regard Mr Miln, then there can be no doubt whatever about his popularity'.[40] However, it is evident that some of the critics were puzzled by the 'novel' ideas Miln imposed on Shakespeare's text. The *Sydney Mail* critic commented that Miln brought 'much that appealed most favourably to the large audience which greeted him, though in his reading there were variations which were hardly acceptable to Shakespearean students'.[41]

Moreover, as we have seen in the reviews at American theatres, Miln was at times a ranting speaker and his acting was excessively artificial. According to the *Sydney Daily Telegraph*, all of Miln's big speeches in the play were too obviously delivered as clap-trap with a view to popular applause, while the melodramatic endings imposed on some of the scenes were no more than a direct appeal to the gallery:

> The new actor has fine eyes and piercing look, which would be more effective were it not resorted to so constantly as to be almost habitual, but this action is characteristic in an impersonation which, in spite of the many good qualities here recognised, *must be described as extremely artificial* [italics added].[42]

However, Miln's oratorical style apparently pleased some reviewers as well as the Australian audience. The *Town and Country Journal* praised Miln as being 'a good face and figure, a voice of considerable power and compass, together with a clear and distinct enunciation',[43] and the critic of the *Brisbane Courier* who saw Miln's *Hamlet* later in Brisbane glorified 'Mr. Miln's rich, deep, musical voice which modulates with much artistic effect'.[44]

After finishing the successful season in Sydney on 26 October 1888 he moved to Her Majesty's Opera House in Brisbane, where he presented several productions of *Richard III, Damon and Pythias, Hamlet, Richelieu* and *The Fool's Revenge*. By this time, Miln had formed his own company of Australian actors. His brief season in Brisbane was a triumphant success. Miln's productions excited not only the audience but also the critics. The reviewer of the *Brisbane Courier* wrote that Miln was 'a first class Shakespearean entertainer'.[45]

Miln's succeeding tours in Australia had a similarly favourable reception as in Brisbane, which ensured him financial success. On 16 March 1889, Miln opened his Melbourne season in the Opera House with *Richard III*, which was followed by *Julius Caesar* and *Hamlet*. The Opera House, which could accommodate 3,000 people, encouraged the actor-manager to present spectacular productions. In particular, Miln's *Hamlet* was vehemently hailed by the public.[46] The writer of the *Table Talk* commented on the performance as follows:

> [Miln's] new readings were full of deep and earnest thought, his departures from the accepted text being guided by a desire to present his idea of the way things should be done. We have so few actors with enough character or brains to depart from stage conventions.[47]

As a whole, Miln's productions at Australian theatres were highly successful.[48] His artificial style gave thousands of people throughout Australia the kind of theatrical experience they craved. However, as we have seen, in the United States he was undervalued as 'not a very good actor'.[49] As Eric Irvin questions, why do the reactions to the actor-manager in Australia differ from those in the States to such an extent? Was it the case that American and Australian audiences were looking for different things? It is evident that Australians welcomed Miln's changes from the traditional *Hamlet*, regarding them as a 'new reading' of the text, while Americans criticized them as 'old-fashioned styles' that pleased just provincial audiences.[50] Whatever the reasons for these different reactions, it is significant that, as we shall see later in this essay, the responses of Japanese intellectuals were as favourable as those of Australians. In particular, his oratorical way of acting pleased Shoyo Tsubouchi.

Shakespearean Productions of the Miln Company in Yokohama

After the highly successful season in Australia, Miln set out for a tour of the Far East from October 1890. He presented several productions in Calcutta, Rangoon, Singapore, Shanghai and Hong Kong. Then in May 1891 he arrived at Nagasaki with his company, including his wife, Louise Jordan Miln. Travelling through Kobe, they went to Tokyo where they produced one performance of *Julius Caesar* especially for a Japanese audience at an ordinary theatre in Tokyo.[51] They ambitiously intended to play *The Merchant of Venice* in front of the Emperor at his court, but the idea was eventually rejected, specifically because a coolie attempted to assault the Russian Tsarevitz who was then visiting Japan, an event which threw the Japanese Court into a state of anxiety.[52] The company visited Yokohama at the end of May, and produced eight performances of Shakespeare plays (*Hamlet*, *The Merchant of Venice*, *Romeo and Juliet*, *Macbeth*, *Othello*, *Julius Caesar* and *Richard III*) at the Yokohama Gaiety Theatre.

It seems that the favourite performance of the company was *Hamlet*, which they presented twice at the Gaiety. Miln played the lead and his wife, Louise Jordan Miln played the part of Ophelia.[53] The *Japan Weekly Mail* reported that their *Hamlet* had had high reputations in the touring of other Asian countries:

> The newspapers of the various communities which they have favoured with a visit on their way to Japan had without exception employed such unequivocal terms of praise in noticing the performances, that, not unnaturally, public expectation in Yokohama was raised to a high pitch, so high indeed that there was danger of disappointment through over-anticipation.

However, the reviewer went on to say that their production in Yokohama was not at all against expectations of the audience: 'But we believe we may say safely that Mr. Miln's acting has quite fulfilled the highest estimates formed of his powers'.[54] As in the States and Australia the outstanding feature of Miln's acting was his oratorical elocution. The reviewer of the press quoted above praised Miln's 'fine and striking declamation': 'Mr. Miln never lapsed from dramatic eloquence which at the very first set the key note of his language'. Thus, as in Australia, Miln's *Hamlet* was favourably welcomed by the audience in Yokohama.

Reactions of Japanese Intellectuals

Among the audience for Miln's productions of Shakespeare at the Gaiety Theatre were Tokoku Kitamura, a famous novelist,[55] several students of Tokyo University who were reading *Macbeth* with a lecturer from the States, and Shoyo Tsubouchi. Through productions by foreign actors such as Miln, Tsubouchi learned the difference of performance techniques such as dialogue, expressions, and elocution between productions in Japan and the West.[56] When the Miln company came to Yokohama, Tsubouchi saw their productions of *The Merchant of Venice* and *Hamlet*. They were, for Tsubouchi, the very first Shakespeare productions he had seen performed by foreign actors. In later years, he commented on their *Hamlet* as follows:

> The director of the company was called Miln, who was short and thickset. I recall that although he was merely an ordinary touring actor, in comparison with another British travelling actor, Alan Wilkie who performed Shakespearean plays at the Teikoku Gekijo [Imperial Theatre] in the first year of the Taisho era [1912], his production was more authentic, by no means self-taught, and was certainly following the old-style productions of Shakespearean plays. I went to Yokohama all the way from my house in Tokyo and saw only *Hamlet* and *Merchant of Venice* of Miln's productions. As his way of directing was in accordance with the old style, the few productions which I saw provided the means to analyse a number of other Shakespearean performances on stage. His productions not only helped my reading of the plays but also became useful when I presented *Merchant of Venice* and *Hamlet* on the stage with Doi, Togi, Minakuchi in the later years.[57]

It is evident that Miln's productions of Shakespearean plays directed in 'the old style' were well appreciated by Tsubouchi, although they were unfavourably criticized for being outdated in the States. The main reason for his preference was, of course, that Miln's productions were the very first performances by foreign actors he had ever seen on stage. Tokoku Kitamura, another member of the audience of Miln's *Hamlet*, was profoundly impressed by Hamlet's soliloquy and Ophelia's mad scene. Even two years after the performance he could not forget the memory and recounted it to a colleague, who described the scene in later years as follows:

> While we were drinking, Tokoku narrated his memory of *Hamlet* which he saw at the Yokohama Gaiety Theatre. As he became

excited, he put his handkerchief on his head ... and danced the dancing of Ophelia in her madness.[58]

It is not surprising that these Japanese were deeply moved by Shakespearean productions performed by foreigners, a form of theatre which they had never seen before. Moreover, as mentioned above, Western art of any kind was the model for Japanese intellectuals in the 1890s. Westernization was considered a process of modernization. In order to be a nation state and be equal with the Western powers, the Japanese believed that it was essential for them to imitate Western culture and society. They had an admiration for the Occident, and at the same time, an inferiority complex in relation to anything from the West.

In addition, Shoyo Tsubouchi favoured Miln's oratorical and rather out-dated acting style because it was similar to familiar forms of artificial acting in Kabuki. Although he wanted to establish a new theatre in Japan which was different from Kabuki, his idea was not to ignore the entire theatrical tradition in Japan, but to combine it with the Western tradition of drama. Tsubouchi himself was extremely fond of Kabuki. He also had a good voice and liked reading play scripts loudly. In his schooldays he was taught by American teachers that reading texts aloud was a useful practice.[59] In 1890 with other lecturers at Tokyo Senmon Gakko, he established the *Rodoku-kai* [reading aloud club – in effect it was a play reading club] where they practised reading texts aloud with student-actors such as Shunyo Doi and Biyo Minakuchi, who later acted parts in Shakespeare productions directed by Tsubouchi in 1907 and 1911.[60] They mainly used texts of historical plays written for the Kabuki stage. At the *Rodoku-kai*, Tsubouchi taught his student-actors a declamatory style of delivery with full body gestures which maintained features redolent of Kabuki acting technique.[61]

It may also be the case that Japanese intellectuals in the 1890s preferred 'the old-style productions of Shakespeare plays' because they had had the image of Shakespeare plays only through reading the texts. As Toshio Kawatake states, the introduction of Shakespeare's plays to Japan was unlike that of other Western playwrights such as Ibsen and Chekhov, whose works were fully translated from the beginning of their introduction.[62] Shakespearean plays had gone through all kinds of adaptations for certain periods before the introduction of wholly translated texts. The history of *Hamlet* is an extreme example. *Hamlet* was primarily introduced as poetry. In 1882, a Japanese version of the fourth soliloquy appeared in a collection of Western poetry which was compiled to stimulate new poets in Japan.[63] Additionally the dramatic plot of the play, which is reminiscent of some of the revenge plays from Kabuki, began to attract writers from the 1870s on.⁶⁴ The introduction of Charles Lamb's *Tales From Shakespeare* in the 1880s promoted interest in the plot of the play even more.⁶⁵ It was only in 1905 that the first attempt at translating *Hamlet* was undertaken. The first full-scale translation was produced by Tsubouchi for the stage production by Bungei Kyokai in 1907.

Thus, the text of *Hamlet* was not initially introduced as a play, but as a piece of poetry and a good story with a dramatic plot. On the stage, it was performed for the first time in 1903 by Otojiro Kawakami. However, this group used an adapted version of the play. Before any proper productions based on complete texts of Shakespeare, there had been a number of staged adaptations.⁶⁶ In fact the very first encounter of the Japanese audience with Shakespeare plays on stage were these adaptations. Like other adapted versions, Kawakami's *Hamlet* was entirely transformed into a Japanese version: the whole story was set in nineteenth-century Japan; all the soliloquies were cut, and all the names of the characters were changed to Japanese names.⁶⁷ It was in 1907 that the complete Shakespeare text, although in a translated version, was presented on the stage for the first time.⁶⁸

Before Miln's *Hamlet* intellectuals could only read Shakespearean texts in their studies. They had their own image of a production of *Hamlet*. Even for Tsubouchi, a man of the theatre who provided Shakespeare texts for actors in later years, Shakespearean plays were basically poetry. When he translated *Hamlet* for a stage production, he used archaic language instead of modern Japanese, which was the standard in other modern productions in Japan. Although he was criticized for its admixture of archaisms, he insisted that Shakespeare is 70 per cent poetry and that ignoring this in translation will destroy the balance between form and content.⁶⁹

Later in 1907 and 1911, Tsubouchi chose *Hamlet* for his productions instead of modern naturalistic drama such as Ibsen or Gorki, because *Hamlet* was a play without any overt social or political implications. The Japanese authorities had been attentive to the subversive power of theatre. Around the 1880s literature with a distinct and oppositional political message became prevalent. In the 1910s, conservative forces attacked Nora and Magda as characters subversive to authority.⁷⁰ It was indispensable for Tsubouchi to escape from unnecessary political involvement. Consequently his choice was *Hamlet*. In his essay 'Nihon ni Shakespeare-geki wo Kyosan to suru Riyu' [The reason why we play Shakespeare in Japan], Tsubouchi declared that one of the reasons why the Japanese need to play Shakespeare is that Shakespeare's plays are so elegant and moderate that there is no need to worry about strict censorship. He continues 'even though such a play as *Romeo and Juliet* is about love romance, it has no obscenity and is therefore suitable to show at any place and to anyone'.[71] Japanese intellectuals presumably had an image of Shakespeare which was close to that of Romantic critics such as Schlegel and Lamb.

The investigation into the touring of George Crichton Miln exemplifies the theatrical practices of travelling companies in the Empire around the turn of the century. The artistic standards of such strolling players were probably quite similar to that of provincial touring companies in Britain and the States. As they were detached from the centres of culture during their long and tiring journeys, they often ignored stage tradition. It is noteworthy that while Miln's outdated performance was criticized in the States, it was ardently welcomed in Australia and Japan where there had not been any long tradition of Shakespearean performances. However, the difference in reactions between the States and Japan is not only a matter of theatrical experience, but also of the cultural difference. Shakespearean productions are in fact constructs of changing values of society and culture. Even though George Crichton Miln was a sheer 'ranter' in the States, his productions of Shakespeare had a considerable influence on the growing Japanese theatre at the end of the nineteenth century.

Notes

[1] Evelyn Ballantyne, 'Some Impressions of the Australian Stage', *Theatre* (April, 1892), 186.

[2] For example, the English actor J.H. Barnes went to America thirteen times between 1874 and 1913. See J.H. Barnes, *Forty Years on the Stage* (London: Chapman and Hall, 1914).

[3] In 1914, for instance, John Martin-Harvey toured to Canada under the auspices of the British Canadian Theatrical Organisation. Geneviève Ward went on a 50,000 mile expedition to Australia, New Zealand, India and South Africa starting in 1879 and lasting two years. See Michael Booth, 'Touring the Empire', *Essays in Theatre* 6 (November 1987), 50 and Geneviève Ward and Richard Whiteing, *Both Sides of the Curtain* (London: Cassell and Company, 1909).

[4] Booth, 56. For information on the tour of the Holloway Company in the Empire, see David Holloway, *Playing the Empire* (London: Harrap, 1979) and Josephine Harrop, 'The Holloways: A Hundred Years of Travelling Theatre History', *Scenes from Provincial Stages: Essays in Honour of Kathleen Barker,* ed. Richard Foulkes (London: The Society for Theatre Research, 1994), 155–66.

[5] See Russell Craufurd, *Rumbling of an Old Mummer* (London: Greening and Company, 1909).

6 Seymour Hicks, who toured North America with the Kendals between 1889 and 1890, describes their exhausting itineraries: 'Many a time I have got into the train after a performance, arriving at the next town we were to appear in at almost twelve the next day, dashed to the theatre, unpacked my trunks, and swallowing a few sandwiches, played at a matinee at two o'clock! Directly the curtain fell the clothes used in the piece had to be put away and those necessary for the evening bill got ready. Then scrambled dinner, back to the theatre, and after playing again everything had to be packed and a rush made to catch the train, often without any supper at all'. See Seymore Hicks, *By Himself* (London, 1910), 87–88, quoted in Booth, 54–55.

7 A. Wilson Barrett, *And Give Me Yesterday*, unpublished ms. (1966), 282, quoted in Booth, 54.

8 Booth, 51.

9 Booth, 51.

10 The number of travelling actors in Asia considerably decreased from the late 1920s through the 1930s. There were various reasons for the decline: first, the spread of motion pictures and talkies, second, political and economic instability in Asia and third, the possibility of war. Information taken from Masahiko Masumoto, 'The Asian Tour Network of Western Performing Arts', unpublished seminar paper at 'Cultural Encounters in the Development of Modern East Asia' (23 July 1996 at Doshisha University in Kyoto), 3.

11 For more information on the breakdown of national isolation, see Makoto Takeuchi, ed., *Kyoyo no Sekai-shi* (Tokyo: Tokyo UP, 1987), 200–201.

12 Michael A. Barnhart, *Japan and the World Since 1868* (London: Arnold, 1995), 7.

13 According to the statistics, *Meiji/Taisho ki Yokohama Iju Gaikokujin*, in 1868 there were 260 British residents out of 570 Westerners in Yokohama; in 1870 there were 513 out of 942; in 1876 there were 635 out of 1,521; in 1890 there were 748 out of 1,593; in 1912 the number rose to 1,575 out of 3,673. Half of the foreigners in Yokohama were from China, but among Western foreign residents the British were always in the majority.

14 Information on the Gaiety Theatre in Yokohama is taken from Masahiko Masumoto, *Yokohama Gete-za: Meiji Taisho no Seiyo Gekijo* [Yokohama Gaiety Theatre: A Western Style Theatre in the Meiji and Taisho Eras] (Yokohama: Iwasaki Kinen P, 1989).

15 For information on the Gaiety Theatre in London, see W. Macqueen-Pope, *Gaiety: Theatre of Enchantment* (London: W.H. Allen, 1949) and Alan Hyman, *The Gaiety Years* (London: Cassell, 1975).

16 John Hollingshead, *Gaiety Chronicle* (London: Archibald Constable, 1898), 30.
17 For information on the Gaiety Theatre in Manchester, see Rex Pogson, *Miss Horniman and the Gaiety Theatre, Manchester* (London: Rockliff, 1952).
18 See *Japan Weekly Mail* (22 March 1884), 270; Eric Irvin, 'Nineteenth Century English Dramatists in Australia', *Theatre Notebook* 30 (1976), 34 and Macqueen-Pope, 148, 380.
19 The father of Maurice E. Bandmann, Daniel E. Bandmann (1840–1905) was a Shakespearean actor in Europe and the States. He toured in Australia three times (1869, 1871–2, 1879–84) and visited Asian countries, except Japan, during his last tour. His wife was an actor called Millicent Palmer (1845?–1926), who was playing in Britain around the turn of the twentieth century. See John Parker, ed., *The Green Room Book 1908* (London: Sealy Clark, 1908), 32; C.E. Pascoe, ed., *The Dramatic List* (London: David Bogue, 1880), 27–33 and Daniel E. Bandmann, *An Actor's Tour, or Seventy Thousand Miles with Shakespeare* (Boston: Cupples, Upham and Co., 1885).
20 Allan Wilkie, born in Liverpool, became an actor in 1899. After several years of acting with provincial touring companies in Britain, he joined Frank Benson's Company. In 1905 he formed his own company and toured all over Britain for six years. Then from 1911 to 1913 he undertook a tour in Asian countries, which was followed by a tour in South Africa and Australia. For information on Allan Wilkie Company, see Allan Wilkie, *All the World My Stage: The Reminiscence of a Shakespearean Actor-Manager in Five Continents* (c.1956), a photocopy of the typescripts of the unpublished autobiography of Allan Wilkie at the Theatre Museum in London; 'Obituary: Mr. Allan Wilkie: Shakespearean actor-manager', *The Times* (8 January. 1970); Usui Kojima, 'Arupinisuto no Nikki' [The Diary of an Alpinist], *Kojima Usui Zenshu* [The Complete Works of Usui Kojima], vol. 10 (Tokyo: Taishu-kan, 1980), 285; John Parker, ed., *Who's Who in the Theatre*, 8th edn (London: Pitman, 1936), 1529; Archibald Strong, 'Allan Wilkie and Shakespeare', *The Australian Quarterly* (June 1930), 77–82; Eizo Tanaka, *Meiji Taisho Shingeki-shi Shiryo* [Materials for the History of Shingeki (New Drama) in the Meiji and Taisho Eras] (Tokyo: Engeki Shuppan Sha, 1964), 112–13; and Eizo Tanaka, *Shingeki Sono Mukashi* [Shingeki (New Drama) in the Past] (Tokyo: Bungei Shunju Shinsha, 1957), 101–103.
21 The name of Tokyo Senmon Gakko was changed to Waseda University in 1902.

22. Tsubouchi's first translation of Shakespeare was *Julius Caesar* in 1884. He finished translating the complete works of Shakespeare in 1928.
23. 'Bungei Kyokai was founded in February, 1906, at the urging of Tsubouchi's students. It was planned to be primarily an extra-curricular study association which would engage in a wide range of cultural activities. The main interest of its core members, however, was in drama, and three of them had been studying *rodoku* with Tsubouchi for several years. As an organization it did not last very long, and apart from publishing a journal and mounting two productions twelve months apart its initial loudly proclaimed promise remained largely unfulfilled at the end of its three-year life'. Brian Powell, 'One Man's Hamlet in 1911 in Japan: The Bungei Kyokai Production in the Imperial Theatre', unpublished paper, (1997), 10; see also Kawatake, *Shingeki Undo no Reimei ki,* 192–93.
24. Shoyo Tsubouchi, 'Hamlet no Koen ni Sakidachite', *Tsubouchi Shoyo Senshu* 12 (Tokyo: Shunyodo, 1927), 590–91.
25. Bungei Kyokai's *Hamlet* in 1911 was a significant beginning for Shakespearean productions in Japan. First of all, they used the genuinely translated text of Shakespeare. There had been numerous productions of *Hamlet* in Japan. Secondly, it was the first modern production to use actresses in female parts. Thirdly, it was one of the first productions directed by a sole director.
26. Powell, 18.
27. Shoyo Tsubouchi, 'Naichi de Hajimete Mita Gaikoku-haiyu no Shakespeare-geki no Insho' [The Impression of Shakespearean Stages Performed by Foreign Actors, Which I Saw for the First Time in Japan], *Shoyo Senshu* [Selected Works of Shoyo Tsubouchi], vol. 12 (Tokyo: Shynyo-do, 1927), 376.
28. Kaoru Osanai, *Osanai Kaoru Engeki Zenshu* [Complete Works of Kaoru Osanai], vol. 1 (Tokyo: Mirai-sha, 1964), 270–80.
29. In 1875 an amateur company performed *Henry V*; in 1879 Boothroyd Fairclogh with Miss Elcia May and amateurs presented scenes from Shakespeare and *The Taming of the Shrew*; in 1887 an amateur company performed *Catherine and Petruchio*; in 1888 the Louise Crawford Company produced an extract of *Hamlet*; and in 1889 the Wonderers Company presented an extract from *Hamlet*.
30. Alan Woods, 'Quality Wasn't Expected: The Classical Tours of George C. Miln', *Theatre Studies* 24/25 (1977–9), 140.
31. *Chicago Tribune* (22 October 1882), quoted in Woods, 140.

32 The repertoire included *Hamlet, Macbeth, Romeo and Juliet, Othello, Richelieu, The Fool's Revenge, The Lady of Lyons* and *Damon and Pythias*.
33 There is a promptbook of his *Macbeth* at the Folger Library in Washington DC: see *Britain's Literary Heritage, Shakespeare and the Stage, Series One: Prompt Books From the Folger Library, Washington DC* (Brighton: Harvester Microfilm, 1985), 86.
34 *New York Mirror* (16 February 1884). One week later the same paper reported Miln's lack of financial success in New York: 'George C. Miln lost $1,200 at the Academy of Music last week, but that was to be expected'. From September 1884, his first nationwide tour, including such major cities as Washington and New York, lasted for eight months. The *Washington Post* (23 April 1885) remarked that 'a polished and consistent performance could not be reasonably expected of Mr. Miln'.
35 Woods, 139.
36 Woods, 144.
37 Eric Irvin, 'George Crichton Miln: An Individualist on the Australian Stage', *Australian Drama Studies* 19 (October 1991), 104.
38 Marion Moore Coleman, *Fair Rosalind: The American Career of Helen Modjeska* (Connecticut: Cherry Hill Books, 1969), 433.
39 *Sydney Morning Herald* (8 October 1888). Moreover Miln cut the final 'to set it right' from the famous line 'the time is out of joint' and ended the speech with 'O, cursed spite, that ever I was born'. In the graveyard scene, Hamlet did not jump into the grave after Laertes.
40 *Sydney Morning Herald* (8 October 1888).
41 *Sydney Mail* (13 October 1888). The writer of the *Sydney Morning Herald* (8 October 1888) did not altogether share the enthusiasm of the audience. Miln, he said, presented a rampantly physical and mad Hamlet, rather than the usual contemplative, philosophical, dreaming Hamlet of tradition, and as a whole the production 'was strangely uneven'. 'There were moments when one felt like saying "This man has some startling indications of tragic strength", and again there were others when one lost interest in him and found the mind wandering to the other characters of the play'. The reviewer of the *Sydney Daily Telegraph* (8 October 1888) found that many cuts in the text were often aimless.
42 *Sydney Daily Telegraph*.
43 *Town and Country Journal,* quoted in Irvin, 95.
44 *Brisbane Courier* (6 November 1888).
45 *Brisbane Courier*. The writer further marked his approval: 'Playgoers were rewarded by an interpretation of what the majority of critics

reckon the greatest play in the English language, if not in any language, which in many respects would compare most favourably with anything seen previously on the Brisbane stage'.

46 The reviewer of the *Table Talk* (7 May 1889) wrote as follows: 'One remarkable trait (sic) of this portion of the audience was that the standers kept their position from eight o'clock to half past eleven without absenting themselves from their coign of vantage during the interval'.

47 *Table Talk* (7 May 1889).

48 After the season in Melbourne, he set off on a provincial tour of Tasmania. Then he returned to Melbourne in September 1889. His production of *Antony and Cleopatra* at the Opera House reminded the audience of Charles Kean's spectacular productions at the Princess's Theatre in London, which were based on archaeological and historical research. Miln wrote in his advertisement: 'Altogether this will be the most brilliant succession of stage pictures and effects ever presented to the English speaking public in connection with this great Shakespearean drama. It will have all the fascination of a magnificent spectacle, and all the sensuous charm of a Glittering Pantomime'. Although his spectacular productions at first impressed the Melbourne audience and critics, the magnificence eventually no longer appealed to them. In the end Miln was declared bankrupt. Once again he toured all over Australia and in 1890 went back to Sydney where he mounted a four-week season. After he completed the tour in New Zealand, which was successful beyond all expectations, Miln and his wife embarked on a professional tour in the Far East. Later in 1896 he produced *Julius Caesar* in New York, but it was totally unsuccessful. The *New York Dramatic Mirror* (14 March 1896) criticized Miln's acting style as ranting: 'Mr. Miln would have done well to avoid New York altogether, for his presentation of Marc Antony ... last evening was not to the liking of his audience so far as his road methods are concerned. There is no disguising the fact that Mr Miln is an arch ranter. And ranting tragedians have seen best days in a Broadway house. It is but fair, however, to concede that Mr Miln possesses various qualities that are most desirable in a tragic star, such as magnetism and dramatic force, but he must amend his ranting methods or the metropolis will have none of him'. After this failed attempt, his name as an actor-manager disappeared from the scene. He went to back to England and became an editor of a right-wing magazine called *The British Realm* from 1897 until 1907.

49 G.C.D. Odell, *Annals of the New York Stage*, quoted in Irvin, 104.

50 Woods, 144.

51 After the tour in the Far East, Louise Jordan Miln published a miscellany of essays on her experience in Asian countries. According to this book, the Miln Company performed *Julius Caesar* especially for a Japanese audience in an ordinary Japanese theatre in Tokyo. But there is no official record of the performance. See Louise Jordan Miln, *When We Were Strolling Players in the East* (London: Osgood, Mcilvaine, 1894), 232.

52 See Miln, 196, 220, 231.

53 Other cast were as follows: Kate Douglas as Gertrude, Frances Ross as queen in the Mouse Trap, Atholewood as Laertes, Stark as Polonius, J.H. Nunn as King, Channcey Edcott as the Grave Digger, Montgomery as Horatio. The band of the *Monocacy*, by kind permission of Admiral Belknap, was present and played a number of selections during the evening. See the *Japan Weekly Mail* (30 May 1891), 632.

54 *Japan Weekly Mail.*

55 See Seiichiro Kawamoto, ed., *Tokoku Zenshu* [Complete Works of Tokoku Kitamura] (Tokyo: Iwanami, 1955), 253 and Banboku Hirata, *Banboku, Ikyou Bungaku-kai Zengo* (Tokyo: Yomogi Shobo, 1943), 35.

56 Tsubouchi, 376.

57 Tsubouchi, 376 (my translation).

58 Banboku Hirata, *Banboku, Ikyo Bungaku-Kai Zengo* (Tokyo: Yomogi Shobo, 1943), 35. See also Toson Shimazaki, *Toson Zenshu* [Complete Works of Toson Shimazaki], vol. 3 (Tokyo: Chikuma Shobo, 1967), 10–11.

59 Powell, 7.

60 For information on *rodoku*, see Shigetoshi Kawatake, *Shingeki Undo no Reimeiki* [The Beginning of Shingeki (New Drama) Movement] (Tokyo: Yuzankaku, 1947), 56–64.

61 Kappei Matsumoto, *Nippon Shingeki-shi* [History of Shingeki (New Drama) in Japan] (Chikuma Shobo: Tokyo: 1966), 23–6.

62 Toshio Kawatake, *Nihon no Hamlet* (Tokyo: Nansosha, 1972), 25.

63 Powell, 3.

64 Revenge drama has always been enormously popular in Japan. The most famous of such revenge plays is *Kanadehon Chusingura*, in which the forty-seven loyal retainers take vengeance for the death of their master.

65 The version of *As You Like It* in Charles Lamb's adaptation was translated by Arashi Aoi in 1883, then in 1886 all of Lamb's tales were translated by Takichi Shinada.

66 In 1885 the first adaptation, *Sakuradoki Zeni-no Yononaka*, an adaptation of *The Merchant of Venice,* was put on stage. It was apparently popular and was performed several times. There were about thirteen adaptations of Shakespeare plays in this period.

67 Powell, 5. For information on the stage history of *Hamlet*, see Kawatake; Yoshio Ozasa, *Nihon Gendai Engekishi: Meiji Taisho Hen* [History of Japanese Modern drama: Meiji and Taisho Eras] (Tokyo: Hakusui-sha, 1985; Takashi Sasaki, ed., *Nippon Shakespeare Soran* [A General Survey of Shakespeare in Japan] (Tokyo: Erupisu, 1990).

68 The Bungei Kyokai presented *Hamlet* at the Hongo-Za in Tokyo in 1907 under the supervision of Shoyo Tsubouchi. Four years later, in 1911, Tsubouchi directed *Hamlet* at the newly built Teikoku Geki-Jo (Imperial Theatre).

69 Shoyo Tsubouchi, 'Nihon de Enzuru Hamlet' [*Hamlet* performed in Japan], *Shoyo Senshu* [Selected Works of Shoyo Tsubouchi], vol. 12 (Tokyo: Shyunyo-do, 1927), 655.

70 Powell, 28.

71 Shoyo Tsubouchi, 'Nihon ni Shakespeare-geki wo Kyosan to suru Riyu' [The reason why we play Shakespeare in Japan], *Shoyo Senshu* [Selected Works of Shoyo Tsubouchi], vol. 12 (Tokyo: Shyunyo-do, 1927), 637.

CHAPTER 4

Interculturalism or Indigenization: Modes of Exchange, Shakespeare East and West

Poonam Trivedi

Interculturalism has been the key issue in performance studies during the last decade, coming into vogue after the success of Peter Brook, Ariane Mnouchkine and Eugenio Barba. Viewed as a progressive cultural exchange, an answer to the failures of 'multiculturalism' and the 'melting-pot' ideals,[1] which will revitalize/explode the 'self protective huddling' of western theatre practice,[2] it has largely remained a metropolitan discourse, a product of the Euro-American postmodernism, which has sanctioned a dislocating and abstracting experimentalism with eastern theatre forms. Rarely has attention been paid to the view from the margins as it were, of how the east perceives and performs the western canon. Rustom Bharucha's critique of the current interculturalism as an exploitative 'cultural tourism'[3] is well known, but it does not confront a longer history of the western penetration and eastern resistance in the processes of colonization and modernization. This paper seeks to redress this balance by investigating the history and the modes of exchange between east and west as exemplified in the performance of the one 'global' author, William Shakespeare, in India. For it is not merely a coincidence that 'India', its image, culture, history and theatrical traditions were and continue to be located centrally in the rise of interculturalism. The name and label of India has in the past decade acquired a new kind of consumerist currency: it authenticates, it sells, it stimulates creativity. It thus becomes imperative to look at the flip side of interculturalism, not just to expose the appropriations of the other, but also to face ourselves in the image of the other.

Such investigations become all the more urgent for, as Dennis Kennedy has argued, 'there is no theory of cultural exchange' of what happens when Shakespeare travels to different cultures.[4] In an attempt to break this new ground, this paper will argue for indigenization as a counter to and an extension of interculturalism in post-colonial cultures where traditional non-illusionistic aesthetics and performance codes were driven underground by the seductive illusionism and realism of the western theatre for over 150 years. In the Indian context, progress continues to lie not so much in receiving other cultures but in localizing and making our own the foreign cultures imposed on us. Indigenization, it will show, through an analysis of two major productions of Shakespeare, *Barnam Vana* (*Macbeth*) and *Othello*, performed respectively in Yakshagana and Kathakali, two traditional folk theatre forms of south-western India, is a significant way out of the double bind of the colonial legacy of over 200 years, which paradoxically has left Shakespeare as both 'foreign' and 'native' to Indians.

Shakespeare as the star of English literature has been the key player in the east-west cultural exchange in India, a process which like Shakespeare is protean and even contrarious. Imposed on educated Indians as part of the colonizing mission of the empire, Shakespeare was, however, initially introduced to India as an entertainer, being performed as early as 1770 (Bombay) and 1784 (Calcutta), even before he was being taught in the classroom (introduced in the English language curriculum, Hindu College, Calcutta, 1817). While the impact of English literature and western ideas created a fundamental shift and schism in the Indian psyche, contact with Shakespeare also provoked a renaissance of classical Indian literature. And while the presence of Shakespeare in the classroom still remains ubiquitous – there is no English language and literature course without some Shakespeare – the primary popularity of Shakespeare came via the stage, through translations and adaptations. And while the academic response to Shakespeare has been mainly reverential, the theatrical engagement, especially in the early years, has been innovative and subversive, producing thoroughly indigenized versions which localized names, characters and situations and interpolated song and dance. Any history of the reception of Shakespeare in India has therefore to confront this matrix of submission and resistance in which a colonizing master text became, and remains to this day, the most translated, adapted, performed and published western author.[5]

It is the performative map which provides a more sensitive record of the reception of Shakespeare in India. The single most crucial, in fact revolutionary, factor rarely remembered is that Shakespeare came to India not as an Elizabethan but enclosed in an eighteenth-century proscenium box-stage. The earliest theatres built in Bengal by the British, the Playhouse (1753–56) and the New Playhouse, also called the Calcutta Theatre (1775) were modelled on the London theatres of the time, which Garrick helped to set up by sending scripts, scenery, actors and artists.

Sophia Goldborne in Hartley House (1789) has left a vivid account of the Calcutta Theatre:

> the house is about the size of the Bath Theatre and consists of Pit and boxes only. ... It is lighted upon the English plan with lamps at the bottom of the stage. ... The scenery was beautiful and dress superb ... my heart several times asked if it could be possible I was at the distance of 4000 miles from the British metropolis.[6]

Such was the novelty and impact of the English performative aesthetic of psychological realism and illusionism that the first Bengali theatres, Lebedeff's (1795) and Hindu Theatre (1831), were built in imitation of the indoor proscenium arch stage, completely overturning native dramatic traditions which rigged up temporary acting spaces, did not use designed costumes, lights or scenery and were acted in a symbolic and stylized manner. Not only did the new histrionic totally hold in thrall, but also generated as a backlash a 'growing distaste for contemporary entertainments provided by indigenous forms'.[7] Traditional theatre was marginalized and relegated to the rural areas. The first private theatre in Calcutta, Prasanna Kumar Tagore's Hindu Theatre, opened on 28 December 1831 with selections (Act 5) of *Julius Caesar* and an English translation of a Sanskrit play, *Bhavabutti's Uttar Ram Charitam*. Colonization seemed complete, but not for long. By 1853 the first translations of Shakespeare in the Indian languages start appearing which are aimed at not only the reading but also the theatre-going public. Almost all the early translations adapt, mutate and interpolate in differing degrees conventions from folk and classical staging. Thus the first Bengali translation and adaptation (1853) of *The Merchant of Venice*, entitled *Bhanumati Chittavilas*, was described as 'Shakespeare's ideas, but given in a Bengali dress'.[8]

Even as Shakespeare was steadily being taught and read in English by the Indians, he was increasingly being performed in different Indian languages and performative styles. This pattern of a free-wheeling 'tradaptation', to borrow Patrice Pavis's coinage, became the dominant mode for the popularization of Shakespeare. And it is the continuity of this performative tradition which this paper seeks to assert, a tradition in which translations produced slyly subversive forms and adaptations became bold and blatant acts of appropriation which localized, indigenized and even reverse-colonized, subjugating the bard into our own.

More than the eastern, it was the western India, Bombay in particular, which consistently staged this transmuted Shakespeare. C.J. Sisson's monograph, *Shakespeare in India: Popular Adaptations on the*

Bombay Stage (1926), based on his experiences as an educator and administrator in India, affords valuable documentary evidence.

> We can trace from 1890 onwards, and probably long before, a continuous series of performances of Shakespeare's plays in vernacular adaptations ... attended by men of all castes, mill-hands, workmen and petty shopkeepers, as well as middle class folk and students.

Sisson, the liberal, justifies the appropriations of the Parsi theatre[9] where according to him:

> Shakespeare is not translated formally, not imitated, but transplanted as a living organism [and where] nightly from 9 p.m. till 1 a.m. the benign Shakespeare might be seen, masking in turban and gorgeous feudal vestments, speaking strange languages, and delighting audiences which were in part not even aware of his name ... many of them probably think that he is still alive and are in the felicity of hoping for inventions of his skill.

He ends with the hope that Shakespeare will be the leaven for the regeneration of Indian theatre.[10] In sharp contrast, R.J. Minney is not so sanguine about this counterfeit Shakespeare. In an *Empire Review* article he revealed the colonialist pride in 'high' Shakespeare presented in English by Bengali women at the Shakespeare Festivals presided over by the Viceroy. But the 'low' Shakespeare, the popular adaptations, produced for the 'simple-minded Indian' was to him nothing less than a travesty.[11] Condemnation or valorization, both, however, erase the fact of the displacement and even effacement of the native folk forms of theatre by this feeble imitation of Shakespeare.

Post-independence, the 'theatre of roots' movement,[12] which began as a search for identity through experimentation with traditional theatre forms, provided a resurgence of this tradition of indigenization, but with a difference. The earlier 1900s adaptations, especially of the Bombay Parsi stage, were usually an amalgam of Victorian music-hall and melodrama with the Marathi sangeet natak. Now attempts were made to incorporate and fuse conventions and performative skills deriving from the purer folk traditions of Indian theatre. Before, adaptations had happily exploited the mechanical benefits of the proscenium stage to draw audiences with spectacular scenic and light changes. Post-independence indigenizations in an act of decolonization rejected the proscenium, explored a variety of performance spaces and sought to restore the actor and audience to a closer interactive relationship, as was originally conceived by the classical performatic aesthetic. If the turn of the century Shakespeare was often bowdlerized out of recognition, late century indigenizations are marked by an artistic scrupulosity towards both the essence of Shakespeare and the folk form. This transformed what earlier were often loose improvised scripts into meticulously structured performative texts in which gesture, voice and movement were carefully balanced with the demands of the text. If, as C.J. Sisson observed, the adaptative energies of the early Bombay stage was similar to the Elizabethan, the later experimentation with alternative staging spaces and styles succeeded in elucidating dimensions of Shakespeare's texts often lost in western contemporary historicist and modernist staging. If earlier the tendency was to exploit and 'use' Shakespeare, now the aim was to reread him in our own terms, to ingest and thereby to extend and to recreate him. Total indigenization of Shakespeare therefore becomes a true interculturalism in which the friction between two opposing performance modes results in a creative cross-fertilization of both.

This indigenous Shakespeare forged out of the very local pressures of colonialism and post-colonialism in India has a place in the larger issues of the theorization of Shakespeare worldwide. As Leonard C. Pronko has convincingly argued, staging Shakespeare in Kabuki or any other Asian style does 'not belittle the greatness of Shakespeare', rather it enables us 'to stretch to the magnitude of the master'. He finds contemporary Shakespeare performance choked by a century of realism and tele-cine techniques, and provocatively suggests that 'what we need is to clear away the smoggy naturalistic air by dropping a bomb – a Kabuki bomb, for example – that would exhibit such theatricality, drama, colour and artifice' as that which inheres in Shakespeare. Pronko strongly advocates Asian theatre: for him the exoticism 'far from distancing, often draws us in, intriguing us by its colourful differences and overwhelming us by its extravagant theatricality' and that 'it is a step in the direction of authenticity, of creating the theatre world of Shakespeare's day with its non-illusionistic presentationalism, ... emotional intensity and the poetic or rhetorical force of the text'. So taking the cue from Pronko we may move 'from Logos toward Mythos ... from West to East'.[13]

Barnam Vana (*Macbeth*) 1979, one of the earliest, much acclaimed, instances of indigenous Shakespeare, and *Othello* in Kathakali (1996), one of the most recent, represent most successfully the variants in the spectrum of indigenization. *Barnam Vana* was a lightly edited Hindi translation which not only preserved names and places but also successfully transposed imagery and idiom into Hindi equivalents. *Othello* on the other hand used a heavily edited, barebones version of the text which, however, managed to retain the essence of the play. *Barnam Vana* made selective use of the Yakshagana form, adapting key conventions to the demands of the Shakespearean text. *Othello*, instead, was a total immersion of Shakespeare in the Kathakali form, with the text, translated into Malayalam, sung in traditional ragas to the accompaniment of the mimed balletic enactment by the actors. *Barnam Vana* modified the costumes and the gestural language of Yakshagana, doing away with its elaborate head-dresses and makeup. *Othello* was a purist production whose only concession was its admission of a story not belonging to the traditional repertoire of Kathakali. *Barnam Vana* was a re-reading and a reinterpretation of both Shakespeare and Yakshagana, while *Othello* recreated a distilled and intense alternative experience of a western play in a eastern form.

Barnam Vana performed by the National School of Drama's repertory was marked by its close engagement with the text, but in terms of the Natyashastra poetics. As the director B.V. Karanth said in this programme note:

> I do not find myself capable of producing Shakespeare in the way he is produced in his own country. Were I to do so, it would be false of me. Therefore, my use of Yakshagana form is not for its own sake but because it is part of my awareness and expression. The tragedies of Shakespeare, especially *Macbeth* overflow with rasas[14] such as valour, wrath, terror or wonder, and the characters and situations have a universality and larger-than-life quality which can be well expressed in the Yakshagana style.

The congruities between a rural Indian folk form and an elite English dramaturgy are more real than apparent. Though its origins may be traced back to the Sanskrit drama of the fourth century, Yakshagana developed mainly around the sixteenth century as a means of mass contact in the face of the growing threat of colonialism, in this case the Portuguese presence,[15] as the Elizabethan theatre was similarly, around almost the same time, patronized by the court to propagate the ideals of nationalism and Tudor unity in the face of Spanish imperialism. The repertoire of Yakshagana, the mythic stories of love, valour and loyalty deriving chiefly from the *Ramayana* and the *Mahabharata*, therefore signify not so much a preoccupation with the past, as a counter to the growing presence of Christianity. The Yakshagana like the Elizabethan evolved as a popular public theatre performed in the open air by itinerant groups of players who move from village to village. They both used fluid shifting stages, minimal props, improvisation in music and dialogue and all-male acting companies. The structure of the acting companies, headed by a Bhagvatar (Narrator), is akin to the non-hierarchical equation between the actors of the Elizabethan groups of players. The flexibility of the Yakshagana stories to communicate at two levels – with the past through mythic themes and with the present through improvised satire interpolated into the dialogue – is also reminiscent of the freedoms of the Elizabethan stage and contributed not inconsiderably to its adaptability to a western text. Karanth's vision enhanced the poetic and mythic archetypes of the play. As he summarized it, 'It was not *Macbeth* in Yakshagana but Yakshagana in *Macbeth*'.[16]

All Indian folk forms are premised on the principle of a continuum between man, nature and supernature. The controlling image of the production was a tree representing the forest, the Vana of the title (Birnam Wood) which was physically literalized on the open air stage by a living pipal tree whose outspreading branches overhung part of the downstage but whose shadows, manipulated by the skilful lighting, seemed to spread their tentacles right up the front of the stage. The poster and the programme depicted the same tree with wild entangling branches in a blood red silhouette against the blackness of the night. This tree as forest became the physical symbol of the interpretative shift from *Macbeth* to *Barnam Vana*. As Karanth elaborated,

> This production has been titled *Barnam Vana* because the theme of *Macbeth* is the labyrinthine jungle of ambition which ensnares and destroys man. The witches that pursue him are a creation of his own mind. Surrounded with fear, he wanders in a dark world of nightmares. His journey, full of suffering, is yet interesting, for it reveals the primitive passions and sensibilities of the human being. The tree as forest Vana was then not just the world of nature but a metaphor for the nature of the world of *Macbeth*.

The witches, figments of Macbeth's imagination, emerged from the dark entrails of the Vana/tree swaying, dancing, covered by hand-held cloth curtains painted with emblematic shapes of grasping roots and branches. As they danced upstage they slowly lowered their curtains, inch by inch till below their shoulders, then dropped them suddenly to reveal half-human, half-demonic owl-like creatures. These witches were the 'withered and wild' dark emanations of the natural world. In the cauldron scene too, the apparitions seemed to float up from behind the vana/tree, outcrops of nature and the nature of Macbeth's desires and fears. With the storming of Dunsinane hill the metaphor of the tree/vana was fully extended. Malcolm's army emerged from behind the overshadowing tree, covered with the familiar hand-held screens, this time green with painted branches, and advanced like its grasping offshoots to deceive and defeat Macbeth, evolving in the process into a concretized image of those deceptive labyrinthine illusions which ensnare and screen him from reality. At the end *Barnam Vana* remained, both living nature and the worldly web of illusion, literally a 'maya jaal', the Vedantic concept of the world as illusion. Karanth's revisioning of *Macbeth* was in terms of Vedantic philosophy which locates the cause of human suffering in man's inability to look beyond this mutable physical world which is only an illusion – 'maya', the only true godhead being Brahman. Incidentally, Kurosawa's *The Throne of Blood* also imaged a forest as a metaphor for the entangling desires which lead Macbeth astray. Its Buddhist perspective shares with Vedantism the concept of the world as illusion.

Stylization of body language and of staging devices like the curtain was another theatrical intervention of the production. Entries and exits in Yakshagana are always heightened and celebratory. Characters enter with a flourish of the drums dancing vigorously, but fully or partially covered by a hand-held curtain. They perform their introductory dance in obeisance to the deity, and then facing the audience, drop the curtain and reveal themselves in spectacular splendour, divine, martial or demonic. All the actors in *Barnam Vana* entered with a rhythmic dancing/gliding movement, arms curved out on the sides and knees slightly bent, the beat and pace of which was varied to suit the mood and type of character. This introduced a lyrical and metrical flow of action which blended with the rhythmic assonance of Shakespearean speech, which the translation had been particularly alert to and which embodied the cycles of temptation, the tragic ebb and flow of the play. The vigorous acrobatic movements of the traditional Yakshagana were adapted to express emotional states through body stance and movement. The actor playing Macbeth held his head high, at an angle, moving with a slight slant, very taut, signifying particularly, in the early part of the play, 'the sharp deadly edge of a sword'.[17]

An innovative use of the hand-held curtain, called 'patt', was made by Karanth, setting free this common folk ritual theatre device of its codified rigidities. In *Barnam Vana* the hand-held curtain/patt became a metaphor of the curtains of the mind which concealed the 'fair' from the 'foul'. Hence the witches wrapped themselves up in the curtain. Lady Macbeth was introduced reading Macbeth's letter behind the patt, held up by two gentlewomen, which alternately rose and fell along with her resolution and fears. In the sleepwalking scene the curtain was a literal manifestation of the fragile divide between dream and reality against which the hallucinating Lady Macbeth was painfully straining. At the end of the scene the curtain dropped signalling her collapse too. In the Banquet scene, the hand-held curtain was chillingly extended into a red drape – interminably long – which came trailing behind Banquo's ghost winding around, ensnaring Macbeth and very vividly materializing on stage the illusions of the mind which led Macbeth into a trail of blood in which he is 'stepp'd in so far, that ... returning were as tedious as go o'er'. At the end the concealing patt as misleading illusion returned with the soldiers of Malcolm's army who carried green drapes painted with leafy branches to camouflage themselves.

A particularly effective piece of indigenization was achieved in the sleepwalking scene by the localization of the gestural language and stage business. It was conceived not so much as a sleepwalking reverie but as a possession by spirits – 'Bhuta' – underlining a parallel to Macbeth. Lady Macbeth moved to the front, with hands outstretched, palms facing the audience, eyes rolling with a crazed glint, accompanied by a mournful choric hum. The action of washing the hands was given an elemental quality, when she used earth, air, water, fire/candle in desperation to erase her nightmare. A reviewer noted how:

> she commands as she cajoles; she rubs as she wheedles: one hand against the palm. On the floor, in the air, she scrubs, she erases: memory against nightmare: lost in some primeval rhythm, steeped in a ritualistic frenzy. The spot grows despite; the smell lingers. ... And when the very elements fail her and nothing can perfume her little hand, Lady Macbeth did not whimper or dwindle: she just burst into a conflagration of scorching torment.[18]

With hair unpinned and arms and fingers outspread she flashed into mad 'possessed' circles and pirouettes till she fell on the stage. This action of uncontrolled mental and physical giddying was straight out of exorcism rituals still staged for women in India today. It gave Lady Macbeth's torment a revisionary edge by re-locating her 'perturbation in nature' in a well-defined patriarchal practice of psychic and social control.

The ultimate indigenizing touch, however, came with the ending. Karanth did not end Macbeth's story with his death in battle. During Malcolm's last speech which lavishes favours on his nobles, Macbeth's ghost, draped in red, entered and sat centre-stage unnoticed by others and watched the cycle of politic planting and harvesting going on. This image of rebirth was inserted to add a restorative closure, insisted upon by classical Sanskrit poetics, which do not admit of the genre of tragedy. For Karanth, the return of Macbeth's spirit observing the happenings on earth, aligned his reading of *Macbeth* to the closing episodes of the *Ramayana*, *Mahabharata* and other traditional myths, where death and slaughter are not finalities and the cyclical rhythms of regeneration are seen to reassert themselves.[19]

Predictably, the production was critiqued for a loss of tragic intensity and empathy which was diluted by the stylized dance movements. In fact the whole production seemed designed to elicit not a passionate emotional response, but a considered thoughtful one. And audiences conditioned to expect an overflow of emotion were baffled with a show that held back from traditional effects. On the other hand this acculturation did provide insights which are often missed in the historicist realistic stagings. The central image of the Vana/forest/tree as literal forest and metaphoric maze provided a linkage into that web of interconnectedness between man and nature – physical, social, political and spiritual – in other words, with that 'great bond' (translated as 'jeevan sutra' – thread of life) which keeps Macbeth pale and tormented. It is the location of this great bond in nature or Dharma, that is, the law of creation emblematized in the tree/vana, both natural and illusory, non-human and human, which was this production's interpretative contribution. Criticism of *Macbeth* shows a curious lack of an in-depth investigation into the workings of nature in Shakespearean tragedy and its philosophical underpinnings. Polarities between nature as a tidy servant maintaining order and degree, and nature as contrary and chaotic remain, leaving Shakespeare's engagement with nature as a tenuous unity between the two. In *Barnam Vana* the great bond is seen in terms of a great chain of being, not a mere hierarchical ladder but a cosmic cycle of deaths and births, redefining the framework of what is called the 'supernatural'.

The fatalism commonly attributed to the eastern world view seems equally endemic in the *Macbeth* universe. There has always been a line of criticism which has been reluctant to categorize the play as a tragedy, seeing it as closer to a morality play. Illusionism in Shakespeare's *Macbeth* is not just a misapprehension but a terrifying condition of the world. R. Sahai's translation of 'Fair is foul' as 'dhoop dhundh' – 'light fog' shifted the entrenched reversal of values to a condition of confusion between knowing and non-knowing.

Similarly, the providential celebratory reading of the ending is more and more subject in criticism to qualification. Critics see chilling signs of a cyclical repetition, of a wheel coming full circle in the images of death and in the rhetoric of the state. Marvin Rosenberg details a number of productions where the ending was dramatized as deeply sceptical.[20] Hence Macbeth's ghost in *Barnam Vana* was not gratuitous; rather, it elucidated submerged areas of the text. Showing Macbeth's tragedy as suffering deriving from illusionism or 'maya' as a condition of the world and of man, of man's failure to comprehend his own 'humankindness', that is, his 'dharma', the law of being, it is perhaps closer to the metaphysical implications of the text.

Suresh Awasthi, a leading theatre critic, wrote of *Barnam Vana* that it made 'Shakespeare our contemporary'[21] and here he meant that it served to establish a continuity with the deeply ingrained philosophic traditions which inform all the traditional performing arts in India. This does not undermine a more radical post-colonial contemporaneity which was also achieved when Karanth used an indigenous folk form originating in opposition to colonialism, to subjugate a master colonizing text.

The Kathakali *Othello* was an all-out transplantation and thus faced the possibility of outright acceptance or rejection. Yet it was not such a curiosity either, for there has developed, recently, a minor tradition of adapting Shakespeare in Kathakali: the *King Lear* performed at the Edinburgh festival in 1990 is the most publicized instance, but before that, in Kerala, in the mid-1970s, Kalamandalam Kesavan's adaptations of *The Tempest* and *Doctor Faustus* were so successful that they continued to be performed alongside the classical repertoire. Nor was it necessarily a fanciful yoking of opposites, for surprisingly, directors have perceived areas of congruence between Shakespeare and Kathakali, particularly in their narratives of the struggle between good and evil, in the heightened emotionality of the characters and their rhetorical rhythmic rendering. Of the choice of *Othello*, the actor/director Sadanam Balakrishnan said:

> unlike many other plays, *Othello* fits very well with Kathakali – it is a very emotional story of a heroic warrior. ... Even though Kathakali does not have tragedy, that is death as an end, it does allow tragic emotion, therefore doing Shakespearean tragedy is not different or alien.[22]

Like all the earlier experimentations, *Othello* too was performed in strict Kathakali with traditionally choreographed dances and gestures, in the conventional costumes, set to the accompaniment of fixed musical scores. It was staged initially, as is traditional, in an open courtyard on a temporarily cleared staging space, lit up mainly by oil lamps with the audience seated a few feet away. The 'close-up' perspective onto the small acting space provided for a total induction effect, in spite of the distancing devices of the exotic costumes and mask-like makeup. And it is this simultaneous intense 'microscopic' experience within the framework of a larger-than-life staging – the actors' crown-like head-dresses, and large billowing skirts and drapes making them tower over audiences viewing from the same level – which is the keynote of the Kathakali style.

This 'double view', both intimate and spectacular, is structured chiefly by the elaborate gestural stylization which is the most characteristic feature of the Kathakali performative code. Stylization, which in the western aesthetic is usually a pejorative term signifying artificiality, is in Kathakali the very life stream. Its highly codified gestural language, especially of the hands and face, forms an alternative mode of rendering content and character. It encompasses both the representational and the theatrical, what Barba has termed the 'daily' and the 'extra daily'. Kathakali mudras (gestures) not only convey meaning with the precision and clarity of words, they also comment upon them: charged with symbolic signifiers, they add new semantic layers to the text. In a very controlled exposition, the actor moves only those parts of the body and those facial muscles which are necessary. The effect of stylization is not of obscuring by distortion, but of a sharpened clarification. As Kenneth Rea has observed, 'watching Kathakali compared to western theatre is like looking into a glass of pure water'.[23]

In the Kathakali *Othello* stylization worked both to abstract and exalt and to acutely express the powerful emotions written into the text, emotions which are so often undercut by today's realistic acting styles which tend to flatten out the rhythmic and poetic patterns. Freed from the tyranny of mouthing the words, the actors could convey with greater subtlety, through the flexible 'abhinaya' (acting), the finer nuances of emotion. The colour-coded costumes and the edited and tightly focused narrative all heightened, not undermined, 'emotionality'. Further, parallels and resonances from the mythic characters of the traditional narratives of Kathakali staged in a similar fashion were set up which energized and at times dislocated moments of the play. Thus Othello, cast as a heroic noble 'pacca' character with a green face but blackened arms and feet, dressed in blue, was very much the 'noble Moor' in line with the traditional heroes of Kathakali, Rama and Nala,[24] who have an innate gentleness and sensitivity. Performed by Sadanam Balakrishnan as the valorous but gentle soldier, Othello was a man led astray by his acute sensitivity. He could not bear the taunts of Iago. The confusions and the tensions of the creeping poison of jealousy were acutely visualized by the facial expressions ranging from disbelief and bafflement to pain and anger. Repeatedly, his hand pressed his forehead thrown back signifying the mental trauma he was undergoing until finally he fell in a faint.

Kathakali is essentially an elaborative form which revels in reinterpretative and renewing improvisation. Therefore reinterpretative sequences of the play took on a new vitalizing energy. The love scene between Othello and Desdemona was a particularly successful rendering of the 'shingara' (erotic) rasa, both tender and passionate, theatrical and realistic, with the two lovers exiting slowly dancing in harmony with arms linked in close embrace. Desdemona, attired in the conventional realistic dress and makeup of the female lead, activated associations of the traditional 'pati-vrata' (husband worshipping) heroines of Indian legends, imparting to her relationship with Othello an unquestioning devotion and purity and suspending any suggestion of a disruptive flirtatiousness or an unbridled sexuality which has almost become mandatory in the mainstream performance of the role. In fact, it was hard to resist, while watching this performance, resonances of the archetypal transgressive lovers of Indian myth, Shiva and Parvati. Othello and Desdemona's passion now acquired a supra-human, near divine sanction: Desdemona like Parvati was entranced by Shiva the uncouth and unconventional 'wild man'; like Sati, Parvati's earlier incarnation, she defies patriarchal authority to follow her love, and like the divine lovers, Othello and Desdemona remain coupled together for ever. Immersed in the colours and conventions of Kathakali, the Shakespearean lovers achieved an instant recognition and mythic sanction which relocated the subversiveness of their love in a cosmic pattern.

In the death scene, Othello, like Shiva in his 'rudra' (angry) aspect, became both lover and destroyer. Staged in a symbolic darkness, Othello moved slowly with a flickering lamp towards Desdemona's bed, his angst articulated in the slow menacing beat, which gradually increased, of the chenda and maddalam drums. This Othello killed out of a terrible duty, equally suffocating for himself: anguished, after the murder, his hands grasped his own throat and his face grimaced into a choking sensation, foretelling his suicide which otherwise is an abrupt collapse.

Another productive relocation was of the nature of evil as embodied in Iago, who was performed as a vicious 'katti' character with black painted face and red nose. This typification was not, as seen by some, reductive of the complexities in Shakespeare. It arose out of the aesthetic history of Kathakali in which the exaggeration and demonization of evil is part of its anti-classicism deriving from folk ritual traditions, originally a form of spirit worship, which constituted a celebration of the demonic as a propitiatory act. Most Indian folk theatre forms treat evil as a fascinating 'Other', presented as spectacular and grossly colourful demons bursting with cunning and tricks who easily upstage, for a time at least, the virtuous characters. Shakespeare's Iago metamorphosed from the mean and jealous ensign into a powerful Satanic anti-hero. His inherent evil was reinterpreted as part of that pull of the demonic which is inexplicable and inextirpable.

As with *Barnam Vana*, the rewriting of the closure was the final indigenizing touch, reinstating Shakespeare in the conventions of the Natyashastra and simultaneously questioning the parameters of the tragic genre. After the death of Othello, the hand-held curtain was removed and Othello rose to perform a 'mangalam', a prayer cum soliloquy in which he recounted his errors and begged forgiveness of the gods.

The Kathakali Shakespeare had a more mixed reception than the Shakespeare in Yakshagana. It was criticized both for not being purist enough and not being radical enough. Suresh Awasthi, who had valorized *Barnam Vana* as 'a most innovatively conceived production', severely indicted the intercultural experiment of the Kathakali *Lear* as 'a complete failure', a 'violation of the aesthetics of the form' which in effect 'crushed a western text'.[25] Further, the Kathakali *Othello* was charged with the erasure of race. Partly the result of pragmatics, 'it was not possible to do it all', said the director, it also brought to the fore the particularity of the problematic of Othello's blackness among a predominantly dark-skinned people whose major deities and demons are dark-coloured too. A fresh configuration of the issue in terms of class and caste was attempted in R. Sahai's Hindi translation (1980) of 'Moor' as 'Kaluta', literally, blackie, but carrying derogatory connotations of a low-caste country bumpkin. For a non-verbal, dance-drama of the sixteenth century, the performance of a western text was in itself a radical stance. What is often not remembered is that both Yakshagana and Kathakali are theatre forms which had become marginalized by the late nineteenth century under the onslaught of psychological realism and the well-made play as popularized by the 'company nataks', by the development of modern literature in the local languages, and later by the rapid growth of cinema. Earlier they had sought to preserve themselves by closing ranks, ridding themselves of pollutant foreign elements. Now their incorporation of Shakespeare is a loosening of the shackles of tradition, an extension of the possibilities of the folk forms, and, as the paper has tried to show, an extension of the staging possibilities of Shakespeare too. For what Awasthi found lacking in the Kathakali *Lear*, 'a creative utilization of and merger of the two cultures on which it drew', has been amply met by the Kathakali *Othello*, as substantiated by the documentation of the performative detail. Even the loss of Shakespeare's words and images was not really felt. For those who knew the play, such a staging enhanced the situations and the moods, and emotion was 'purified' and 'essentialized' in a newly satisfying manner. As a viewer put it, in realistic staging, 'Othellos always seem to rave and rant'.

Such transculturalism and acculturalism as a result of indigenization function as processes compensatory of colonization, unlike the Brook and Mnouchkine dislocating appropriations of Indian theatrical traditions which border dangerously on versions of neo-colonialism. What was earlier imitation and borrowing is now a forging of an alternative aesthetics, where an indigenous 'play' with western texts and forms is a step in the direction of decolonization, where Shakespeare and Indian theatre need not remain as 'chalk and cheese', but as the two ends of the same performative spectrum.[26] Performances of exchange must lead to change.

Notes

[1] Richard Schechner, 'Comment', *The Drama Review* 36.4 (Winter 1992), 7.
[2] Patrice Pavis, 'Introduction', *The Intercultural Performance Reader* (London: Routledge, 1996), 19.
[3] Rustom Bharucha, 'Collision of Cultures: Some Western Interpretations and Uses of Indian Theatre', in *Theatre and World* (New Delhi: Manohar, 1990), 15.
[4] Dennis Kennedy, 'Afterword: Shakespearean Orientalism', in *Foreign Shakespeares: Contemporary Performance* (Cambridge: Cambridge University Press, 1993), 297.
[5] Sisir Kumar Das, ed., *A History of Indian Literature, Volume VIII, 1800–1910 Western Impact: Indian Response* (New Delhi: Sahitya Akademi, 1991), 110, 227.
[6] Quoted in *The Indian Theatre*, Hemendra Nath Das Gupta, 1st reprint (Delhi: Gian Publishing House, 1988), 187–9.
[7] Sushil Mukherjee, *The Story of the Calcutta Theatres 1753–1980* (Calcutta: K.P. Bagchi and Company, 1982), 13. Mukherjee also recounts how in 1826 an editorial appeared in *Samachar Chandrika* rallying opinion and financial support for a theatre on the English model, 13.
[8] Reverend Long, 'Foreword', *Bhanumati Chittavilas* (Calcutta: Purnachandroday Yantra, 1853).
[9] The commercial theatre in Bombay 1880–1930, so called after the predominantly Parsi community who financed and organized it.
[10] C.J. Sisson, *Shakespeare in India: Popular Adaptations on the Bombay Stage* (London: The Shakespeare Association, 1926), 14, 7, 24.
[11] R.J. Minney, 'Shakespeare in India', *Empire Review* (May 1925).
[12] Suresh Awasthi, 'Theatre of Roots: Encounter with Tradition', *The Drama Review* 33.4 (Winter 1989).
[13] Leonard C. Pronko, 'Approaching Shakespeare Through Kabuki', *Shakespeare East and West*, eds Minoru Fujita and Leonard C. Pronko (Richmond: Japan Library, 1996), 23–6.

[14] Rasa = flavour, essence or joyful consciousness. The central aesthetic concept of the Natyashastra (c. fourth century BC), treatise of Sanskrit poetics.

[15] Kapila Vatsyayan, *Traditional Indian Theatre: Multiple Streams* (New Delhi: National Book Trust, 1980), 36.

[16] B.V. Karanth, interview, *Dainik Jagran* (9 January 1995); phrase coined by S. Awasthi, 'Yakshagana in Shakespeare', *Dinman* (9–15 December 1979).

[17] S. Awasthi, *Dinman* (9–15 December 1979).

[18] Reeta Sondhi, *Enact* (1979).

[19] Karanth, interview with the author (June 1996).

[20] Marvin Rosenberg, *The Masks of 'Macbeth'* (Berkeley: University of California Press, 1978).

[21] S. Awasthi, 'The Intercultural Experience and the Kathakali *"King Lear"*', *New Theatre Quarterly* 9.34 (May 1993), 178.

[22] Sadanam Balakrishnan, interview, Hindu College, Delhi University (20 November 1996).

[23] Kenneth Rea, 'Theatre in India: the Old and the New, Part 1', *Theatre Quarterly* 7.30 (1978), 21.

[24] Leela Venkataraman, 'Shakespeare Speaks in a New Voice', *Hindu* (26 April 1996).

[25] S. Awasthi, 'The Intercultural Experience', 178.

[26] John Russell Brown, interview with author, March 1997.

CHAPTER 5

Berlin–Zürich–Düsseldorf: Aspects of German Theatre During the Nazi Period and After

Wilhelm Hortmann

The subject is vast. Theatre historians have written weighty volumes on this period. Obviously I cannot unroll the whole canvas. I propose instead to present three sharply focused snapshots and to contextualize them.

Theaterstadt Berlin

30 January 1933. The Nazis take over power. Less than a month later, the Reichstag, the seat of the Imperial Parliament, goes up in flames – a symbolic occurrence, as many people felt. By June, all other parties except the National Socialists had been outlawed. The new rulers lost no time in bringing the nation into line. Communists, Jews and Social Democrats were removed from office and replaced by members of the Nazi Party. Opposition was ruthlessly crushed.

In cultural matters the programme of 'Gleichschaltung', the enforced alignment or conformity, was promoted with equal rapidity and rigour.[1] 'Cultural Bolshevism' was to be stopped and the Jewish influence on German culture eliminated. 'Un-German' books were blacklisted and removed from libraries; free speech, critical thought and exchange of ideas were derided as shibboleths of rootless, Westernized, Jewish intellectuals. When, on 10 May, Nazi students of Humboldt University in Berlin staged their eerie ritual of publicly burning thousands of undesirable books, this auto-da-fé signalized the gravity of the changes that had been set in motion.[2]

The consequences of the Nazi take-over were equally profound for the theatres. During the first weeks of terror, most of the Jewish and Communist actors and directors who, with very few exceptions, were on the Nazi blacklist, fled the country. Those who did not went in fear of their lives. Private theatres under Jewish ownership were closed down or confiscated. Max Reinhardt, to forestall expropriation, bequeathed his theatres to 'the German People', transferred his activities abroad and ultimately went to America.[3]

Josef Goebbels, Minister of Propaganda, needed the theatres for cultural propaganda.[4] Coercion, therefore, was only a last resort. Theatres were to be showcases of German culture rather than mere propaganda tools, just as opera and symphony orchestras were expected to demonstrate the high standard of German art. Thus, given the right person at the top, a theatre might pursue a course which kept Nazism at a (relative) distance.

Goebbels was well aware of the lack of enthusiasm among the heads of theatre whom he convened on 8 May 1933 to acquaint them with his vision of a 'steely romanticism'. They had other worries and other ideals. The best among them had been trained up in a spirit of liberal humanism and saw themselves as guardians of 'Geist' and culture, and hoped to conserve this spirit at their institutions. In other words, they hoped to weather the storm in a niche which they kept clear from all too obvious Nazi influence. There were many such niches, some imaginary, others not.

Yet it would be wrong to think of the theatres as pockets of active resistance or breeding grounds of anti-Fascism. Inside Germany, the very terms were virtually unknown. As mental concepts they were certainly not common property.

The saddest chapter of all is that of the Jewish artists who were thrown out of work and stayed on, partly because they were not prominent enough to find jobs outside, partly because they hoped the situation would mend. About a quarter of them found a temporary haven in the 'Kulturbund deutscher Juden' ('Cultural Association of German Jews') soon forced to rename itself into 'Jüdischer Kulturbund', not being allowed to claim the 'honour' of carrying 'German' even in the title. The idea was to establish a separate cultural life for Jews, although of the 92 branches only those in Frankfurt and Hamburg and above all the central institution in Berlin can be said to have fulfilled the purpose. Here, under the tutelage of Dr Hans Hinkel, a high-ranking SS-officer responsible for Jewish personnel and the Aryanizing (in Nazi terminology the 'de-Jewification') of German culture, and under constant surveillance by the Gestapo, the 'Kulturbund' started its brave attempt to ensure cultural participation for its members. In the first year alone it produced ten plays, four operas, one ballet, twelve concert programmes and over a hundred lectures. Kurt Singer and his Jewish board of governors tried to maintain the links to German culture, but plays by Goethe, Schiller and Kleist were forbidden them, as was the music of Beethoven after 1936, with Bach, Mozart, Schubert and Schumann disallowed within the next two years.

The 'Kulturbund' struggled against impossible odds. Its members inclined towards the culture they were at home in, which was German.

Hinkel pressed for a greater share of Jewish composers and playwrights, but the progress towards a specifically Jewish cultural identity was slow. Financially barely afloat, the greatest difficulty for the 'Kulturbund' arose from artists dropping out of productions through sudden arrest, emigration or defecting while on tour abroad. Kurt Singer, Fritz Wisten, Julius Bab and others responsible for running the organization were torn between satisfaction at people escaping Nazi clutches and dismay at having to fill another gap and see quality deteriorate under makeshift solutions. The six Shakespeare productions put on by the 'Kulturbund' during its existence from 1933 to 1941 (*Othello*, 1933; *Twelfth Night*, 1934; *A Midsummer Night's Dream*, 1936; *Much Ado About Nothing*, 1938; *The Winter's Tale*, 1939; *The Taming of the Shrew*, 1940; all except the first two directed by Fritz Wisten) therefore should not be judged primarily on artistic merits, nor can they. The organization and history of the 'Kulturbund' happen to be exceptionally well documented,[5] but reviewing in the ordinary sense no longer existed. The few Jewish publications still permitted could not afford to be trenchant about cultural activities produced under duress. These productions, therefore, have to be seen first of all as a determined staking of claims in the German theatrical heritage, even if non-Jewish Germans were forbidden to attend.

Gründgens and Hilpert

The situation in Berlin was in many ways exceptional. For years, the Nazi press had vilified the Deutsches Theater under Max Reinhardt for its 'Jewishness', and had lambasted the Staatstheater for its cultural Bolshevism. They were now under pressure to prove they could do better, especially since both theatres, under interim management installed by Nazi authorities, were lapsing into mediocrity. A radical remedy was called for. Hermann Göring, who as Prussian Minister of the Interior had control of the three state theatres of Prussia (in Berlin, Kassel and Wiesbaden) and jealously guarded this privilege against encroachments from the Minister of Propaganda (who controlled all the rest), gave Gustaf Gründgens full charge of the Berlin Staatstheater. This was a bold move considering Gründgens' age (thirty-four), homosexual tendencies and left-wing past (in the twenties he had acted in a political cabaret in Hamburg together with Erika Mann) – yet the brilliant outcome justified Göring's choice. Goebbels, to avoid losing face, had no option but to follow suit and appoint a professional of proven worth and ability, and irrespective of his political inclinations, namely Heinz Hilpert, as head of the Deutsches Theatre. These two appointments assured the predominance of Berlin in the world of the German theatre for another ten years. The theatrical achievements of these two men and the story of how they managed, at the very centre of Nazi surveillance, to preserve the spirit of their institutions, to shield endangered individuals from persecution, to fend off infiltration and minimize concessions to the regime, have become legendary and are proof of honourable conduct under adverse and even dangerous circumstances. Gründgens, a flamboyant figure, was the more exposed and needed all the protection Göring could give him and all his own suave adroitness to keep the Staatstheater, where unruly directors like Jürgen Fehling went as far as they dared, from getting into serious trouble.[6] Goebbels kept Hilpert on a much shorter rein, but he could not prevent Hilpert's quiet and persistent humanism from determining the attitude of the Deutsches Theatre, his own pet venue. Two niches, under the very eye of the devil's advocate himself.

The rivalry between Göring and Goebbels and their vanity to have 'their' respective theatres acclaimed as the best in the land had some strange consequences. The man who took the most daring liberties was Jürgen Fehling. His case is indicative, both for what was just about possible under exceptional circumstances as well as for the mental and ideological limitations of the age in which Nazis and anti-Nazis alike were caught up. To Goebbels and his henchmen he ranked as a 'Kulturbolschewist', yet so powerful and electrifying was his grip on texts, acting and design that other productions lost much of their lustre when compared with his unique and penetrating renderings.

2 March 1937, Staatstheater Berlin / 'Richard III' directed by Jürgen Fehling

Theatre historians regard this production as a milestone in the theatre history of the Third Reich and beyond:

> Jürgen Fehling was a genius. ... His productions were the talk of the town, but none was awaited with greater impatience than *Richard III*. Fehling, a passionate anti-Nazi ... took a devilish pleasure in turning the last scion of the house of York into a likeness of the club-footed Minister of Propaganda with all his lies, treacheries and womanising.[7]

John Newmark, the Canadian pianist and composer, who described the production fifty years later, was a uniquely placed observer. Fehling had engaged the unemployed Jewish musician, then still Hans Neumark, to collect and arrange the incidental music and to play the piano accompaniment to the march of the armies in the fifth act. To have Aryan soldiers marching to the tune of a Jewish pianist was a deliberate affront and quickly suppressed. But that was Fehling.

The production contained further political dynamite. Richard's bodyguard wore uniforms reminiscent of the feared SS. The murderers of Richard's brother Clarence committed their crime dressed in white coats. When they turned round their coats swung open to reveal SA-type uniforms underneath, for no more than a second, but it electrified audiences. The audience caught their breath once more immediately before the interval. In the play there is a small part for a Scrivener who only has one short monologue. He has been working on the indictment of Lord Hastings for eleven hours, but five hours ago Hastings was still a free man. 'Who is so gross / That cannot see this palpable device? / Yet who so bold but says he sees it not?' This question he shouted into the auditorium just before the lights went up. It is reported by some as being spontaneously applauded, by others as creating 'an uncanny silence'.[8]

There was an equally impressive closing scene. Richmond, the glorious saviour, only had to lift his sword for Richard to fall as if struck by lightning. 'Richard dies without having received his stroke of death', wrote a critic, 'he dies because he is *ripe* for extinction, because the divine order claims to be re-established'.[9] After Richard's fall there was a short blackout and when the lights went up, the previously empty stage was filled with Richmond's army on its knees singing a Bach *Te deum* giving thanks for their deliverance from the tyrant. The lights going up at the same time in the auditorium included the audience in this hymnic relief.

Most critics of this literally breathtaking production felt, but naturally could not comment on, the provocative nature of what they had witnessed. A direct analogy between Richard and any of the then Nazi potentates would have been too risky, although Gloucester taking his time at the beginning to limp the full fifty yards from the back of the stage right up to the footlights to explain his coming devilries is said to have been thought by many as an unmistakable allusion to Goebbels. Certainly, Goebbels was furious. He had Fehling's passport withdrawn (so that he could no longer visit his Jewish girlfriend Lucie Mannheim in London), and Göring also was seriously displeased. But somehow all concerned must have been under some kind of shock or illusion which made it impossible for them to realize the full extent and meaning of the production they had witnessed. As a piece of daredevil provocation it could have been squashed. Bernhard Minetti, who played Buckingham, is probably right when he suggested that 'the full representation of a work of art (of the kind of format Fehling cared to deal with) offered a view of the world which the regime could not cope with'.[10]

With an audience painfully alive to the nature of their times, correspondences to the current political state of affairs did not have to be laboured. What had to be transmitted was a sense of the scale of events. For this Fehling found convincing metaphors.

Was this production an act of rational opposition, of politically conscious resistance? Fehling would not have understood the question. He lived and worked, loved and hated, as D.H. Lawrence would have said, from the solar plexus, from the creative impulses of his anarchic soul, not from critical intellect. His vision of history – as that of many Germans at the time – was pan-demonic. History for him was not a calculable sequence of cause and effect, but a struggle of primal and uncontrollable forces. The rational values of Enlightenment were not highly regarded at the time, certainly not by a man of Fehling's cast of mind and soul. The sources of his art were instinct and intuition. They fed his great achievements, and at the same time denoted their limitations.

This particular limitation can be studied in his production of *Julius Caesar* (1941). Contemporary observers often noticed that classical plays proved surprisingly relevant to the political situation.[11] A request like 'Sire, please grant freedom of thought', by Marquis Posa in Schiller's *Don Carlos*, rarely failed to elicit prompt audience response. The many calls to freedom in Schiller's *Wilhelm Tell*, and Tell's decision to kill the tyrant, led to the banning of the play in 1942. Some of Shakespeare's plays would seem to have been equally *a propos*. When Colonel Claus von Stauffenberg, who directed the coup against Hitler and planted the bomb in Hitler's headquarters on 20 July 1944 was arrested, there was an open copy of *Julius Caesar* on his desk in which the relevant speeches by Brutus were underlined.[12] Had he perhaps seen Fehling's production of the play at the Staatstheater in 1941? But then, Fehling, a confirmed anti-Nazi, read the play completely differently. The reviews are unanimous about one thing, namely that the director had done everything in his power to enhance the role of Caesar and mark him out as the man of the future. His fall, therefore, must appear as a historical catastrophe, and his murder a crime of mythic proportion. It was obvious that this was not a performance designed to vindicate the spirit of Republican Rome and its ancient virtues. Fehling's reading of history and of the play led him to stress the tragedy of Caesar's fall. Fehling's fascination for Caesar, the man of power, cannot be overlooked. History, according to a much quoted dictum by the historian Heinrich von Treitschke, was made by (great) men and Caesar, the epitome of greatness, being murdered at the threshold of a new era and by his very fall bringing about the historical change for which he is killed – the subject was too tempting to resist. Erich Engel's analytic intellect might have withstood the Caesar myth, Fehling's anarchic soul vibrated to its suggestions.

Caesar is much more revolutionary than his opponents who kill him in the name of freedom ... They act ... from blind idealism but they look backward and do not understand Caesar's visionary projection into the future.[13]

It would be difficult to claim that a production built on these lines was an invitation to tyrannicide. In fact the director did everything in his power to raise the tragedy of Caesar's fall to mythic proportions. The murder at the Capitol, according to all reports, was one of the most soul-stirring theatrical experiences imaginable: the memory of this scene must have given pause to any potential conspirator. Fehling's obsessive compulsion 'to drill down to the deep layer of things',[14] as Minetti remarks, stopped short, in this case at least, of rational analysis. Theatre as a didactic strategy, as part of a programme of ideological manipulation or in the service of specific causes or general enlightenment, all this was alien to Fehling's nature. The world, in his personal and his theatrical cosmos, was not a system of cause and effect. It was determined by the presence of dynamic forces, by characters in thrall to their 'daimon' (or destiny) in the Goethean sense, not by rational constructs or figures spouting propaganda. Brecht, he told a scandalized audience of dramaturgs in 1953, was a 'pied piper ... a highly gifted cat burglar ... whose first plays of thirty years ago are ten times as powerful as anything he is writing today'.[15] And, looking back on his legendary successes, he declared that the German public was

> ideal for the theatre. And it is a calumny to the vital force of this idiotically young people still struggling in the swamps of its Teutonic forests ... to deny its burning curiosity and passion for true and vital theatre, i.e. a theatre not of the 'Brechtian' kind, but of deliberate pathos.[16]

It is obvious that a man thus bent on exploring the irrational sources of character and action had only limited sympathy with Brutus's careful self-examination. He thrilled instead to the agglomerate of passions and impulses he saw contained in the part of Mark Antony. Gustav Knuth as Antony was directed to eliminate all traces of conscious planning and scheming from the role. He was to appear as the warm, open-hearted friend, unsuspecting and generous, dragged into politics almost against his will but, once involved, an unstoppable force.

History in the making, pushed towards anarchy or order by headstrong agents, characters in paroxysms of passion or moving as under a doom – this was the scale and temper Fehling envisaged for *Julius Caesar*.

In other words, a theatre of 'deliberate pathos'. Can his production of *Julius Caesar* be said to have contained a topical message or to have had a political effect? It was certainly worlds apart from agitatory theatre such as Piscator's in the twenties, and equally far removed from the political didacticism Brecht was at that time putting into dramatic form. Fehling was caught in the limitations of his approach: to preserve and repossess the classical heritage, to heighten its impact, to vivify, vitalize and intensify, but not to surmount or overcome it. Any contemporary political relevance had to be achieved by purely theatrical means. It had to remain below the level of rational discourse and remained, presumably, below the horizon of intellectual insight. Fehling believed in the cathartic power of theatre and strove with all his might to stir the emotions and shake the hearts of his audience. Should he have instructed it? If so, about what? 'About the need for tyrannicide, of course', a later generation would exclaim. Fehling, the impassioned anti-Nazi, did not see (or care to make) the connection. There were theatre people outside Germany who did.

The 'Zürcher Schauspielhaus': Swiss Bastion Against Hitler

When Oskar Wälterlin, on the first night of the 1944–5 season, stepped before the curtain to announce that all German theatres had been closed for the duration, his Swiss audience was well aware of the symbolic significance of the statement: their theatre in the heart of Zurich with its ensemble of less than thirty actors had become the only professional stage (devoted solely to drama) in operation in the German-speaking world. Two years before, when German troops had overrun Europe from Norway to Greece and from outside Leningrad to the Bay of Biscay, there had been almost 300 theatres in operation, quite a few also in the occupied areas: after all, the Germans thought of themselves as bringers of culture. Now, on 2 September 1944, only one was left, and that one outside Germany. An unusually negative form of cultural politics.

The Zurich Schauspielhaus was in many ways an anomaly.[17] The company was made up of reputed actors and directors, most of them Jewish or Communist émigrés from Nazi Germany who had gravitated to Zurich since 1933. They were reinforced by another influx from Austria in 1938. At the beginning of the Nazi period, Ferdinand Rieser, the Jewish director, had helped endangered individuals to escape the clutches of Nazi authorities by inviting them to work at his theatre. In some cases this was a mere fiction, but once in safety, the fugitives could emigrate to other countries. They were brought together by Kurt Hirschfeld, dramaturg to Gustav Hartung at the Landestheater Darmstadt. Both men had been publicly dismissed from their posts in the very first speech of the Hessian Gauleiter, and Hirschfeld, once hired by Rieser, lost no time in bringing the best available talents to his notice. Within a few months after Hitler's coming to power Rieser had a unique team of hand-picked actors at his disposal. It was virtually an all-German ensemble, an unusual feature even for Switzerland where German personnel, especially in opera, sometimes made up a large part of the casts. The new team at the Schauspielhaus was young, well-trained and politically wide awake; they were expatriates either by choice or necessity and ideologically far more left-wing than the money-minded Rieser had bargained for. He hated having his theatre called a 'den of Bolshies' by the right-wing Swiss press or made the target of repeated interventions by the German embassy. Yet he was also proud of the rising fame. He had sunk his fortune in the 'Pfauentheater' (the theatre's older name) in 1926 to provide Zurich society with a lavishly appointed place of fairly light entertainment. He now found himself with a team of actors and advisers who pressed for a greater share of serious, contemporary and political drama and were willing to prove that even the classics were sound business.

Rieser, with a businessman's sense of a shift in the market, followed the trend, but on his own conditions. Yet neither his extreme penny-pinching nor the unbelievable workload of one première per week could stop the impetus. When he sold out in 1938 to emigrate to America, Oskar Wälterlin took over a theatre conscious of its political mission and ready to play its part in strengthening the will of the Swiss nation to resist Nazi pressure under the threat of another 'Anschluss'.

Rieser began his first season with the new ensemble with *Measure for Measure* (8 September 1933). This was by no means a fortuitous choice. Gustav Hartung as director, a breathtakingly outspoken and uncompromising anti-Nazi,[18] apparently worked out the analogies between Angelo and Hitler in such a manner that they could not be overlooked. Goebbels was furious. He sent Hartung a message that he would have him quartered should he ever venture on German soil again. That was German Goebbels-style. Winston Churchill treated actors differently. He had himself announced in Laurence Olivier's dressing room to apologize for having constantly whispered during performance. But, he said, *Macbeth* was the only Shakespeare play he knew completely by heart, and he had not been able to deny himself the fun of testing his memory in what must have been a very audible form of unsolicited prompting. Of course Laurence Olivier melted. Goebbels knew nothing by heart.

Under Rieser as owner and general director the Schauspielhaus performed 19 plays by exiled German and Austrian dramatists.[19] Of these Ferdinand Bruckner's *Die Rassen* and Friedrich Wolf's *Professor*

Mannheim created the greatest stir. Their reception is indicative of the political climate of the time.

Die Rassen ('Races'), a simple play about a young 'Aryan' student breaking with his Jewish friend Siegelmann and his Jewish girlfriend Helene in the first flush of Nazi enthusiasm but being murdered by his own comrades when he prevents Helene's arrest, would not have had the formidable reception without its burning topicality. In the words of Curt Riess about Ernst Ginsberg who had the part of the Jewish victim,

> It was only during rehearsals that he realized this was not a role he was playing, but reality. 'His' Siegelmann – that was the Munich lawyer Siegel, who had really been chased through town with cut-off trousers and a placard on his chest 'I am a Jew'. To play Siegelmann meant more than play-acting, it meant accepting responsibility towards life and contemporary history.[20]

The Zurich Schauspielhaus apparently started on its new era with a bang. Almost exactly a year later Friedrich Wolf's *Professor Mannheim* (8 November 1934) brought an even bigger explosion. As far as artistic quality was concerned *Professor Mannheim* (better known under the title of *Professor Mamlock*) hardly had the edge of Bruckner's *Die Rassen*, but it was ideologically more pointed. It showed the fate of a Jewish doctor whose liberal humanism and belief in German culture incapacitates him for grasping and adequately reacting to successive instances of humiliation and degradation. He is ultimately driven to suicide. A young communist worker from Berlin is given the gratifying part of explaining the background to the shocking events from the standpoint of class-conscious anti-Fascism.

The play was an instant success, its propagandistic appeals were spontaneously applauded. There was also considerable resistance. Swiss Nazis organized demonstrations, and when the play was transferred to the Stadttheater for a few cheap-ticket performances, armed riot police had to protect the actors and effected almost a hundred arrests. The Zurich Schauspielhaus had arrived. There was not another German-speaking theatre in Europe with such a brave record.

Productions causing such spectacular successes were rare. But the Zurich Schauspielhaus was a beacon of light for exiled German drama. For everything that was modern, critical, intellectual and innovative during the Nazi period, there was only one address, and that was Zurich. Brecht's famous *Mother Courage* had its world première here on 19 April 1941.

Shakespeare was the most frequently performed author. From 1933 to the end of the 1944–5 season twenty-one plays were performed, seven of them (*Troilus and Cressida, Othello, Henry IV, Richard III, Julius Caesar, The Taming of the Shrew* and *Much Ado About Nothing*) coming out in several productions, some under different directors. The productions do not seem to have been unusual as regards directorial interpretation or visual presentation. For one thing, there was no need to give the Histories, for example, additional ideological twists. Other than in Berlin, *Richard III* (17 May 1934) could here be played straight and still be understood as a parable referring to the clique ruling beyond the border. Quite fortuitous aspects also played a part. The aged Albert Bassermann, one of the great masters of realistic acting, was Richard. He had left Germany because his Jewish actress wife Else had been banned from German stages. In other words, Bassermann, a victim, played the dictator whose present reincarnation had driven him into exile – the contradictions were too obvious and poignant to need labouring. The play was taken up again in March 1942 in the course of a planned but incomplete cycle of History plays. By then the parallels between Richard and Hitler were much clearer. *Richard III* was preceded in the same season by *King John* (18 September 1941) directed by Leonhard Steckel who, in the meantime, had become one of the three foremost directors next to Lindtberg and Wälterlin.

> The opening of the cycle with *King John* had an artistic as well as an ideological reason. For one thing, ... *King John* had not been played before, for another, the political brigandry determining European politics in those days was presented in a manner highly symbolical of the present time.[21]

In fact, the whole of the cycle must have appeared as a theatrical comment on the times. Wälterlin was responsible for one of the clearest instances at the Schauspielhaus of turning a Shakespeare play into a political comment. *Troilus and Cressida* (1 September 1938) with which he opened his first season as the new head of the 'Schauspielhaus Ltd.', is described by several observers as containing a highly pertinent message.

> this Ajax is still busy spouting his suicidal war propaganda ... he lives just across the border, he is Hitler, Göring, Goebbels, Mussolini. To underline this, Wälterlin has one of the actors come on in a Mussolini mask ... How topical is the parable of Hector's death! The one who did not want the war is killed ... just at the moment when he has disarmed. In other words: death to the defenceless.[22]

This was a year before Switzerland ordered general mobilization on the eve of Hitler's attack on Poland. The Schauspielhaus, by pointing the lessons contained in *Troilus and Cressida* and warning Switzerland not to be caught unarmed like Hector, was doing its bit. The frenetic applause accompanying the performances showed that the message had been understood.

The conditions under which the plays were produced were close to scandalous. A new play every week (under Rieser), or even every fortnight (under Wälterlin) meant that there was no time for deeper analysis or thoroughgoing dramaturgic preparation. That the merciless tempo did not result in slovenly work is a miracle. The answer seems to be that the ensemble consisted of quality-conscious actors to begin with and that singular dedication, commitment, and comradeship under a common fate made the impossible possible. To make a virtue out of necessity seems to have been a highly perfected art at the Zurich Schauspielhaus.

Compared with the scrupulous and disciplined production of Shakespeare's plays as theatrical *Gesamtkunstwerke* at the top theatres in Germany, the methods at the Zurich Schauspielhaus were slipshod, the results showed signs of hasty work; there simply was no leisure for profound premeditation. As Gustaf Gründgens was to say in a different context later on, 'You can make a virtue out of necessity, but not a style'.[23]

There certainly was no 'style' at the Zurich Schauspielhaus in the Gründgens sense, and the ensemble did everything to avoid it. Conditions prevented 'style' and forced the actors to develop a direct, no nonsense, no frills approach. This soon came to be regarded as the hallmark of their productions. There was neither time for calculated stylizations nor room for star cult. They were all 'stars', or certainly actors in full command of their craft. Rieser had encouraged many actors to try their hand at directing so that ultimately next to Wälterlin, Lindtberg and Steckel, there were six others, namely Wolfgang Heinz, Kurt Horwitz, Ernst Ginsberg, Robert Trösch, Karl Paryla and Wolfgang Langhoff who more or less frequently operated as directors. This also meant they all controlled each other.

The predominance of the actor-director had positive consequences. It not only prevented a star cult but above all focused dramaturgy on those effects that could be achieved by acting. There was little else. The sets by Teo Otto, a designer of genius, simply could not compete with what the Staatstheater in Berlin or the Burgtheater in Vienna could put on view. Theirs was poor theatre. It was rich only in one aspect – acting. They made the most of this capital. Their different artistic temperaments and approaches complemented each other and created what Kurt Hirschfeld later termed 'humanist realism' as the prevailing form.

There could have been, as Hans Mayer pointed out later,[24] no greater contrast than that between the type of theatre Gründgens had perfected at the Staatstheater, a theatre of nobility of style and high-polish form, of deliberate artificiality and abstention from overtly mixing politics and art – and the equally deliberate realism, directness and determined anti-Fascism practised at the Zurich Schauspielhaus. When the war was over and the German theatre had to be rebuilt, these two traditions confronted each other. They did not mingle easily. The Gründgens tradition had another lease of life during the post-war restoration period and was finally abandoned in the late fifties. The Zurich tradition of a politically activist theatre quickly established itself in East Germany.

'Die Stunde Null' – Zero Hour Continuity or a Fresh Start?

When the Nazi nightmare ended with Hitler's suicide on 30 April 1945 and the unconditional surrender of all German forces eight days later, Germany was in ruins. Her cities and factories were heaps of rubble and twisted metal, the military losses came to about six million, and two million civilians had lost their lives either under aerial bombardment or on the trek to the West in their flight from the Red Army. The survivors who thought their cup was full learnt with shock that other nations had suffered even worse, above all Poland and Soviet Russia where the death toll exceeded the twenty-million mark. And by stages people also awoke to that ultimate horror, the Holocaust, and the thousands of lesser crimes their nation had been guilty of. The full recognition of what Germany and Germans had perpetrated would take years to grow and decades to come to terms with. It was to be a determining factor in German politics and a crucial element in German intellectual life well into the 1980s and beyond.

It is still a cause for wonder how quickly some sort of theatrical life was re-established. It had of course nothing to do with show business in the old sense. Half the theatres had been totally destroyed, the other half more or less seriously damaged. Few had survived unscathed. Performances were held in temporary halls with whatever props or costumes had been salvaged, and the hungry spectators in winter would sit wrapped in greatcoats and mufflers. There were also many new groups which made no pretence at all to imitate established theatre. Calling themselves 'Junge Bühne', 'Studiobühne', 'Zimmertheater', or even 'Kellertheater', (usually followed by the name of the town or the year in which they were founded), they operated in whatever venues were available – barns, halls, classrooms, lofts and cellars. In winter spectators were expected to bring a briquet of brown coal wrapped in a newspaper to help maintain a minimum of animal comfort. It was a theatre of bare necessity but the new groups responded to a deeply felt need. For twelve years people had been cut off from a substantial part of their own tradition as well as from practically all foreign writing. A whole generation of young Germans had been robbed of all chances of cultivation. There was an immense hunger to make up for the lost time, to fill the gaps in one's literary education, to develop a mental culture, to find a voice. Carl Zuckmayer, one of the first émigrés to return from the United States and travelling through Germany in the service of the US Military Government, noticed everywhere

> a ravenous desire for clarification and insight, a thirst for spiritual renewal. It was, in spite of the general sorrow and destruction, a great time of hope. Whatever cultural nourishment came from abroad ... was passionately seized upon ... the unheated theatres were packed with people who often had to walk for hours to reach them, people poorly clad, their faces tinged yellow with hunger but with burning eyes, ... and ready to have their minds and emotions stirred.[25]

However, the programmes of the new theatre groups were hardly extraordinary and often depended, in the beginning at least, on the available texts. Nor were they revolutionary in form. But the conditions under which they worked did not permit type-acting and broke down the barriers between actors and audience, their scripts were often intellectually demanding, they represented a ferment or source of renewal when theatrical life, in the years of the 'economic miracle' in the early fifties, returned to normal.

The Nazi past, in its most shameful aspects, was still too painful to handle. What people sought in the theatres (as in the crowded churches of the time) was reassurance, guidance, spiritual orientation, some form of hope, not flat confrontation with the unthinkable and ineffable. German theatre after 1918 was proudly revolutionary. After 1945 it tried to regain its spiritual bearings by becoming conservative.

Decades later, this development was derided as theatre's contribution to 'Adenauer-Restauration', that spirit of going back to Christian basics which dominated a great part of Konrad Adenauer's long term (1949–63) as Chancellor of the Federal Republic. At the time it seemed to be the logical course. Wherever a theatre re-opened with Lessing's *Nathan the Wise* and its call to reconciliation, tolerance and forgiveness, the target was not revolutionary renewal as in the twenties but an attempt to regain lost humanist traditions. Regeneration, it was felt, could only be effected on the basis of values and institutions least discredited under Nazism, namely Christianity and the classical tradition of the Occident. Christian humanism as the central ethos also explains the German vogue of plays by T.S. Eliot, Christopher Fry, Thornton Wilder, Paul Claudel, Jean Anouilh, of Max

Frisch and Friedrich Dürrenmatt, and of the few German exponents, for example Stefan Andres, of the same spirit.

I wish there was a simpler story to tell. Namely, that post-war developments on the German stage were a matter of clear-cut oppositions: on the one hand the old directors, big-shots of the Nazi period, attempting to re-establish previous conditions – on the other side the young, poor, enthusiastic but powerless new groups. It is much more difficult than that. The 'old' ones, Gründgens, Schalla, Stroux, Hilpert, Sellner, were men in their forties and still well able to learn and re-adapt. Only Fehling was past it. He demanded that as unquestionably the best director and proven anti-Nazi, he be given charge of all theatres in Berlin. He even got a licence for a few months for his own, the Jürgen-Fehling-Theatre, but after an uncritically grandiloquent obituary for Heinrich George, who died in a Russian internment camp in 1946, Fehling was no longer 'acceptable'. George had been a Nazi. This is what Fehling, the anti-Nazi, had left unmentioned – *de mortuis*.

In Berlin, the Cold War made itself felt. Many good people left. The city quickly lost its role as a theatre metropolis. The new centres were Düsseldorf (under Gründgens, 1947–55), Darmstadt (under Gustav Rudolf Sellner, 1951–61), Göttingen under Hilpert, Bochům under Schalla, only Munich had to wait till 1949, when Fritz Kortner, the unsurpassed star actor of expressionist Berlin in the twenties, came back from America and started directing in a manner which is still a legendary memory with theatre fans. In the same year, Brecht took up his work in East Berlin: on 12 February 1949 Helene Weigel as Mother Courage for the first time drew her cart across a German stage.

But, returning émigrés and those who had stayed did not get on. Biographies had diverged too crassly and they had become sensitized to completely different things. Kortner suspected anti-Semitism behind every contradiction and spent much time writing letters of apology. Fehling, irritated by Kortner's fame, remarked he would rather have read Kortner's name on a gravestone in Auschwitz. It took years before Kortner forgave him. Fehling in any case had been suffering for some time from mental disturbances.

But even where nerves were not so raw mutual understanding was difficult. Those who had stayed were allergic to criticism from people who, as they thought, had been sunning themselves in California while *they* had spent their nights in air-raid shelters. The returnees could not understand why post-war theatre in West Germany did not try to re-establish contact with the revolutionary aesthetics of Piscator and Brecht. For those who had stayed it was clear that, at least in West Germany, there was no social basis for such a move. They sought instead to link up to the uncompromised achievements of the thirties, a phenomenon which naturally jarred on the sensibilities of returning émigrés. 'Reichskanzleistil' (hollow pathos, fake nobility of gesture and declamation, the groundless neo-expressionism Kortner hated) was Berthold Viertel's blistering verdict in 1954.

Nobody doubted, however, that theatre's prime task at that time was to contribute to the ethical regeneration of a dejected and morally compromised people. This ethos determined the choice of play and the manner of presentation. For the lessons to be palatable, they had to be indirect. The shock techniques of frontal assault contained in the future plays of Heinar Kipphardt, Rolf Hochhuth or Peter Weiss, would have been unbearable at this early period. The message, instead, had to be couched in a more general form, as allegory or parable, and related to a metaphysical frame of reference, not pronounced as a direct and historically concrete accusation. Lessons of such general validity (and sufficiently unspecific in character) were found in the plays of Wilder, Eliot, Fry, Giraudoux, Anouilh, Sartre, Dürrenmatt and Frisch – Priestley's *An Inspector Calls* ran for years – and they helped audiences to make sense of their experience and understand their place in a moral scheme of things without immediately finding themselves in the dock or at the pillory.

The only Shakespeare play to serve this deeply felt need was *Measure for Measure*. It could be interpreted as a sublime debate between Justice and Mercy, a mystery play where an overzealous idealist merely wants to clean up a world rotten with immorality and decadence, yet overshoots the mark and becomes criminal and guilty himself, an Angelo Germanicus as it were, whose life by rights was forfeit were it not for the godlike Duke who only wanted to test the young firebrand, teach him a stern lesson but then dispense mercy – just as the Germans after the war stood in need of mercy before justice. That is how *Measure for Measure* was frequently played, as a parable: moral arrogance falling into crime and guilt, being severely chastised and corrected before being granted final absolution. A most reassuring conception.

How to regain a humane 'image of Man', how to rebuild theatre in the spirit of 'classicist humanism', those were the concerns of the important post-war directors. For Brecht, Piscator and Kortner, who were about to give theatre a much sharper edge, such concepts were red rags to a bull, nothing but subterfuges and obscurantism. But the authoritative directors of the fifties (Gründgens, Schalla, Stroux, Sellner, Hilpert, Schuh) were convinced that they had passed the test, had got through the Nazi era without too many concessions and that the best they could do was to uphold the principles they had developed then, namely: abstraction, sparsity, stylization and spirituality. They had avoided realism then, and avoided it even more so now. The catastrophe that had overtaken Germany, so they thought, could only be grasped as a form of metaphysical abandonment, a dimension, they felt, which could only be reached through symbolic form, in the words of Oscar Fritz Schuh, by a 'theatre of existential spiritualization'. One can positively hear Brecht and Piscator grind their molars.

In Düsseldorf, Gründgens continued to rely on his well-proven categories of 'form and style'. In Nazi times they had been his answer to 'blood and soil'. The theatre should not be a tribunal, but a place of art, if possible timeless art. In Gründgens's repertoire in Düsseldorf there was not much place for the so-called Enthüllungsdramatik, that is the immediate post-war plays revealing Nazi crimes. Wolfgang Borchert's *The Man Outside* was produced (18 September 1948), but already Carl Zuckmayer's absolute best-seller on the German stage, *The Devil's General* (totalling 2069 performances in the 1948–9 season) was not seen by Düsseldorf audiences.

Was this by intention or by chance? Gründgens never left anything to chance. He brought new foreign authors on the German stage, he established Sartre in Germany, he directed Cocteau, and helped to establish T.S. Eliot, Christopher Fry and Thornton Wilder. But these were authors presenting the time's outrages from a philosophical distance, who transposed the actual monstrosities into unspecific generalization and symbolic configurations. It was only in this fairly distanced form that he, and with him the dominant directors of the fifties, found that the 'hot irons' could be handled.

The 'Düsseldorf Manifesto against Directorial Licence' of 1952 confirms the devoted service to the interests of the poet that had always inspired his work. 'The secret of art is more easily revealed in a stringent form', he wrote in 1948, 'and the wonders of the spirit will become more easily transparent when the interpretation is objective'.[26] The few Shakespeare plays he directed after the war followed this line of unquestioned authority of the classical heritage.

Günther Rühle granted that Gründgens had created a 'theatre of great form', showing the qualities of 'human truth, spiritual discipline, noblesse and elegant acting'. What more can one want? The time was coming when very much more was wanted, when Rolf Hochhuth, Heinar Kipphardt and Peter Weiss would be asking questions much more directly, when student theatres in Frankfurt, Berlin, Tübingen and Erlangen rebelled and turned the stage into a tribunal – or when Peter Zadek took on Shakespeare, squashed all nobility of form and turned the severe German educative theatre into a garish playground and vital circus.

But that is a different story.

Notes

1 See the collection of documents and letters in Joseph Wulf, *Theater und Film im Dritten Reich: Eine Dokumentation* (Gütersloh, 1964), equally Jutta Wardetzky, *Theaterpolitik im faschistischen Deutschland: Studien und Dokumente* (Berlin, 1983) and, for a brief survey, John Willett, *The Theatre of the Weimar Republic* (London, 1988), 179–89.

2 For a comprehensive documentation of the campaign against 'un-German' books see *Die Bücherverbrennung*, ed. Gerhard Sauder (München, 1983). *Dort wo man Bücher verbrennt*, ed. Klaus Schöffling (Frankfurt, 1983) contains essays by and the reactions of authors whose books were burnt.

3 Reinhardt's son Gottfried called his father's letter to the Hitler government 'an empty gesture and a misguided attempt' to maintain a fictitious position of neutrality. *Der Liebhaber: Erinnerungen Seines Sohnes Gottfried Reinhardt an Max Reinhardt* (München, 1973), 201.

4 See Boguslaw Drewniak, *Das Theater im NS-Staat: Szenarium Deutscher Zeitgeschichte 1933–1945* (Düsseldorf, 1983). Hans Daiber even sees a correlation between the theatricality of the spectacular Nazi rallies and the new government's overestimation of the effects to be achieved through theatre. 'With no government in Germany before or after was theatre in such high repute. The quantitative proof: in 1933 there were 147 theatres employing 22,000 people, in 1940–1 the figure had risen to 248 and the number of those employed to 44,000'. *Schaufenster der Diktatur: Theater im Machtbereich Hitlers* (Stuttgart, 1995), 11.

5 See, e.g., Herbert Freeden, *Jüdisches Theater in Nazideutschland* (Tübingen, 1964); Eike Geisel and Henryk M. Broder, *Premiere und Pogrom: Der Jüdische Kulturbund 1933–1941: Texte und Bilder* (Berlin, 1992); *Geschlossene Vorstellung: Der Jüdische Kulturbund in Deutschland 1933–1941*, ed. Akademie der Künste (Berlin, 1992), the highly informative catalogue of an exhibition; Hans Daiber, *Schaufenster der Diktatur: Theater im Machtbereich Hitlers* (Stuttgart, 1995), the relevant chapters.

6 It is hardly surprising that at the beginning and especially from the outside, Gründgens's conduct must have appeared as ambiguous and questionable. Even his closest associates inside Germany were never sure of his real convictions. The published documents, however, reveal a stunning blend of self-control, tactical skill and bravado, and do not support any of the allegations levelled against him in *Mephisto*. This fact is also borne out by Curt Riess who – as Gründgens's German-

American-Jewish biographer above suspicion of complicity – draws a quite different picture and takes very decided issue with Klaus Mann's biased presentation of the case. See Curt Riess, *Gustaf Gründgens* (Hamburg, 1965), 154–6 et passim.

7 John Newmark, '... so halb Totschläger und halb Gestapo', in *Frankfurter Rundschau* (31 October 1987).
8 E.g., Curt Riess, *Gustaf Gründgens*, 213, resp. John Newmark in the article quoted.
9 Quoted in *Das Theater des Deutschen Regisseurs Jürgen Fehling*, 182.
10 From an interview with Kurt Kreiler, quoted in *Das Theater des Deutschen Regisseurs Jürgen Fehling*, 168.
11 Riess, *Gustaf Gründgens*, 214f.
12 Minetti, 108.
13 Biedrzynski, 18.
14 Quoted in *Das Theater des Deutschen Regisseurs Jürgen Fehling*, 166.
15 Ibid., 34f.
16 Ibid., 35.
17 The eventful history of the Zurich Schauspielhaus has been variously described. The most colourful story is presented by Curt Riess, *Sein oder Nichtsein: Zürcher Schauspielhaus – Der Roman eines Theaters* (Zurich, 1963), enlarged and reissued as *Das Schauspielhaus Zürich: Sein oder Nichtsein eines Ungewöhnlichen Theaters* (Munich, 1988). The war years are focused by Günther Schoop, *Das Zürcher Schauspielhaus im Zweiten Weltkrieg* (Zurich, 1957), while the East German scholar Werner Mittenzwei, *Das Zürcher Schauspielhaus 1933–1945 oder Die Letzte Chance* (Berlin, 1979) concentrates on the ideological background and development of the theatre as a whole as well as its most prominent actors, especially Wolfgang Langhoff.
18 Cf. Mittenzwei, 26.
19 According to the lists in Mittenzwei, 67f.
20 Riess, *Sein oder Nichtsein*, 61.
21 Ibid., 81.
22 Ibid., 151.
23 Quoted in Paul Rose, *Berlins Große Theaterzeit*, 140.
24 'Staatstheater und Emigrantentheater', in Hans Mayer, *Die Unerwünschte Literatur* (Frankfurt, 1992), 227–30.
25 Quoted Eugen Schöndienst, *Geschichte des Deutschen Bühnenvereins seit 1945* (Frankfurt, 1981), 16f. Adorno was equally surprised by the intellectual climate of post war Germany. In place of the expected 'barbarism' and 'loss of culture' he encountered a veritable 'intellectual passion'. Joachim Kaiser who quotes these observations (24–5) explains that young intellectuals in 1945 emerged as from a

tunnel 'into the realm of intellectual freedom' (23). 'It was ... like an addiction. For the generation of Grass, Walser, Enzensberger, Ingeborg Bachmann the years between 1945 and 1953 were "our golden twenties"' (24). J. Kaiser, *Wie ich sie Sah ... und wie sie Waren* (Munich, 1985).

[26] *Wirklichkeit des Theaters* (Frankfurt, 1977), 177.

CHAPTER 6

Gentlemen You Are Welcome to Elsinore: *Hamlet* in Performance at Kronborg Castle, Elsinore

Niels B. Hansen

The known sources of Shakespeare's *Hamlet* do not connect the story in any way with a Renaissance setting or the castle at Elsinore twenty-five miles north of Copenhagen. So it has been surmised that it was on the basis of personal familiarity with the place that Shakespeare chose the newly erected castle for the setting of his version of Saxo's legendary tale. There is, however, no proof that Shakespeare had any first-hand experience of the place, but it is quite possible that he may have heard about it from Englishmen who had visited the royal court at Kronborg Castle. Itinerant troupes of entertainers of various kinds are known to have been there in the late sixteenth century, and one of the names recorded in the accounts is that of Will Kempe, who was later a member of Shakespeare's company. What touches of local colour the play contains are not very detailed or accurate, though.

Nevertheless, the story of Hamlet has for centuries been linked with Elsinore in the minds of readers and playgoers throughout the world, and the 'rottenness' of Denmark has become a byword. So it is hardly surprising that the idea of staging the play where it is set should arise. It arose as early as 1816 when it was performed in a Danish translation/adaptation somewhere around the castle precincts to celebrate the bicentenary of Shakespeare's death. A hundred years later, in 1916, actors from The Royal Theatre in Copenhagen once again played *Hamlet* at Kronborg, but this time outside the actual castle walls, on the ramparts overlooking the Sound and Sweden across the water.

Not until 1985 was *Hamlet* again performed in Danish at Kronborg, but in the meantime a tradition of playing *Hamlet* at Elsinore had been established. This sequence of international performances at irregular intervals started in 1937 on the initiative of a Danish organization which called itself The National Open-air Stage. They invited the Old Vic Company to give a performance of *Hamlet* in the courtyard of the castle.

The weather conditions on the opening night made it painfully clear that it will always be a hazardous affair to stage open-air performances in the Danish summer. It was pouring down so badly that the performance proper had to be cancelled. A memorable indoor version on a makeshift stage in a nearby hotel took shape at few hours' notice, but the following night it was possible to proceed according to plan.

Undaunted by climatic adversity The National Open-air Stage continued its activities. When they finally gave up in 1954 they had organized ten performances, three before the war and seven after. The play was performed in English by British companies in 1937, 1939, 1950 and 1954, by an American company in 1949 and by the Irish Dublin Gate Theatre in 1952. In addition there was a much publicized German production in 1938 by the Staatliches Schauspielhaus, Berlin with Gustav Gründgens starring; plus visiting companies from Norway in 1946, Finland in 1947 (performing in Swedish) and from Sweden in 1951.

Twenty-five years passed after the English production in 1954 before the circumstances were right to revive the tradition. In 1979 the Old Vic was back in the courtyard at Elsinore with Derek Jacobi in the title role, performing to an audience seated in a semicircular amphitheatre, a timber construction which solved some of the problems of the highly atmospheric but by no means acoustically and visually ideal venue. This was to be a once-only solution to the practical problems of playing in the courtyard. In 1985 a production originally staged at the Royal Theatre in Copenhagen was recreated at Kronborg, but this time on a new (covered) stage outside the Castle up against the east wall. This stage was used again in 1986 when Kronborg was visited by the Oxford Playhouse with David Threlfall as Hamlet, and most recently in 1988 when Kenneth Branagh's Renaissance Theatre Company played not only *Hamlet* (directed by Derek Jacobi and with Branagh himself in the title role) but also *Much Ado About Nothing* and *As You Like It*.

This completes the succession of the open-air '*Hamlet* plays' at Kronborg, but to this survey the most widely seen *Hamlet* at Kronborg should be added, namely the TV version starring Christopher Plummer which was filmed inside and outside the castle in 1964 to mark the 400th anniversary of Shakespeare's birth.

To play *Hamlet* 'on location', as it were, raises a great number of problems concerning acting technique, sound projection, lighting, costumes, etc., and last but not least the choice of set and the use of the surrounding buildings. Many of these problems would have had to be dealt with in a very short on-the-spot pre-performance phase, commonly adapting a production that had in the first place been created for an entirely different space.

My central concern in this paper is with the question of how different companies have addressed themselves to the issues of staging the play in this particular setting. The material available for dealing with this question is quite limited, especially as regards the earlier productions. The most useful material is photographs, but programme notes and reviews must also be taken into consideration. The technically best photos are often of the leading actors posing for the photographer against the castle architecture; actual performance shots, insofar as they exist, are often technically inferior and not terribly informative.

Even with such limitations in the scope of the inquiry and in the documentation this paper does not allow me time to deal with fourteen productions, or even the ten that make up the first series. I shall therefore here limit myself to a description and a discussion of the first four British productions to visit Elsinore, two before and two after the Second World War.

In the summer of 1937 Lilian Baylis took her Old Vic Company to Denmark to perform a *Hamlet* which had premiered in London earlier in the year. The play was directed by Tyrone Guthrie, and the parts of Hamlet and Ophelia were performed by Laurence Olivier and Vivien Leigh. The interest and the enthusiasm were overwhelming, partly due to the inauspicious but highly successful indoor opening of the open-air production due to the inclement Danish weather, but chiefly because of the quality of the acting, the director's imaginative and lively production, his use of the space and the quite special atmosphere created by the interaction between the play and the place.

Two years later, after the German *Hamlet* of 1938, John Gielgud followed in Olivier's footsteps to Elsinore. This was Gielgud's fourth Hamlet during the 1930s, a production which he himself directed. It had had a brief session in London at the Lyceum before it came to Denmark, but as Gielgud wrote in the London programme, 'I have naturally had to consider the conditions with which we shall be faced at the open-air performance at Elsinore next week for which the setting and the production have been primarily designed'. According to Danish reviewers the evening was above all a personal triumph for Gielgud, whose Hamlet made a very powerful impression, not least because of his diction and noble bearing, which were almost inevitably compared to Olivier's more agile and energetic, but also more declamatory Hamlet two years earlier.

The third great English actor to play Hamlet at Kronborg was Michael Redgrave. This was in 1950, the fourth post-war performance organized by the Danish festival committee. It was again an Old Vic production, directed by Hugh Hunt. It was greatly appreciated for its classical dignity against the background of an American *Hamlet* the previous summer, which Danish audiences generally had found too highstrung and peculiar for their liking. There was praise for Redgrave's Hamlet, but it seems that he did not tower above the rest of the company like Gielgud: it was the *ensemble* that impressed.

The fourth and last Hamlet to be considered here is Richard Burton's in 1954. Once again it was produced by the Old Vic Company, directed by Michael Benthall. This *Hamlet* had been designed for an indoor stage, and there seemed to be no attempt to adapt it to the Kronborg Castle setting. Richard Burton's Hamlet was characterized as 'sporty', full of energy and vitality, but not particularly sensitive or moving. In fact, if any one member of the company was singled out for special praise it was Claire Bloom as Ophelia.

To give an idea of the basic conditions under which these four productions were shaped and the ways in which they used the surroundings in creating their acting space I shall refer to the four figures appended to this essay. As appears from the four pictures the seating arrangements were more or less identical. Within the quadrangle of the castle walls the audience were placed on benches in many long rows across the entire space and directly on the flat surface of the courtyard. With a capacity of some 1800 seats such factors clearly influence, or at least ought to influence the actual set. In all four performances the audience faced east. In other words the stage was placed against the east wall of the courtyard, presumably because this gives the easiest access to the stage from behind.

The acting space was built up in two essentially different ways. In 1937 (fig. 1) and 1950 (fig. 3) an open plan had been adopted using a rather wide stage with a number of platforms at different levels and a system of stairs or ramps to connect them. In both productions a tower-like structure was erected on the right-hand side of the stage, the flat top of which in 1937 provided an extra level of acting space, whereas the somewhat taller 1950 tower was capped. These two productions shared the advantage of having an acting space which could be seen fairly well by every member of the audience, even those placed at the ends of the rows. The open plan without any kind of backdrop also allowed the castle to play a quite prominent part in the performance.

In clear contrast to this design the 1939 (fig. 2) and 1954 (fig. 4) stages were enclosed and covered, or canopied, and blocked off the castle wall. In 1954 the stage had quite considerable width under draperies supported by lance-like poles, whereas the 1939 stage was quite confined, although it seems to have had a narrow platform extending beyond the banners on either side of the picture frame stage. Both these stages had an apron-like space in front and a recess or inner stage of somewhat different character. It may seem surprising that Gielgud's design was the outcome of a visit to the castle which he had paid well in advance, especially as he claimed to have chosen it with a view to an open-air performance in this particular space. This is how he justified his choice in the programme for the Kronborg performances:

> When I saw the beautiful Courtyard of Kronborg Castle, I felt the play should be given there in a swift, concentrated production. Motley, who have designed the scenery and costumes, have helped me to create the atmosphere of a luxurious and splendid Court. But although, at first, I was tempted to employ the wide platforms and fine proportions of the stage used at Kronborg in previous years, I decided after some thought that I preferred a more intimate stage, of which I might convey more easily that feeling of council chambers, passages and anterooms, where Hamlet walks, where his uncle father and aunt mother pass their days in feasting and debauchery, where Polonius and Rosencrantz and Guildenstern are ever lurking and spying, and where Ophelia is set on to trap the Prince whom she loves.

It is quite likely that Gielgud chose a set which suited his own particular style of acting, but whether it suited the particular venue is another matter.

In what follows I shall consider in more detail the various sets and attempt to evaluate their effect, largely by drawing on reviews in major Danish national dailies. The performances were also reviewed in British newspapers, but typically in less detail, and as the productions had already been reviewed when they were first shown in Britain, the reviewers tend to concentrate more on the event.

The sense of an event in which 'Hamlet comes home' was particularly strong in 1937, and not only because of the quite unusual and unexpected first night. English reviewers had flocked to Elsinore to cover the visit, and one of the Danish daily newspapers carried a review by the distinguished British critic Ivor Brown, who found the open platform stage quite similar to Shakespeare's Globe both in the demands it made on the actors' technique and the opportunities it created for them. What this stage resembled was perhaps not so much the Globe Theatre with its tiring-house and its roof supported by pillars as the pre-Elizabethan acting space consisting of a platform set up in an enclosed courtyard. In this case, however, the stage consisted of several platforms at different levels, the highest of which was a kind of rostrum, a cube of about six by six by six feet, which towered above the rest of the set. The various levels were connected by a quite elaborate set of stairs. Everything was designed and painted as rectangular slabs of stone which merged with the façade of the castle wall behind the stage. This set, which was essentially the same as had been used for the indoor performances in London, was very suitable for the location. The voices carried well, and the enclosing castle walls were felt to call to mind the prison-like state of Denmark, and as the lingering light of the Danish June night gave way to the dusk and the artificial lighting, the shadows of the characters were clearly outlined larger than life on the wall behind the stage. The set suited not only the castle setting but also the demands of open-air theatre as well as Guthrie's and Olivier's talents. It was spacious and flexible and gave Guthrie fine opportunities for working with bold colours, strong contrasts and plastic crowd scenes. The large court scenes with 'The Mousetrap' and the duel, which both made effective use of the high rostrum, seem to have been specially captivating because of the possibility for large, rapid and tumultuous movements. Claudius and Gertrude were seated up here during the play-within-the-play, which provided a strong focus for the King's horror and anger at being caught in the mousetrap and the general confusion upon his hurried exit, followed by Hamlet's frantic dancing. From the same rostrum Claudius and Gertrude also watched the duel which led to the Queen's highly dramatic dying fall of fifteen feet. The general verdict was that the performance was a great success for the actors and the director alike, because Guthrie had had the good sense to relinquish exquisite and delicate details of voice and facial expression in favour of a perhaps less subtle, more physical and energetic style of acting, and to concentrate on the larger lines in the drama, which came powerfully across in his imaginative and skilful use of his actors, his supers and his space.

The difference between the dramatic assets of Laurence Olivier and John Gielgud, which Gielgud much later summed up by saying 'Larry had the legs, I had the voice', may well lie behind the quite different production Gielgud staged at Kronborg two years later. Gielgud was both the director and the leading actor, and as explained above he had given a good deal of thought to the set he wanted for the outdoor performance in the courtyard of the castle. He settled for 'a more intimate stage' than the one Guthrie and Gründgens had used, and it would appear that it worked well for some scenes, but let him down in others. Upon much the same basic four foot high structure of imitation castle wall stonework across the east side of the courtyard was erected a kind of picture-frame stage, an approximately 24 feet wide and 15 feet tall, dark, roofed box with a wooden arch attached on either side. It had a curtain at either side and also one at the back, which when drawn aside gave access to the stage down a flight of steps. This casket-like stage, which also had a blue curtain in front, served for all indoor scenes. In front of it was a fairly small, level acting space accessible via the arches. Above the box stage was a light superstructure with a coat of arms and a banner at either corner, and the whole erection was flanked by seven larger heraldic banners. It was generally felt that this did not quite work. *The Times*'s drama critic put it like this:

> The set designed by Motley, admirably as its flags and dark colour composed with the castle walls and green roofs of copper, seemed too small for its surroundings. It suggested a Punch and Judy booth set down in an immense open space.

The problem with this set was that, in clear contrast to Guthrie's production, in the ensemble scenes the actors were cramped in the narrow space, and the outdoor scenes with the gravediggers and the ghost did not quite work in front of the elegant curtain and pillars. The illusion of darkness and horror in the ghost scenes in particular was unconvincing, partly because of the strong daylight in the early part of the performance. Later, it would seem, the spotlights on the castle walls made the surroundings interact with the play in a striking *son et lumiere* show. But what stood out in the 1939 *Hamlet* at Kronborg was not so much the director's achievement as the leading actor's. 'The world's best Hamlet' wrote the reviewer in the Danish daily *Politiken*, and he devoted most of his piece to a glowing tribute to Gielgud's looks, his stage presence, his eyes, and above all his voice, and the critic reviewing for *The Times* also found that Gielgud 'though unaccustomed to act in the open air, quickly found the range of the courtyard, and the subtlest of his gestures and intonations carried to the most remote seats'.

When the Old Vic returned to Kronborg in 1950 it was with a 'vigorously conventional' production which had been adapted to the new setting, with performances by the leading actors which, according to *The Times*'s reviewer, had grown in the process: Mark Dignam's Claudius became 'more formidably clearcut' and likewise Wanda Rotha's Gertrude improved 'by the enlarging effect of the open-air stage', and Michael Redgrave's Hamlet 'has now what formerly it lacked – the quality of excitement'. Even so Redgrave's Hamlet, though occasionally reminiscent of Gielgud's, did not spark off the same enthusiastic responses. His physique was impressive, his diction clear and beautiful and full of nuances, but he seems to have lacked some of the pathos, the inner drama. The dramatic tension seems rather to have expressed itself between the characters in the perfectly attuned ensemble. Suiting not only the action to the word and the word to the action but also the set to the style of acting, the set for this production was fairly unobtrusive. Returning to the basic idea of the 1937 set, it consisted of a series of platforms at several levels. The main platform could be reached via ramps leading off from the front both left and right. There was also access to the main platform through a portal on the left and from behind a tower on the right. Centre stage there were three steps up to a narrower platform which also allowed actors to enter from behind. The tower stood on another platform, which could be reached by five further steps, on which the ghost appeared. On either side of the tower and the portal were screening walls across the whole east wing with additional doors where the ramps got down to the floor of the courtyard. Simpler than it sounds in description, this stage lent itself to fluent, varied and continuous dramatic movement. Neither the set nor the costumes were assertive. What was most striking about this unassuming set was the way it allowed the castle to play its part in the developing tragedy. The final tableau appears to have been very stirring, where Fortinbras's army entered across the full breadth of the stage from behind, headed by ten large, waving, scarlet banners like a wave rolling over the pale face of the dead prince as he was carried out by four knights in armour and Fortinbras picked up the crown.

The set for the Old Vic's 1950 production of *Hamlet*, designed by Margaret Harris, had clearly been created, or recreated, for the occasion, whatever it may have looked like before it was taken to Kronborg. When the Old Vic returned in 1954 with a production directed by Michael Benthall and designed by Kenneth Rowell, they had made absolutely no concessions to the special venue. It was an indoor production which depended for many of its special effects on artificial lighting to the extent that the daylight in the first half vitiated or downright destroyed some of these special effects. The director had clearly not taken into account that at midsummer (the first night was on 18 June); it does not begin to get dark in Denmark till around 10 p.m. Nor had he apparently wanted to adapt his performance to the courtyard or in any way use the castle in creating the set and the atmosphere of the play. It was the stage of the Old Vic transported to Elsinore, and several critics observed that it would have made no difference if it had been placed out in the woods or in front of the Copenhagen Town Hall. This time the wooden structure on which the set was raised did not imitate the stone walls of the castle, and the set itself virtually excluded the background. A towering canvas structure supported by lance-like poles, rising in the middle to a gigantic canopy some 25 feet above the stage floor, somewhat lower on either side, but here too with the castle curtained off effectively by draperies. The depth of the stage on the two sides suggested galleries, but the middle section, rising six steps above the floor of the apron, was more like a large hall with huge candelabra extending backwards. The response of the major Danish critics to this was on the whole negative, even if they were prepared to admit the effectiveness of the design on its own terms, in what one of them called an overwrought baroque style like a Handel opera, with strong colours in draperies, pennants and costumes, heavy and garish black and yellow, red and blue colours gradually giving way to a hectic, phosphorescent, putrid green as the artificial light began to work as intended. Though Richard Burton's Hamlet had had plenty of time to develop in a long run which had started at the Edinburgh Festival, it failed to impress the Danish critics as a performance to match in depth, nobility and subtlety his English predecessors at Kronborg.

This marked the end of an era in *Hamlet* performances at Kronborg. When the tradition was resumed 25 years later with yet another Old Vic production it was acted on a stage and in an auditorium which excluded the castle ambience pretty effectively from the experience. Since then there has been only one (Danish) *Hamlet* in the courtyard of Kronborg Castle, and it is not likely there will be another. The new location outside the castle, which was used as lately as the summer of 1996 for a *Hamlet* ballet, has obvious advantages, but also obvious drawbacks. Not least there is a strong local interest in reviving the *Hamlet* Festivals, but the obstacles are considerable: the availability of a first-rate touring version of the play, the financing and the unreliability of the Danish climate, just to mention the most obvious ones.

We are left with incomplete and hazy impressions of an important epoch in the stage history of *Hamlet*. To reconstruct and interpret the scenic realization of the ten *Hamlets* at Kronborg under the auspices of The National Open-air Stage is at the same time an intriguing and a frustrating task, fraught with most of the problems of historical performance studies. The available material, textual and pictorial, gives us a fairly good insight into what the stage looked like each time, but only a very limited idea of what the actual performance was like. Along with the methical research problems which I have touched upon intermittently, the '*Hamlet* plays' at Kronborg raise the question of the *raison d'être* of (open-air) performances at 'topical' venues. Why and when is it a good idea to play *Hamlet* at Kronborg? It seems safe to conclude that the more the unorthodox theatrical setting is given a genuine role to play in the proceedings, the more sense it makes to use it. The conclusions to be drawn from the analysis of the four productions discussed in this paper would by and large be confirmed if all the ten productions were considered. There were basically two types: the 'self-contained' set and the 'open' set. The open set, doing away with the paraphernalia of the traditional naturalistic theatre, the backcloth, the wings, the proscenium arch and the curtain, has on the whole proved to work best. In other words, the style of the first of the international Kronborg *Hamlet*s in 1937 rather than that of the last one in

1954. It is ironic that since the 1950s the trend in performing Shakespeare has been towards the open, flexible, suggestive set.

6.1 Kronborg, 1937 production, dir. **Tyrone Guthrie**, Laurence Olivier as Hamlet

6.2 Kronborg, 1939 production, dir. **John Gielgud**, John Gielgud as Hamlet

HAMLET IN PERFORMANCE AT KRONBORG CASTLE, ELSINORE 119

6.3 Kronborg, 1950 production, dir. Hugh Hunt, Michael Redgrave played Hamlet

6.4 Kronborg, 1954 production, dir. Michael Benthall, Richard Burton as Hamlet

CHAPTER 7

Culture Clustering, Gender Crossing: *Hamlet* Meets Globalization in Robert Lepage's *Elsinore*

Nigel Wheale

In the Theatre

A lute rendering of 'Walsingham' plays as ambient mood music; we are presented with a screen, close-up to the front of the stage, onto which is projected an indigo, fluid patterning, damasked, somehow Moorish; the lute may begin to sound like an oud, its middle-eastern relative. The *mise-en-scène* also suggests an Islamic grace in the framing of Ophelia by a central vertical rectangle, hinting at retired seclusion and the modesty conventions of pre-modern societies. We only see Ophelia indistinctly through a lace veil which is stretched across this aperture as she reflectively addresses her mirror, the dubious double-emblem of vain folly and/or self-knowledge. The lace membrane is not perfect, but broken by three mandorla-shaped piercings; we seem to see the actor through a lattice, like one of the filigree wooden screens enclosing balconies in some traditional middle-eastern houses, an image of seclusion, the female withdrawn from the early-modern social world, but able to look over the street below. The scene is a wordless tableau, intensely moving in its pathos: Ophelia's naked torso is patterned by the projected shadows of the modesty veil, as if she is comprehensively damasked. But there is an anomaly; her upper chest has the mass and shape of a well built, fleshy male, and more than this, s/he sports a neo-Jacobean moustache and goatee beard.

    This viewing of pensive Ophelia is scene nine in the version of Robert Lepage's one-man *Elsinore* which was world-touring throughout 1996, a production which was arguably one of the most contentious of the current wave of radical-adaptive versions of Shakespeare on the global circuit. In 1992, at the invitation of Richard Eyre, Lepage became the first North American to be invited to direct a production at the Royal National Theatre of Great Britain, and his *A Midsummer Night's Dream* provoked strong reactions in critics and audiences alike.[1] Lepage's adaptations of

Shakespeare can offend well-informed theatre patrons, but they also attract audiences whose medium-of-choice is more usually film, video or even television: in other words, *Elsinore* is a prime example of a production which divides its patrons to the extent that they seem to have been attending quite different events. In this essay I focus on the scenes which include Lepage's playing of Ophelia, Gertrude, and their modulations into the Prince, as a way of exploring three related issues:

- the nature of Lepage's adaptation of *Hamlet* with his company Ex Machina;
- a critique of the notion of 'the body-as-site' in performance criticism as a way of accounting for our 'lived response' to drama;
- and very briefly, Lepage's cross-gendered performance in reference to western appropriations of Japanese and Chinese dramatic conventions.

Male-to-female drag artists and transvestism have always enjoyed a powerful presence in popular theatre and vaudeville, and there's a lot of it about in all sorts of vibrant forms in contemporary entertainment, including in the UK the splendid Lily Savage (when will the RSC make her an offer?), and the hugely popular Eddie Izzard (a 'gay woman trapped in a man's body'). Theatrical practice in many different cultures has traditionally taken female impersonation as a central convention, for a variety of reasons.[2] But as Lepage's *Elsinore* shows, cross-gendered acting is now also making a come-back in 'classical' western theatre. Toby Cockerell's Katherine was reckoned to be one of the star performances in Mark Rylance's *Henry V* which opened the 'new' Globe 1997 season in Southwark, and there is even a return of 'boys' companies': the cast of twenty-five from Sandbach Boys Comprehensive won a place in the Finals of the BT National Connections Youth Theatre competition, presenting Bryony Lavery's *More Light*. Adapting the conventions of the (all-male) Peking Opera they enacted the drama of court concubines immured in the tomb of their emperor; *The Independent*'s Louise Jury declared that the Sandbach Boys' performance shed light 'on what it means to be a woman'.[3] Male playing of female roles currently and unsurprisingly raises two related issues: first, the claims on male roles which can be made by actresses, as in Deborah Warner's direction of Fiona Shaw in *Richard II* [4] and Helena Kaut-Howson's Young Vic production of *Lear* starring Kathryn Hunter; and second, the proposals to systematically 'regender' roles in classical dramas so as to produce new perspectives and create more opportunities for underemployed female and ethnic minority actors, as in the Washington DC 1997 all-Black *Othello*, the only exception being

Patrick Stewart in the title role. There is not space to deal with these topics in this essay, but they are associated issues in the wider debate.

Charles II, kept waiting for *Hamlet* to begin at Davenant's Theatre, sent behind the stage to ask why the delay, and was told that '"The Queen was not *shaved* yet": The King, whose good Humour loved to laugh at a Jest, as well as to make one, accepted the Excuse, which served to divert him, till the male Queen could be effeminated'.[5] It took only two years after the Restoration in 1660 for women to begin playing female roles, since the old convention had become ridiculous to the new audiences. *Hamlet* has a particular and complicated history in relation to the convention of cross-gendered playing, since from the late eighteenth century in Europe and America there was a consistent tradition of actresses taking on the role of the Prince. Citing only the best-known performers, Sarah Siddons is thought to have been the first woman to play the part, in Birmingham in 1776, continuing to at least 1802; Charlotte Saunders Cushman, the first great native-born American actress, played Hamlet in 1851 – she was also Romeo to her own sister Susan's Juliet[6] – a psycho-sexual agenda of potentially paralysing complexity. In the 1860s Alice Marriott played Hamlet at Sadler's Wells to popular and critical acclaim, but the greatest of the Hamlettes was surely Sarah Bernhardt in Marcel Schwob's adaptation of 1899, when at the age of fifty-four Bernhardt undertook 'to impersonate a youth of twenty summers'.[7] During the 1890s Millicent Bandmann-Palmer gave nearly a thousand performances of the Dane in English provincial theatres: she was touring with the part in Dublin on 15 June 1904, and the *Freeman's Journal* of the following day commented on her performance 'to say the least [she] sustained it credibly',[8] all the more creditable since she was by then sixty and weighed a rheumatic fourteen stone.[9] Man-in-the-street Leopold Bloom noticed a poster for this performance: 'Hello. *Leah* tonight: Mrs Bandman Palmer [sic]. Like to see her in that again. *Hamlet* she played last night. Male impersonator. Perhaps he was a woman. Why Ophelia committed suicide?'[10] Bloom as usual has very modern views, and is unknowingly repeating the critical theory of Edmund Vining's *The Mystery of Hamlet* (1881). Vining argued that the Prince was in fact a Princess, whom Gertrude had disguised as a boy to ensure his succession when she feared that Old Hamlet would not return from his campaigning against Norway; the notion adds all kinds of possibilities to the role of the Prince in relation to Gertrude, Horatio and Ophelia, as Bloom demonstrates. And in cinema Svend Gade and Heinz Schall directed Asta Nielsen in the German *Hamlet: The Drama of Vengeance* (1920) using a narrative like that suggested by Vining, to produce 'one of the finest silent interpretations of Shakespeare'.[11] This sketchy survey of cross-gendered playing may begin to suggest the variety of effects which it can generate, and the very different motivations which may lie behind 'perverse' casting and direction. But the return of males taking the female roles in Shakespeare (and his contemporaries) must carry extra resonance for scholars and historians of drama, because it activates a number of debates about the nature of the first performances of drama on the early modern London stages. Does Lepage make a distinctive contribution to this long history?

Elsinore is the third of Robert Lepage's solo performance shows, after *Vinci* (1986) and *Needles and Opium* (1991), and it also extends his attempts to engineer a 'cinematic integration between actor and technology'.[12] The production ran for about 110 minutes without interval, drastically filleting the text of *Hamlet* into a series of tableaux. Lepage was the only actor, taking on all the surviving roles – Hamlet, Claudius, Polonius, Ophelia, Gertrude, Laertes, Horatio, grave-digger – though in two crucial scenes the production made use of a 'body double' (Pierre Bernie). *Elsinore* is therefore only the latest in a long line of interpretations which propose that *Hamlet* is the tragedy of isolated subjectivity, a critical response as old as the Earl of Shaftsbury's remark of 1720 that the play is effectively 'a Series of deep Reflections, drawn from one mouth . . . . It may be properly said of this Play, if I mistake not, that it has only ONE *Character* or *principal Part*'.[13] The staging and *mise-en-scène* were remarkable; set designer Carl Fillion contrived a mobile cube construction which continuously (and silently) metamorphosed to create different kinds of playing space. A central plane with two side panels and top frame moved so as to alter the volume of the stage and selectively frame the action in a different way for each of the twenty three scenes; the central panel was a complex arrangement with a circular revolve including a rectangle which is used as a door, a grave or viewing-slot as the action dictated. The combined effects of the design, Robert Caux's synthesized score, and video and slide-projection combined to powerfully envelop the audience, and generate a potent concentration on the playing (or else drive to distraction!).

A significant part of the success of the performance for many members of the audience must have been the astonishing ingenuity of this staging; the 'closet' scene was contrived so that the audience joined Polonius behind the arras and saw him stabbed by the back-projected shadow of the Prince, and as he fell he pulled down the tapestry to reveal the 'bedroom' beyond. Claudius's propositioning of Laertes (4.7.125–37)[14] was viewed through the central rectangle as if we were observing from above the table at which they were seated (with Laertes an implied,. not a visible presence); and most extraordinarily, the duel scene was played by Lepage and his body-double Pierre Bernier with the help of video relays viewed from the points of the protagonists' swords. These images were projected on to the central flat, and the duellists emerged singly at key moments to left and right of the screen: as they die their images were 'grabbed' and frozen on the central panel, allowing the next character to emerge in the contest. *Elsinore* was therefore a highly technicized performance, impressive in its ingenious use of devices – although if you were not charmed by the techno-magic, then you might denigrate it by saying it is not *echt* theatre, and more like a Genesis concert or a Peter Gabriel stage-set (just two of Lepage's sources of inspiration in fact) – or even worse (overheard in the bar) most like a multinational corporate presentational sales pitch. But Lepage also drew on the simplest effects within this elaborate machinery in order to convey drama. Much of his training and development was in improvisation and the techniques of 'poor theatre', where it is the impure, carnal presence of body and voice, phrased by dramatic lighting, which must capture our attention, and there are several scenes in *Elsinore* where I would argue that this was successful, most particularly in the roles of Ophelia and Gertrude.

How do we (successfully) describe 'successful' performance?[15] Lepage's impersonation of the Prince is best thought of as a sketch of what the role might be, a 'walk-through' of aspects of *Hamlet* as a part of Lepage's larger Shakespeare cycle (which has already included *A Midsummer Night's Dream* and *Coriolan*); Lepage stated that *Elsinore* was itself a device which helped him to prepare for the direction of a full-scale production which will draw on 'proper' actors. On this description, *Elsinore* was therefore already an 'alienated' *Hamlet*, an approach to the text rather than an authentic realization in performance. Lepage's Hamlet was pursy (like the 'times', 3.4.155, and his role is after all 'fat and scant of breath' – 5.2.209), his hair and beard more than faintly ridiculous: not a good-looking Prince who will work an easy seduction on the audience. And as in Lepage's *A Midsummer Night's Dream*, it is possible to criticize the delivery of the lines: too hasty, not inhabited and inflected enough, not given as if for the first time – this weakness in itself may be enough to make the seasoned playgoer 'tune out'. The virtues and excitements of the performance therefore have to be found elsewhere, and for some viewers these may be in the most stylized and anti-realist moments of the performance – the roles of Ophelia and Gertrude – which consequently raise issues about cross-gendered playing in different times and places.

Following the viewing of Ophelia in scene 9, described above, scene 10 presented 'To be or not to be' in a more conventional playing space, with the mobile frame withdrawn, and minimal technical modelling, though there was some use of an angelic 'white noise' from Robert Caux's synthesizer. Hamlet delivered the soliloquy by his father's tomb side, but at

'Soft you now, the fair Ophelia' the top flat descended as the Prince took off his white shirt to raise his arms vertically, so neatly inserting himself into the three piercings of the lace 'veil' which had framed Ophelia in scene 9. The flat descended to stage-floor level, leaving the former Hamlet draped pyramid-wise in the lace screen which had now become a hieratic dress, leaving only his bearded face and drab, lank hair clearly exposed; this Prince was definitely having a 'bad-hair day'. The tense exchange between Hamlet and Ophelia from 3.1 coalesced into this isolated double-figure: when Ophelia spoke, the dress remained white, a sharp pyramid of anguish, and her lines were delivered in a higher tone. The Prince's attacks on her, 'Are you honest?', and 'I have heard of your paintings' were given under a blue fluorescent light which transformed the dress into a wedge of aggression. The delivery was therefore static, but the switching between roles was complete, modelled only by the lighting changes. The dialogue was constructed as a three-layered score, given in a rising, choric register: there was an echo playback of 'What a noble mind is here o'erthrown' which formed a ground-base, over which the voices of Hamlet and Ophelia were themselves 'doubled', but also very clearly distinguished by the light-modelling and variations in voice tone. At the end of the scene the figure struggled free of its dress-carapace, metamorphosing through a kind of birth to leave the vulnerable half-naked male figure as if delivered from the female costuming. The figure-now-become-the-Prince was fully and murderously resolved: 'I'll no more on't, it hath made me mad' was played in voice-over, as the flats rose to vertical and the forbidding battlement projection returned, Hamlet stalking off left, his dagger unsheathed, suggesting starkly that the resolution of revenge had been born out of the hatred and disgust addressed to the figure of Ophelia – which was inseparably also himself.

There was no interval in the 1996 version of *Elsinore*, but the curtain did fall at 4.3 after Claudius's exasperated command '[To] England', and there was a brief interlude where an animated cartoon of Hamlet's voyage and encounter with the pirate ship was projected onto the front curtain (perhaps a vestige of Lepage the failed-geography-teacher's persistent interest in travel, mapping and tectonics). This was followed by the 'Walsingham' refrain as in scene 9, and the composite figure of Ophelia/Gertrude stepped in front of the curtain, a sombre claret dress, crownet – beard and moustache still in place. She sang a moving version of 'How should I your true love know', again electronically treated to give the voice a shadowing echo. Ophelia was then displaced by Gertrude's 'There is a willow grows aslant a brook', addressed straight to audience, and still front-of-curtain; the figure modulated finally to Ophelia desperately singing 'And will ye not come again?' who shed the regal claret dress and wrapped herself in a white wedding robe which was simultaneously a sere cloth shroud, to sing 'Tomorrow is Saint Valentine's Day', at last drowning in the central grave rectangle.

On Reflection

Anthony B. Dawson's stimulating article 'Performance and Perception'[16] may be helpful as a way of thinking about the effects of Lepage's cross-gendered playing. Dawson is concerned to explore the limitations of 'cultural materialist' and 'discourse theory' criticism in relation to our experience of theatrical performance, partly – best of all critical methods – in order 'to pay delighted attention to the particular and the concrete' (30), and partly to contribute to the revaluation of criticism from the 1980s which had been inspired by the work of philosopher-theorists such as Foucault and Althusser. Both of these aims are also part of a more general movement in the 'human sciences' to re-establish the claims of subjectivity on terms other than those of pure subjection, and which therefore are attempting to examine what may be the 'givenness' of our experience rather than its 'constructedness', but where the 'given', crucially, weaves our life inextricably into the surrounding life-world.[17] This broadly based critical effort might be characterized by saying that it attempts to integrate the privileged access to bodily experience claimed by classical phenomenology with the remorselessly contextual paradigms of the structuralisms which first displaced existential phenomenology forty years ago. These 'post-poststructuralist' approaches therefore argue that some kinds of emotion and intuition are irreducible, and so are effectively transcendental, because they are not susceptible to 'anti-foundational' critique: we do not experience many of our emotions as if they had been scripted for us by external, determining structures, rather we live them as authentically and inherently our own, and what we are. Reflection and self-consciousness may of course also be telling us that our feelings in a real sense are not quite coincident with what we hope for, or with what we ought to feel, and we can describe others and ourselves to a significant degree as influenced by all kinds of external agency – class, age, gender, ethnicity: but this second-order reflection may only revise and cannot cancel utterly the comprehensiveness with which our feelings first present themselves and which may be concerted with decisions and actions that are in no sense determined by the contextually driven demands of supposed 'discourses'. Something like this was Maurice Merleau-Ponty's conclusion to 'La liberté', the final section of his *Phénoménologie de la Perception*:

Rien ne me détermine du dehors, non que rien ne me sollicite, mais au contraire parce que je suis d'emblée hors de moi et ouvert au monde. Nous sommes de part en part *vrais*, nous avons avec nous, du seul fait que nous sommes au monde, et non pas seulement dans le monde, comme des choses, tout ce qu'il faut pour nous dépasser. Nous n'avons pas à craindre que nos choix ou nos actions restreignent notre liberté, puisque le choix et l'action nous libèrent seuls de nos ancres.[18]

[Nothing determines me from outside, not because nothing acts upon me, but, on the contrary, because I am from the start outside myself and open to the world. We are *true* through and through, and have with us, by the mere fact of belonging to the world, and not merely being in the world in the way that things are, all that we need to transcend ourselves. We need have no fear that our choices or actions restrict our liberty, since choice and action alone cut us loose from our anchorage.][19]

Attending plays may particularly provoke thoughts about this 'firstness' of our feelings which are 'true through and through', and the ways in which we subsequently revise them from the point of view of categorical, analytical descriptions; responding to the audio-visual representations of cinema almost certainly relies on quite a different kind of affectivity, and this raises interesting complications in the case of performances which combine live and electronic mimesis (as does Lepage). What I take to be new in Anthony Dawson's article is that he usefully addresses this doubleness in our response to performance: the agency of our feelings as we emotively respond, and the agency of the actor as they demonstrate the simultaneous authenticity and performativity of character, role and action. In his complex discussion of Henry Jackson's record of a boy actor's performance of Desdemona in 1610 (35), and in his analysis of Lady Macbeth's sleepwalking scene (39–43), Dawson acknowledges the dimension of subjection in these early modern representations, but he includes the emotive value of acting and of viewer response as ways of qualifying what might otherwise be a purely ideological description of the female roles as victims within patriarchy's oppressive theatricalization. By means of meta-theatrical devices in plotting and dialogue, and additionally by the fact of the boy actor bearing the female roles, Dawson argues that Shakespeare characteristically 'stages the conflict between body and meaning in a way that locates fundamental, though not of course exclusive, signifying power in the theatrical body' (44, n. 8). If this is true, then the plays do not necessarily 'stage patriarchy' through repressively tolerant devices, but rather offer ways of reflecting on the nature and consequences of hierarchy and representation, together with as it were bodily intuitions of quite different possibilities: 'The theatre, by concentrating on the body, may indeed limit its power as a discursive practice – but this limitation may paradoxically free it, shifting the ground to focus on the power to move audiences and hence to incite who knows what kind of passionate participation' (42). Dawson therefore argues that the place of the 'body' in a performance is not simply a 'site' of ideological construction and conflict, because this simplifies our somatic experience as pure subjection to social stresses such as gender politics and class structure, which are the inflections of an abstracted (and therefore unanswerable) conception of 'power': 'The body in this view is important only for what it says, for how it is transformed from sentience into discourse' (31).

Let's now try and bring these thoughts to bear on *Elsinore*. Lepage founded his production company Ex Machina in 1994, beginning work on *The Seven Streams of the River Ota*; his intention was to create a company which was able to restore playfulness to contemporary theatre, so that performance took precedence over writing as the arena of invention through developing co-operative activity which produced the drama. Ex Machina was inspired by Lepage's work with Jacques Lessard's Théâtre Repère in Quebec, which had in turn been influenced by Anna and Lawrence Halprin's dance company in San Francisco.[20] In the late 1970s Lepage had also studied in Paris with Alain Knapp who encouraged his students to combine the roles of writer, actor and director: Lepage describes this integral creativity as the 'global' method, and as a 'globalist' Lepage draws on a diverse but consistent range of cultural traditions, such that 'My shows are usually about travelling, about culture clustering'.[21] Lepage's stated ambitions for his performance practice include emphases which taken together indicate a very traditional, even antique, perspective, combined with a desire to renew theatre arts using the most up-to-date resources. Lepage describes the best theatre as a 'vertical' form in utterly physical terms, where scenery and actors may ascend and descend before our eyes, but 'vertical' also in the oldest sense of a medium which 'has a lot to do with putting an audience in contact with the gods'.[22] He seems to mean by this the way in which the experience of effective drama can call an audience to itself, suddenly alert to the aspiration and risk of the lived performance which it is watching, or more accurately, as French has it, the 'réalisation' of the play text at which each member of the audience 'assists'. The attempt to refresh the audience's experience of theatre is of course perpetual, and Lepage shares this ambition with every innovative twentieth-century practitioner, from Gordon Craig onwards (who for example dreamt of a metamorphosing playing space, as fulfilled in Carl Fillion's mobile cube). For Lepage the deadly enemy today is a theatre of 'acting' rather than 'playing' where engineered spectacle reduces the audience to a new kind of passivity as it consumes the safely technicized routines of *Les Misérables*, *Phantom of the Opera*, or the multimedia extravaganzas of Las Vegas and the Columbia Studio Experience. Therefore Lepage hopes to recreate dramatic risk by integrating cinematic and audio-visual conventions with a theatrical playing which includes the barest, essential traditions of 'poor theatre', thereby producing a 'vertical cinema' animated by the intangible, fifth dimension of sacred drama.

This is an ambition full of pretension (maybe in both senses), and it is surely the case that Lepage's performance of Ophelia and Gertrude sporting a natty moustache-with-goatee is a part of what he terms the 'risky' element of Ex Machina's drama. But when an actor convinces and moves us by their performance, as Dawson has argued, a complex simultaneous transaction of effect and reflection may occur, and cross-gendered playing prompts these kinds of second-order reflection on the way we receive roles in very particular ways, because the assumption of the other sex's gendered appearance and behaviour may demonstrate what is performative about all gendered experience, and even what may be intrinsic to sexed experience. Lepage takes the (as it were fundamentalist) view that since Shakespeare's female roles were written to be performed by males, there may be strategic losses when they are performed by women, even today. He must therefore accept the argument that the fact of gender impersonation could be an active component of the roles for early modern audiences, perhaps creating the complex distantiation effects such as those explored by Anthony Dawson in respect of Desdemona and Lady Macbeth. Lepage's female impersonation cannot figure the women's roles in the ways which they were originally played by youths such as Nathan Field (Ophelia), Alexander Cooke (Lady Macbeth), or Robert Goffe (Juliet and Cleopatra), and it goes without saying that the gender cultures of early seventeenth-century London and the contemporary cosmopolitan venues where Lepage now performs effectively belong to different planets. How can his risky personation be contextualized?

One of the games which may be played via consideration of *Elsinore*'s female roles derives from the director-actor's eclectic but persistent interest in oriental cultures. Lepage claims that his work takes inspiration from study of Japanese Kabuki conventions, particularly the onnagata, or male bearers of the female roles. Stephen Orgel asserts of early modern Europe that 'No contemporary continental public theater restricted the stage to men',[23] but on the other side of the world in Kyoto around 1600, a female dancer named Okuni was inventing Kabuki, a kind of 'citizen comedy' drama, initially performed by prostitutes, which satirized contemporary Japanese urban life for the first time on stage. The ruling Shogunate however banned women from performance in 1629, and boy actors were also proscribed by 1652: the onnagata, clans of highly proficient male players of female roles, developed from this date in Kabuki – they had long been present in 'classical' Japanese and Chinese drama.[24] Their manner, which evolved over three centuries, was intended to convey the sense of a 'third sex' combining masculine 'strength' and feminine 'delicacy', a kind of gestic playing in which neither sex is unambiguously present:

> The onnagata's art is the dramatisation of gendered identity as constructed and represented in a precarious balance between becoming the onnagata as 'fictitious' woman and revealing his 'real' identity as man.[25]

Did Shakespeare visit Japan and draw on this rich stylization for his later plays? Well, probably not, but William Adams of the Company of Barbary Merchants may have been the first Englishman (and Jacobean) to see Japanese drama. Adams arrived in Japan aboard a Dutch ship in 1600, and went on to advise the shogun Tokugawa Ieyasu (1543–1616) on ship construction; Ieyasu patronized the Kanze troupe of Noh players, and it is tempting to imagine Adams attending their performances, or those of Kabuki, a form which has often been compared to the contemporaneous drama in England.[26] Lepage also draws a contemporary parallel: 'the British actors I love have that quality [which is] very close to Japanese theatre where everything is happening inside and it takes half an hour for an actor to cross the stage ... a modesty that has been lost in theatre in North America'.[27]

Lepage's insistence – however charmingly apologetic – on depriving contemporary actresses of some of the greatest roles in the classical repertoire therefore may derive from his interest in the pathos of the contemporary male body seeking to mimic the gender and sexuality which it can never be, sustaining sexual difference even as he presents gender similitude in the manner of the onnagata. The bearded female impersonator in scene 9 of *Elsinore* may become in this way the Prince's longing for the grace of Ophelia's person and figure, from which he is excluded, together with the audience on the other side of the modesty veil. Further, the male player may be embodying the knowledge that the 'feminine' for which he yearns is in crucial respects already a construction rendered for his benefit, and at the expense of actual female interiority. His Gertrude might be said to have a different kind of status, where her regal, frankly political maturity is at one level reinforced by the corporeality of the masculine player. But if that aspect of the Queen's role is endorsed by gender-cultural conventions, then it is in plain conflict with her maternal role where again the male performer embodies the fact of impersonation most keenly – this male as a sex can be no mother. Is this playing an example of theatre alerting us 'to the complex theatrical construction and the historical specificity of the Elizabethan drama, which might provide a salutary disruption of the authority of their images of womanhood'?[28]

Acting in the manner of an onnagata is therefore an extreme example of formalized playing which for western audiences, as it were, coats the performance with an additional, estranging layer, and it is best compared to other severe mimetic strategies such as puppetry or mime – both repertoires exploited by Lepage. By minimizing psychological naturalism and filtering the delivery of role through stylization, the assisting audience may be prompted to new thoughts about how we each inflect, and are inflected by, the performance of role – female or male, hetero-, bi- or homo-sexed:

> The reason why I'm so fascinated by Japanese and Chinese culture is because they seem to have a three-dimensional concept of what things are, and their way of writing is both a sound and an image. It's both a drawing of a word and at the same time it's the sound of the word, and they alternate between them ... So your mind is always switching and that's why the Japanese theatre and Chinese opera is [sic] the most refined three-dimensional, sculptural hologram form of theatre, because stories are told on these two levels all the time.[29]

This seems to indicate that Lepage hopes to encourage a simultaneous appreciation of his performance both emotively and conceptually, so that within Carl Fillion's fluid, hologramatic playing-device we observe a demonstration of the roles of Ophelia, Gertrude, and Hamlet, and the gender-crossing of the drama is elaborated by Lepage's orientalist 'culture clustering' approach to play-making and performance. At this point another range of questions appears: is Lepage merely reproducing a characteristic western misconception about the nature of Asian drama, in the manner of Brecht's 'creative misunderstanding' of the Noh?[30] As Yoko Takakuwa puts this, 'are the female roles impersonated by the onnagata the metaphors of woman [which are] constitutive of man's symptom?'[31] Why should 'stylization' promote reflection more effectively than 'naturalization'? Is 'culture clustering' just another version of cultural appropriation?[32] But perhaps these troubling, endless enquiries are also implicit within the global remit of Robert Lepage's stimulating enterprise.

Notes

1. Richard Eyre, 'Robert Lepage in Discussion with Richard Eyre', in *The Twentieth-Century Performance Reader*, eds Michael Huxley and Noel Witts (London and New York: Routledge, 1996), 237–47; Barbara Hogdon, 'Looking for Mr. Shakespeare after "The Revolution": Robert Lepage's Intercultural *Dream* Machine', in *Shakespeare, Theory, and Performance*, ed. James C. Bulman (London and New York: Routledge, 1996), 68.
2. Peter Ackroyd, *Dressing Up – Transvestism and Drag: The History of an Obsession* (London: Thames and Hudson, 1979); Lesley Ferris, ed., *Crossing the Stage: Controversies on Cross-Dressing*, (London and New York: Routledge, 1993); Sabrina Petra Ramet, ed., *Gender Reversals and Gender Cultures: Anthropological and Historical Perspectives* (London and New York: Routledge, 1996).
3. Louise Jury, *The Independent* (26 May 1997).
4. Deborah Warner, 'Exploring Space at Play: The Making of the Theatrical Event', *New Theatre Quarterly* 12.47 (August 1996), 229–36. Interviewed by Geraldine Cousin.
5. Colly Cibber, *An Apology for the Life of Colly Cibber* (1740) quoted in Ann Thompson, 'Women/"Women" and the Stage', in *Women and Literature in Britain, 1500–1700*, ed. Helen Wilcox (Cambridge: Cambridge University Press, 1996), 102.
6. Joseph Leach, *Bright Particular Star: The Life and Times of Charlotte Cushman* (New Haven: Yale University Press, 1970), 170.
7. Jill Edmonds, 'Princess Hamlet', in *The New Woman and Her Sisters: Feminism and Theatre 1850–1914*, eds Viv Gardner and Susan Patherford (London: Harvester Wheatsheaf, 1992), 71.
8. Don Gifford with Robert J. Seidman, *'Ulysses' Annotated. Notes for James Joyce's 'Ulysses'*, 2nd edn (Berkeley, Los Angeles, London: University of California Press, 1989), 88.
9. Edmonds, 71.
10. James Joyce, *Ulysses*, with an introduction by Declan Kiberd (Harmondsworth: Penguin, 1992), 93.
11. Luke McKernan and Olwen Terris, eds, *Walking Shadows: Shakespeare in the National Film and Television Archive* (London: BFI, 1994), 48.

[12] Nancy Copeland, rev. of *Elsinore*, Toronto 20–27 April, in 'International Shakespeare', *Shakespeare Bulletin* 14.3 (Summer 1996), 27.
[13] Anthony Shaftesbury, *Characteristics of Men, Manners and Times* (1714), quoted in Eric Griffiths, '"A Hearing for the Sick at Heart": Romances for One: The Potent, Technological Vaudeville of Robert Lepage's Hamlet', *Times Literary Supplement* (27 December 1996).
[14] Quotations from Harold Jenkins, ed., William Shakespeare, *Hamlet* (London and New York: Methuen, 1984).
[15] Anthony B. Dawson, 'The Impasse over the Stage', *English Literary Renaissance* 21.3 (1991), 309–27, and 'Performance and Participation. Desdemona, Foucault, and the Actor's Body', in *Shakespeare, Theory, and Performance*, ed. James C. Bulman (London and New York: Routledge, 1996) 29–45.
[16] Dawson, 'Performance and Participation'.
[17] Peter Dews, *The Limits of Disenchantment. Essays on Contemporary European Philosophy* (London and New York: Verso, 1995), Chapters One, Two and Four.
[18] Maurice Merleau-Ponty, *Phénoménologie de la Perception* (Paris: Gallimard, 1945), 520.
[19] Merleau-Ponty, *Phenomenology of Perception*, trans. Colin Smith, (London: Routledge and Kegan Paul, 1962), 456.
[20] 'Robert Lepage in Conversation with Alison McAlpine at Le Café du Monde, Québec City, 17 February 1995', in 'Robert Lepage', *In Contact with the Gods? Directors Talk Theatre*, eds Maria M. Delgado and Paul Heritage (Manchester and New York: Manchester University Press, 1996), 133.
[21] Nigel Hunt, 'The Global Voyage of Robert Lepage', *Drama Review* 33.2 (1989), 104, 115.
[22] 'Robert Lepage in Conversation', 143.
[23] Stephen Orgel, *Impersonations: The Performance of Gender in Shakespeare's England* (Cambridge: Cambridge University Press, 1996), 10.
[24] Thomas J. Rimer, 'What More Do We Need to Know about the Noh?' *Asian Theatre Journal* 9.2 (Fall 1992), 215–23; Yoko Takakuwa, 'Masquerading Womanliness: The Onnagata's Theatrical Performance of Femininity in Kabuki', *Women: A Cultural Review* 5.2 (1994), 151–61; Sophie Volpp, 'Gender, Power and Spectacle in Late-Imperial Chinese Theater', in *Gender Reversals and Gender Cultures: Anthropological and Historical Perspectives*, ed. Sabrina Petra Ramet (London and New York: Routledge, 1996), 138–47.
[25] Takakuwa, 157.

26 Richard Tames, *Servant of the Shogun: Being the True Story of William Adams, Pilot and Samurai, The First Englishman in Japan* (Tenterden: Paul Norbury Publications, 1981); William Corr, *Adams the Pilot. The Life and Times of Captain William Adams: 1564–1620* (Folkestone: Japan Library, 1995); Andrea J. Nouryeh, 'Shakespeare and the Japanese Stage', in *Foreign Shakespeare: Contemporary Performance*, ed. Dennis Kennedy (Cambridge: Cambridge University Press, 1993), 254–69; Zeami Motokiyo, *On the Art of the No Drama: The Major Treatises of Zeami*, trans. J. Thomas Rimer and Yamazaki Masakazu (Princeton, NJ: Princeton University Press, 1984); James Brandon, 'Noh', 716–17 in *The Cambridge Guide to Theatre*, ed. Martin Banham (Cambridge: Cambridge University Press, 1992), 716–7, and see also his entries on 'Kabuki', 533–4 and ancient and traditional Japanese theatre, 508–15.

27 Eyre, 245.

28 Kathleen McLuskie, 'The Act, the Role, and the Actor: Boy Actresses on the Elizabethan Stage', *New Theatre Quarterly* 3.10 (May 1987), 130.

29 'Robert Lepage in Conversation', 154.

30 Poh Sim Plowright, 'The Birdwoman and the Puppet-King: a Study of Inversion in Chinese Theatre', *New Theatre Quarterly* 13.50 (May 1997), 106–18.

31 Takakuwa, 155.

32 Rustom Barucha, 'Collision of Cultures: Some Western Interpretations and Uses of the Indian Theatre', in *Theatre and the World. Performance and the Politics of Culture* (London and New York: Routledge, 1993), 13–41.

CHAPTER 8

'The Homestead of History':
Shakespearean Medievalism on the
Mid-Victorian Stage

Richard W. Schoch

It is not possible to write a paper on historicism without first invoking the spirit of Nietzsche who, in his untimely essay *On the Advantage and Disadvantage of History,* asserted that 'every past is worth condemning'. Though surely not possessed of a Nietzschean historical forgetfulness, the Victorians had this much in common with the German philosopher: an ambivalence toward history. For no other society had so rapidly and completely embraced technological innovation, and yet sought so desperately to reanimate its past. No people since the Renaissance combined such confidence in their own powers with so much antiquarian retrospection. But the Victorians' aggressive identification with both the past and the future betrayed, not surprisingly, a profound discontent with an unstable and ever-changing present. As Matthew Arnold recognized, the nineteenth century was an age of self-conscious transition, 'Wandering between two worlds, one dead, / The other powerless to be born'.[1] The Victorians' fear of being lost within history – and of being dememorialized in their own time – impelled their return to the past. Far from being passively picturesque or merely nostalgic, nineteenth-century historical mindedness was an urgent defence against the combined shocks and dislocations of mechanization, political economy and continental revolution.

Yet which past should be restored? Which relic prized above all others? For the nationalistic nineteenth century, the Middle Ages was the chief touchstone and the rehabilitated Gothic style occupied a privileged position in a northern European campaign of historical search and seizure. As Alice Chandler and Lee Patterson have demonstrated, medievalism in Victorian Britain was a complex and often contradictory bundle of social, political and spiritual ideals which were nonetheless united by a shared desire to make a 'home' in history.[2] When the Middle Ages finally transcended an aesthetic of contemplative melancholy, it re-emerged as the cornerstone of English civil society: the age when English language, law and literature were born. And thus it is not surprising that in a period of constitutional crisis, ideologues and reformers of all stripes would invoke the medieval past, equally hoping to benefit from its stabilizing *auctoritas*.

While we tend to associate Victorian medievalism with architecture, painting, literature and the arts and crafts – with Pugin, Rossetti, Ruskin, Disraeli and Morris – theatrical performance was also an active partner in the effort to recover the Middle Ages. Performance was a powerful agent of historical consciousness because it realized the past with a 'bold and master hand'[3] greater than that of literature, painting, or even photography. In the words of one nineteenth-century tragedian, performance 'endows the creations of the painter's art with animated reality'.[4] In the theatre, at least, the past was not dead. It was not even sleeping. It was alive and well and appearing nightly. Archaeological eclecticism flourished in the Victorian theatre, where a lively range of historical places, personages and events was recreated for eager and ever-expanding audiences.

In 'performing' the Middle Ages, the Victorian theatre turned first to Shakespeare, whose English chronicle plays were widely regarded as history books written in dramatic verse. Charles Kean, the actor-manager of the Princess's Theatre in London from 1850 to 1859, was the most ardent and aggressive historicizer of Shakespeare in the nineteenth century. Indeed, in only nine seasons, Kean recreated not merely the medieval and Tudor England of Shakespeare's history plays, but also Renaissance Italy (*The Merchant of Venice*), Magna Grecia and Bithynia (*The Winter's Tale*) and Periclean Athens (*A Midsummer Night's Dream*). The 'present age demands that all dramatic representations must of necessity be accompanied by a certain selection of scenery, dresses and music', he wrote in 1853 and '*truth* in these matters is preferable to *inaccuracy*' (italics original).[5] Endorsing that very preference for historical truth, the *Builder* admitted to having happily

> trod with Macbeth the wilds of Scotland and visited its pre-Norman fortresses; seen the eighth Henry in his voluptuous court ... [and] contemplated a portraiture of the architecture, costume, and domestic manners of the Greeks never before attempted upon any stage.[6]

So enamoured of Kean's complete 'view of Universal History' was Britain's leading journal of architectural criticism that it later reproached the actor-manager for staging *Henry V* as his farewell production at the Princess's in 1859. From the *Builder*'s 'scenic point of view', either *Coriolanus* or *Antony and Cleopatra* would have been more desirable, as a

Roman play would have made Kean's 'series complete in an architectural and ethnological point of view'.[7] While Kean's historical interests were impressively global – and thus consistent with the nineteenth century's rapacious designs on the past – his chief legacy undoubtedly resides in his grand revivals of Shakespeare's English (and, in one instance, Scottish) chronicle plays: *King John* (1852), *Macbeth* (1853), *Henry VIII* (1855), *Richard II* (1857) and *Henry V* (1859).

Kean's antiquarian and spectacular productions were remarkable for their sets and costumes of unprecedented historical precision, re-enactment of historical events not dramatized by Shakespeare (such as the return of Henry V to London after the Battle of Agincourt), and pseudo-academic editions of the plays, annotated by Kean himself, which were sold in the lobby of the theatre. So fastidious was Charles Kean in his insistence upon 'authentic' sets, properties and costumes that his detractors at *Punch* dubbed him not the 'Upholder' of Shakespeare, but the 'Upholsterer'. Unlike most students of Shakespeare in the Victorian theatre, I believe that Kean's antiquarian dramaturgy was not a naïve fascination with historical trivia – not interior decoration with a vengeance – but was, in fact, historicism in action: the reanimation of the past through the combined arts of the playwright, the actor and the scenographer. By studying Kean's productions as enactments of nineteenth-century theories of history and historical representation, I hope to disclose the centrality of a neglected tradition of theatrical performance in Victorian cultural mythology.

Consider, for example, how Walter Pater, as an eighteen-year-old, was enraptured by the luxuriant sensuality of Charles Kean's *Richard II*. In the repose of middle age, he recalled that 'those who were very young thirty years ago' might have witnessed at the Princess's Theatre

> much more than Shakespeare's play could ever have been before – the very person of the king based on the stately old portrait in Westminster Abbey ... the grace, the winning pathos, the sympathetic voice of the player, the tasteful archaeology confronting vulgar modern London with a scenic reproduction, for once really agreeable, of the London of Chaucer. In the hands of Kean, the play became like an exquisite performance on the violin.[8]

Pater's anecdote gracefully brings together several of the principal strategies and features of Charles Kean's historicist *mise-en-scène*: the use of primary visual sources (the 'stately old portrait'), the theatrically effective recreation of historical sites ('tasteful archaeology'), the embodiment or realization of historical personages ('the very person of the king'), the continued importance of acting even in the midst of spectacle ('the winning pathos, the sympathetic voice of the player'), the recognition that performance is the event when an ideal past meets a degraded present ('confronting vulgar modern London'), and the Victorian theatre's attempt to surpass the limitations of previous performances ('much more than Shakespeare's play could ever have been before').

Most critically significant of all is that Pater's fond recollection of his adolescent theatregoing reiterates, at a personal level, the general phenomenon of Victorian medievalism. That is, Pater recalling having seen *Richard II* as a teenager is analogous to Victorian England affectionately gazing upon the 'Young England' of its medieval (but by no means middle-aged) past. The poetic narration of English history, the astonishing accuracy of scenery and costume, and the presence of live actors recreating legendary events collectively established the theatre of Charles Kean as a place where the traditional parts of history were reclaimed and restored.

Referring to his earlier stagings of *The Winter's Tale* and *A Midsummer Night's Dream*, Kean wrote in the playbill essay for his revival of *Richard II* that in

> Quitting the far-famed regions of classical antiquity, I now *return to the homestead of history*, and offer to the public one of those exciting dramas drawn from our own annals, in which our national poet has depicted the fierce and turbulent passions of our ancestors, and thus immortalised events of the deepest importance to every English mind ... I have endeavored to produce a true portrait of mediæval history ... [The stage settings] are all either actually restored, or represented in conformity with contemporaneous authorities.[9]

Like his belletristic counterpart Thomas Carlyle, Charles Kean intuited the connection between a theatricalized history and an historicizing theatre: that historical 'annals' were composed of exciting 'dramas', that the collective memory of historical events was safeguarded by 'our national poet', and that the restoration of public buildings and monuments was most thoroughly accomplished not by architects, but by theatrical scene-painters.

Of course it really will not do merely to demonstrate that mid-Victorian productions of Shakespeare were a serious and legitimate part of the Gothic revival. That much is obvious. Indeed, it would be more remarkable if the theatre were *not* part of the Gothic revival. If theatre ignored history. But it did not. And so we must ask why the theatre was an especially provocative site for the recovery of England's medieval past and, moreover, what these theatrical provocations had to do with cultural nationalism. For medievalism was nothing if not an attempt to create a genealogy of national identity.

We can begin this exploration by noting that Charles Kean's audience at the Princess's Theatre included not only John Bull in the gallery but also the respectable middle class family, the clergy, the aristocracy and the sovereign herself. Indeed, when Queen Victoria took her children to see Kean's productions of Shakespeare – when her daughter, the Princess Royal, drew sketches of those productions during the performance – the aristocracy could no longer retreat to Covent Garden on the grounds that the national drama lacked royal patronage. Similarly, bourgeois moralists and low-church pamphleteers could no longer dismiss the playhouse as a pit of iniquity, seeing that it was good enough for the instruction of the monarch's children. And for the middle-class family, which had by mid-century internalized Charles Lamb's dictum that 'the practice of stage representation reduces everything to a controversy of elocution',[10] the visits of Victoria to the Princess's Theatre, recounted at length in the London press, were a potent and unmistakable signal that the mental pleasures of the solitary reader could not compare to the physical delights awaiting the community of spectators. To those previously unwilling to set foot into a playhouse, Victoria's patronage of Charles Kean sounded a reassuring and encouraging 'all's clear'.

For the first time since the late eighteenth century, a London theatre audience achieved something resembling class integration. Even one of Kean's critics was forced to admit, in the otherwise excoriating poem *The Celebrated Eton Boy*, that at the Princess's Theatre,

> Royalty sat, in curtain'd state;
> The Noble and the Gentle came (early or late),
> The general Public throng'd the Pit,
> The Clergy of course in Stalls would sit'.[11]

The artisans and sailors in the gallery were presumably not worth mentioning. This diversity of the mid-Victorian theatre audience, building upon the social cohesion symbolized by the Great Exhibition of 1851, suggests that theatre was important to the development of nineteenth-century British nationalism because it offered one of the few opportunities – perhaps the only opportunity – where, as Marc Baer has written, a variety of social orders could 'learn together how to be English'.[12]

So what exactly did this socially integrated audience learn from Charles Kean's productions of Shakespeare's history plays? Like other forms of the Gothic revival, Kean's productions authorized a model of nationalism rooted in the medieval origins of English liberty. For as Shakespeare's John of Gaunt proclaimed on his deathbed, Englishmen were a 'happy breed', dwelling in an island fortress built by Nature herself to protect them from 'infection and the hand of war' (2.1.43–4). This prescriptive model of a collective national identity – of political superiority fortified by geographic insularity – looked back to the Middle Ages as its founding moment.

By going to the theatre and seeing the history of England recalled to life – to misquote Dickens – the urban working and middle classes of the Victorian era gained an increased sense of their own cultural rights at the precise moment when they exercised newly-won political rights. Indeed, those rights were inseparable, and antiquarian revivals of Shakespeare were the cultural equivalent of the franchise. Metaphors drawn from core principles of liberal democracy – public opinion and majority rule – were used by Kean himself to explain the attraction of his revivals of Shakespeare's history plays. In the playbill for *Richard II*, Kean wrote that his theatre was 'supported by the irresistible force of public opinion, expressed in the suffrages of an overwhelming majority'. This triangulation of historicized dramaturgy, national identity and emancipatory rhetoric secures, I believe, the position of Shakespeare's Victorian stage as a dynamic and socially inclusive articulation of national identity.

Let me now shift the focus of my analysis from performance as social phenomenon to performance as signifying act – presuming, of course, that we can even make such a distinction. The question I want to ask now is really one of historical poetics: what was the value of *performing* the Middle Ages? To answer that, we need to remind ourselves that the Victorian theatre was a public forum for antiquarian display and spectating. To be sure, the theatre's obsession with antiquarianism ran counter to the development of nineteenth-century historical thought and the hegemonic ascendancy of positivism. And antiquarians themselves have long been dismissed as half-baked scientists, forgers, dilettante aristocrats, or dry-as-dust bookworms. Yet antiquarianism has made something of a theoretical comeback in the past decade, most notably in the writings of Stephen Bann, who does not dismiss antiquarianism as a failed, unscientific historical method but rather exalts it as a distinctive mode of relating the past to the present. Antiquarianism, in Bann's estimation, liberates 'the historical object from the ahistorical zone of Neoclassical perfection' and then places this rehistoricized object within a synecdochic process whereby an isolated and particular fragment both participates in and reveals a wider historical experience.[13]

Bann's notion of antiquarianism as cultural synecdoche, as *pars pro toto*, is useful because it helps us to theorize the liberating contribution of theatre to nineteenth-century medievalism: the diverse fragments of *mise-en-scène* (costume, scenery, acting, music, dance) reassimilate in the moment of performance to evoke the presence, material continuity and oneness of the past. The hermetic excesses of antiquarianism could be checked only by performing the past, by turning the self-indulgent display of fragments and artifacts into a public encounter with the materiality of history.

Consider the following example of how theatrical 'fragments' of the medieval past led their audience out of exile and back to the 'homestead of history'. In his 1857 revival of *Richard II*, the production which secured his election to the Society of Antiquaries, Kean recreated a medieval interior to represent the bedroom of John of Gaunt. He boasted, in the playbill essay, that 'in this scene ... the walls are covered with paintings, selected from the very beautifully illuminated manuscripts in the British Museum, containing 120 miniature representations of scenes from the legendary lives of St Edmond and St Fremond'. Kean's official biographer, J.W. Cole, contended that this 'room in Ely-House' and, indeed, the entire performance of *Richard II*

> brought back the past to the eyes of the present, and bewildered the spectators with a mingled sensation of astonishment and admiration. ... The spell was rendered still more potent by the knowledge that we saw passing before us a resuscitation of a memorable passage from our own domestic chronicles.[14]

Despite the predictable hyperbole of commissioned biographies, Cole's interpretation of the *effect* of the performance reiterates a process whereby spectators behold a reanimated version of the past and come to identify with it as their own. First, the historical fragment is put on display ('brought back the past to the eyes of the present'); then the spectators are absorbed within the historical fragment, an experience of both pleasure and disorientation ('bewildered the spectators with a mingled sense of astonishment and admiration'); and finally, the spectators recognize that the fragment stands for the fullness of their own restored history ('a resuscitation of a memorable passage from our own domestic chronicles').

In a formation that has rapidly become canonical in British historiography, the mid-Victorian years were the 'age of equipoise':[15] a collective sigh of relief at having successfully negotiated the land mines of electoral reform, Chartist agitation and revolutionary phobia. For a generation that wanted nothing more to do with crisis, the Middle Ages was a guarantee from across the centuries that the future, however 'powerless to be born', would turn out all right because it would be modelled upon a revered and cherished past. The Middle Ages shone forth as the dream of order which alone could ease the wide-awake anxiety of the Victorians. If, as John Ruskin proclaimed, 'the Middle Ages are to me the only ages',[16] then Shakespeare in performance was the best, if not the last hope of Victorian medievalism. For only through the perpetual present of theatrical performance could the Middle Ages be revived and embraced not as a cold and lifeless corpse, but as a living body with a steady pulse, flashing eyes and warm touch. The Victorian devotion to the past was not, as Susan Sontag would have it, a disastrous form of unrequited love, but an affair to remember.

Notes

[1] 'Stanzas from the Grand Chartreuse', in *The Poetical Works of Matthew Arnold*, eds C.B. Tinker and H.F. Lowry (Oxford: Oxford University Press, 1950), 299.

[2] Alice Chandler, *A Dream of Order: The Medieval Idea in Nineteenth-Century English Literature* (Lincoln: University of Nebraska Press, 1970) and Lee Patterson, *Negotiating the Past: The Historical Understanding of Medieval Literature* (Madison: University of Wisconsin Press, 1987).

[3] 'A Few Words in Defence of the Stage Addressed to its Religious Objectors', *Tallis's Dramatic Magazine* (April 1851).

[4] Charles Kean, playbill essay for *Richard II*, Princess's Theatre, London (March 1857).

[5] Charles Kean, playbill essay for *Macbeth*, Princess's Theatre, London (February 1853).

[6] *Builder* (21 March 1857).

[7] *Builder* (2 April 1859).

[8] Walter Pater, 'Shakespeare's English Kings', *Appreciations* (London: Macmillan and Co., 1924), 195.

[9] Kean, as note 4 above (italics added).

[10] Charles Lamb, 'On the Tragedies of Shakespeare' (1811).

[11] *The Celebrated Eton Boy* (London, 1859), by a 'Theatrical Squib'.

[12] Marc Baer, *Theatre and Disorder in Late-Georgian London* (Oxford: Clarendon Press, 1992), 195.

[13] Stephen Bann, *The Clothing of Clio: A Study of the Representation of History in Nineteenth-Century Britain and France* (Cambridge: Cambridge University Press, 1984), 38.

[14] J.W. Cole, *Life and Theatrical Times of Charles Kean, F.S.A.* (London, 1859), 226.

15 The phrase comes from the title of Walter Burn's 1964 landmark study of mid-Victorian Britain, *The Age of Equipoise* (London: Allen and Unwin, 1964).
16 *Collected Works*, eds E.T. Cook and Alexander Wedderburn, vol. 37 (London: George Allen, 1903–12), 189.

RENAISSANCE CONTEXTS

CHAPTER 9

Falstaff's Page as Early Modern Youth at Risk

Mark H. Lawhorn

In his cinematic version of *Henry V*, Kenneth Branagh as Henry slogs across the muddy Agincourt battlefield carrying the corpse of a boy. The young victim, Falstaff's former page, is held up as an emblem of the terrible cost of war. The obvious irony of the moment is unsettling: God is to be praised for fighting on the side of the English and yet all the English boys have been slaughtered.[1] As director, Branagh has given the slain boy the spotlight after the Agincourt victory, but he has also decisively cut most of the lines that Shakespeare has given the character, including the boy's moderately lengthy speeches at 3.2.24–45 and at 4.4.53–61.[2] Similar truncations appear frequently in dramatic and cinematic productions of *2 Henry IV*, where Falstaff's page is introduced. It is common theatrical practice to cut lines and rearrange text to speed a production along, to remove the difficulty of outdated jokes and references and, in some cases, to adapt to the limitations of actors available to perform various roles.[3] Making such cuts may also be seen as part of a cultural process that both responds to and shapes societal attitudes. When the directorial knife renders a character inconsequential or merely emblematic, it is not surprising that 'some elements are actually lost'.[4] Despite efforts by directors to 'see' an old script in fresh ways, theatrical traditions often work against serious re-examination of the dramatic uses of marginalized characters. The page boy's history of dramatic treatment as a character of little importance may be partly based on a general impression of his line count. In *2 Henry IV*, for example, the character has only twenty-nine lines.[5] Nevertheless, the page 'appears' in seven out of the play's seventeen scenes. A third of the play's lines are spoken while the boy is on stage. The boy's presence for such a large portion of the play certainly presents the possibility of a greater significance than modern productions or analyses of the play would suggest. In making this claim, I am assuming that dramatic tension and interest can be created, cultural attitudes examined and audience expectations disrupted when the speech or behaviour of performers compel attention to a silent presence.[6]

Perhaps, in too hastily dismissing those figures with few or no lines, we overlook their potential dramatic uses. For example, the King's page in *2 Henry IV* makes a speedy exit at the beginning of Act 3, scene 1 after the King utters a three-line command for the boy to depart in haste with letters for the Earls of Warwick and Surrey. This brief appearance of an obedient, quiet royal page is arguably an important counterpoint to the role of Falstaff's page.[7] The order for the page to deliver letters mirrors a similar order given by Falstaff to his page in the previous act. A page serving in the royal household could look forward to social advancement of the sort that Geoffrey Chaucer enjoyed. But, Falstaff's page has been placed among rogues. The question of whether the boy will survive the corrupting influences of the adult rogues with whom he appears is expressed in Bardolph's dark-humoured jest to Falstaff and his companions: 'An you do not make him hang'd among you, the gallows shall have wrong' (2.2.96–7). The sight of the boy associating with scoundrels and knaves for much of *2 Henry IV* does not suggest a future of social advancement for him. From his first appearance, Falstaff's page prompted dramatic tension associated with societal concerns regarding youth and vagrancy.

The problem of youthful vagrancy was an enormous concern during the time the Henriad was composed and first performed. According to A.L. Beier, the little evidence that exists regarding the ages of vagrants 'suggests that youth predominated'. For example, over half of those incarcerated in London's Bridewell correctional facility in 1602 were under 16 years old.[8] Bridewell, which was established in 1553, not only provided work and punitive correction for 'sturdy vagabonds' but also served 'to train up the beggar's child in virtuous exercise, that of him should spring no more beggars'.[9] The successive poor laws of sixteenth-century England suggest a growing concern for youth at risk. While 'the first poor law of 1531 made no mention of children', the Act of 1536 recognized the societal benefits to be gained from seeking to rescue from a future of vagrancy and crime those children who might otherwise grow up knowing no other way of life.[10] The Acts of 1572 and 1576 were both attempts to deal with issues surrounding vagrant children. 'Until 1597', as Beier observes, offenders 'aged from 5 to 14 were usually to be placed in service, although a statute of 1572 ordered them stocked and whipped. Those over 14 were to be gaoled, whipped and burnt through the ear'.[11] At about the time that Shakespeare was composing *2 Henry IV*, the English enacted, after many years of concern and experimentation, a comprehensive poor law that sought to provide a systematic response to early modern children at risk,[12] a group that constituted a 'problem of huge proportions'.[13]

The precarious nature of the page's situation is introduced in *2 Henry IV* almost from the moment the page enters in the second scene of Act 1.

At the boy's initial appearance, Falstaff describes him as a lone piglet following along behind his large mother who has 'overwhelmed' the rest of her offspring. While the scene has been played for the physical comedy which may arise from the casting of a particularly small boy behind whom the bulky Falstaff may try to hide, audience awareness that pigs occasionally devour their young might lend an even more grotesque colouring to the monstrous shadow looming above the lad. Some members of an Elizabethan audience might have caught in the pig imagery an allusion to the Vice figure of morality interludes with whom Falstaff has often been associated. In Richard Wever's *Lusty Juventus*, a mid-sixteenth century interlude with a prodigal son theme, Satan's offspring Hypocrisie apologizes for comparing his 'father's voice unto a sow's groaning'.[14] If there is dramatic tension associated with youth tempted by vice in the Henriad, it does not reside in the prodigal figure of Prince Hal in part because he is a historical personage whose fate is well known.[15] Falstaff's page does, however, seem to provide such a focal point for audience suspense. In a few brief examples, I will illustrate how tension over what will become of the youth is maintained throughout his 'stage life' from *2 Henry IV* to *Henry V*. Because the world of *The Merry Wives of Windsor*, where Falstaff has a page named Robin, is a safer, more stable place whose youth generate more affection than societal anxiety and because there is little in that comic 'by-product of the English history plays'[16] which focuses attention on the boy's precarious socioeconomic state, I will not be examining the page in the context of that play.

During the page's first scene in *2 Henry IV*, where he enters with a urinalysis report from Sir John's doctor, several elements combine to situate the character in an insecure socioeconomic environment as a virtual apprentice to roguery. First are the specific references to Falstaff's lack of funds. Asked what the cloth merchant has told him about Falstaff's request for satin cloth, the boy informs his master that the man 'liked not the security' (1.2.24–5), meaning that he doubted Falstaff's ability to pay. When Falstaff asks the boy at the end of the scene, 'What money is in my purse?' the boy's response, 'Seven groats and twopence', reveals just how desperate Falstaff's fortunes are. Falstaff aptly describes the state of his purse as 'consumptive'. Its contents have been consumed, perhaps coughed up in fits of riotous spending. While the boy engages in some brief banter with Falstaff at the beginning of this scene and answers several questions put to him, for the most part he is a silent observer of an exchange between Falstaff and the Lord Chief Justice, who at first sends his servant ahead of him to accost Sir John. Besides the topics of beggary and poverty, youth itself is a recurrent subject throughout the scene. When the servant addresses Falstaff – 'Sir John!' – Falstaff replies, 'What? a young knave and begging? is there not wars? is there not employment? doth not the King lack subjects? do not the rebels need soldiers?' (1.2.58–60). In pretending to mistake the Justice's servant for a beggar, Falstaff alludes to the problem of youthful vagrancy while performing an act of dissembling for which rogues and beggars were noted. His reply also foreshadows the dramatic destination of the page in *Henry V*, namely the battlegrounds of France. The problem of masterless men roaming the countryside is linked to military service in Shakespeare's day. Beier claims that 'no occupational groups increased as much as sailors and soldiers among vagrants from 1560 to 1640'. Not only were released military men likely to become vagrants, but soldiers were mainly 'recruited from the poor and criminal classes'.[17] Falstaff's speech here effectively suggests several of the themes woven through the stage life of his young page.

During the lengthy dialogue between the Justice and Falstaff, the two younger actors (the servant and page) watch and, presumably, learn. Ultimately, Falstaff's audacious request of a thousand pounds 'to furnish ... [him] forth' drives the indignant Justice from the stage. Unabashed, Falstaff turns to the page with instructions to deliver several letters designed to con money from the wealthy. Although he laments the diseased state of himself and his finances, Falstaff tells the boy, 'A good wit will make use of anything: I will turn diseases to commodity' (1.2.194–5). Here endeth the boy's first lesson in roguery. Falstaff's disease metaphor resonates powerfully with period comments on the way that beggars trained their children to counterfeit disease and disfigurement. Unfortunately, there are also horrific accounts of children who were considered too young to master the 'histrionics of disfigurement' and who were therefore mangled and broken by their parents 'to achieve the same status as the counterfeits'.[18] The page-boy, however, is a fit pupil.

In his next scene, the boy appears in the unwholesome setting of a tavern frequented by whores and their clientele, where he intervenes during a brawl between Falstaff and Mistress Quickly to shout, 'Away, you scullian, you rampallian, you fustillarian! I'll tickle your catastrophe!' (2.1.45–6). It is the boy's only line in the scene but its tang of roguish cant sufficiently indicates how his education is progressing under the tutelage of Sir John.[19]

In the following scene, Falstaff's metaphor of the commodification of disease shifts into a trope that emphasizes the boy's commodification of Falstaff's teaching. When the boy enters with Bardolph in Act 2, scene 2, Prince Hal, who has been chatting with his crony Poins, immediately notes a striking change in him, exclaiming, 'And the boy that I gave Falstaff: 'a had him from me Christian and look if the fat villain have not transformed him ape' (2.2.53–4).[20] When the page offers a clever rejoinder laced with references to alehouses and prostitutes, the prince jokes, 'Has not the boy profited?' (2.2.64). The prince's ironic observation on the profits of Falstaff's teaching is echoed by the boy himself in *Henry V*, where he presents in a moderately lengthy monologue a jaded perspective on his 'teachers' Bardolph, Nym and Pistol, whom he finally recognizes as 'sworn brothers in filching' (3.3.38). Thus, the boy's initial exposure to Falstaff causes one transformation and the boy's later experiences provoke another, a moral turning that echoes the prodigal pattern that informs both parts of *Henry IV*.

As many critics have noted, Prince Hal is a prodigal figure who eventually rejects Falstaff and the other bad influences of his 'wilder days'. His harsh treatment of Falstaff is a moment whose painfulness to audiences is heightened by their appreciation of the load of laughter Falstaff's character has supplied them. Few eyes turn to examine the state of the page at this juncture. Yet there is good reason to question Hal's treatment of the page. Shakespeare twice calls our attention in *2 Henry IV* to the circumstance by which the page came into Falstaff's service – in the lines spoken by Falstaff upon the boy's introduction in 1.2 and in 2.2 as noted above. In the first instance, there is some ambiguity about whose service the boy is in. When the boy uses his wit at Falstaff's expense, Falstaff threatens to send the boy back to 'the juvenal prince ... [the boy's] master' (1.2.14). In scene 2 of the following act, however, when he pays Bardolph and the page to keep mum about his presence in town, Prince Hal says to them, 'no word to your master', meaning Falstaff (2.2.123).

Despite some minor ambiguity expressed by Falstaff, Hal's assertion that he has given Falstaff the boy (2.2.53–4) establishes a clear link between Hal and the page that is subtly underscored elsewhere. In Act 4, scene 2 of *2 Henry IV*, at the mention of Poins's name, Hal's royal father ruminates on his wayward son:

> Most subject is the fattest soil to weeds,
> And he, the noble image of my youth,
> Is overspread with them ... (4.2.54–6)

The blighted garden image echoes a joke that Poins has earlier made about the page, 'O that this blossom could be kept from cankers!' (2.2.71). Just before Hal uproots himself from his weedlike companions, he transplants into their earthy ground a young shoot in the form of the page. Within the world of the play no reasons emerge for the prince's action and we are given no further information about the boy's origins. We are, however, frequently directed to consider the ends to which his roguish education will lead. This thematic concern links the boy via the prodigal figure Hal with the figures of youth at risk in earlier morality drama. Shakespeare has replaced the simple didactic structure of the morality play with a situation far more complex. Does the play raise the issue of the accountability of those who place children into the service of others? If so, by only tracing the boy's history for us as far back as his service to the prince, what questions are being raised about the prince's responsibilities at that moment and perhaps later when he is king and Falstaff has died? Is there any indication that Hal offers the page the sanctuary of royal service again when the boy is left without his master?

At the close of *2 Henry IV*, Falstaff and 'all his company' (5.5.93) are led to prison. It is not uncommon for directors and critics alike to assume that the Falstaff's page is somehow exempt from arrest, as Krupski does:

> The Page-Boy is a wordless witness to these proceedings. In the time gap between them and his reappearance, still as Falstaff's servant in the first scene of Act 2 in *Henry V*, we must surmise that he was on his own until, by means unknown to us, Falstaff and Co. were released from prison and restored to the freedom of the London streets.[21]

As I have already pointed out, however, the house of correction seems to have been particularly designed to reform youth so that, as the Act of 1576 declared, they would 'be accustomed and brought up in labour and work and ... not ... grow to be idle rogues'.[22] Thus, the most logical theatrical interpretation of the end of *2 Henry IV* would reveal the boy being taken with the adults to prison. Such staging might reveal some early modern concerns about the actual effects of imprisonment. In Middleton's play *Your Five Gallants*, the character Bungler, speaking about time spent in Bridewell prison, claims ''a will learn more knavery there in one week than will furnish him and his heirs for a hundred year' (3.5.138-9),[23] a sentiment which ought to sound quite familiar to us today. The moment of Falstaff's incarceration is a crucial one for the page character. There is nothing in *2 Henry IV* to indicate that the boy avoids a trip to jail. In fact, his first appearance in *Henry V* suggests that he has never been separated from Falstaff and his companions. Although there is no discussion by these roguish elements of their recent imprisonment, the play holds up the penal institution for a measure of critique. The rogues who appear before us in *Henry V* seem in no way to have been 'corrected'. Thus, the end of *2 Henry IV* presents the audience with an image of a 'reformed' figure assuming the powers of the state, casting off his former companions and eschewing personal involvement with them in favour of a new reliance on an official state institution of correction. Hal is apparently ignorant or indifferent to the function of prison as a breeding ground for criminals rather than a reformatory. It is at this moment, when the different stations of the former prodigal Hal and the youth at risk page are most evident, that the dramatic tensions connecting the two might be powerfully realized in performance. The main focus of the scene will always be the exchange between Hal and Falstaff. But Falstaff's language as he addresses the new king as 'most royal imp of fame' and 'my sweet boy' may call to mind a potentially important silent presence who is still appropriately called 'boy'.

At Falstaff's death in *Henry V*, his page becomes a masterless boy and ventures with Bardolph, Nym and Pistol to France, as Pistol says, 'to suck, to suck, the very blood to suck' (2.3.43–4), indicating that are profits to be taken by those not shy of knavery. Just as the boy's movement into full-fledged roguery seems complete, however, he has an epiphany regarding his leechlike companions and reflects on his place among such unsavory types. The following speech is often cut in performance, along with most of the boy's other lines. His first sentence suggests what he has been doing during his many on-stage silences.

> As young as I am, I have observed these three swashers. I am boy to them all three, all they three, though they would serve me, could not be man to me, for indeed three such antics do not amount to a man. For Bardolph, he is white-livered and red-faced, by the means whereof a faces it out but fights not. For Pistol, he hath a killing tongue and a quiet sword, by the means whereof a breaks words and keeps whole weapons. For Nym, he hath heard that men of few words are the best men and therefore he scorns to say his prayers lest a should be thought a coward, but his few bad words are matched with as few good deeds, for a never broke any man's head but his own and that was against a post when he was drunk. They will steal anything and call it purchase. Bardolph stole a lute-case, bore it twelve leagues and sold it for three halfpence. Nym and Bardolph are sworn brothers in filching and in Calais they stole a fire-shovel. I knew by that piece of service the men would carry coals. They would have me as familiar with men's pockets as their gloves or their handkerchiefs, which makes much against my manhood if I should take from another's pocket to put into mine, for it is plain pocketing up of wrongs. I must leave them and seek some better service. Their villainy goes against my weak stomach and therefore I must cast it up. (3.2.24–45)

Although the boy has discovered that sucking the blood of France is not to his taste, there is no hotline for troubled youth amid the 'vasty fields of

France'. When he next appears, doing able service as an interpreter of French, he aids Pistol in his efforts to extort ransom from a captured Frenchman. In his final monologue, the boy reveals that Bardolph and Nym 'are hanged' and hints that he himself may be perilously near his doom. In a short time, Falstaff's former page is killed when the French commit a serious breech of the rules of war by going behind the lines to attack the defenceless boys left to watch over the English baggage.

Citing a number of post-Second World War productions in his introduction to the Cambridge edition of *Henry V*, Andrew Gurr suggests that, from the 1950s when 'it became standard to show the Eastcheap Boy being killed by French soldiers on stage' to Branagh's 1989 film, the figure of the dead child has been highlighted on stage and screen as a means of underscoring 'Henry's ambivalence and sensitivity to the horrors of war'.[24] It seems both appropriate and ironic to have the king confront the dead body of the page. The vision of Branagh carrying the dead page may well be a comment on Henry's feelings about war, but the boy need not be simply an emblem of innocence cut down. The page and Henry have a 'history' with important societal implications. We might consider King Henry as an emblem of privilege, of state power and control and the boy as simply a boy struggling against the vagaries of a society that might better serve its youth. It is no surprise that Burgundy's appeal for social healing at the end of the *Henry V*, which also adopts the blighted garden motif associated with Hal and the page, culminates in an appeal to consider the nation's youth:

> And as our vineyards, fallows, meads and hedges,
> Defective in their natures, grow to wildness,
> Even so our houses and ourselves and children
> Have lost, or do not learn for want of time
> The sciences that should become our country,
> But grow like savages, as soldiers will
> That nothing do but meditate on blood,
> To swearing and stern looks, diffused attire,
> And everything that seems unnatural. (5.2.54–62)

Of course, Burgundy is talking about a country that has now been 'properly' reunited through violent efforts. His speech, by refusing to exempt the victorious soldier from criticism, forces even the king to confront his recent behaviour. Just as the prodigal Hal's reformation at the end of *2 Henry IV* does not indicate that the character has achieved the pinnacle of wisdom, his victory at Agincourt, as the Chorus so pointedly reminds us at the close of *Henry V*, does not indicate that he and England have forever thwarted the unpleasant twists of Fortune, which 'made his sword / By which the world's best garden he achieved' (5.3.6–7). Henry's achievement is tempered by our sense of its historical effervescence. Just as Henry's stirring rhetoric of glory in battle may seem hollow in retrospect, his placement of the boy into Falstaff's care, though providing dramatic moments of both humour and pathos, takes on a more complex hue by the time the boy is dead. In subtle and not so subtle ways, the stage life of the sometimes witty, sometimes wise, often silent and yet very present, character of Falstaff's page focuses attention on the state's relationship to early modern youth at risk.

Notes

1. Another layer of irony may be created out of the realization that it was Prince Hal who gave the boy in service to Falstaff and who has had no contact with the page character since seeing Falstaff and his companions sent to prison at the end of *2 Henry IV*.
2. William Shakespeare, *King Henry V*, ed. Andrew Gurr (Cambridge: Cambridge University Press, 1992); all subsequent references are to this edition.
3. As Ann Blake has observed about the continuing practice in our time of cutting lines for children in Shakespeare's plays, 'it may be partly attributed to the difficulty the actors have in speaking Shakespeare's verse' ('Shakespeare's Roles for Children: A Stage History', *Theatre Notebook* 48.3 (1994), 133).
4. Blake, 122.
5. William Shakespeare, *The Second Part of King Henry IV*, ed. Giorgio Melchiori (Cambridge: Cambridge University Press, 1989); all subsequent references are to this edition.
6. My contention that a character does not have to be speaking to maintain a powerful presence on stage and to engage dramatically with discursive matrices formed by both speaking and silent characters and by the social affections and anxieties circulating among an audience is a logical extension of Philip McGuire's convincing argument that the silence of characters present on stage at the conclusion of many plays unsettles the possibilities of dramatic closure; see Philip C. McGuire, *Speechless Dialect: Shakespeare's Open Silences* (Berkeley: University California Press, 1985).
7. For a discussion of the positions for children in medieval aristocratic households, see Nicholas Orme, *From Childhood to Chivalry* (London and New York: Methuen, 1984).

8   A.L. Beier, *Masterless Men: The Vagrancy Problem in England 1560–1640* (London and New York: Methuen, 1985), 54.
9   Quoted in Ivy Pinchbeck and Margaret Hewitt, *Children in English Society, Volume One* (London: Routledge and Kegan Paul, 1969), 132–3.
10 Pinchbeck and Hewitt, 94–5.
11 The 1597 Act for the Relief of the Poor, which, among other progressive moves, exempted those under seven years old from prosecution, held a foundational position in English law until the early nineteenth century.
12 Pinchbeck and Hewitt, 138.
13 Beier, 10.
14 Richard Wever, *Lusty Juventus* in *The Dramatic Writings of Richard Wever and Thomas Ingelend*, ed. John S. Farmer (Guildford, England: Charles W. Traylen, 1966) [a facsimile of the 1905 edition, London: Early English Drama Society], 16.
15 It seems to me that the age and size of the boy might also have stimulated audience affection and concern in ways that Prince Hal's figure would not. Hal is no longer a child, even by Elizabethan standards; he is a young man on the brink of assuming the throne, which the historical Hal did at age 26. The page, whose diminutive size is the subject of commentary, clearly is much younger, although in modern productions casting for the role has ranged from the pre-adolescent (as in Welles's *Falstaff: Chimes at Midnight*) to the late adolescent (as in Bogdanov and Pennington's English Shakespeare Company film of 1989).
16 T.W. Craik, ed., William Shakespeare, *The Merry Wives of Windsor* (Oxford: Oxford University Press, 1990), 11.
17 Beier, 93, 94.
18 William C. Carroll, *Fat King, Lean Beggar: Representations of Poverty in the Age of Shakespeare* (Ithaca and London: Cornell University Press, 1996), 49.
19 One of the intriguing features of the page is the variety of expression given to the character. The boy's speech seems to shift according to his environment. In the tavern, the boy's speech is rather rude and sassy. In France, he has a better working knowledge of French than his nominal master Pistol. In his monologues the tone is strikingly without roguish qualities. Although these variable linguistic registers might be dismissed as authorial inconsistencies, they might illustrate the child's proverbially impressionable nature and further underscore the character's struggle with his environmental influences.

[20] The prince's observations in this scene on the boy's dress and performance suggest a thread that I do not have time to pursue at length here. As William Carroll has noted, 'Every rogue book from Copland on attributes superlative histrionic powers to the sturdy beggar', (Carroll, 42) and it was a commonplace that beggarly parents instructed their children in the dissembling arts (Carroll, 50). It is the shape shifting ability of the sturdy beggar that generates some of the anxiety revolving around vagabondage. Antitheatrical tracts and sermons of the day illuminate the link between theatre and the corruption of youth. Besides their warnings of the detrimental moral and political infection to which patrons were exposed in the generally unhealthy playhouse environment, antitheatrical writers often commented on the dangers of youth taking the stage. The attitude expressed by William Crashawe in a sermon he preached in 1607 is typical of these age-related anxieties: 'hee that teacheth children to play, is not an instructor, but a spoiler and destroyer of children' (William Crashawe, *The Sermon preached at the Crosse, Feb. xiiij 1607* (1608), 170). The way that the character of Falstaff's page illustrates youth at risk while at the same time reflecting the ability of the youth's conscience to discern the morally compromising nature of his surroundings and teachers effectively works against the criticism of theatre as a destroyer of children.

[21] Jadwiga Krupski, *Shakespeare's Children*, (unpublished PhD dissertation, McGill University, 1992), 137.

[22] Quoted in Beier, 165.

[23] Thomas Middleton, *Your Five Gallants* in *The Works of Thomas Middleton*, ed. A.H. Bullen (London, 1885–6).

[24] Gurr, 54.

CHAPTER 10

Fashion, Nation and Theatre in Late Sixteenth-Century London

Janette Dillon

Why, presently this great linguist my master will march through Paules Church-yard, come to a booke binders shop, and with a big Italian looke and a Spanish face aske for these bookes in Spanish and Italian; then, turning, through his ignorance, the wrong end of the booke upward, use action on this unknowne tong after this sort: first looke on the title and wrinckle his browe; next make as though he red the first page and bite the lippe; then with his nayle score the margent, as though there were some notable conceit; and lastly, when he thinkes hee hath gulld the standers by sufficiently, throwe the booke away in a rage, swearing that hee could never finde bookes of a true printe since he was last in Padua (*2 Return from Parnassus*, 1277–89).[1]

This is Amoretto's page describing his master's behaviour in Part Two of *The Return from Parnassus*, a play performed at St John's College, Cambridge during the Christmas season of 1601–2. What emerges most conspicuously from this description is the importance of language to the fashionable image. Language here is an object almost as material as the books Amoretto holds upside down, to be picked up or cast off according to caprice. So socially desirable, apparently, is a knowledge of other European languages that Amoretto is portrayed as willing to waste substantial amounts of time looking at books he does not understand merely to impress the bystanders. And a verbal display is even more impressive than a silent one, where the gallant can produce it. Gullio, a character in the slightly earlier St John's play, *The Return from Parnassus* (1599–1601) boasts that

> It is my custome in my common talke to make use of my reading in the Greeke, Latin, French, Italian, Spanishe poetts, and to adorne my oratorye with some prettie choise extraordinarie sayinges. (1134–7)

This is not an affectation specific to the *Parnassus* plays, with their university auspices, but one widespread in plays that cluster around 1599–1601, including especially the plays usually grouped together under the heading of the 'War of the Theatres', and written predominantly for the indoor, private theatres.[2] The passage quoted from *2 Return from Parnassus* above may in fact be alluding to an earlier play, Jonson's *Every Man Out of His Humour* (1599), where Cordatus says that Clove 'will sit you a whole afternoone sometimes, in a booke-sellers shop, reading the Greeke, Italian, and Spanish; when he understands not a word of either: if he had the tongues, to his sutes, he were an excellent linguist' (3.1.29–32).[3] Criticism dealing with the War of the Theatres plays up to now has tended to focus on identifying which individuals are supposedly targeted by particular characters and allusions. In the present context I am not interested in continuing this game of riddles, but in the self-evident fact that all of these plays manifest an obsessive interest in linguistic decorums, fashions and excesses, an interest which is marked by its difference from the nationalistic concerns dominating so many public-theatre plays of the late 1580s and 1590s and continuing to drive many of the Admiral's Men's productions at the Fortune after 1600.

Like the *Parnassus* plays, the War of the Theatres plays generally show a tendency to treat verbal styles as commodities. Words are portrayed as quasi-material objects to be picked up or discarded at will in the conscious and careful process of manufacturing a public persona. Amorphus, coaching Asotus in the language of courtship in Jonson's *Cynthia's Revels*, performed by the Chapel Children at the Blackfriars in 1600–1601, is explicit about this:

> Your pedant should provide you some parcells of french, or some pretty commoditie of italian to commence with, if you would be exoticke and exquisite. (3.5.91–4)

Words here, it is clear, are not conceived of as signs expressive of a preexistent identity, but as fashion accessories.

Foreign languages are only one of the linguistic commodities on display. English too is displayed as composed of a variety of modes of discourse, some of which are to be cultivated at the expense of others in particular social settings. Amorphus is as enthusiastic about a laboured rhyming couplet that Asotus has devised in English as he is in recommending that Asotus acquire fragments of French or Italian:

> O, that peece was excellent! if you could picke out more of these play-particles, and (as occasion shall salute you) embroider, or

damaske your discourse with thém, perswade your soule, it would
most judiciously commend you. (3.5.118–22)

English viewed against the fashion for foreign language and culture, becomes visible as an assembly of constituent parts. It becomes, in Bakhtinian terms, perceptibly heteroglot to its own speakers, who may be recognized as speaking in different tongues. And it extends *heteroglossia* beyond the mere social reality of different discourses into the realms of the fantastic. Not only does it literally borrow from other languages, it also creates 'foreignness' at the limits of its own parameters, inventing styles and modes of expression that are barely intelligible and distinctly un-English. Peter Womack, identifying this conspicuously useless language in Jonson's work, describes it as 'linguistic *junk* – that is, a cultural object ambivalently compounded of alienation, bad taste, cheapness, freedom, fun, superabundance, uselessness, waste'.[4] It is language dedicated to the display of its own substance, language, in effect, as fetishized commodity, its materiality so foregrounded that its usefulness, or referentiality, disappears under the excessive weight of its self-reference.

The fashionable maker of epithets on the Elizabethan stage is a figure intimately linked with the development of capitalism. Though Marx's explanation of commodity fetishism postdates Amorphus's choice of the word 'commoditie' in 1600 by nearly three centuries, the Marxist exegesis offers a theoretical context after the fact for making sense of the eruption of this alienated discourse at the end of the sixteenth century.[5] As Jean-Christophe Agnew has argued, the development of a 'volatile and placeless market' during the early modern period produces a 'crisis of representation', problematizing the process of representation itself, so that the kinds of characters the stage now chooses to represent are conscious performers, inhabiting multiple identities without embodying any one of them. 'Just as London's Exchange enforced an ideal of financial liquidity, so London's theatres enacted a vision of this new sociological and psychological fluidity. And why not, since the world was at once a market and a stage?' Amorphus might stand emblematically as the Elizabethan designation of what Agnew calls '"Protean man" – the plastic, polymorphous, performative figure that is both the ideal and the nightmare of modernity', and who must be understood, as Agnew shows, to be 'the collective dream work of commodity culture'.[6]

The key concept underpinning the representation of the Protean man on the late-Elizabethan stage is fashion. The fluidity of character is directly linked to his reliance on a quality transient in itself, as opposed to any groundedness in some more stable matrix of identity. The fashionable persona is constructed via selection and practice, conscious dipping into stylistic junk; and this fashionable user of fetishized verbal styles, whether those styles are made up of literally foreign elements or alienated vernacular fragments or both, is in distinct opposition to the plain-speaking Englishman celebrated in so many history plays of the 1590s, whose identity is firmly grounded in a national and nationalistic framework. As with Marx's theory of commodity fetishism, another, much later theoretical discourse seems to offer a useful model of analysis for this self-producing, image conscious figure. In Walter Benjamin's writing on nineteenth-century Paris the *flâneur* is by definition a creature of the expanding city. More specifically, he is a creature of the arcades, 'glass-covered, marble-panelled passageways, ... lighted from above, ... lined with the most elegant shops, so that such an arcade is a city, even a world, in miniature'.[7] As Benjamin argues, the arcades represent 'a cross between a street and an *intérieur*', and the *flâneur* who haunts them emerges out of 'a new and rather strange situation, one that is peculiar to big cities'.[8] He is a figure constantly on view as well as viewing. As he inspects the commodities on display in the arcades he simultaneously, and ironically, presents himself for inspection.

Yet the *flâneur*, as later critics have pointed out, is more than merely a historical phenomenon. He, or rather it, has achieved the status of a theoretical model, and may function as 'the representation of a way of experiencing metropolitan life, a literary motif, and an image of the commodity in its relation to the crowd' (though, as John Rignall, author of these words, points out, once he is equated with the commodity, he ceases to be the figure Benjamin conceives of, a figure who still stands balanced on the edge of 'the alienating system of commodity exchange into which he will eventually be absorbed'[9]). As Chris Jenks argues, the *flâneur* as theoretical model 'is a multilayered palimpset that enables us to "move" from real products of modernity, like commodification and leisured patriarchy, through the practical organization of space and its negotiation by inhabitants of a city, to a critical appreciation of the state of modernity'.[10] And though Jenks's interest is in how the figure of the *flâneur* may be appropriated for analysing the whole period that follows, the details of his argument point as logically to the early modern as to the postmodern. 'Commodification' and 'leisured patriarchy' are visible products of the early modern that merely reach different stages of development in the modern and postmodern.

Though urban capitalism is much more developed by the mid-nineteenth century than it is in the late sixteenth, both periods respond to the threatening speed of social and economic change by producing figures who self-consciously try to hold back the pace of things. Benjamin notes a brief fashion around 1840 for taking turtles for a walk around the arcades and letting them set the pace;[11] the extended fashion-conscious play with words on the part of the sixteenth-century stage-gallant is a similar device aimed at creating a deliberate and extended pause. Both figures signal a need to create a different sort of time and space around themselves from the kind of rushing time and crowded space they feel pressing in on them from outside. Their devotion to producing the self as 'personality' may be read as signifying 'the protest of a fading aura in the face of commodity production'.[12] As Jenks emphasizes, the *flâneur* offers a model for opposing commodification: he chooses an alternative pace that is deliberately and consciously out of step with the rhythm of the city, providing the space for ironic reflection on the direction of social change. Despite the pursuit of fashion and novelty that identifies the *flâneur*, he is a figure paradoxically, yet necessarily, tinged with nostalgia. His mannered cultivation of stylish fragments seems to arise out of an attempt to compensate for an imagined wholeness, now lost. As a recent critic has argued of mannerism generally,

> there is always some degree of nostalgia for a lost unity, a longing to overcome the compression of disparity, to compensate for the absence of logic, to recentre the composition around the main subject and restore the correlation of the sign and the referent.[13]

The *flâneur*, carefully fashioning the gap between sign and referent, signals regret for the impossibility of an 'authentic' existence of inherent usefulness and value.

There is an important distinction to be made, of course, between the *flâneur* as urban social phenomenon and the *flâneur* as urban theatrical phenomenon, though the necessity for this distinction need only imply that the theatrical phenomenon had no social correlative. Indeed much satirical writing outside the drama suggests that affected speech was a fashion cultivated in urban society as well as in literary and dramatic texts. Everard Guilpin's fifth satire (published in 1598), for example, pokes fun at a ridiculous 'cavalier' who is not only dressed in the height of fashion, but is in his speech

> the Dictionary of complements,
> The Barbers mouth of new-scrapt eloquence,
> Synomicke Tully for varietie,
> And Madame Conceits gorgeous gallerie,
> The exact patterne which Castilio
> Tooke for's accomplish'd Courtier ... (143–8).[14]

Dekker too advises his gull, 'where planting yourself in a stationer's shop ... to look in your tables and enquire for such and such Greek, French, Italian or Spanish authors whose names you have there but whom your mother for pity would not give you so much wit as to understand'. He is also explicit about the way urban fashion may model itself on theatrical fashion, recommending his gull to 'hoard up the finest play-scraps you can get'.[15] The point is that the nostalgia attaching to sixteenth-century fictional *flâneur*-figures belongs not to them but to their creators. The ennui that characterizes the nineteenth-century Parisian *flâneur* as social phenomenon is not shared by his fictional precursors on the sixteenth-century stage, and not necessarily anticipated by the sixteenth-century social phenomenon to which such fictions may be linked; but it is anticipated by the creators of those fictions, the writers driven to produce the alienated figures of the simultaneously fashionable and satiric stage.

The truism that dramatic characters are distinct from real people applies with particular point to these plays, with their lack of interest in the concept of coherent or realistic 'character'. Just at the point when some other playwrights are beginning to develop the kind of play that seeks to represent real people in real worlds, these plays are preoccupied with *dramatis personae* explicitly manufactured out of disjointed fragments, figures whose modes of speech might be transferred to other characters in other plays and who might 'themselves' be appropriated by other dramatists for other purposes. It is not that these plays are uninterested in the concept of a 'real', or authentic, self; it is rather that they convey their anxiety about authenticity through a self-reflective emphasis on performance.

Despite the fact that both Benjamin's *flâneur* and his predecessor in late sixteenth-century drama are characteristic products of the developing city, both are defined in opposition to the figure of the citizen. Just as Benjamin develops an argument that opposes Hugo and Baudelaire as, respectively, '*citoyen*' and 'hero'/'*flâneur*',[16] so the *flâneur* of 1590s drama is defined against citizen-types and what they represent. The *flâneur* both needs and holds himself back from the city; he is drawn to the crowd at the same time as he maintains a sceptical detachment from it. He demands 'elbow room', is 'unwilling to forego the life a gentleman of leisure' and only escapes the sense of his own isolation by entering imaginatively into the life of strangers or inorganic things.[17] In the sixteenth century this is partly because the *flâneur* comes bearing the traces of the court. Up to this point, the concepts of wastefulness, excess and display would have tended to find their imaginative location in the environment of the court; only now was the city beginning to look like a viable alternative arena for social display. The 1590s *flâneur* is effectively Castiglione's courtier, with his carefully manufactured social persona, in process of transformation into a specifically urban phenomenon as he is adjusted in relation to this new and commercialized arena of display; but the courtly environment traditional for self-display is not yet fully accommodated into its new urban setting. By the time Dekker's *Gull's Hornbook*, a kind of *flâneur*'s handbook, was published in 1609, the link between the *flâneur* and the city is explicit and understood, so that Dekker quite naturally organizes five of his eight chapters around characteristically urban locations, examining how a gallant should behave himself in Paul's Walks, an ordinary, a playhouse, a tavern and passing through the city by night. But a decade or so earlier, the theatres are staging the *flâneur* in terms that are more oblique. Thus Fastidious Briske, for example, in *Every Man Out of His Humour* (1599), is conceived as a courtier in a city setting, while *Cynthia's Revels* (1600–1601) is entirely set in the court.

The opposition between the *flâneur* and the citizen also organizes two different theatre cultures at the turn of the century. On the one hand, a group of plays predominantly associated with Rose, and later the Fortune, begins to stage London and its citizens to and for those same citizens in a celebratory way. These plays revel in the guild structure underpinning the city's wealth, as well as in the city's role in guaranteeing the safety of king, court and nation. They create scenes which will offer the opportunity to display the red gowns of civic office: it is no accident that there is so much play with Simon Eyre's mayoral robes in *The Shoemaker's Holiday* (1599) or that Hobs the tanner mistakes the mayor for the king in *1 Edward IV* (1599). At the same time they also highlight the dependence of this finery on individual achievement and commercial success rather than noble birth: any man, however poor, they suggest, can reach this status by sheer hard work.

On the other hand the group of plays that stage *flâneur*-types is associated with the children's theatres (Paul's and Blackfriars) and the Globe, and with a satirical style that approaches the city from a very different angle. When these theatres, in the first decade of the seventeenth century, begin to develop the genre known as 'citizen comedy', they displayed a more sceptical, often cynical, attitude than the typical Rose or Fortune play of the same date towards merchants, entrepreneurs and commercial success. The two theatrical trends point to a city in transition becoming increasingly self-aware about its own status. What is happening is that Londoners are coming to terms in different ways with a geographical expansion of the city, an invisible expansion of liquid capital and a corresponding awareness of the city as a centre of power that, via its growth in size, wealth and commercial energy, is emerging as a real alternative to the power of the court (and negotiations between King James and the city of London in the first decade of the seventeenth century were to show that new power proving itself in very material ways).

The War of the Theatres is a dispute about the proper place of theatre and theatricality in the city. The 'War' plays are fascinated not only by linguistic excess, but by the theatrical implications of staging and focusing on that excess. At the heart of these plays is a conundrum: the affectations this theatre seeks to expose may be described as fashions, humours or the games people play; but, in using the stage to expose those affectations as games, the plays themselves become part of a similar fashionable game. In the same way as railing and satire are often accommodated in these plays by being made to acknowledge their own fashionability,[18] so the moral edge of the drive to expose affectation is blunted by its own participation in affectation. The ritual unmasking to which these plays almost necessarily lead is predicated on a morality that denounces masking by definition as guile; but the medium of denunciation is itself a mask. It is a reformulation of the old problem of theatre addressed by its attackers, from Lollards to Puritans, the problem that theatre is constructed on pretence; but the problem is now posed in particularly urgent relation to the developing city, with its heightened awareness of the 'look' and its push towards a notion of the self as no more than the sequence of its multiple social stagings.

The very structure of these turn-of-the-century plays highlights their self-reflexivity. Just as so much of their spoken dialogue is about itself as linguistic object, so their shapes are predominantly circular rather than linear. The Induction to *Cynthia's Revels* has one of the children 'tell all the argument of [the] play aforehand' in a fit of pique because he is not allowed to speak the prologue. So tangential is the notion of plot to this play that it foregrounds the show of openly discarding its secrets. Even those plays that are more conventionally plotted still seem perpetually poised to deviate from their plots for the purpose of exposing linguistic foibles. They willingly devote whole scenes to linguistic play which is barely attached to plot, thereby playing with questions about what drama is, and what it is to be on stage at all. The extraneous nature of certain scenes and characters is sometimes openly acknowledged, as when Mitis and Cordatus in *Every Man Out* describe Clove and Orange as 'meere strangers to the whole scope of our play; only come to walke a turne or two, i' this Scene of Paules, by chance' (3.1.17–19). Clove is, furthermore, a figure whose language seems to step out of the play to parody the language of an earlier character in an earlier play (Chrisoganus in Marston's *Histriomastix* (1598–9)). Self-conscious reference to, and appropriation of characters from, one another is very much a feature of the 'War' plays, and one that shows the plays performing in the same way as their *flâneur*-figures, in manufacturing simulacra as substitutes for expressive function.

These plays seem to drive towards a staging of the moment that will encapsulate the visibility of pretence and pretentiousness almost emblematically rather than seeking to advance a narrative. Part of the point is often that there is no narrative to advance, since narcissistic characters who play with words for pleasure as opposed to meaning are constructed as by definition going nowhere. Hence, in a play like *Cynthia's Revels*, the dominant sense of waiting for something real to happen is germane to the audience's experience of the play. The inane word-games that the courtiers devise to pass the time and that substitute for plot in the play are representative of the sham world they construct for themselves to inhabit, where time is passed rather than used. Words are not required to be actively engaged in such a world; they are mere counters filling a gap in time. Yet the sense of purposelessness does not merely operate as a negative hermeneutic attaching to certain characters within the fiction of the play; it also expresses some radical doubts about what performance is and how theatrical performance intersects with social performance. This kind of drama seems to want to strip the theatre of as many elements as it can in order to see what resists that stripping. It pushes against theatrical form, seeking to find whether there are any limits to that form, in order to test whether there is anything that may be defined as 'core', in relation to either theatre or the human self. If such a 'core' could be isolated as germane to one rather than the other, the worry about the resemblance between the two would be resolved.

Sometimes the attempt to incorporate exploration of the parallel between social and theatrical performance is dizzying in its self-reflexiveness, as when Mercury and Cupid decide to disguise themselves as pages in *Cynthia's Revels*. Mercury urges on Cupid the need to practise the right speech and behaviour in order for them to pass themselves off as 'cracks' ('pert boys'):

> since we are turn's cracks, let's studie to be like cracks; practise their language, and behaviours, and not with a dead imitation: act freely, carelessly, and capriciously, as if our veines ranne with quick-silver, and not utter a phrase, but what shall come forth steept in the verie brine of conceipt, and sparkle like salt in fire.
> (2.1.3–10)

The word 'cracks' here is a reminder that the speakers of these lines are precisely that already, since this is a Chapel Children's play. So the boy-actors, or 'cracks', speak for characters who are 'turn's cracks' and who must therefore 'studie to be like cracks'. The layers of self-reference work to expose and problematize the gap between performer and role, since they simultaneously show performers constructing roles while reminding the audience that 'selves' too are performed.

It is hardly surprising that such a 'limit-drama' has sometimes been suggested to be unperformable. Anne Barton, writing on the plotlessness of *Every Man Out of His Humour*, argues that none of the extant editions of it represents a performable text. She notes the prominence of set-piece descriptions of character 'designed more, it seems, for readers than for theatre audiences' and speculates on the probability that such descriptions were cut or abbreviated in performance.[19] Admittedly the early quartos of Jonson's *Every Man Out* explicitly state that they contain 'more than hath been Publickely Spoken or Acted'; but is it legitimate to read back from these statements a fundamental unperformability attaching to this particular mode of speech? The kind of speeches Barton identifies as unperformable are not mere occasional hiccups in the texts, but deeply embedded in and essential to the nature of these particular plays, and we have the evidence of numerous other contemporary plays that these supposedly unperformable speeches were highly fashionable in this particular theatrical mode.

Marston's satire, *The Scourge of Villanie*, offers an interesting sidelight here. In this poem the figure of Luscus is described as one who has

> made a common-place booke out of plaies,
> And speakes in print, at least what ere he sayes
> Is warranted by Curtaine plaudeties.[20]

This seems first to confirm that the fashion for thickening up speech or cultivating linguistic excess was a recognizable aspect of social performance, not one restricted to stage-performance; but it further suggests that this kind of speech on stage produced spontaneous applause. Characters in plays, then, thickened up their speech, or spoke 'in print', because audiences wanted them to. This would place verbal excess at the opposite extreme from unperformability, suggesting instead that audiences responded to them as highlights of performance.

What is needed in order to make a space for these speeches as performance is a different model of performance. Elizabethan culture was attuned to various kinds of static and emblematic performance and to the formal delivery of set pieces. Though these plays lack the visual spectacle that accompanied the prolonged static speech of, say, pageantry, they are addressing an audience that still valued the skills of oratory and recitation and still gathered voluntarily to listen to sermons. A parallel from more recent times is music hall, or variety, which centres on the skill, and sometimes outrageousness, of the individual 'turn'. A bastardized derivative of music hall in fact suggests a quite precise analogy: in the 1960s television show, 'The Good Old Days', Leonard Sachs, the presenter who introduced the various turns, made himself into a turn by the simple device of speaking in a thickly textured, arcane and alliterative register, isolating each long and special word by a combination of pause and voice inflection, in a way that encouraged the audience to roar its outrage or approval. As in the Elizabethan plays considered here, persona gives way to 'textuality', and the 'writtenness' of this eccentric dialect becomes the primary focus of attention. The example perhaps suggests the kind of context in which material designated unperformable by a culture that finds it alien can be seen to be performable; and not merely, or barely, performable, but consciously outstripping its own excesses for the delight of the audience.

The pleasures of this kind of theatre are, like those of any theatre, entirely bound into the expectations of the genre and the artfulness of variation within certain parameters of predictability. They are furthermore closely tied to the particular talents of known troupes and star performers and often provide the added attraction of a certain topical edge. The plays of the 'War', with their self-referentiality, their knowing allusions to, and recognizable parodies of, one another, and their ties to the same two or three theatre companies (and perhaps specifically to individual actors, known for their ability in particular kinds of parts) may find their performability within such a model of performance.

There is a further dimension to the problem, however. While music hall may offer a model for understanding the pleasures of a show that seeks to dazzle through a sequence of *tours de force*, it does not offer a model for a show that seeks to moralize its own highlights. As Cupid's comment on the practised speech of cracks suggests, these plays are characteristically hung between admiration for speech that sparkles 'like salt in fire' and disapproval of cultivating sparkle for pure effect. The critical tone emerges most clearly in the trio of adverbs qualifying the verb 'act': 'freely, carelessly, and capriciously'.[21] This notion of careless whimsicality implies a familiar moral take on the surface/depth binary; it carries the suggestion that cultivation of the surface is fraudulent, inauthentic and amoral. The issues theatre addresses in confronting the conditions of its own representation are, as Agnew has shown, the same as those of the market: 'authenticity, accountability, and intentionality'.[22]

Cupid's moral stance is even clearer in his explicit disapproval of the courtiers' folly. It is he who speaks the condemnation of flamboyant speakers who, 'when they have got acquainted with a strange word, never rest till they have wroong it in, though it loosen the whole fabricke of their sense' (2.4.15–18). But this moral frame of disapproval functions in tension with the play's own dedication to displaying that same exhibitionism of which it disapproves. The pleasure of shared jokes, collective play and stylishly conscious performance encounters the fear that such celebration of the surface covers up emptiness. The dramatists reflect on the fragments pieced together to dazzling effect and worry about the consequences of working with fragments and surfaces. And this worry manifests itself as a moral discourse that upbraids the dialect that wallows in the surface of the sign as evidence of cultural bankruptcy. A society that seeks to cultivate the sign at the expense of the referent, it is implied, is idolatrous, irresponsibly unconcerned about its own inner state.

Characters who speak in fragments are often explicitly noted for this attribute in the world of the play. Jonson's Amorphus, as we have seen, consciously assembles his speech out of 'remnant[s]' (*Cynthia's Revels* 1.4.80–2), while Marston's Puff is noted as one 'whose phrases are as neatly deckt as my Lord Maior's Hensman' (*Jack Drum*, Act 1, 191).[23] Other characters recognize and classify this kind of speech as a 'humour', or affectation. When Valentine first comes across his friend Juniper speaking like a dictionary, he at once enquires how long 'this sprightly humour' has affected him (*The Case is Altered*, 1.4.9).[24] Promiscuous and indiscriminate speakers of fragments are condemned as themselves fragmented and fragmenting, mere pastiche personae deliberately assembled as the occasion requires. They 'are' in one sense the words they speak; but the words are presented, not as having a productive function, but as commodified objects waiting to be put on display. Speakers tell us before they speak how they will do it, and practise their chosen registers in front of us. Figures who seem to fashion their social personae 'freely, carelessly, and capriciously' are presented as decentred beings. Cultivating singularity, yet lacking wholeness, they appear to threaten the wholeness of the community. Since the meanings of words are established by communal agreement, those who seek out singularity for its own sake are seen as threatening to collective values. Hence a figure like Gullio, who maintains his right to create new language ('we of the better sort have a privilege to create Latin, like knights, and to say, Rise up Sir Phrase' (*The Return from Parnassus*, 1435–7)), is not only a fool, but a dangerous fool. Clearly, theatre's focus at this time on the dangers and/or attractions of individuals 'wholly consecrated to singularity'[25] speaks of an anxiety around the meaning and coherence of 'civil society', an anxiety linked to ideas about both the city and the state.

The problem is deeply related to what theatre understands its role to be. Now that it is firmly established 'for sale' in permanent theatre buildings in and around the city, it has truly entered the marketplace. These plays respond to market demand by developing a particular kind of flamboyant set-piece in response to audiences' expression of approval for this kind of thing; but they also feel the need to reprove the audience for enjoying such display for its own sake. The dramatists respond to the commodification of their product with ambivalence, giving audiences prolonged and conspicuous displays of the verbal glitter they like, but seeking simultaneously to position such displays as invalid or excessive. Even as the theatre stages the excesses of fashion that audiences clamour for, it registers discomfort about its own complicity with the market. At the same time as it begins to understand itself to be a fashionable commodity, it seeks to reject that status and to validate its own authenticity via its capacity to recognize the theatrical forms that need to be disowned.

Notes

[1] Quotations from the Parnassus plays are taken from *The Three Parnassus Plays*, ed. J.B. Leishman (London: Ivor Nicholson and Watson, 1949).

[2] The plays usually considered to constitute the 'war' are (in probable chronological order): *Every Man Out of His Humour* (1599), *Jack Drum's Entertainment* (1600), *Cynthia's Revels* (1600–1601), *What You Will* (1601), *Poetaster* (1601) and *Satiromastix* (1601). *Histriomastix* (1598–9) is sometimes added to this list as the trigger for the parody of Marston in Jonson's *Every Man Out of His Humour*. *Every Man Out* was first performed by the Chamberlain's Men; *Cynthia's Revels* and *Poetaser* were written for the Chapel Children; *Jack Drum's Entertainment* and *What You Will* were written for Paul's Boys. *Histriomastix* has been attributed to Paul's Boys, but was more probably written for the Middle Temple (see Philips J. Finkelpearl, 'John Marston's *Histriomastix* as an Inns of Court Play: A Hypothesis', *Huntington Library Quarterly*, 29 (1966), 223–34), while Dekker's *Satiromastix* was performed by both Paul's Boys and the Chamberlain's Men. As excellent short narrative of the 'War', explaining the personal allusions encrypted in the plays, is Cyrus Hoy's account in *Introductions, Notes, and Commentaries to Texts in 'The Dramatic Works of Thomas Dekker'*, edited by Fredson Bowers, vol. 1 (Cambridge: Cambridge University Press, 1980), 179–97. Although this affectation is particularly conspicuous in plays performed around the turn of the century, it is in evidence occasionally before that date. Shakespeare's *Love's Labours Lost* (c. 1595) may

well have been a trigger for the burgeoning interest in fashionable language in subsequent plays.

3   All quotations from Jonson's plays are taken from *Ben Jonson*, eds C.H. Herford and Percy Simpson, 12 vols (Oxford: Clarendon Press, 1925–52).

4   *Ben Jonson* (Oxford: Blackwell, 1986), 101.

5   The term 'commodity' was itself undergoing a change in use during this period. Initially used to mean any kind of good or benefit, including abstract benefit, it was coming to refer more frequently to material objects; see Douglas Bruster, *Drama and the Market in the Age of Shakespeare* (Cambridge: Cambridge University Press, 1992), 41.

6   Jean-Christophe Agnew, *Worlds Apart: The Market and the Theatre in Anglo-American Thought 1550–1750* (Cambridge: Cambridge University Press, 1986), 59, 98, 14.

7   Walter Benjamin, *Charles Baudelaire: A Lyric Poet in the Era of High Capitalism*, trans. Harry Zohn (London: NLB, 1973), 36–7. Benjamin is quoting a guide to Paris from 1852. The term '*flâneur*' is appropriated by Benjamin from Baudelaire, but developed by Benjamin in directions sometimes at odds with Beaudelaire's own brief pronouncements (see further note 17 below).

8   Benjamin, *Charles Baudelaire*, 37.

9   John Rignall, 'Benjamin's *Flâneur* and the Problem of Realism', in *The Problem of Modernity*, ed. Andrew Benjamin (London: Routledge, 1989), 113, 112.

10 Chris Jenks, 'Watching Your Step: The History and Practice of the *Flâneur*' in *Visual Culture*, ed. Chris Jenks (London: Routledge, 1995), 148.

11 Benjamin, *Charles Baudelaire*, 54.

12 Terry Eagleton, *Walter Benjamin, or Towards a Revolutionary Criticism* (London and New York: Verso, 1981), 26.

13 Pierre Maquerlot, *Shakespeare and the Mannerist Tradition: A Reading of Five Problem Plays* (Cambridge: Cambridge University Press, 1995), 26.

14 *Skialetheia, of A Shadowe of Truth, in Certaine Epigrams and Satyres*, ed. E. Allen Carroll (Chapel Hill: University of North Carolina Press, 1974), 86.

15 *The Gull's Hornbook*, in *The Wonderful Year, The Gull's Hornbook, Penny-Wise, Pound-Foolish, English Villainies Discovered by Lantern and Candlelight and Selected Writings*, ed. E.D. Pendry (London: Edward Arnold, 1967), 109, 96.

16. Benjamin, *Charles Baudelaire*, 57–66. 'Hugo', Benjamin concludes, 'placed himself in the crowd as a *citoyen*; Baudelaire sundered himself from it as a hero' (66).
17. Benjamin, *Charles Baudelaire*, 54–5. The ambivalence surrounding the *flâneur's* relation to the crowd seems to arise partly out of Benjamin's misreading of Baudelaire's interpretation of Poe's story, 'The Man of the Crowd' (see Rignall, 116–21).
18. See, for example, Quadratus's dry response to Lampatho Doria's denial of the charge of railing in *What You Will*: ''tis now grown fashion; / What's out of railing's out of fashion' (2.1.580–81). And though Lampatho Doria denies the charge here, he acknowledges the fashionability of railing later in the play:

> This is the strain that chokes the theatres,
> That makes them crack with full-stuff'd audience.
> This is your humour only in request,
> Forsooth to rail; this brings your ears to bed,
> This people gape for; for this some do stare;
> This some would hear, to crack the author's neck;
> This admiration and applause pursues. .
> Who cannot rail? (3.2.1142–9)

Quotations are taken from M.R. Woodhead's edition of the play for Nottingham Drama Texts (Nottingham: Nottingham University Press, 1980).
19. *Ben Jonson, Dramatist* (Cambridge: Cambridge University Press, 1984), 65, 70.
20. *The Poems of John Marston*, ed. Arnold Davenport (Liverpool: Liverpool University Press, 1961), Satire 11, lines 43–5. I owe the reference to these lines to a note by Reavley Gair in his edition of *Antonio's Revenge* (Manchester: Manchester University Press; Baltimore: Johns Hopkins University Press, 1978: note to 1.3.22).
21. Jonson had already drawn attention to the word 'capricious' in *The Case is Altered* (2.7.74–83). When Valentine first makes reference to 'a few caprichious gallants', Juniper interjects to note the word as object ('Caprichious? stay, that word's for me') before allowing Valentine to continue with his disapproval of such types, who, he says, find fault with everything (the word is highlighted by italics in the 1609 Quarto text). Herford and Simpson note the reappearance of the word amongst those isolated for scorn in Dekker and Chettle's attack in *Patient Grissel* (1600) on those writers who 'chew between their teeth terrible words, as though they would conjure'.
22. Agnew, *Worlds Apart*, 11.

23 The quotation is cited from H. Harvey Wood's edition of Marston's plays (3 vols (Edinburgh and London: Oliver and Boyd, 1934–9)), which has no line numbers.
24 Though the primary, physiological sense of the word points to the essential interior make-up of the person, it was also in fashionable use to denote affectation, whimsicality, or grotesquely caricatured behaviour. A 'humour', then, can be 'a quality of air or water' specific to the individual human body; by extension it can be the mere pretence of such possession, so that 'if an idiot / Have but an apish, or fantastic strain, / It is his humour'. (Quotations are taken from Jonson's classic exposition of humours in the Induction to *Every Man Out of His Humour*.)
25 The phrase is part of Jonson's description of Puntarvolo in the list of *dramatis personae* preceding *Every Man Out of His Humour*.

CHAPTER 11

The Italian Job: The Poetics of Graced Performance in the Commedia dell'Arte and in Jonson's Humour Plays

Rocco Coronato

Then you have derision, which you can make by corrugating your nose, twisting your mouth or showing your teeth ... or also by lifting up the middle finger and uniting all the others together, which is highly vituperative (Andrea Perrucci, *Dell'Arte Rappresentativa*).

To lovers of soccer and Renaissance drama, the recent flow of Italian football players into British Premiere League may seem to have renewed the controversial encounter between refined acting and vigorous carriage already ignited by the arrival of the Commedia dell'Arte in England. Although any direct influence on Elizabethan drama may be soundly dismissed, the relevance of the Commedia dell'Arte to our appreciation of the figure of the modern actor and of the acting job itself is hardly questioned.[1] However, it has been a zany sort of survival. In fact, the Commedia dell'Arte has not still recovered from its mythical reduction to a grotesque bunch of masks, replete with a set of conventional speeches.

Part of the problem is that such influence has been mainly assessed by studying the extant *scenari* and their cursory similarities with Elizabethan plots, not infrequently with a malicious emphasis on the description of acting vices, rather than trusting the self-portrait provided by the actors themselves. Acting was in fact associated to the correct performing of the rhetorical virtues of the orator.[2] It purported to be a sort of absolutely orthodox body-talk, which could be conveyed even through manual gesture, 'whose language is as easily perceived and understood as if man had another mouth or fountain of discourse in his hand'.[3] In this sense Thomas Wright refers to the 'discovery' of passions by external actions, 'for indeede, words & actions spring from the same roote, that is, vnderstanding and affections'.[4] One may expect then all acting rules duly to espouse the rhetorical tradition of composure and the doctrine of the imitation of passions in both the Commedia dell'Arte and Elizabethan acting.[5] Yet one problem with the latter is that its consideration is impaired by the abundance of disparaging comments on contemporary theatrical practice and, conversely, a lack of additional comparative evidence.[6] Elizabethan acting can be hardly recovered through the commonplace descriptions of acting defects.[7]

I would like then to explore the possibility of a literal sort of 'interacting' comparison. The testimonies actually left by some Italian actors, beyond their obviously apologetic aura, reveal a sort of dignified awareness of the acting role together with a practical description of how to translate this grace into theatrical actions. Thus, the concept of grace was distinctly propelled back to its religious root, underlining the intervention of an almost divine redemption of the body and the actions of the actor. Resting on the actual treatises written by some of the most prominent Italian actors,[8] it is my purpose to try to decode such sort of grace and compare it with the comic performance exemplified by Jonson's parody of Italianate *grazia* in his humour plays.

Thomas Coryate was probably one of the few to praise the 'admirable volubility and plausible grace, even extempore' displayed by the mountebanks he saw in Venice.[9] Together with distorting their visages and bodies, in fact, the *buffoni* provided the touchstone of diabolic dexterity, as well as of obnoxious imitation, to both Italian antitheatrical polemicists and refined actors. The further end of this realistic continuum was occupied by the *attarantati,* a sort of amateur actor who counterfeited the violent effects of the tarantula's bite in their writhing bodies. But the diatribe did not invest only in such monsters. Meaning to play down the skills of all actors, Tommaso Garzoni first mentions their ability to imitate the distorted features of a blind or a hanged man. Then he reviles the overwhelming presence of excellent imitation, criticizing what could be otherwise considered the signs of perfect theatrical carriage. In their replies, actors detect the main faults of popular acting in the repetition of stock gestures and speeches, dismissing the parrot-like imitation that goes unaccompanied by intimate knowledge. Accordingly, the difference between the *buffone* and the *attore* is that only the latter can counterfeit the former – the *buffone* is, while the *attore* pretends. Such distaste for sheer imitation may be detected in Andrea Perrucci's taxonomy of ridiculous actions. Actors can make people laugh when they directly represent moral and corporal vices through the imitation of hunchbacked, lame or defective servants; by means of similitude when they imitate the foreigners, the lunatics or the drunk; by means of derision (*dispregio*), carried out through rude gestures and, finally, by means of verbal indecency or rusticity. These actions of monstrous imitation, marked by a continuous flow of jibing ripostes, are polemically opposed to the actors' interpretation of laughter as the didactic end of comedy. The adroit sort of laughter is aroused not just by a disproportionate speech or gesture, but by a carefully studied representation of the same.[10]

Talking about graced comic performance, actors stray into sanctity.[11] Another defect which can be blamed to the buffoon is his lack of virtue, a term which the pious actors took in an almost religious sense. Their portrait of the good actor overlaps with the refined gentleman and, more generally, with the accomplished Christian man living in a world of vulgarity and profanity, a sort of perfect being that knows all deft gestures and lines in advance and lavishes all the talents he has received from heaven and nature. One practical reason for insisting on the religious orthodoxy of skilled acting was that the printed texts were destined to (and revised by) religious censors. The actors are not ashamed to report the stories of actors-saints, or of actors on whose death-bed a cilice was promptly discovered, secretly playing on the lexical ambiguity of *recitare*, the Italian word for acting, which also means saying one's prayers. They prudently report to be habitual churchgoers and to observe at least a fasting day during the week. Acting itself falls short of shrift, as all human sins are represented, that is, reported to the audience as in a confession and accordingly shunned. These religious overtones are however to be found also in the less self-interested accounts coming from the antitheatrical writers. Garzoni refers to the sort of wonder aroused by the *grazia* and *gentile discorrere* of the skilled actor, and also mentions the famous Isabella Andreini, a living handbook of theatrical art, who boasted a perfect decorum in her proportioned gestures, harmonic movements and dignified bearing. Within this framework of virtuous acting, even the Protean ability to transform one's body according to the varying moods, usually censored in the buffoons, may be redeemed as yet another token of theatrical excellence.[12] Grace must then have provided the choicest term to define the physical aura of perfection that only the accomplished Italian actor was able to emanate.

Grace is a distinctive quality even amongst the actors, as the most talented can move to laughter merely by their appearance on stage or their performance of trivial gestures. If Nicolò Barbieri seems to opt for a restricted election, Perrucci argues for a slightly enlarged redemption. Proudly conscious of the founding comparison between acting and oratorical eloquence, he defends the *arte rappresentativa* as an opportunity for refining the gentleman, a school for learning the right doctrine of good speaking, gesturing and having decorous social intercourse. He conversely argues that the comic parts should be assigned to those who received this grace from heaven, since well-timed gestures and movements will infallibly move to laughter if accompanied by decency. Finally, coping with the question whether the prominence must be assigned to grace or to knowledge, he revamps the Catholic compromise between grace and deeds. Grace is a special gift from above, a smashing letter of reference; but if it is not refined by art, it will remain like an uncultivated tree: it is art that can prevail over nature, not the other way round. Only the graced comedians can dispense with such training, as they are helped by natural grace or by readiness of wit.[13]

The actors' interpretation of grace also redeems imitation and laughter from their dangerous contiguity with the marketplace. A novel stress is ultimately laid on the acting profession, qualifying what could have otherwise seemed a clear-cut opposition between the monstrous incongruity of the buffoon and the proportioned grace of the actor. Perrucci argues that all ridiculous actions generally consist in blunders, deformities or counterfeited visages. Only if represented with masking and grace can these comical ingredients be converted from compassion into laughter. Despite the precept against close imitation, the ultimate theatrical ridiculous derives from the graced rendition of all types of blunder and disproportion, where the ridiculous gesture, being perceived as utterly natural, becomes a telling picture of the vices that are being emended through representation. Then grace imposes a redeeming sign on buffoonish actions too. The audience will be legitimized to laugh even at a Zane displaying his counterfeited visage, making ridiculous gestures as ambling in the pose of a knight, saluting with his hat or even acting as a grotesque king.[14]

From a more practical standpoint, the physical expression of such grace sees these accomplished actors resort to chastened language and prudent gestures. Acting grace is vividly translated by Perrucci into the ideal of physical firmness (*essere sodo*), thus graphically portraying the redeemed body of the graced actor. Similarly, Pier Maria Cecchini reports that as gesture is the spirit that informs the body of narrating, it has to diverge from the affectation of those actors who roll their eyes, stir their arms and utterly discompose their bodies to the point of making the spectacle of a person suffering from a colic less disturbing. Gestures must reveal the intimate emotion (*l'affetto interno*). Thus the 'naked' gesture, being an affection coming from the soul, must precede the tongue in its expression, as for example when the tongue says 'sky', the eye must immediately point at it. Just like any other public speaker, the actor must boast his whole body as a speaking, ordered part of his oration: head, arms, feet and eyes will move in time, with method, order and sense of measure.

As for the voice, the pronunciation must be so softened as to convey the concept to the audience in a gentle style (*istile amabile*). Still, natural graces can be compensated with art, provided that the actor's voice be proportioned to the task of giving satisfaction to his audience. Finally, words and actions are to be generated as synchronic twins: the voice will be followed by gestures, but they both must come out and be united in time, with the gesture obeying the voice, so that any superfluous element is ruled out.[15]

The grace of the *attori* is ultimately made of rules of containment and refinement that can be translated in practical precepts and conventional actions. Some of them are directly described, thus giving us an idea of their possible performance. Grace is extended to even the smallest particles of acting, such as saluting with one's hat: one has to begin by the gesture of the head, taking off one's hat with grace and nobility, together with the type of reverence dictated by the character and his country of origin. A general sense of mediocrity is extended to all the parts of the body, consciously evoking the refined posture of the fencer. The eyebrows are 'vicious' when they keep still or move too much, and can be corrugated to signify wonder, but without abandoning decency or becoming signs of foolery; the nose and the lips are not to be twisted, but have to stay firm, moving in due order and time; the neck has to stay stiff and upright, in order to help release a smooth flow of voice; raising up or lowering down the arms become the Zani; the hands must not raise any higher than the eyes, nor, when they lower down, are they to touch the breast; the right hand must not touch the right arm, and the left hand has to move synchronically with the other one; finally, the actor must display his waist upright with modest gravity and no sense of haughtiness: at the beginning of his speech he will put the right foot ahead, as if he were about to play a fencing bout. In a word, the actor has to be 'physically' modest, differing from those comedians that, like *attarantati*, shake their heads, roll their eyes and make gestures with all their limbs. In Perrucci's final portrait the graced actor will always respect physical firmness, without jumping all about on the stage, making demented actions or superfluous, incomplete gestures or looking for buttocks to pinch (sic).[16]

Arguably, the English stage had its own quota of imperfect actors looking for buttocks to pinch, so that it need not look at the *attori* for polemical inspiration. It may also be that Perrucci's theorizing, though consistent with earlier testimonies such as the works by Pier Maria Cecchini and Giambattista Andreini, was partly influenced by a much more didactic, refined type of acting that corresponded to late seventeenth-century fashion. Still, it is indeed revealing to approach Jonson's humour plays from the theorizing framework I have tried to suggest and find some arguable hints of direct parody and reinterpretation of the Italian grace. Rather than reiterating the elaborated discussion on the theory and practice of humour,[17] it is indeed possible to propose a typological approach to the acting roles of the humour plays as seen through the Italian perspective of grace and nature.

Every Man in His Humour seems to consist in a general rehearsal, where the most humorous characters are unflinchingly drilled into practising the part of the boasting soldier. If we had to pick a peculiar scene (Perrucci's *azione apparente*) that conveys this rehearsal principle, that would be the act of drawing one's sword up to the climax when 'they all draw' (Q: 3.4.135).[18] The role of the *miles vanagloriosus* is however divided into several constituents, each reflecting a debatable union of grace and nature.

Stephano and Matheo are, accordingly, the practising actors that try to imitate the external action of the accomplished soldier. Lorenzo Senior's reproaches of Stephano apparently pertain to the celebration of the sober style of acting we have seen in the Italians: 'Let not your carriage and behavior taste of affectation ... lay by such superficial forms, and entertain a perfect real substance' (Q: 1.1.68–9; 74–5). He should be comparable to an oncoming gentleman who, confronting him, 'contains himself / In modest limits', whereas Stephano's 'kind of carriage' is as 'void of wit as of humanity' (F: 1.1.120). But Lorenzo Junior remarks that Stephano is *per se* ridiculous because of his pretence to enact the ridiculous role of the soldier. His mock-encomium, praising such 'a man so grac'd, gilded, or rather ... tin-foil'd by nature', actually portrays this gullible modesty through the predictable transparency of the excellent actor:

> Come, wrong not the quality of your desert with looking downward, coz; but hold up your head, so; and let the idea of what you are be portray'd i' your face, that men may read i' your physnomy: 'Here, within this place, is to be seen the true, rare, and accomplish'd monster, or miracle of nature'. (F: 1.2.104–9)

Whereas both Stephano and Matheo desperately try to acquire grace by parroting outward actions, Bobadilla embodies the accomplished actor, whose grace is marked by a sort of modest melancholy. He strives 'not [to] be so popular and general as some are' (Q: 1.3.114–15). Indeed, the rules he willingly imparts to Matheo uncannily evoke the actorial grace under the reductive disguise of the fencing skills:

twine your body more about, that you may come to a more sweet, comely, gentlemanlike guard. So, indifferent. Hollow your body more, sir, thus. Now, stand fast on your left leg, note your distance, keep your due proportion of time – oh, you disorder your point most vilely! ... Why, you do not manage your weapons with that facility and grace that you should do. (Q: 1.3.190–95, 205–6)

This excellent actor, talented with sophisticated, albeit denatured grace, proudly asks to be perused in his ability to swear, his distaste for prolixity and his physical grace that is lost on Matheo: 'you do not give spirit enough to your motion; you are too dull, too tardy. Oh, it must be done like lightning, *hay!*' (Q: 4.2.10–11). Bobadilla also boasts his familiarity with Italian grace, as he saw in Venice 'your *Nobilis*, your *Gentilezza,* come in bravely upon your reverse, stand you close, stand you firm, stand you fair, save your *retricato* with his left leg, come to the *assalto* with the right, thrust with brave steel, defy your base wood!' (Q: 4.4. 9–13). Part of his ludicrous aspect can be obviously interpreted by means of the disproportion between such boasting and his defeat at the hands of the choleric Giuliano, who is devoted to a more violent, sudden type of acting. But contemporary comic performance must have gained momentum also from his 'inter-acting' display of Italianate grace. Babbling about his acting skills, Bobadilla translates positive terms as balance, spirit and distance into denatured accomplishments.

The point is made clearer by Musco, the third component of the boasting soldier. He consciously counterfeits not just the real type, but the acting role, which he translates into would-be tokens of grace within his 'borrowed shape': 'now must I create an intolerable sort of lies, or else my profession loses his grace ... I must practice to get the true garb of one of these lance-knights' (Q: 2.1.2–4, 17–18). He is equally conscious of the verbal quality required by his part, for instance when he boasts about his campaigns 'in all the provinces of Bohemia, Hungaria, Dalmatia, Poland' (Q: 2.1.55–6), as well as of the exterior tricks he readily dismisses when shifting to another role: 'this brass varnish being wash'd off, and three or four other tricks sublated, I appear yours in reversion' (Q: 2.3.187–8). After imitating the 'fine, easy amble' of decayed gentlemen, he has approached the testing case of any acting grace:

Into the likeness of one of these lean Pirgos had he moulded himself so perfectly, observing every trick of their action, as varying the accent, swearing with an emphasis, indeed all, with so speciall and exquisite a grace. (Q: 3.2.13–17)

He is comical, then, in so much as he has translated acting skills into telling signs of theatricality. As in Bobadilla, the tokens of Italianate refinement are decoded as grace devoid of nature. However, he is aware of having usurped all these acting roles until fulfilling his identity:

> Well, of all my disguises yet, now am I most like myself, being in this varlet's suit. A man of my present profession never counterfeits, till he lay hold upon a debtor and says he rests him, for then he brings him to all manner of unrest. (Q: 5.2.1–4)

Obviously, the play is an indictment against 'self-love and affectation', especially if 'fed by folly' (Q: 3.1.147–8), and other more innocuous humours as the wantonness of unbridled youth. But the triad of characters respectively impersonating the would-be graced, the too graced actor, and the in-and-out of grace actor, may suggest that, from the standpoint of comic performance, this purgation of humours could have taken place in an inverted portrayal of Italianate acting grace. This suggests that for Jonson true grace can be reached by increasingly depriving the acting self of its ready-made, if consciously refined, technique, ultimately advocating natural grace instead of graced nature.

As for *Every Man Out of His Humour*,[19] the actorial ratio may be interpreted according to the recurring figure of the courtier, a mere compound of the conventional fawner and the Italian *innamorato*. But whereas the grace of the *attori* playing the roles of the effete courtier is detected in the extent to which they stick to the convention without exaggerating, as their masks are already grotesque, Jonson's characters underline the theatricality of the trick without ever getting to the actual beginning of the performance. Their true performance consists in their training to acquire grace.

Carlo and Macilente instruct all the other characters by means of downgrading otherwise positive skills – thus the precepts imparted by Carlo to Sogliardo mock the sanctimonious, 'graced' impersonation of the gentleman:

> you must observe all the rare qualities, humours, and complements of a gentleman ... be sure, you mixe your selfe stil, with such as flourish in the spring of the fashion, and are least popular; studie their carriage, and behaviour in all ... You must endeuour to feede cleanly at your Ordinarie, sit melancholy, and picke your teeth when you cannot speake ... That's a speciall grace you must obserue. (1.2. 21–3, 43–5, 55–7, 60–61)

Far from being a buffoonish performance, this lecture means to aggravate the comic transparency of the character by twisting the refined skills of the Italian school of acting. Actors, not the real types, are being imitated through the exposure of their conventional acting. In a sense they are always *before* the part, stuck in the realm of unnatural grace.

Puntaruolo, then, is the actor too much in the part, going through all the practical steps of his dignified role as lover. His embodiment of the enamoured knight smacks of too much grace, as for instance in his manner to accost his own wife: 'I will step forward three pases: of the which, I will barely retire one; and (after some little flexure of the knee) with an erected grace salute her (one, two, and three)' (2.2.10–12). He even anatomizes the different components of the action ('the *superficies,* is that we call, place; the *puntilio's,* circumstance; and the *gnomon,* ceremony') in order to become a perfect stranger and stage that 'designement of his owne, a thing studied, and rehearst as ordinarily' (2.2.35–6). A great part of the trick lies on exaggeration, as shown by his stiff, upright way of walking. But the abusing jargon is derived from the handbook of the perfect actor, with which Puntaruolo also seems to be familiar in other everyday situations: 'Stand by, retire your selues a space: nay, pray you, forget not the vse of your hat; the aire is piercing' (2.3.20–21).

Another similar actor is Fastidious Briske, the courtier who explicitly browses through the instructions of the Italian school of grace:

> doe you know how to goe into the presence, sir? ... You must first haue an especial care so to weare your hat, that it oppresse not confusedly this your predominant, or fore-top; because ... you may, with once or twice stroking vp your fore-head thus, enter, with your predominant effect: that is, standing vp stiffe. (3.3.5–11)

He is the acknowledged master of courtship, as the hardly reliable Fallace remarks: 'How comely he bowes him in his court'sie! How full hee hits a woman betweene the lips when hee kisses! How vpright hee sits at the table! How daintily he carues! How sweetly he talkes' (4.1.34–7). The satirical usage of positive acting skills as signs of foppery resorts again to the equivocal conception of grace, as Macilente notes that this accomplished performance has not been well received ('grac't') by the true gentlemen:

> they should shew the frothie foole,
> Such grace, as they pretend comes from the heart,
> He had a mightie wind-fall out of doubt.

> Why, all their Graces are not to doe grace
> To vertue, or desert. (4.4.81–5)

The graced actor will then show his defect by separating acting art from nature. The return of Sogliardo on the scene is marked by a final set of instructions, as if the whole play were intended to be a continuous rehearsal. Macilente instructs this actor who is continuously *before* grace to mistake the refined act of courtship as a symbol of foppery:

> be sure to kisse your hand often inough; pray for her health, and tell her, how *more then most faire* she is. Screw your face at' one side thus, and protest; let her fleere, and looke a skaunce, and hide her teeth with her fanne, when she laughs a fit, to bring her into more matter, that's nothing: you must talke forward. (5.1.53–9)

There is no need to think only of a disgraced actor that undermines perfect acting with some awkward malapropos. He could legitimately be a good actor in a denatured context. Laughter then derives from a more serious, ontological type of disproportion, namely, the divergence betwixt nature and the sort of Italianate acting which is constantly praised by Puntaruolo: Sogliardo 'speakes the languages with that puritie of phrase, and facilitie of accent, that it breeds astonishment: his wit, the most exuberant, and (aboue wonder) pleasant ... hee doth so peerelessely imitate any manner of person for gesture, action, passion, or whateuer' (5.1.28–31, 40–42).

Consistently with this contention between nature and art, the play offers other examples of severing imagery. Sogliardo and Shift are dubbed '*Countenance and Resolution*' (4.5.67); the latter stands also for the volatile mutability of too graced actor: 'he has so varied himselfe, that if any one of 'hem take, he may hull vp and downe i' the humorous world, a little longer' (2.6.195). Also Orange and Glove are recognisable through their tags and catch-phrases: 'nothing, but *Salutation*; and, *O god, sir;* and, *it pleases you to say so, Sir;* one that can laugh at a iest for company with a most plausible, and extemporall grace; and some houre after, in priuate, aske you what it was' (3.1.24–8).

More generally, the concept of grace is exposed as utterly devoid of nature even in its most refined acting embodiments. The logical progression of acting leads to the end of close mimesis. Fungoso, finally redeemed of his humour, proclaims to 'haue done imitating any more gallants either in purse or apparell, but as shall become a gentleman, for good carriage, or so' (5.9.3–5). But we could also take the humour as an acting ratio that decidedly heads for violent, graphic depiction of nature despite the refinements of the Italian school of acting. This becomes apparent in the scene where Sordido tries to hang himself, an uncanny flashback to the Italian distaste for the buffoons and their grotesque actions. He violently reacts against the *rustici* that have come to save him as if he were possessed by 'some desperate furie'. But then he accomplishes his true conversion through a distorted, grotesque type of acting marked by weeping:

> Sordid. I am by wonder chang'd; come in with me
> And witnesse my repentance: now I proue,
> 'No life is blest, that is not grac't with loue.
> Rvst. 2. O miracle! see when a man ha's grace! (3.8.55–8)

The typical spectacle staged by the *attarantati* saw a *guidone* (the leading man) escort his shaking fellow, who was bound with two long iron chains. A great concourse of people flocked to see such amateurish acting, made up of much grinning, bubbling, staring and shaking, despite the *guidone*'s false bit of advice against contagion.[20] In a sense, the Italian school of graced acting consciously fenced off the similar type of contagion coming from naturalistic imitation. To the eyes of these early modern actors, grace was a commodity signifying the duty both to refine their gestures and words and to redeem their natural actions from buffoonish laughter. On the other hand, the Jonsonian parody of such graced acting seems to suggest that his comical characters were not intended to be afraid of such contagion. His characters are meant to be ridiculous insofar as they are set in a denatured context, rather than in their fictional inadequacy to perform their respective roles. Jonson's ultimate idea of the comic was not very humorous, after all: it functions as a disproportion between natural and Italianate grace, rather than between the imaginary essence of the character and his shortcomings. Jonson's humour plays seem thus to be ridiculing not just the excesses of the Commedia dell'Arte, but its best parts. If there was indeed a grace within the acting role, it was probably a fruitful kind of contagion that could lead contemporary audiences to laugh at these actors always auditioning for the roles and, at the same time, to praise the natural acting which did not require any training skills or quasi-religious theorizing.

Notes

[1] The best study of this topic remains K.M. Lea, *Italian Popular Comedy. A Study in the Commedia dell'Arte, 1560–1620. With Special Reference to the English Stage*. New York: Russell and Russell, 1962,

especially vol. 1, 355–7, 411–12, 453. Cf. also S. Ferrone, 'Dalle parti "scannate" al testo scritto. La commedia dell'arte all'inizio del secolo XVII', *Paragone* 34.398 (1983), 38–68; D. Pietropaolo, *The Science of Buffoonery: Theory and History of the Commedia dell'Arte* (Ottawa, 1989); S. Ferrone, *Attori Mercanti Corsari: La Commedia dell'Arte in Europa tra Cinque e Seicento* (Turin: Einaudi, 1993).

2   This rule even applied to the single gestures, as is apparent in the translation of Quintilian's oratorical virtues into different gestures and related meanings made by Giovanni Bonifaccio, *L'Arte de' Cenni* (Vicenza, 1616), 548f. The rhetorical tradition of *actio* was fully expounded by Abraham Fraunce in his description of utterance as 'a fit deliuering of the speach alreadie beautified' by the rhetorical figures of speech, in *The Arcadian Rhetoric* (London, 1588), sig. H6v.

3   John Bulwer, *Chirologia: or the Natural Language of the Hand* [1644], ed. James W. Cleary (Carbondale: Southern Illinois University Press, 1974), 15.

4   Thomas Wright, *The Passions of the Minde* (London: 1601), 196.

5   The common heritage of classical *actio* is made evident by Abraham Fraunce: 'The gesture must followe the change and varietie of the voyce, answering thereunto in euerie respect: yet not parasiticallie as stage plaiers vse, but grauelie and decentlie as becommeth men of greater calling. Let the bodie therefore with a manlike and graue motion of his sides rather followe the sentence that expresse euerie particular word. Stand vpright and straight as nature hath appoynted: much wauering and ouercurious and nice motion is verie ridiculous' (*The Arcadian Rhetoric*, sig. I7v).

6   The point is convincingly made by Lise-Lone Masker, 'Nature and Decorum in the Theory of Elizabethan Acting', in *The Elizabethan Theatre II*, ed. D. Galloway (London, MacMillan, 1970), 87–107, especially 94–5. In a shrewd remark, Daniel Seltzer says that 'the paucity of detailed information about acting styles points to the truth of the matter: such observations would hardly have informed Londoners of anything they did not know already' ('The Actors and Staging', in *A New Companion to Shakespeare Studies*, eds Kenneth Muir and S. Schoenbaum (Cambridge: Cambridge University Press, 1971), 35). On the notorious difficulty of describing Elizabethan acting, and the questions of decorum and apprenticeship, see Michael Hattaway, 'Acting Styles', in *Elizabethan Popular Theatre: Plays in Performance* (London: Routledge and Kegan Paul, 1982), 72–9. For the studies on contemporary acting, see for instance A.J. Downer, 'Prolegomenon to a Study of Elizabethan Acting', *Maske und Kothurn* 10 (1964), 625–36; B.L. Joseph, *Elizabethan Acting* (New York:

Octagon Books, 1964); Muriel C. Bradbrook, 'The Triple Bond: Audience, Actors, Author in the Elizabethan Playhouse', in Joseph G. Price, ed., *The Triple Bond: Plays, Mainly Shakespearean, in Performance* (University Park: Pennsylvania State University Press 1975, 50–69; M. Clermont, 'L'acteur et son jeu au XVIIe siècle', *Revue d'Histoire du Théâtre* 33.4 (1981), 379–88.

[7] See B.L. Joseph, 'Acting and Rhetoric', in *Elizabethan Acting* (Oxford: Oxford University Press, 1951), 1–18. The dependence of acting on rhetoric is described as a progressive shift along the emphasis laid on passion, character and grace in Jane Donaworth, 'Shakespeare and Acting Theory in the English Renaissance', in *Shakespeare and the Arts*, eds Cecile Williamson Cary and Henry S. Limouze (Washington DC: University Press of America, 1982), 165–78.

[8] It is fairly safe to assume that, even though some of these treatises were written in the second half of the century (Perrucci's, for example, was published in 1699), the type of acting rules seem to refer to the customary early seventeenth-century practice of the most famous Italian companies: see C. Jannaco, 'Stesura e tendenze letterarie della commedia improvvisa in due prologhi di Flaminio Scala', *Studi Teatrali* 1 (1960), 199; D. Gambelli, '"Quasi un recamo de concertate pezzette": le composizioni sul comico dell'Arlecchino Biancolelli', *Biblioteca Teatrale* 1 (1971), 47–95; L.G. Clubb, 'The State of the Arte in the Andreini's Time', in G.P. Biasin, ed., *Studies in the Italian Renaissance* (Naples: Societa Editrice Napolentena, 1985), 263–81; R.L. Erenstaein, 'The Humour of the Commedia dell'Arte', in C. Cairns, ed., *The Commedia dell'Arte from the Renaissance to Dario Fo* (Lewiston: Mellon, 1988), 118–40; A. Cerbo, 'Ragioni e virtù del comico (G.B. Andreini)', *Annali dell'Istituto Universitario Orientale di Napoli*, 33.2 (1991); S. Ferrone, *Attori Mercanti Corsari*, 199f. Richard Andrews, 'Scripted Theatre and the Commedia dell'Arte', in *Theatre of the English and Italian Renaissance*, ed. J.R. Mulryne (London: Macmillan, 1991), 21–54.

[9] Thomas Coryate, *Crudities* (London, 1611), 273.

[10] See T. Garzoni, *La Piazza Universale delle Professioni del Mondo* (Venice, 1587), 815–16; Andrea Perrucci, *Dell'Arte Rappresentativa Premeditata, ed all'improvviso* (Naples, 1699), 81, 310; Nicolò Barbieri, *La Supplica. Discorso Famigliare Intorno a Quelli che Trattano de' Comici* (1634), ed. F. Taviani (Milan: Il Polifilo, 1971), 22–3.

[11] Jane Donaworth notes that the ideal of grace, originated with classical rhetoricians, was adapted by Heywood to the special ends of acting,

thus combining 'convincing portrayal of character, and idealized symbolic gesture' (173–4).

[12] See Nicolò Barbieri, *La Supplica*, pp. 26–8, 35–7, 110; G.B. Andreini, *Teatro Celeste,* in V. Pandolfi, *La Commedia dell'Arte*, vol. 3 (Florence: Sansoni, 1957), 342–53; Tommaso Garzoni, *La Piazza Universale*, 737–8; 'Orazione d'Adriano Valerini Veronese in Morte della Divina Signora Vincenza Armani, Comica Eccellentissima' (Verona, s.d.), in V. Pandolfi, *La Commedia dell'Arte,* vol. 2, 147–8.

[13] Barbieri, 34; Perrucci, 17, 83–4, 109. Cecchini also refers to the natural instinct of learned persons, equally awarded with good manners and a desire for virtuous acting (Pier Maria Cecchini, 'Discorso Sopra l'Arte Comica con il Modo di Ben Recitare', in V. Pandolfi, *La Commedia dell'Arte,* vol. 4, 84).

[14] Perrucci, 340–41.

[15] Barbieri, 116; Pier Maria Cecchini, *Frutti delle Moderne Comedie, et Avisi a chi le Recita* (Padua: 1628), 16; Pier Maria Cecchini, Discorso Sopra l'Arte Comica, 84–7; Perrucci, 112.

[16] Perrucci, 112–23. Cf. the precepts given by Saviolo, a famous Italian fencer, on the teaching of the ward: the body of the learner must 'rest more vpon the lefte legge, not steadfast and firme as some stand, which seeme to be nayled to the place, but with a readiness and nimblenes, as though he were to performe some feate of actiuitie' (*Vincentio Saviolo His Practise* (London: 1595), sig. 8v).

[17] Classical interpretations of the humour plays are: Jonas A. Barish, 'Rhetoric's Tinkling Bell', in *Ben Jonson and the Language of Prose Comedy* (Cambridge, Mass.: Harvard University Press: 1960), 98–113; B. Millard and D.H. Brock, 'Jonson's Humour Plays and the Dramatic Adaptation of Pastoral', *English Miscellaney* 16 (1965), 125–55; Alan C. Dessen, 'Jonson and the Morality Tradition: The Early Plays', in *Jonson's Moral Comedy* (Evaston, IL: Northwestern University Press: 1971), 44–54; R. Shenk, 'The Habits and Ben Jonson's Humours', *The Journal of Medieval and Renaissance Studies*, 8.1 (1978), 115–36.

[18] For ease of reference, all quotations come from J.W. Lever, ed., Ben Jonson, *Every Man in His Humour: A Parallel Text Edition of the 1601 Quarto and the 1616 Folio* (Lincoln and London: University of Nebraska Press, 1971), with the prefixes 'Q' and 'F' respectively referring to the Quarto and to the Folio texts.

[19] All quotations are from *Ben Jonson*, eds C.H. Herford, P. Simpson and E. Simpson, vol. 3 (Oxford: Clarendon Press, 1954).

[20] Raffaele Frianoro, 'Il Vagabondo' (1621), in *Il Libro dei Vagabondi*, ed. Piero Camporesi (Turin: Einaudi, 1973), 133–4.

CHAPTER 12

The True Physiognomy of a Man: Richard Tarlton and His Legend

Peter Thomson

The figure of Richard Tarlton, in book-designer's oval frame, decorates the front cover of the 1979 paperback re-issue of Muriel Bradbrook's *The Rise of the Common Player*.[1] It is taken from the sepia wash drawing in the Pepysian Library at Magdalene College, Cambridge. We do not know when and how the drawing came into Pepys's possession. It is a sanitized reworking of John Scottowe's resourceful miniature, set inside a capital 'T' to accompany some indifferent memorial verses.[2] The cast in the eye is less prominent, the squashed nose straightened, the face and body slimmed down. Most significant, though, is the minute adjustment of the mouth. Scottowe's Tarlton, standing on the flimsy whorls at the foot of his circular 'T' and penned in from behind and above by a trelliş and a triffid, contrives nonetheless to exult in his one-man-band virtuosity. The drumstick is firmly held, the gaze compels the viewer's attention and the lips are slightly pursed around the pipe that he is nonchalantly playing. Fleetingly (the impression varies as I contemplate the comedian imprisoned in his letter), Scottowel has captured the powerful presence of a man who does not so much invite as command laughter. Pepys's copyist has given Tarlton a looser hold on the drumstick and allowed the pipe to hang from smiling lips like the neglected cheroot of a chain-smoker. There is no puff in this mouth. It is as if this alternative Tarlton is watching us rather than demanding that we watch him. The smile is so kindly, the whole demeanour so gentle. The bullneck has gone and the right shoulder sunk, taking the barrel-chest with them. Compared with Scottowe's, this Tarlton is almost a stooge.

It is not as a stooge that Tarlton has descended from contemporary anecdotes into the adjudications of twentieth-century scholars, but his status and his impact remain matters of controversy. My supposition is that Tarlton is most familiar to students of Shakespeare worldwide as an editorial footnote to Yorick's skull, 'a fellow of infinite jest', the archetypal entertainer who could always 'set the table on a roar'.[3] There is a natural extension from that comfortable stereotype: Yorick's skull as *memento mori* translates into Tarlton as tragic clown. 'He was nobody out of his mirths', wrote Sir Roger Williams within two years of Tarlton's death.[4] That is to say that the composite literary sketch, for those whose concern for performative values is marginal, might be of a funny man whose public humour camouflaged private melancholy and whose time, however regrettably, has passed. Yorick, then, is Shakespeare's affectionate requiem to a jester who no longer matters. It is an incidental concern of this essay to counter so partial a view. My primary intention is threefold: first, to summarize four recent assessments of Tarlton, second, to re-examine his legend as it is preserved in the published book of *Tarlton's Jests*, and third, to investigate afresh Shakespeare's representation of the clown who died when Shakespeare was twenty-four years old.

Bradbrook's Tarlton, though certainly not a stooge, is, like the Magdalene College drawing, comparatively benign. She records his drunken act, 'a stock item with all clowns',[5] but not his drunkenness. She stresses his physical agility in popular 'feates of activity' and as a Master of Fence, but singles out an occasion (not wholly characteristic) when, at Norwich in June 1583, he intervened to dissipate a dangerous quarrel.[6] The chivalric model for such intervention between drawn swords is Romeo, but Bradbrook averts her gaze from the Tybalt in Tarlton. Most insistently, she presents him as a metropolitan 'Common Player of uncommon brilliance',[7] whose impact was such as to confirm the distinction between clowning and country pastime. This Tarlton is a clown who specializes in 'give-and-take with the audience',[8] a phrase which implies an allowance of equality contradicted by even those milder anecdotes which Bradbrook selects for mention. Her source-books are literary, or only marginally sub-literary, and she is inclined to discount the most extreme of the recorded jests, although stating, without cited evidence, that 'Tarlton hit out at both Papists and Puritans with more force than decency'.[9] Bradbrook prepares the way for her conclusion with the sort of sleight-of-hand to which all scholars are liable. 'The most revealing portrait of Tarlton', she writes, 'is Henry Chettle's', thus implying that it is not personal bias but cultural consensus that impels her judgement. '*Kind Heart's Dream* (1592)', she continues, 'provides the first printed vindication of popular pastime'.[10] Bradbrook's gist is that Tarlton was the champion of 'honest recreation'[11] against the killjoys of radical Protestantism and the hierarchically jealous established Church. This is a Tarlton who cannot claim to represent the spirit of agrarian festivity, but who propagates traditional irreverent humour in the urban environment: 'He was a household jester who also took the whole City for his home'.[12]

Robert Weimann[13] employs Tarlton in the service of a more coherent cultural project. His Tarlton is prominent among the irresistible forces that retarded the rejection of a popular tradition by the literary high culture of the Elizabethan renaissance. The 'first plebeian artist to achieve national recognition in England',[14] Tarlton was the ancestor of the Shakespearean clown (performed by his successor, Will Kemp) and the Shakespearean fool (developed by his pupil, Robert Armin). It was Tarlton who created the prototype out of a composite of 'the morality Vice and the outmoded court fool'.[15] As a master of riddle and word-play[16] and a parodist of legal and religious rhetoric,[17] Tarlton increased the range and enhanced the vocabulary of dramatic prose. Insofar as he 'completely secularized the Vice',[18] Tarlton gave popular impetus to the secularizing of drama. In his constant 'double-dealing with illusion and reality',[19] Tarlton helped to ensure that 'the actor-audience relationship was not subordinate, but a dynamic and essential element of dramaturgy'.[20] For Weimann, then, Tarlton played a central historical role in the reconciliation of folk-culture with the professional stage.[21] It is an important strand in his argument that London's first playhouses were located where the people had traditionally assembled for their sports and pastimes, in Finsbury Fields and on the Bankside. It was before such assemblies that Tarlton developed a personal performance style that slowly transformed the rural Jig into 'a balladesque performance that combined dance and song'.[22] Most controversially, Weimann's portrait of Tarlton the plebeian innovator is painted against a background of social and cultural homogeneity: 'In matters of social custom and dramatic taste there was as yet no clear division between the rural plebs and the London middle classes'.[23] Weimann is referring here to the years from 1570 to 1585 that saw Tarlton at the height of his fame, and it is his underlying assumption that an essential unity prevailed in England until the ideology of Puritanism had gathered sufficient strength to destroy it. Tarlton's jesting days, according to this historical scheme, predated the onset of plebeian alienation. The tripartite division of *Tarlton's Jests* – His Court Witty Jests, His Sound City Jests, His Country Pretty Jests – is proposed by Weimann as evidence of 'the broad social base of his appeal'.[24] It is readily apparent that such pronounced divisions might be read in an entirely contrary way.

The approach of David Wiles[25] is less overtly tendentious. His treatment of Tarlton is the prelude to a particularly intimate account of Will Kemp's career and idiom, though he has no doubt that Tarlton's was a 'seminal influence'[26] on Elizabethan clowning. He too emphasizes the consanguinity of Tarlton's clown and the Morality Vice, but the fusion he sees is not, like Weimann's, between Vice and court fool, but between Vice and rustic. 'The rustic transposed to an urban setting was the type that Tarlton made his own'.[27] The rustic clown of Tarlton's invention is envisaged by Wiles as a response to London, an immigrant's way of establishing sympathetic contact with the many other immigrants in his audience. But the proposition is subtler than that: 'His comedy cut across barriers of class ... because most people could accept the proposition that beneath every human exterior there lurks a coarse anarchic peasant'.[28] Whilst recognizing class-barriers that Weimann is inclined to deny, Wiles ascribes to Tarlton a significant contribution to fostering in the Londoners of his day 'a new sense of community, shared values, and active participation in the making of a culture',[29] and he believes, like Weimann, that this sense of community was dwindling by the early 1590s. Tarlton's death in 1588 coincided, then, with the end of an era. Not even Will Kemp had the power of personality to straddle the three worlds of 'the stage, the tavern, and the banqueting hall'[30] as Tarlton had, and cultural shifts had, by then, created social fissures which even Tarlton might have been unable to bridge. It is Wiles's central contention that Tarlton's clown was, historically, 'a synthesis of three different types of medieval entertainer: the professional minstrel, the amateur lord of misrule, and the Vice'.[31] Tarlton's style of solo performance was more combative than the minstrels', and the Vice was soon to be ousted from the professional playhouses. It is Tarlton's vestigial links with the amateur lords of misrule that Wiles is keenest to trace. Centrally engaged in ceremonial combat, the lord of misrule could prove himself worthy of office by losing, as Tarlton did when he jousted with sword and longstaff against Queen Elizabeth's dog: 'When Tarlton engaged in verbal duels with spectators in the theatre, and manoeuvred himself into a losing position, he drew upon a rich vein of folk humour'.[32] It is, then, a complex composite that Wiles presents, a Tarlton who contains, and may express in various combinations, Vice, minstrel, rustic clown, lord of misrule, anarchic peasant and community cheerleader. Generated by an oral culture,[33] he is a man whose anti-intellectualist gut responses invite any 'instinctual response from the audience'.[34] Wiles's Tarlton is the inspirational figure of sixteenth-century dramatic orature.

In the nightmare world of Martin Buzacott,[35] terrorized by actors who threaten to annexe his will with their deadly charm, Tarlton has once again an important place: 'The similarity between Tarlton's clown, the Vice, Carnival agitators and political dictators exists not only in this simultaneous presentation of cruelty and comedy, but also in his love of strutting and attracting attention from the moment he enters the drama'.[36] Buzacott's Tarlton is a Chaplinesque great dictator imbued with a real-life lust to kill. He is the product of 'a vicious theatrical and social history dedicated to the oppression and humiliation of revellers and moral miscreants'.[37] When he invokes the world of carnival, Buzacott has in mind a satanic malevolence utterly opposed to C.L. Barber's festive comedy and without the positive social purpose adumbrated by Bakhtin and Bristol.[38] He presents Tarlton as the embodiment of the viciousness and ritualized cruelty that were the 'true' expression of carnival licence. Here was a man, he implies, who used his very ugliness to aid in the transformation of the Vice into 'a modern stage figure'.[39] Worse than that, like the Pakistani (why Pakistani?) beggars who repeatedly break their children's limbs so that these artificially deformed creatures will elicit sympathy-money from passers-by, Tarlton exploited his deformity to excite pity in his audience: 'He was so ugly, so pitiable, so laughable, and so talented, that his transgressions of the Carnival licence to mayhem were rarely likely to result in the whip or pillory'.[40] This is the kind of silliness by which Buzacott is always liable to spoil his plausibility. His character-assassination of Derick, the part Tarlton played in *The Famous Victories of Henry V*, is almost equally excessive. And yet he has a point. You do not have to read between the lines of the surviving anecdotes of Tarlton's offstage antics to recognize his capacity to do damage. He was, in a manner too often neglected, dangerous. Bradbrook's benign portrait is as partial as Buzacott's malign one. It may be taken as evidence of a cultural shift over the second half of the twentieth century that, whilst Bradbrook did not consciously understate her case, Buzacott feels the need to overstate his. To persuade a society accustomed to violence that Tarlton was not a lovable comic, he has re-invented him as a diabolic terrorist. The making of mischief is something he perceives as insufficiently oppositional to convey his meaning, and the legitimacy of that position is certainly arguable. As Meg Twycross has recently indicated, 'The process of history has landed us in the camp of the Vices: they are the norm instead of being an entertaining but unstable divergence from it'.[41]

To various degrees, all the four critics whose work I have reviewed elide the historical Tarlton with his legend. It is not possible, perhaps not desirable, to separate true tales from tall tales: not desirable, certainly, if the veracity of a dictum of Oscar Wilde's were to be accepted. 'What is true in a man's life', Wilde observed, 'is not what he does, but the legend which grows up around him. ... You must never destroy legends. Through them we are given an inkling of the true physiognomy of a man'.[42] The Tarlton legend, his 'true physiognomy', is best preserved in the posthumously published book of *Tarlton's Jests*. The precise status of this collection of anecdotes (scarcely 'jests' in a modern sense) has never been established. The second of the three parts was entered in the Stationers' Register in 1600, twelve years after Tarlton's death, but the first extant edition of the whole is dated 1611. The first part may have been in circulation during the 1590s, but even as late as 1611 Tarlton was too recently dead to be utterly falsified. Whether or not individual 'jests' are true records of incidents is comparatively unimportant. The significant thing is that the figure of Tarlton they cumulatively represent must have seemed to the anonymous compiler sufficiently plausible to convince people who had known him alive. We can, for example, accept the compiler's word that 'God a mercy horse!' was a contemporary catchphrase, and such acceptance lends authority to the accompanying anecdote:

> There was one Banks, in the time of Tarlton, who served the Earle of Essex, and had a horse of strange qualities, and being at the Crosse-keyes in Gracious streete, getting mony with him, as he was mightily resorted to. Tarlton then, with his fellowes, playing at the Bel by, came into the Crosse-keyes, amongst many people, to see fashions, which Banks perceiving, to make the people laugh, saies: signior, (to his horse,) go fetch me the veryest foole in the company. The jade comes immediately, and with his mouth drawes Tarlton forth. Tarlton, with merry words, said nothing, but 'God a mercy horse.' In the end, Tarlton, seeing the people laugh so, was angry inwardly, and said: sir, had I power of your horse, as you have, I would doe more than that. What ere it be, said Banks, to please him, I will charge him to do it. Then saies Tarlton: charge him to bring me the veriest whore-master in the company. The horse leades his master to him. Then 'God a mercy horse, indeed,' saies Tarlton.[43]

The jest is typical in many ways. It takes place in an ambience of alcohol; it implies that the very appearance of Tarlton acted as a provocation (in this instance, to Banks); it shows Tarlton, as so often, initially outfaced; it lets us into the secret that Tarlton was angry, and that it was his anger that excited his combativeness; and it shows Tarlton turning the tables with a minimum expenditure of words. But there are other features, less immediately apparent, in the chosen phrasing of the jest. For different reasons, two of them merit closer attention.

In the opening sentence, we are provided with the apparently gratuitous information that Banks 'served the Earle of Essex'. Tarlton would have known two Earls of Essex, but the readers of the *Jests* would have been familiar only with the second, the Queen's executed favourite. Robert Devereux, who inherited the title on the sudden death of his father Walter in 1576, was the most intensely factional figure of the last years of Elizabeth's reign. By slipping in the information that Banks was one of Essex's men, the author of the *Jests* is hoisting a political flag. Devereux was, with his stepfather the Earl of Leicester, a spokesman for the radical

Protestants who were to evolve into Puritans. After Leicester's death in 1587, and despite a personal life-style that showed little evidence of Puritan restraint, Essex became a figure-head for the anti-Catholic extremists whose powerful presence threatened the Elizabethan settlement during the Queen's declining years. If, then, we read between the lines of this anecdote, Tarlton humiliates a Puritan adversary by uncovering his concealed activity as a pimp. The punishment of the hypocritical Banks has, from this perspective, a Jonsonian rigour, and it is not altogether inappropriate to read several of the anecdotes that comprise the published *Jests* as Jonsonian comedies writ small. The foolish hero of the anthology is a scourge of folly, a detective of hypocrisy, a social corrector. What is more, he may well have a political programme of his own.

The second concealed feature to which I wish to draw attention is a matter of style rather than of content. 'Tarlton, with merry words, said nothing, but "God a mercy horse".' The sentence is a curious one. Its evident reference is to a technique articulated by Bertolt Brecht in his 'Short description of a new technique of Acting which produces an alienation effect' (c. 1940). The actor Brecht has in mind will, during a performance,

> besides what he actually is doing ... at all essential points discover, specify, imply what he is not doing; that is to say he will act in such a way that the alternative emerges as clearly as possible, that his acting allows the other possibilities to be inferred and only represents one out of the possible variants.[44]

Tarlton's silence in the jaws of the horse was evidently a loaded one. It subsumed the merry words he might have spoken. That is to say that he conveyed to the onlookers the fact that his failure to react was not necessary, but elective. The improvising comedian, thinking laterally, implies what he might do whilst doing something completely different. Brecht's 'new technique' may be at least as old as Tarlton.

At the merely technical level, Tarlton's calculated silence has no more significance than a skilfully executed double-take. It is the combination of technique and combative purpose that distinguishes the Brechtian performer. There is, in the published *Jests* and anecdotes, sufficient evidence of that combination (broadly speaking, the technical and the political) in Tarlton to justify the allusion to Brecht. Tarlton's recorded victories were rarely easy. Many of them involve a recovery from humiliation; a recovery, what is more, that sometimes divides the bystanders into opposing camps. His was a comic persona, like Gethin Price's in Trevor Griffiths's *Comedians* or Lenny Bruce's worldwide, that made even his admirers uncomfortable. But neither Gethin Price nor Lenny Bruce ventured as far towards personal ignominy as Tarlton did. There was a Tarltonian sequence on British television in 1994–5. It began with coverage of a football-match between Manchester United and Crystal Palace. Not for the first time, Eric Cantona, Manchester's volatile French star, was sent off by the referee. The camera followed his shameful walk along the touch-line towards the changing-room tunnel and accidentally caught the precipitate descent of an irate Crystal Palace supporter to the low railing that divides the crowd from the arena. We could see, though not hear, the supporter shouting abuse at Cantona from the distance of a few feet; and there must have been shocked intakes of breath in sitting-rooms all over Britain when Cantona suddenly launched a Kung-Fu kick over the railing and into the throat of his abuser. This time (you could almost hear the accumulated volume of outraged British decency) Cantona had gone too far. Like most of the sporting public, I could see no way in which Cantona could recover from the humiliation consequent on this *in flagrante* camera-capture. His circumstance, after all, was dire. He is, everybody admits, an extremely gifted footballer, but his temperament had always been suspect, and his quickly aroused anger was not easily distinguishable from vengeful spite. Heavy-eyebrowed and swarthy, he is ugly in the peculiarly masculine way that carried Humphrey Bogart and Yves Montand (and, perhaps, Tarlton) to stardom. Like Tarlton, he was known to all spectators, home and away, and his bearing and style of playing are provocatively arrogant. You might admire his ball-control, but you would not want to get on the wrong side of him. It seemed undeniably just that, having flirted with danger for so long, this gifted outsider had met his come-uppance. Manchester United had no choice but to suspend him, pending a court-case. Many of us thought that he would never play football in England again. At the trial, however, account was taken of the xenophobic abuse hurled into his face by the Crystal Palace fan, and the sentence was a lenient one. Public opinion hovered during the press conference that followed, but Cantona maintained a silence that could easily be read as sullen – until the very end. Then, with the eyes of the nation trained on him, he said, 'When the seagulls follow the trawler it is because they think the sardines are going to be thrown into the sea', stood up and left the room. Almost unbelievably, with a single enigmatic sentence, Cantona/Tarlton had somersaulted off the hook of public obloquy.

We do not know whether Cantona wrote his own script, as Tarlton certainly did in the years that preceded his emergence as a professional player. Among the biographical snippets that have been preserved, the most persistent establishes him as a publican, perhaps the landlord of an inn in Colchester, more certainly of the Saba Tavern in London's Gracechurch Street. Immigration to London may temporarily have lowered his status, since inns stood higher than taverns in the hierarchy of drinking-places. The staple income of an inn was derived from the provision of lodging to those rich enough to pay for it. Taverns (drinking houses) came next, but, by an Act of 1553, the number of taverns in the City of London was limited to forty, and the humble alehouse sprang up to supply the needs, primarily, of the labouring classes. By 1618 the City Fathers, observing the daily increase of alehouses, considered it 'high time to suppress the number of them'.[45] There was little they could do about the multitude of unlicensed ale-sellers (or 'tipplers') who undercut the alehouses. Ale and beer (ale with hops added) were the favoured drinks of labourers, many of them immigrants to London. In his persona as rustic clown, Tarlton advertised himself as an immigrant, and, by his drinking, he identified himself with those displaced countrymen who took refuge in alcohol from the harshness of urban conditions. We know that, once his fame was established, Tarlton's familiar face appeared on alehouse signs, implicitly endorsing the oppositional humour that tends to accompany the swilling of ale as the hours pass. Tarlton's 'swine-face' was used to advertise the proletarian alehouse, but it is a reasonable deduction that he developed his skills as a tableside entertainer in his own tavern. It may have been at the Saba that he inaugurated his 'themes' – extemporized (often rhymed) responses to subjects set to challenge his ingenuity. If so, the possible move from the Saba to an ordinary (eating-house) in Paternoster Row may be read as a quest for a quieter, more responsive audience. But there is no evidence of a change of style to accompany the changes in performance environment from tavern to ordinary to playhouse. Sir John Harington, writing in 1596, recalls that the word 'prepuce' was 'admitted into the theater with great applause by the mouth of Mayster Tarlton, the excellent comedian'.[46] True to the spirit of carnival, Tarlton concentrated on the lower half of the body, and popular culture's relishing of bodily functions is reflected in the reports that his face adorned Elizabethan privies as well as alehouses.

One of the published jests aptly associates Tarlton with privy and playhouse. It concerns a certain Mr Sunbank, a wealthy citizen of Bristol. Pleased to be among those who welcomed the Queen's Men on their visit to the city, Mr Sunbank nevertheless took time off to marry his maidservant – in secret, as he hoped. But Mr Sunbank had a problem: his neck was so rigid that he was unable to turn his head without swivelling his whole body. Having entertained Tarlton and his fellow-players at the St James Fair in Bristol, he was relieving himself against a wall when Tarlton came up behind him, clapped him on the shoulder and congratulated him on his (secret) marriage. Bound by courtesy, Mr Sunbank 'suddenly turnes about, body and all, in the view of many, and showed all: which so abasht him that (ashamed) hee tooke into a tavern'.[47] The current of cruelty that runs through the Tarlton legend is subdued here, but less so in another urinary jest. Hearing of a quack who practised and profited in Islington, Tarlton half-filled a urine bottle with wine and carried it to the quack for diagnosis:

> He viewed it, and tossing it up and downe, as though he had great knowledge, quoth he: the patient, whose water it is, is full of grosse humors, and hath need of purging, and to be let some ten ounces of bloud. No, you dunce, replyed Tarlton, it is good, and with that drunke it off; and threw the urinall at his head.[48]

The jest is good enough, and perhaps the quack deserved it, but the last clause is chilling. Tarlton 'threw the urinall at his head'. I find that hard to believe, as much because a practised comedian does not readily spoil a joke as because a thrown bottle is liable to inflict a serious injury. That moment of unnecessary violence is necessary only to the narrator, who is bent on ornamenting a posthumous legend. The dead clown is being recreated as an urban terrorist.

I begin to wonder about the project on which the unknown compiler of *Tarlton's Jests* was engaged. His hero is a prodigious plebeian, whose jests at court border always on insolence, and whose jests in city and country are much more often sour than joyful. To be fair, this is a matter of degree rather than of kind, since the Jest-Book genre habitually appealed to a taste for the corrective application of what we would now call practical jokes. The point is that *Tarlton's Jests* contains more savagery than most of its kind. The received image of Tarlton remains less harsh, tending more to Bradbrook than to Buzacott, perhaps because it has been the custom to quote selectively from the *Jests*, usually according to the benign taste of the quoter. There is even some selectivity in the edition that has been my present source, published in 1866 as part of the series of Old English Jest Books. The editor, W. Carew Hazlitt, has omitted the eighth of the Court Witty Jests because he considers it 'pointless and too indelicate to print'.[49] The censored anecdote records an occasion at court when Tarlton so offended a lady that she threatened to cuff him. To her consternation, Tarlton agreed, provided only that they reverse the consonants. The coarse sexuality of a very masculine Tarlton surfaces quite often in the *Jests*. We see him sharing dirty jokes – or sexual innuendoes at least – with the Earl of Sussex, with whose company of players he may first have encountered the literary drama, although, interestingly, we do not hear what they say.

Such behaviour is broadly acceptable. In its mellow aspect, as in the discourses of Falstaff, we may even find it mildly endearing. It is an enduring part of the Shakespeare legend that the creation of Falstaff owed something to Shakespeare's memories of Tarlton, but there is very little of Falstaff in the legendary hero of the *Jests*. Even at court, perhaps because Elizabeth I licensed it, an unattractively throbbing vein of misogyny obtrudes. The third jest, utterly unfunny to a modern sensibility, runs as follows:

> Upon a time, Tarlton being among certaine ladies at a banquet which was at Greenwich, the queene then lying there, one of the ladies had her face full of pimples with heat at her stomake; for which cause she refused to drinke wine amongst the rest of the ladies: which Tarlton perceiving, for he was there of purpose to jest amongst them, quoth he: a murren of that face, which makes all the body fare the worse for it! At which the rest of the ladies laught, and she, blushing for shame, left the banquet.[50]

Such repartee belongs aggressively to the masculine world, as do all the jokes against his wife that establish Tarlton at the head of a stand-up-comedy tradition. Invariably, women were Tarlton's butts. It is an example of folk culture merging with plebeian sexism, and the Tarlton myth should not be permitted to blur its unpleasantness.

Commentators have been reluctant to acknowledge the sheer ill temper of the hero of *Tarlton's Jests*. This is something more profound than dyspepsia or the enflamed susceptibility of a hang-over. The constant impression is of a man barely able to suppress his anger at the way of the world. An honest reading of the *Jests* will not sustain Weimann's argument that Tarlton united Court, City and Country in a pre-capitalist England of cultural harmony. On the contrary, the clown-as-hero insistently defeats the efforts of those in authority to preserve the outer dressings of social stability. It is Falstaff, not Tarlton, who seeks to accommodate himself to Court, City and Country (Prince Hal, Mistress Quickly, Justice Shallow). Tarlton, if he introduced to Court the dialect of the City, to the City the dialect of the Country, and to the Country the dialects of Court and City, did so in order to display cultural disparity towards the end of a century that had already witnessed the breakdown of the old order. That, at least, is the legend propagated by the compiler of the *Jests*, and, unless we are to argue that he has totally re-invented Tarlton in defiance of the many readers who would have known him, it is a legend of which account must be taken. The precise content of most of Tarlton's improvised responses to hecklers has been lost. What the recorded jests most securely preserve is his style. We can, I think, assume that he was quicker of tongue than Falstaff, quicker to recover from humiliation, quicker altogether. And he was certainly combative. Tarlton's entry into any space – a tap-room, a moot-hall, a platform in playhouse or village square – raised the temperature, introduced an aura of competition. It is to the crucial theatrical act of 'entering' that I now turn.

At the beginning of his famous description of Irving's initial appearance as Mathias in *The Bells,* Edward Gordon Craig writes, 'The *manner of coming on* made it extraordinary with great actors. It was this manner of timing the appearance, measuring its speed and direction, which created a rhythm that was irresistible'.[51] A parallel perception about Tarlton is implicit in Wilson's *Commendation of Cockes and Cock-fighting* (1607), which recalls a Norwich cock aptly called 'Tarlton' 'because he always came to the fight like a drummer, making a thundering noyse with his winges'.[52] This is a reference to something more than the fact that Tarlton's rustic clown often announced himself with a tabor: it describes the whole impact of his first appearance. David Mann has alertly proposed the use of the ornithological term 'jiz' to define the combination of outline, bearing and voice that immediately identifies a performer.[53] Tarlton's jiz was not unlike the jiz of a cockerel, and he was a specialist in entrances, varying them according to context. In one of the best known of all Tarlton anecdotes, Thomas Nashe recalls the occasion on which a provincial potentate was provoked into self-parody:

> Amongst other cholericke wise justices he was one that, having a play presented before him and his touneship by Tarlton and the rest of his fellowes, her Majesties servants, and they were now entring into their first merriment (as they call it), the people began exceedingly to laugh, when Tarlton first peept out his head. Whereat the justice, not a little moued, and seeing with his becks and nods hee could not make them cease, he went with his staffe, and beat them round about vnmercifully on the bare pates, in that they, being but fermers and poore countrey hyndes, would presume to laugh at the Queenes men, and make no more account of her cloath in his presence.[54]

Here we have a mischievous Tarlton, on tour with the Queen's Men, creating mayhem by breaking theatrical convention. Eric Morecambe would similarly disconcert Ernie Wise by poking his head through the upstage curtain when Wise had launched himself into one of his futile exercises in audience control. Like Morecambe, Tarlton was a comic master of the secret art of entrances (and exits), so often dependent on the utterly inappropriate interpolation of the non-fictional self into the fictional circumstance. The basis of Tarlton's theatrical technique, David Wiles has suggested, 'was to recreate in the theatre the intimate atmosphere of the table-side, making spectators feel like participants'.[55] In such an atmosphere, what is actually said may be comparatively unimportant. The spectators pluck laughter out of the air. But a dialogue with the audience that may be conventional in a tavern or an ordinary is a distinct breaking of convention in a playhouse. According to the legend fed by Thomas Nashe, Tarlton's appointment to the Queen's company of players in 1583 did not tame him, and the significance of that fact should not be overlooked. At the head of the new profession stood a man who could not be relied on to obey its rules, one who displayed very little of his colleagues' evident anxiety to be accepted into respectability.

Tarlton was already a personality before he became a player, and it would be a pious anachronism to argue that he attempted to suppress his personality in the playhouse. There is a hugely popular annual pantomime in the Dartmoor village where I live, a popularity that has nothing discernibly to do with standards of performance. What audiences seem to relish is the sheer ungainliness of well-known villagers performing themselves in somebody else's clothes. It is the inevitable failure of any attempt at impersonation that creates the greatest hilarity. The vivid incompetence of the actors endears them to the fun-seeking spectators. Professionally honed, this performative inability to adapt to fictional circumstance has characterized the most popular clowns throughout the history of stage and film. Will Kemp inherited it from Tarlton, and, despite the best endeavours of good taste and Stanislavsky, it has survived triumphantly in the cinemas and theatres of the twentieth century. Once they had invented themselves as performers, when did W.C. Fields or Mae West ever try to re-invent themselves as characters? Who cares about the plot of a Marx Brothers film? Or the periodicity of any of the *Carry On* series? Even before they reach the lines, the jokes are in the casting – the twiglet Charles Hawtrey as a macho Indian chief, or Kenneth Williams as any kind of heterosexual. If the compiler of the *Jests* is to be trusted, a transvestite Tarlton in a post-play Jig may have tapped into a vein of more subversive grotesquerie, might even have joined Joel Schechter's troupe of Groucho Marxists,[56] but here the relationship of legend to truth is in the government of speculation. The part of Derick, presumably made to Tarlton's measure by the authors of *The Famous Victories*, is inconclusive on this point, and it is one of the few things that binds Tarlton to dramatic (as distinct from theatrical) history. Shakespeare was presumably alluding to the double-act of Derick and John Cobbler when he composed the royal charade of Falstaff and Prince Hal,[57] and it may be that the authors of *The*

Famous Victories were there exploiting Tarlton's off-stage reputation for irreverence. It is possible, also, that they expected many in the audience to catch the nominal echo of the irascible Garter King-of-Arms (Sir William) Dethicke in Derick. It was an age that delighted in detecting correspondences between dramatic fictions and contemporary politics. But Derick reveals more about Tarlton's style than it can about his personal politics. The part is a composite of *lazzi*, in which what was *done* must generally have had greater impact than what was said; but what also characterizes this raw text is the parade of opportunities it offers to Tarlton as Derick to indulge his metatheatrical talent as a maker of exits and entrances. On the open stages of Elizabethan London, it was impossible to enter or leave the platform unobtrusively. Actors entering at the opening of a scene must first locate themselves in order to place the narrative: actors leaving must have a reason to go. Either way, they have a distance to cover from or to the stage door. That distance was Tarlton's playground, and *The Famous Victories* furnishes it richly.

The legendary Tarlton whom I have been exploring was, then, hard-drinking, provocative, often forced to recover from ignominy, outstandingly short-tempered, a misogynist, an adversary of radical Protestantism, anti-Catholic too, a man who habitually joked about the functions and appurtenances of the human body's lower half, verbally as well as physically agile, not infrequently violent and almost always competitive. As a performer, he specialized in entrances, had an assertive jiz and enjoyed breaking the theatrical conventions imposed by the imperatives of dramatic fiction. Some, at least, of those attributes were in the possession of the historical Tarlton, but it remains difficult to determine his precise significance in the history of the theatre. Wiles, as we have seen, considers that Tarlton's was the seminal influence on Elizabethan clowning, and the received view is that, within Shakespeare's company of players, Will Kemp was Tarlton's direct heir, whilst the advent of Robert Armin signalled or followed a dramatic shift from clown to fool. Such judgements have always to be qualified, and it would be an obvious naivety to argue that Tarlton's influence came to a sudden end with Armin's arrival at the Globe. There is, for one thing, no reason to suppose that London's other companies lost faith in their clowns. Nor is it extravagant to trace Tarlton's legacy through the clowns of Jacobean and Caroline drama, the country bumpkins of Restoration comedy, the low comedians of the eighteenth- and nineteenth-century theatre, to the music-hall and the variety stages, and to the occasional casting of stand-up comedians (George Robey, Frankie Howerd, etc.) in Shakespearean roles during our own century. My concern here is not, however, with a genealogy of performance. I intend, rather, to argue for a neglected but discernible Tarltonian presence in two of the plays Shakespeare wrote between the death of the great clown in 1588 and the death of Elizabeth I in 1603. The argument requires, as a preface, a further examination of Tarlton's special relationship with his audience.

We have very little evidence on which to base an assessment of Tarlton's attitude to his fellow-players. His will, unlike those of many men with whom he acted, lists no bequests to playhouse colleagues,[58] but such negative evidence is unsatisfactory. There may, after all, have been good reason for Tarlton's anxiety to secure the future of his natural son to the exclusion of virtually all other considerations. The will, incidentally, includes no mention of the wife of whom he makes such sport in the *Jests*. But there is more than Hamlet's advice to the players to support a view that Tarlton was a disconcerting person to share the stage with. He was surely more at ease with the spectators in the playhouse than with the less compatible creatures of dramatic fiction. His own extraordinary appearance ensured that the well-known figure of Tarlton would obtrude through any persona that he was required to adopt, and it is unlikely that he made any attempt to disguise the undisguisable. More probably, he milked the dichotomy of the actual and the purported self for all it was worth. As a clown, he was licensed to neglect the purposes of the plot, with or without the encouragement of the playwright. The Launce of *The Two Gentlemen of Verona* is a Shakespearean gesture of assent. If the text constrained him, the clown, in collusion with the audience, broke the constraints. There was political, as well as moral, danger in such unruliness, and the preachers and pamphleteers who inveighed against the evils of the professional stage surely had a point. The occasional licence of carnival was, in the bodies of boy-players as well as clowns, exercised every day in the new playhouses. In retrospect, we should be more surprised by the little harm the players inflicted on the urban *status quo* than by the alarm expressed by their early adversaries. The implication would seem to be that, as the profession developed over the last decades of the sixteenth century, its dangerousness diminished, and this evident diminution lends weight to an argument that the inherent subversiveness of 'playing' was diverted as players became increasingly subservient to their roles. According to such an argument, the threat of the act of acting was dampened by a shift in audience expectation, away from an admiration for the overwhelming performer towards an admiration for the subtle impersonator. Shakespeare's was the supreme contribution to this shift, since it was in his work that the dramatic 'character' most vividly emerged. The ideology of character is implicitly confirmative of the *status quo*, the idea of the player implicitly a threat to it.[59] Tarlton, never in character, scarcely an actor, irredeemably a player, pre-dated the triumph of the literary drama. Against the humanist tide, he maintained the robust traditions of an oral culture. The young Shakespeare, whether or not he 'knew him well', felt the force of Tarlton. His hectoring clowns, assertive against ignominy, recall it (Jack Cade, Launcelot Gobbo, above all Bottom). As time passes, this clown loses power. Lavache imports to *All's Well that Ends Well* the clown's privilege of outspokenness, but his is a flailing, failing rhetoric that carries him towards Thersites and the world of the malcontent. It might even be argued that the ultimate fate of Tarlton in the Shakespearean canon is his entrapment in the deformed body of the disempowered Caliban. But it is, I believe, in two quite different characters that Shakespeare most notably summons up the memory of Tarlton in all his dangerous authority.

We do not know which playhouse hosted the first performance of *Richard III*, and we can only presume that the afternoon began with the famous soliloquy that opens the received text. The man who played Richard had first, in the tiring-house, to deform his body, and then to make an effective entrance. The jiz of the entering actor was, for the play's first audiences, unavoidably reminiscent of Tarlton's jiz: two Richards in one body, the future King of England as Vice/clown. It is an extraordinarily bold trope, and one which is variously deployed as the drama unfolds. Richard is a Tarltonian jester, adept at improvising his way out of danger. This is a role for a player/performer, not for an impersonator, one in which the image of monarchy is perilously aligned with carnival inversion. Richard's competitive style, as well as his appearance, invokes the insolent plebeian. It is doubtful that Shakespeare would have taken such a risk with any other English monarch.

Richard's irreverent response to religious authority calls readily to mind the Tarlton of the *Jests*. Papists and Puritans were Tarlton's targets, and he tilted constantly at puffed-up provincials and petty officials. My proposition that the figure of Malvolio invoked the memory of Tarlton is of a different order from that linking him with Richard III. It was people like Malvolio whom Tarlton most zealously exposed to ridicule. A living Tarlton, to be sure, would not have hidden behind a box-hedge to deal Malvolio his comeuppance, but there is no such brazen clown in *Twelfth Night*. Malvolio's most effective adversary is a female servant. Only when his humiliation is complete does the Armin-fool attend to gloat in the guise of Sir Thopas. Northrop Frye has uncovered, in this pairing of adversarial outsiders, a Shakespearean pattern – Gobbo/Shylock; Touchstone/Jaques; Lavache/Parolles; Feste/Malvolio.[60] But of these, only Gobbo and Touchstone exhibit any of the masculine provocativeness of Tarlton. It is almost as if Malvolio in his pomp exposes the lack of a Tarlton-clown. The stage type that Tarlton represented may sometimes have administered cruel punishment to the pretentious, but that punishment was summarily carried through, and usually face-to-face. The humiliation of Malvolio, on the contrary, is prolonged, secretive, and eventually disconcerting.

The presence of the Armin/fool might equally well be said to have drawn the first audience's attention to the absence of the Kemp/clown, but there are two further points to be made in explanation of my emphasis on Tarlton. Suffering in cross-garters, Malvolio confesses that he wears them only to 'please the eye of one', offering in further explanation the words of the very true sonnet, 'Please one and please all'.[61] This is, in fact, the refrain of a well-known and slightly bawdy song, marketed as 'A pretty new Ballad entitled The Crow sits upon the wall'. Possibly incorporated in a Jig, the song was published under the signature of R.T., and was generally ascribed to Tarlton. What the first audience heard, then, were Richard Tarlton's words on the lips of 'a kind of Puritan'.[62] The association of Malvolio with a particularly mealy-mouthed Puritanism is eventually challenged by Maria, but in terms that reinforce rather than undermine that association. The Globe audience might justifiably have linked their more recent clown Will Kemp with an anti-Puritan lobby, but Shakespeare's concealed allusion is to Tarlton. The background history to this, which forms the substance of my second and final point, has been recently explored by Patrick Collinson.[63]

Collinson's suspicion that the 'stage' Puritan ante-dated the historical Puritan – that the word was brought into currency by its oral deployment in, for example, satirical Jigs – hinges on the style and personality of Tarlton. He recognizes in the street-ballads and pamphlets of Elizabethan controversy an interplay of orality and literature. We can carry this further by reference to Gabriel Harvey. Even at the time, Harvey saw fit to emphasize the kinship of the gifted pamphleteer Thomas Nashe and Tarlton. Nashe's meanings, he noted, were 'right-formally conueied, according to the stile and tenour of Tarltons president, his famous play of the seauen Deadly sinnes ... now pleasantlie interlaced with diuers new-founde phrases of the Tauerne'.[64] Few people were better equipped than Tarlton to redirect the dialect of the tavern into satirical channels. The spoken word and the written word had not yet been decisively separated in cultural reception. It is not, then, especially surprising that their first readers read into the Marprelate Tracts the sprightly voice of the recently dead and already-missed clown. Collinson goes so far as to suggest that, in a way, 'Martin was the resurrected persona of the comedian Richard Tarlton'. It is a matter of record that Martin Marprelate was transformed by the anti-Martinist pamphleteers into an image of obnoxious Puritanism, despite the fact that this new stereotype was utterly unlike the iconoclastic and street-wise original. The scurrilous Jigs, with their Martinist caricatures of bishops and their anti-Martinist caricatures of reforming

Protestants, have not survived in printed form. Tarlton's own lost Jigs may have been a model. We know that, but cannot altogether show how, the playhouses took a leading role in the Marprelate war, and we can be confident that Tarltonian clowning conditioned its inflection. The Stage Puritan was so well established by the end of the sixteenth century that Shakespeare could invoke his image in Malvolio without any reference to religion, and then, by a semi-cryptic allusion, invite an audience to speculate on his likely fate if Tarlton were still around. What we can never recover, however, are the lost semiotics of live theatrical performance. Shakespeare has provided Malvolio with all manner of wonderful entrances. I would not be surprised if some of them were visual jokes echoing the jiz of Tarlton's entrances as a posturing Puritan in Jigs of his own devising.

Notes

1. I am referring here to the 1979 republication by Cambridge University Press for the book first published by Chatto and Windus in 1962. John Astington has effectively dismissed the claim that the Scottowe drawing is a likeness of Tarleton.
2. Harley MS 3885, fol.19, British Library.
3. *Hamlet*, 5.1.201f. Line references here and elsewhere are to the Oxford Shakespeare edition of *The Complete Works*, ed. W.J. Craig (London: Collins, 1919).
4. The quotation is from the prefatory address to the reader in Williams's *A Brief Discourse of War* (London, 1590).
5. Bradbrook, op. cit., 163.
6. Bradbrook, 164.
7. Bradbrook, 165.
8. Bradbrook, 166.
9. Bradbrook, 167.
10. Bradbrook, 170.
11. Bradbrook, 171.
12. Bradbrook, 177.
13. Robert Weimann, *Shakespeare and the Popular Tradition in the Theater*, ed. Robert Schwartz (Baltimore: Johns Hopkins University Press, 1978).
14. Weimann, 186.
15. Weimann, 187.
16. Weimann, 138.
17. Weimann, 24.

18 Weimann, 187.
19 Weimann, 191.
20 Weimann, 213.
21 Weimann, 158.
22 Weimann, 186.
23 Weimann, 185.
24 Weimann, 186.
25 David Wiles, *Shakespeare's Clown* (Cambridge: Cambridge University Press, 1987).
26 Wiles, 11.
27 Wiles, 12.
28 Wiles, 23.
29 Wiles, 23.
30 Wiles, 14.
31 Wiles, 17–19.
32 Wiles, 21.
33 Wiles, 23.
34 Wiles, 139.
35 Martin Buzacott, *The Death of the Actor* (London: Routledge, 1991).
36 Buzacott, 75.
37 Buzacott, 71.
38 The essential references here are to C.L. Barber, *Shakespeare's Festive Comedy* (Princeton: Princeton University Press, 1959); Mikhail Bakhtin, *Rabelais and His World,* trans. Helen Iswolsky (Cambridge, Mass: M.I.T. Press, 1968) and Michael Bristol, *Carnival and Theatre* (London and New York: Methuen, 1985).
39 Buzacott, 72.
40 Buzacott, 73.
41 Twycross Meg, 'The Theatricality of Medieval English Plays', in Richard Beadle, ed., *The Cambridge Companion to Medieval English Theatre* (Cambridge: Cambridge University Press, 1994), 82–3.
42 Cited in Richard Ellmann, *Oscar Wilde* (London: Penguin, 1988), 42.
43 Hazlitt, W. Carew, ed., 'Tarlton's Jests' in *Shakespeare Jest-Books*, Vol. 2 (London: Willis and Sotheran, 1864), 217–18.
44 Willett, John, trans. and ed., *Brecht on Theatre* (London: Methuen, 1964), 137.
45 Cited in Peter Clark, *The English Alehouse* (London: Longman, 1983), 49.
46 Cited in Edwin Nungezer, *A Dictionary of Actors* (London and New Haven: Yale University Press, 1929), 358.
47 *Tarlton's Jests*, 226.
48 *Tarlton's Jests*, 208–9.

49 *Tarlton's Jests*, 195.
50 *Tarlton's Jests*, 189.
51 Craig, *Henry Irving*, (London: J.M. Dent and Sons, 1930), 55.
52 Cited in Nungezer, 356.
53 David Mann, *The Elizabethan Player* (London: Routledge, 1991), 27.
54 Cited in Nungezer, 356–7.
55 Wiles, 93.
56 Joel Schechter, *Satiric Impersonations* (Carbondale: Southern Illinois University Press, 1994), 93.
57 The passages I am here referring to are in *The Famous Victories of Henry V*, scene 4, 95f. and *Henry IV Part One*, 2.4.418f.
58 For Tarlton's will, see *Playhouse Wills*, eds E.A.J. Honigmann and Susan Brock (Manchester: Manchester University Press, 1993), 57–8.
59 The argument I am here advancing has been put forward, cogently and at length, by Lesley Soule in an as-yet-unpublished thesis at the University of Exeter: *Character, Actor and Anti-Character*, 1994, 180f.
60 See Northrop Frye, *A Natural Perspective* (New York: Harcourt, Brace and World, Inc., 1965), 93f, where Frye develops the contrast between two spectator-types in Shakespearean comedy, one which he nominates fool/clown and the other *idiotes*.
61 *Twelfth Night*, 3.4.24–6.
62 *Twelfth Night*, 2.3.153–4.
63 Patrick Collinson, 'The Theatre Constructs Puritanism', in David L. Smith, Richard Strier and David Bevington, eds, *The Theatrical City* (Cambridge: Cambridge University Press, 1995); see especially, 164–7.
64 Cited in Weimann, 207.

CHAPTER 13

' 'Tis a pageant / To keep us in false gaze': *Othello*, Virtual History and the Jacobean Audience's Turkish Expectations

Mark Hutchings

Early on in *Othello* it is made clear that Othello's chief attribute is his generalship: his narratives of military success win over Desdemona, and his reputation is such that, as the Duke implies, his role is crucial if Venice is to prevent the Turks capturing Cyprus.[1] Yet Othello's position has already been undermined by Iago, who has primed Brabanzio even before Othello first appears on stage, and it is clear to the audience that even as an 'international' conflict seems likely, a 'domestic' intrigue is in the offing. The play thus suggests that it will dramatize Othello's domestic weakness against the backdrop of the more pressing, international concern – the impending Turkish attack. For the audience, witness to Brabanzio's anger and Iago's plotting, it is apparent that Othello is wholly dependent on this opportunity to display his military prowess: when the Turkish fleet is destroyed by a storm, his position is jeopardized.[2] Subsequent events illustrate how absolute his military value is, and yet equally how that value, unexchangeable, becomes worthless under the changed conditions of a peacetime economy. The play's abrupt transformation of Othello from successful general to vulnerable, jealous husband unfolds a 'domestic' drama that, reasonably enough, demands the attention of most critics; yet the deployment of the traditional Turkish threat to Europe in the play requires rather more interrogation than scholars have allowed. Indeed, while critics may find the 'psychological' material of betrayal or the treatment of race particularly interesting, the audience in 1604 may well have focused instead on the dramatically attractive offering of a Turkish invasion of Cyprus which the play enticingly (and with historical accuracy) advertises but does not deliver. Insofar as the play operates on the premise that its audience recognizes the potency of the Turkish threat to Mediterranean Europe, it seems reasonable therefore to investigate further what the deployment of the Turkish motif might have meant to Jacobean playgoers.

Despite the importance of the Turkish threat to Venice in *Othello*, a threat of such historical force for its contemporary audience that it must have been recognized for the 'Renaissance commonplace'[3] it was, the role of Turks in the play has elicited little discussion from scholars. Critics have tended to follow the implied logic of the text: the Turkish threat disappears so that the main business may begin, as in the New Cambridge Shakespeare editor's view that while the shift from Venice to Cyprus

> is motivated on the narrative level by the continuing Christian crusade against Turks[,] ... this matter is hurried from the audience's attention in a couple of scenes. Its dramatic value lies largely in enabling Shakespeare to have the ideal conditions for his domestic drama.[4]

Thus the implied narrative of the play – *Othello* as 'domestic drama' – is both established and consolidated by critics, while the international context in which the action is set is marginalized. Ironically, then, just as the play dispenses with the Turkish threat without much ado, so critics enable the text to depend entirely it seems on its own utterances, and dispense with the Turkish spectre as soon as it becomes clear that the main issue, apparently, is Othello's position in Venetian society. Since the opening scenes focus on Brabanzio's and Iago's responses to the elopement, the undramatized threat posed by the Turkish navy appears to be secondary, which its non-appearance confirms.[5]

It is perhaps only Othello's ethnicity (itself of course the subject of considerable debate) that keeps the Turkish issue alive in criticism of the play. Dispensed with in Act 2, scene 1, the Turkish motif is recalled by Othello himself in Act 3 scene 3, when he compares his firm resolve to the waters of the Bosphorus and the Dardanelles (implying movement *from* the Ottoman Empire, rather than *to* it, incidentally):

> Like to the Pontic sea,
> Whose icy current and compulsive course
> Ne'er knows retiring ebb, but keeps due on
> To the Propontic and the Hellespont. (3.3.456–9)

Here Othello implicitly allies himself with the Turks, identifying himself with the 'compulsive course [that] / Ne'er knows retirring ebb', which is plainly symbolic of the Turkish threat to Mediterranean Europe, and, more pertinently here, to Venice. Perhaps of greater significance is the play's closure, where the Turkish motif is realigned with Othello, confirming or contradicting the racist judgements the play offers. As John Gillies remarks, 'his symbolic association with the Turks is a critical commonplace';[6] Othello 'becomes' and/or destroys the Turk in the moment of his suicide:[7]

> Set you down this,
> And say besides that in Aleppo once,
> Where a malignant and a turbaned Turk
> Beat a Venetian and traduced the state,
> I took by th' throat the circumcisèd dog
> And smote him thus.
>   He stabs himself. (5.2.360–65)

In killing himself, Othello either destroys the Turk in an act which ironically recalls the heroic actions on which his military appointment depended, or endorses the identification between himself and the Turkish enemy the play urges, thus glossing the lack of distinction between Turks and Moors and underwriting a conventional racial stereotype. As Gillies observes, Othello's 'Africanness is constantly being telescoped into other notorious forms of exoticism: Turkish, Egyptian and Indian'[8] – a telescoping that functions ideally as an enabling device, encouraging (on stage and in the audience) a unified Christian opposition to this 'general' or generic Other.[9] For a 'pessimistic' reading of *Othello* which argues that it underwrites rather than undermines its deployment of racial stereotypes, linking Othello with the Turkish enemy sustains the play's apparent racism, both in structural terms – for Othello, if 'Turkish', becomes the *de facto* enemy, regardless of the actions of Iago[10] – and in the implicit offer it makes to its audience to identify with its representation of racism in sixteenth-century Venice.

The lack of interest in exploring a more sustained analysis of the Turkish presence in *Othello* is unsurprising, however, since despite the burgeoning interest in cultural approaches to early modern English drama there has been only a limited critical engagement with the playhouse's Turkish narrative. Yet between 1581 and 1642 some seventy plays depicted Turks in considerable detail, in addition to many more plays whose incidental Turkish references were presumably recognized and interpreted by spectators; indeed, almost half of the plays in the Shakespeare canon alone make reference to Turks. This suggests that the early modern playgoer was familiar with numerous (and surely not 'identical') representations of Turks, performed representations or images which cumulatively produced a degree of awareness of Turks which in turn created expectations and implied spectator recognition of the dramatic device. The dramatized Turk has, however, been treated in isolation, if at all, by critics, and the extent of the collective effect of the frequency of the image on stage has not been sufficiently investigated. Moreover, where the motif has been identified, individually in plays (invariably those that are considered canonical), it has been assumed that the image of the Turk functions always as a negative foil, as part of a consistent narrative of otherness. This can be seen clearly in the criticism of *Othello*'s Turks.

The only full-length study of the subject of the stage Turk was published sixty years ago;[11] articles and chapter-length surveys that have focused on the Turkish motif have tended to endorse a traditional view of east-west relations dependent on a binary opposition separating and differentiating between Moslems and Christians. Unfortunately, this undertheorized, unquestioned reliance on a model which further investigation places under severe strain has contributed to the neglect of the subject. The image of the Turk in early modern Europe has become so firmly established by critics as always already manifesting itself unambiguously as a threat, military and cultural, to Christian Europe, that the subject has been deemed unworthy of further investigation, or interrogated in simplistic terms. Thus Virginia Mason Vaughan's otherwise informative study of the play makes the conventional claim that 'by Shakespeare's day "the Turk" represented all that was barbaric and demonic, in contrast to the Christian's civil and moral code',[12] and thereby endorses a traditional view of the image of the Turk that is rarely questioned. It is then entirely consistent with the narrative of criticism of the image of the Turk that she argues that 'Othello's final speech and culminating suicide is civilization's last victory over the Turk',[13] since such hyperbole is commonplace. Vaughan cites the important work of Edward Said in support of her position,[14] but ironically Said's approach, rather than opening up the subject of early modern conceptions of the Orient, has reconstituted the binary opposition as a structuralist model apparently justified by hundreds of years of history.[15] Said's immensely influential study, though not directly concerned with exploring the image of the east in early modern Europe (its focus is on western conceptions of the Orient in the eighteenth and nineteenth centuries),[16] does briefly set out early modern origins of western perceptions of the east, and it is partly to this that scholars of the stage's dramatization of the east are indebted. Said claims that

> not for nothing did Islam come to symbolize terror, devastation, the demonic, hordes of hated barbarians. For Europe, Islam was a lasting trauma. Until the end of the seventeenth century the Ottoman 'peril' lurked alongside Europe to represent for the whole of Christian civilization a constant danger, and in time

European civilization incorporated that peril and its lore, its great events, figures, virtues, vices, as something woven into the fabric of life.[17]

The binary structure on which Said's thesis depends reads in the European fear of Turkish military conquest a clear manifestation of the west's demonization of the east. Thus the historical Turkish threat both explains and underwrites the narrative of binary conflict which critics who have investigated the early modern English stage's interest in representing the Turk have sought to establish.[18]

The positioning of Turks in *Othello* is often seen to fit this binary model remarkably well; indeed, Said's argument has a bewitching simplicity. Because much of Europe *was* legitimately fearful of the Turkish threat during the fifteenth, sixteenth and seventeenth centuries, and because *Othello* (like *Tamburlaine*, *The Jew of Malta* and numerous other plays) draws on the general historical truth of this threat, the critical tendency has been to gloss this historical 'background' as if it were simply a small part of the text's infrastructure. Thus the simplified truth of the European perception of the Turkish threat is deemed sufficient to justify no further critical investigation, despite the fact that this is of course to accept at face value early modern historiography without subjecting it to scholarly, historical and textual exegesis. This undertheorized approach is dependent on two conditions which ought to be questioned by scholars. First, whether the employment of the binary opposition distinguishing between Christians and Moslems is useful when discussing *English Protestant* views of Turks in the early modern period:[19] if 'it is specifically in the context of the Turkish threat in the East that Europe becomes a synonym for the Christian world',[20] then 'Europe' is a construct which, after the Reformation, is always already out of date. Second, if the production and reception of *Othello* is to be considered in its historical context, then current critical assumptions underlying audience negotiation with the Turkish element in the play may be shown to be fundamentally inaccurate, for the imposition of a European historical consciousness on the Jacobean playgoer may in fact constitute an *ahistorical* position, since the paradigm on which it is based is inapplicable and misleading.

To view the Turkish motif on the early modern English stage through the lens of a binary, Christian-Moslem opposition is to map onto England a narrative that was European in outlook and interest. Criticism's endorsement of the binary opposition thus allows the Turkish threat (always already present, according to this critical paradigm, in the Turkish motif) to impose a fictional unity on the west under the terms of which

England is glossed as 'European': Christian Europe is thus situated in *de facto* opposition to the Moslem threat. Consequently, the danger posed by the Ottoman Empire is not so much historicized as dehistoricized and re-presented in blanket terms, ironically underpinning a religious opposition that must be sustained, apparently, at all costs. Commentators accept the apparent 'universality' of the Turkish threat so that it is seen to operate in England on the same terms as it does in the Mediterranean.[21]

Although it has become orthodox to question the validity of the *grand recit*, the European narrative of the Turkish threat, for which the Christian-Moslem binary opposition is its structural and legitimating model, has enjoyed extraordinary longevity. Indeed, the underlying assumptions governing the historical image of the Turk would seem to be constant to this day, religious difference only partly displaced by a fundamental cultural impasse that proclaims modern Turkey's exclusion from Europe.[22] Yet the endurance of this narrative (whereby the structuring assumptions are upheld, even if the more virulent expressions of difference are suppressed or reformulated) testifies not to a deep-rooted historical tradition in which the Turk was demonized by the English, but signifies instead a blurring and dilution of ('western') national boundaries, a simplification of historical differences which allows the binary opposition purchase. In fact, the narrative's origins are indeed solidly European: what has remained constant has been Europe's (rather than England's) preoccupation with the Ottoman threat (metamorphosed into its residual essence – the very cultural difference that sustained opposition to the Turks even after the military threat waned); it is this tradition that has been allowed to speak, outside of history, as it were, for England, when England's perceptions of Turks in the early modern period were not only not in tune with those obtaining in Europe, but in fundamentally important political and strategic respects diametrically opposed to 'European' interests.

The modern narrative, according to which the Turkish presence in south-eastern Europe is constituted as a constant threat, a narrative which is at once historical and, subsequently, in its later formulations 'literary' or 'cultural', since it underpins not only immediate fears of military conquest but, in more recent times, shores up residual concerns that are cultural and racial, has its origins in Christian responses to the capture of Constantinople in 1453 by Mehmed II.[23] Although Constantinople was long considered vulnerable to the Turks, this nonetheless spectacular Turkish success galvanized European fears of Ottoman expansion, fears that were to be realized in the following hundred years at the expense of south-eastern Europe, the eastern Mediterranean and the coast of north Africa.[24] The capture of the city was of great symbolic importance, generating a simple narrative of fear underwriting a desire for a united Christian military response, a register of anti-Turkish sentiment that may for convenience but also for its historical momentousness be termed the '1453 narrative'. To adapt Hayden White's formulation, the 1453 narrative is both 'historical' and 'literary', for its subsequent deployment tropes history in the service of a narrative that, in effect, projects itself into the future.[25] This narrative was then not simply a means of understanding in religious terms the fundamental threat to Christian expansion which Turkish expansion posed, but also a historical project which demanded that the Turks be repelled by a Christian force – a narrative which was of course linked implicitly to its crusader 'ancestor', thus recalling the example of Christianity's victory over the infidel. Successive popes sought a Christian crusade against the Turks, but their attempts to impose the 1453 narrative's cumulative logic on Christian Europe was doomed to fail, since the binary opposition underpinning the crusades no longer held, and instead sixteenth-century Christian 'Europe' was riven by division and distrust. As Jacob Burckhardt remarks,

> great as was the terror felt for the Turks, and the actual danger from them, there was yet scarcely a government of any consequence [in fifteenth- and sixteenth-century Italy] which did not conspire against other Italian states with Mohammed II [Mehmed II (1451–81), conqueror of Constantinople] and his successors.[26]

The 1453 narrative is then to be seen only in part as a response to the capture of Constantinople, and rather more importantly in the context of a discussion of *Othello* as a narrative whose value was perceived to be greatest in the sixteenth century, when Ottoman forces most threatened Europe, and when simultaneously the Reformation threatened to destroy the 1453 narrative's logic from within. The Reformation may have made a crusade effectively impossible; for Protestant England the 1453 narrative was itself undesirable.

Because the 1453 narrative was driven and theorized by the papacy, it was a narrative which both reflected and promoted Catholic interests; it is for this reason that Protestant England was always unlikely to subscribe to its aims, a stand that further redefined the concept of a Christian crusade against the Turks as a *de facto* Catholic project.[27] Indeed, given England's own fear of Catholic power on the continent, a strong Turkish presence which threatened Europe's Catholic powers was in England's interest. In particular, since Turkish naval strength in the Mediterranean challenged England's main rival Catholic Spain's desire for control of the lucrative north African coastal trading ports, the Turkish threat worked to England's advantage.[28] Not only did the constant fear of the Turks keep the Catholic powers occupied (looking east rather than west), it allowed England to pursue her own economic, political and strategic interests independently of other Christian powers, and perhaps with a little less concern about Catholic intentions against England.

But England's 'Turkish policy', for so it may be styled, given its design and its effect, was not merely a passive, opportunist attempt to take advantage of Europe's weak flank, but a strategy in its own right, an attempt by Elizabeth I to extend England's sphere of influence and expand the country's economic reach. English merchants had been trading with the Ottoman Empire since the reign of Henry VIII, notably in 'Turkey carpets', which were prized by the court, and whose popularity and symbolism can be seen in paintings such as Holbein's *The Ambassadors* (1533),[29] but it was under Elizabeth that England's mercantile and political relations with the Turks were put on a firm footing and given the royal seal of approval. Her decision to send William Harborne to Constantinople in 1581 as both a trading and a court representative was to have far-reaching consequences, both in terms of England's relations with Catholic Europe and, most pertinently for a discussion of *Othello*'s audience, in terms of the perception of Turks in England. Far from England falling into line with Europe and subscribing to the 1453 narrative – which remains the underlying assumption governing criticism of this topic – England pursued an independent policy which served her own interests and implicitly damaged Catholic Europe's security. Indeed, at the height of the crisis with Spain in the 1580s, when England feared invasion, Elizabeth sought a military alliance with the Turks to defeat their common enemy, Spain.[30]

A striking example of the extent to which Elizabeth was willing to antagonize the Pope in her pursuit of an independent, 'non-European' strategy was her decision to allow English merchants to supply tin and other military materials to the Turks, supplies that could only have fuelled Turkish attacks on Europe.[31] Not only did this promote English trade and extend her sphere of influence, but it gave a thoroughly modern and materialist emphasis to its Protestant resistance to Catholic hegemony. The presence of England's second ambassador to the Ottoman Empire, Edward Barton, accompanying Sultan Murad III on his Austrian campaign in 1594, and in Hungary in 1596, with Sultan Mehmet III's war machine,[32] dramatically identified England's mercantile support for the Turkish military effort with diplomatic attempts to cement further the political and strategic implications of such co-operation. This ambassadorial recognition of Ottoman hegemony in Europe suggestively illustrates the dramatic change in attitudes that England underwent, a paradigm shift from

'Christian' to 'Protestant', as it were, that undermined the 1453 narrative's relevance for early modern England.

Nevertheless, that these changes were momentous is testament also to the residual authority of the 1453 narrative for people in England in the late sixteenth and early seventeenth century: that despite the imperatives of contemporary international politics, the Ottoman Empire remained an unknown culture, defined largely by its military prowess (which was marvelled at by historians such as Richard Knolles[33]) and its potential for frustrating Catholic Europe's desire for unity, but also identified in terms of the *fear* it provoked – fear which theorists identify as fear of the Other; if Turks were framed in terms of England's European anxieties, the racial-political stereotypes that *Othello* deploys were nonetheless still valid in England in 1604.[34] Simon Shepherd has argued that stage representations of Turks signified not only Turks *per se*, but also, for example, Spanish Catholics.[35] Thus in Shepherd's reading the Turk was a more complex – though still overwhelmingly *negative* – motif than has been allowed; but crucially the potential for allegorical interpretation for which Shepherd argues acknowledges the role of the audience in negotiating with stage representations of international politics. The image of the Turk on the early modern English stage therefore allowed neither the simplistic, ahistorical, 'European' sign of the Turk to function unproblematically, but nor was it able to erase this image from the minds of spectators who were at least as familiar with the 1453 narrative as they were with the newly defined Turk, who was at once the infidel and, as Catholic Spain's enemy, England's potential ally. The stage Turk that results, in the eyes of the audience, is then in critical terms a dialectical representation, and in effect a manifestation of the audience's power to interrogate.

It is in England's response to the Turkish defeat at Lepanto in 1571, and the later reincarnation of this response in *Othello* thirty years later, that this dialectical conflict between the 1453 narrative's residual purchase on English *Christian* sympathies and English *Protestant* fears of Catholic invasion can be seen most clearly. One year after the Pope excommunicated Elizabeth I, the success of the Holy Alliance's naval forces against the Turks at Lepanto in 1571 was celebrated across England, as it was throughout Europe;[36] one year after her death the battle was re-staged (albeit *offstage*) in Shakespeare's play, as if, in once again ensuring a Turkish defeat, the performance could 'erase' Elizabeth's Turkish policy from the audience's consciousness. The symbolic importance of the comprehensive defeat of the Turks at Lepanto can hardly be exaggerated (though its historical consequences were markedly less spectacular); undoubtedly the popular response in England was in line with the crusading rhetoric of Catholic Europe, despite the fact that, buoyed by the

Holy Alliance's victory, 'Philip II even thought of attacking Elizabeth at this time, so incapable of resistance did she appear'.[37] Yet when the victory at Lepanto was recalled thirty years later on the stage, it may be doubted that the response was so euphoric.

England's policy towards the Turks, established a decade after Lepanto, did not of course simply displace cultural attitudes, and indeed England's complex religious politics during the sixteenth century must have confused and disorientated many: the 1453 narrative's insistence on a Christian-Moslem binary opposition must still have appeared to be 'common sense'[38] for years and perhaps decades after Elizabeth's death in 1603, particularly when James I inaugurated a regressive policy against the Turks in keeping with the political logic of his 1604 peace with Spain.[39] But it is in popular perceptions of James's politics, as much as in the undoubted growth in knowledge of the Ottoman Empire that London merchants, travellers and adventurers must have experienced – and the stage registered – that prevents the Turkish motif from resuming, as it were, its role in the binary structure which Elizabeth's political strategy so clearly undermined. Crucially, then, it is both the changing political climate under Elizabeth, which enabled the Turk to be seen, gradually, as a potential ally, and the popularly-perceived Catholic tendency of James to move closer to Europe that renders the demonizing of the Turk inherently problematic. Thus it is significant that 'formal relations between England and Venice began soon after James's succession',[40] since it suggests that the new king's policy was European in outlook and implicitly at variance with Elizabeth's Turk-orientated foreign policy. Indeed, it is surely relevant to a discussion of *Othello* (and particularly pertinent with regard to the court performance of the play) that, according to the Venetian ambassador's report to Venice of 25 December 1603, James's 'European' political views had been made abundantly clear:

> The King [James I] openly shows that he has no affection for the Turkish alliance [established by Elizabeth], and that he thinks all Christian Princes ought to unite for the destruction of their common foe.[41]

Othello's Turkish properties are not therefore 'in themselves' significant, for to attempt to isolate the Turkish motif from its playhouse context would be implicitly to endorse the 1453 narrative, which the Reformation and Elizabeth's foreign policy had rendered weak and ineffectual (though at a rhetorical level this narrative undoubtedly retained some of its power); rather, *Othello*'s significance as a 'Turkish play' lies not in its relationship (however tenuous) to Elizabeth's policy, but in the perceived and actual relationship between this policy and England's apprehension of Catholic Europe in general and Spain in particular. Of much greater significance than the question of whether Turks *per se* were 'positive' or 'negative' factors in the early modern play is the resultant dialectic that the politically-aware Protestant audience is able to identify: how far the demonizing of Turks follows a *Catholic* agenda. Staging the Turkish threat results in a complex interpretive negotiation that displaces the 1453 narrative from its implied centre in English politics. Instead of dispensing with the Turks as *Othello* does so effortlessly, therefore, the play-text may be opened up by a sceptical audience able to participate parochially and politically in this version of Mediterranean history, and this audience may well resist the play's assertions on the basis that it too, like the play, is historically aware, and is not easily persuaded by the historical fiction that *Othello* imposes.

Tracing the Turkish motif in *Othello* is therefore a process of historicizing the text through the politically-aware audience. This is not to suggest that some or all of the spectators were political in their motivations; rather, that the text releases the potential for recognition which the contemporary playgoer might then use as the basis for a more thorough interrogation of the European political picture which the play invokes but cannot sustain. For it is *Othello*'s re-presentation of recent European history in the mode of 'what if' history, or 'Virtual History',[42] that may have raised the audience's suspicions and in turn led to a productive engagement with the text. As a 'counterfactual', fictionalized history play,[43] *Othello* appears to both call up the 1453 narrative and in doing so call that very same narrative into question: it produces a logical closure of the 1453 narrative – defeat of the Turks – that, because it is at once at variance with historical fact and out of tune with popular anti-Catholic sentiment, allows the audience to question the text's deeper political motives. Far from employing the Turkish motif then as a mere background device, as critics contend, *Othello* not only depends on that motif for its political, pro-European, pro-Catholic strategy, but leaves itself open to a specifically *Protestant* reading of its content that encourages the spectator to interpret the text against the grain, because of the sheer velocity of the historical content it distorts.

As Emrys Jones notes, *Othello* depicts recent European history: it is set in 1570–71, when Cyprus, held by Venice since 1473, was attacked by the Turks. Moreover, according to his reading, it is likely that the play 'was intended to reflect James I's opinions and tastes', for the king published a commemorative poem on the battle of Lepanto in 1591,[44] which was reprinted on James's accession to the throne in 1603.[45] Thus the performance by the King's Men at court on 1 November 1604[46] may well have been a tribute to the new king's political views: James's desire for better relations with Spain, together with his more conventional (more 'Christian') pro-European view of the Turks might seem to be satisfied by a play in which the Turks are vanquished and European power reasserted. The destruction of Othello may then be regarded, albeit in rather crude terms, as a further, symbolic defeat of the Other, reasserting a European, Catholic purity over the forces of the Crescent – the latter formulation merging 'Turk' and 'Moor' indiscriminately. This recasting of Christianity as united against the Moslem Other clearly subsumes Protestantism under the umbrella of a European Christianity, which is of course effectively European Catholicism.

The point at which *Othello*'s reliance on recent European history becomes problematic, rather than merely anachronistic, is when the text rescues Cyprus with the aid of its *deus ex machina*, the storm that destroys the Turkish fleet.[47] The text steers a dangerous course, at once 'quoting' history and rewriting it, demanding that it be 'remembered' and 'forgotten' simultaneously. As Jones reminds the modern reader,

> The Turks had landed in Cyprus in 1570; one of the two chief Cypriot towns, Nicosia, soon fell; the other, Famagusta, underwent a long siege. It was these events which led to the Lepanto engagement. But the victory of Lepanto did not in fact restore Cyprus to Venice. Famagusta fell to the Turks on 1 August 1571, which left them in possession of the island. At the time of *Othello*'s composition therefore (c. 1602–4), Cyprus had been in Turkish hands for over thirty years.[48]

In fact the battle of Lepanto took place *after* the loss of Cyprus, on 7 October 1571; the Holy Alliance had given up on the prospect of their forces being able to aid Cyprus. Unfortunately for the Holy Alliance, wintry conditions in the Mediterranean made the deployment of large fleets hazardous, and the advantage that the Lepanto victory afforded over the Turks was not pursued.[49]

The problem, clearly, is that in historicizing the audience's consciousness the text also demands a suspension of disbelief. This is not to suggest that the audience was *acutely* aware of recent history and contemporary politics[50] – rather, that the 1453 narrative overdetermines the reception of the text so that it becomes impossible to separate the two fundamental features of the 1453 narrative from the play's simultaneous historical and ahistorical fiction. If the 1453 narrative is at once a narrative of failure and faith in that it registers defeat as a condition of its will to rebirth, its desire for victory predicated on its knowledge of past disaster (and present disappointment), then *Othello* may be seen to attempt through a dramatized fiction of the events of 1570–71 to impose its own logic on a narrative that is divided against itself. Insofar as the narrative espoused by the Catholic European powers aspires to victory in the future, its past and present history articulate the reverse: *Othello* attempts to circumvent a history which must always deconstruct itself.

'In Act 1', Emrys Jones observes,

> everything seems – or perhaps would have seemed to Shakespeare's first audience – to be moving towards the naval action which culminated in Lepanto and which was fought over the same issue as that presented in the play: the possession of Cyprus. ... Given the fame of Lepanto, Shakespeare's audience could not have been blamed if they had expected the play to run along lines much more true to history than the play they were actually given. ... [But] the military and naval clash which we seem led to expect never takes place.[51]

What *Othello* offers, therefore, instead of the historically accurate version of events which it encourages its audience to anticipate, is a rewriting of history which both depends on and challenges the 1453 narrative. The text can be seen then to epitomize the 1453 narrative's implicit contradictions, for in the historical 'moment' of Lepanto recast in *Othello* the battle is fictionalized as a victory which prevents the historical loss of Cyprus. While Cyprus's loss was of greater significance to Venice than to Europe, Lepanto was of immense symbolic significance for the Holy Alliance, and it was desirable for contemporary and later historians to lessen the importance of Cyprus in their accounts and heighten the value of Lepanto. However, in *Othello* the two events are intertwined and redeployed, refashioned as a fiction. The text of *Othello*, its narrative self-fashioning,[52] demands that the audience register the salvation of Cyprus in the defeat of the Turks – a fabrication that can only draw attention to its fiction. Indeed, since, as Jones observes, spectators were likely to have expected the dramatization of the Turkish attack – it is after all presented as overriding all other considerations in Act 1, scene 3 – it is in the text's very failure to *stage* its fiction that its historical untruth is, paradoxically, rendered visible. The Turks must instead be destroyed offstage by a storm, and removed from the audience's consciousness. Indeed, if the storm in *Othello* reminds the audience of the destruction of the Spanish Armada in 1588[53] – similarly, an event which took place 'offstage', as it were – it may do so of course ironically, in effect redirecting the 1588 cultural memory in *Othello* against the Turks and in the service of a pro-Spanish policy.[54]

What is important therefore is not whether 'Shakespeare had the events of 1570–1 in mind' when he wrote *Othello*,[55] but how the play might have been interrogated by an audience that perhaps knew that Cyprus was captured by the Turks in 1571, and certainly was familiar with the traditional European anti-Turkish narrative. *Othello* thus offers an instance of an early modern play whose interpretation on the Jacobean stage was conditioned, the critic can be reasonably certain, by a core of knowledge or contextual familiarity shared by many of the spectators present. This is not to claim that *all* playgoers interpreted *Othello* in the way suggested here; rather, that the play's high-risk gamble with history, and with the audience, may have spectacularly backfired.[56]

Othello dramatizes the 1453 narrative and projects it back into history to secure a future victory. Yet whatever its destination as a text, however it is activated by its interlocutors, its design is fundamentally *ironic*: that is, it undermines its own project even as it asserts it, and reveals its politics even in the act of concealment. In rescuing Cyprus from the Turks *Othello* metamorphoses the Battle of Lepanto, refiguring it in the form of a storm[57] (as if sent by God), a wish-fulfilment on behalf of Christians whose desire is emblazoned across its own fictionality, a fantastic *deus ex machina* device in which only the devout can believe. The storm is a preposterous fantasy, a conjuror's trick with history which displays its fiction so visibly because its desire for enactment is underwritten by European history's 'common' narrative, Christianity's fear of the Turks. *Othello*'s problems with history arise not simply because it depicts an event that did not happen – the Christian salvation of Cyprus – but because it 'quotes' Lepanto, thus elevating the symbolic Catholic victory over the Turks and so undermining the play's historical validity. It is *Othello*'s attempt to offer a 'virtual history', producing an ahistorical Christian triumph, that illuminates its own ideological agenda.

The audience reception of *Othello* in performance cannot be predicated entirely on a spectatorial historicizing of the performance-text, unless there is also a contextual relationship established which focuses in turn on the likely prejudices of the London playgoer. Given the residual cultural resistance to Turks the 1453 narrative encourages, it is unlikely that the historical infelicities of *Othello* alone, or the gradual emergence of Anglo-Turkish discourse as a result of trading and political links filtering into London life, would encourage a playgoer to interrogate the text to the extent suggested here; presumably the shock of the disappearing act that accompanies the apocalyptic quotation that is the Turkish threat would give way to an engagement with the domestic politics which the play (by critical consensus) deals. But if the Elizabethan playgoer enjoyed plays which attacked the unpopular Catholics (invariably Spanish or Italian), and since the stage had begun to register the new English interest in Turks that clearly went beyond the religious demonizing of the 1453 narrative, then the Jacobean playgoer was almost certainly aware of the change in political climate which the new regime inaugurated. James's treaty with Spain was deeply unpopular and suggested to the popular imagination a desire to foster closer relations with England's bitter rival. Similarly, in the context of his attitude to the Turks, which manifested itself most clearly in an attempt to dismantle the Levant Company which Elizabeth had fostered,[58] James's poem *Lepanto* is an early indication of both his anti-Turkish stance and his pro-European politics which the poem's implicit support for the 1453 narrative, and its progeny the Catholic Holy Alliance, illustrates. The reception of *Othello*, then, may have been mediated by the same process that underwrote Elizabeth's Turkish policy, namely the secondary effect of indirectly undermining Spain. If the popular perception of James was that he was dangerously pro-Spanish, and if this resulted in responses to 'European' plays which registered this unease, then it may well be that *Othello*'s treatment of Turks was perceived as not being not simply anti-Turkish but implicitly, and, as it were, secretly, pro-Catholic.

In this respect, *Othello* as a 'European' play, as a text that offers less an English view of events than a pan-Christian (Catholic) attempt to reinvigorate the 1453 narrative in Protestant England, participates in a process of textual transaction which situates the active, historically-aware audience in opposition to the politics of the text. *Othello* becomes, in this reading, an advocate of not only the 1453 narrative, but of the pan-Catholic Holy Alliance.

Whether the text can deliver its Catholic project, simply by demonizing Othello – the somewhat inevitable consequence of seeking a united Christian front in opposition to the Moslem threat, since the binary system demands a reductionist simplicity in order for 'Christianity' to function at all – must surely be open to question. For in removing the Turkish threat from the play the drama is left without its historical antagonist,[59] and is then as it were determined on destroying the non-Christian general. But far from encouraging its audience to adopt a 'European' attitude towards the Turks, whether as a consequence of the depiction of the destruction of the Turkish navy[60] or in the play's gradual undermining of Othello, the play surely exposes its own ideological and political divisions, the very disunity that lay at the heart of the historical failure of Christians (or rather Catholics) to repel the Turkish threat. Indeed, *Othello* accurately portrays Burckhardt's description of intrigue that characterized the precariousness of the Venetian state, oscillating as it did, historically, between war and trade (sometimes both) with the Ottoman Empire:

> Within the ranks of the [Venetian] nobility itself, travel, commercial enterprise, and incessant wars with the Turks saved the wealthy and dangerous from that fruitful source of conspiracies – idleness.[61]

The 'idleness' that ensues after the destruction of the Turkish fleet in *Othello* allows the play's nascent conspiracies to blossom. In its domesticating of international affairs, therefore, *Othello* may have suggested to its audience *not* the ideal of a European unity under a Christian, anti-Turkish banner, but ironically a more realistic, and pessimistic, view (underwritten by the audience's knowledge of actual, rather than virtual, history) of European *dis*unity and disarray. Following the removal of the Turkish fleet in *Othello* the 'domestic' politics which thereafter dominates the play may have been interpreted as historically *accurate*, as a version of European failure to unite which is not, under Protestant eyes, a *Christian* failure, but a symptomatic failure of the Catholic church. In this reading *Othello* offers, despite itself, a version of Europe's failure to capitalize on Lepanto. The insertion of the historical battle into history to freeze the moment of danger merely highlights its status as a flash in the pan: its success in *Othello* merely points to its failure in European history.

After the storm that destroys the Turks Othello orders a banquet, a celebration that may be regarded as ironic by the spectators (and rather less enticing than the promise of a sea battle dramatized on stage).[62] Indeed, the banquet scene not only compromises the play as a historical narrative but highlights the failure of Lepanto to inaugurate a new Christian crusade. The text has already foreshadowed Othello's vulnerability, and the celebrations of Cyprus's deliverance are clearly premature, even, and especially, in terms of the 'domestic' politics of the play; but in historical terms this 'domestic' scene reveals its 'international' conceit: laid bare is *Othello*'s sub-narrative – the failure, not success, of Lepanto. *Othello* cannot simply 'quote' Lepanto as a Christian victory, then, without also signalling its long-term historical failure; ironically, this dual narrative is in keeping with the 1453 narrative's unending crisis.

If the play is interrogated by a sceptical audience as a boastful, empty fiction, then its depiction of treachery and malice may have been interpreted as representing the bickering and division that characterized Catholic Europe's attempts to act in concert. As Patricia Parker has observed, 'it has often been remarked what an extraordinary emphasis is given in *Othello* to narrative and the demand for narrative, to the relating of a story or report'.[63] Stephen Greenblatt has described this as the '*submission to narrative self-fashioning*', and observes that Iago performs a 'ceaseless narrative invention' which tricks the play's other characters so that, ultimately, 'they have always already experienced submission to narrativity'.[64] But this obsession with narrative is not only an internal property of the text; it is not only a facet of the text in performance which necessarily makes narrative demands on the spectators, who also narrate. Narration in *Othello*, while clearly undermining the play-world's domestic economy, also draws attention to its own narrative gambit: its conflicting narratives further undermine its attempts to carry through its political project.

Othello is 'a pageant / To keep us in false gaze', a ruse to fool the audience, a sign of Shakespeare's own religious beliefs perhaps,[65] and/or an attempt to flatter the new king, as Emrys Jones suggests; but more importantly the text engages with a historical narrative of Turkish terror that Protestant England was beginning to question. Indeed, *Othello* may in this respect, straddling as it does the reigns of two very different monarchs, be regarded as pivotal in regard to the changing image of the Turk in early modern English drama: despite itself, it belatedly recognizes, in the urgency of its Catholic project, the changing perception of Turks in early modern England that Elizabeth's foreign policy and Philip II's invasion plans had laid the foundations for fifteen years previously, and which had now been brought up to date in the popularly perceived Catholic sympathies of the new monarch. Though the critical history of the play's Turkish properties has endorsed rather than questioned its recourse to virtual history, its quest for the 1453 narrative's wish-fulfilment lays bare its Catholic credentials: Jacobean spectators may have been alert to this strategy, and have seen through the text's Catholic project. Gary Taylor observes that 'in early modern England the relation between Englishness and Christianness was important, contested, and uncertain. It was impossible not to have a position, and any position entailed an opposition'.[66] Because Christianity was disunited, the Turkish motif on the early modern English stage did not, and could not, operate at the binary level, since it had no natural antagonist; instead, it was inserted into the complex opposition between English Protestantism and European Catholicism. The battle of Lepanto did not re-establish the 1453 narrative in England, and even in Europe it was a false dawn for those seeking to reinvigorate the myth of an anti-Turkish crusade; its appearance in *Othello*, empty of its historical content, merely exposes it as a fantastic fiction, a fiction to which its Protestant audience would be unlikely to be sympathetic.

In his discussion of the historical significance of Lepanto, Braudel remarks on the difficulty the historian faces in narrating this immensely important *symbolic* event:

> Lepanto was the most spectacular military event in the Mediterranean during the entire sixteenth century. Dazzling triumph of courage and naval technique though it was, it is hard to place convincingly in a conventional historical perspective. One certainly cannot say that this sensational feat was the logical outcome of preceding events. ... People have always found it surprising – and Voltaire found it amusing – that this unexpected victory should have had so few consequences. The battle of Lepanto was fought on 7th October 1571; the following year the allies were unsuccessful at Modon. In 1573, Venice abandoned the struggle, exhausted. In 1574, the Turks triumphed at La Goletta and Tunis, and all dreams of a crusade vanished in the wind.[67]

Although Braudel concludes that the Holy Alliance victory in 1571 signalled that 'the spell of Turkish supremacy had been broken',[68] his treatment of the battle and its (lack of) consequences as a *problem* for contemporary commentators and subsequent historians draws attention to its ambiguous status; it is the difficulty of inserting Lepanto into a historical narrative that problematizes it as a historical *event*. For if Lepanto can be seen to have been a false dawn – and was seen as such during the years immediately following the battle – then clearly there opened up a yawning gap between the symbolic significance of the Christian victory and the actual ramifications of the Turkish defeat. If the 1453 narrative was driven by its (narrative) recognition of the 'fall' of Constantinople, an event all too real, foreshadowing as it did Turkish inroads into Europe, its need to symbolize Lepanto, to rejuvenate itself, may be seen to have resulted, in terms of practical results, in failure. As *Othello* demonstrates, Lepanto and its aftermath may be seen to epitomize the internal divisions in Europe that the 1453 narrative registered, almost as a condition of its narrative power. Shakespeare's play inserts Lepanto into a symbolic virtual history the 1453 narrative can never secure, at once registering and participating in the epistemological crisis Braudel identifies: the impossibility of Lepanto delivering what it 'should'.

Notes

[1] All references to *Othello* are to the edition prepared by Walter Cohen, in Stephen Greenblatt, gen. ed., *The Norton Shakespeare* (New York and London: W.W. Norton and Company, 1997), 1.3.19–20, 1.3. 221–6.

2   On Othello's absence from the beginning of the play, see Janet Adelman, 'Iago's Alter Ego: Race as Projection in *Othello*', *Shakespeare Quarterly* 48.2 (Summer 1997), 125–44; 125.
3   See C.A. Patrides, '"The Bloody and Cruell Turk": The Background of a Renaissance Commonplace', *Studies in the Renaissance* 10 (1963), 126–35.
4   Norman Sanders, ed., William Shakespeare, *Othello* (Cambridge: Cambridge University Press, 1984), 18.
5   See John Gillies, *Shakespeare and the Geography of Difference* (Cambridge: Cambridge University Press, 1994), 32 where Gillies suggests that the Turkish threat to Cyprus parallels the 'threat' Othello poses to Desdemona. In structural terms therefore the Turkish threat is legitimately displaced, since the more important threat in the play is that foregrounded by Iago in the opening scene.
6   Ibid. See also Edward Berry, 'Othello's Alienation', *Studies in English Literature* 30 (1990), 315–33, 330. Dennis Bartholomeusz argues that 'Othello surely is not meant to think well of himself, for he groups himself with a "turbaned Turk", the "circumcised dog" he once destroyed'; see Bartholomeusz, 'Shakespeare Imagines the Orient: The Orient Imagines Shakespeare', in Stanley Wells et al. eds, *Shakespeare and Cultural Traditions* (London and Toronto: Associated University Presses, 1994), 188–204, 193.
7   As Walter Cohen remarks, 'he is and is not the Turk', 2098.
8   Gillies, *Shakespeare and the Geography of Difference*, 32.
9   The terms 'Turk' and 'Moor' were both used quite freely in early modern English drama to denote a range of geographically diverse peoples. There is a substantial body of criticism on the image of the Moor on stage: see for example Anthony Gerard Barthelemy, *Black Face, Maligned Race: The Representation of Blacks in English Drama from Shakespeare to Southerne* (Baton Rouge and London: Louisiana State University Press, 1987); Ania Loomba, *Gender, Race, Renaissance Drama* (Manchester: Manchester University Press, 1989); Jack D'Amico, *The Moor in English Renaissance Drama* (Tampa: University of South Florida Press, 1991); and Joyce Green MacDonald, ed., *Race, Ethnicity, and Power in the Renaissance* (London: Associated University Presses, 1997).
10 As Virginia Mason Vaughan notes, 'despite Venice's need for Othello's military acumen, the Venetian outlook in Shakespeare's play is predominantly racist'; see Vaughan, *'Othello': A Contextual History* (Cambridge: Cambridge University Press, 1994), 65.
11 Samuel Chew, *The Crescent and the Rose: Islam and England During the Renaissance* (Oxford: Oxford University Press, 1937; rpt 1965).

There have also been a number of unpublished PhD dissertations on the subject.

[12] Vaughan, 13.

[13] Ibid., 34.

[14] Ibid., 13–14.

[15] See Edward Said, *Orientalism: Western Conceptions of the Orient* [1978] (London: Penguin, 1991), and *Culture and Imperialism* (London: Chatto and Windus, 1993). For a wide-ranging critique of both Said's approach and the narrative he seeks to establish, see Bart Moore-Gilbert, *Postcolonial Theory: Contexts, Practices, Politics* (London: Verso, 1997), especially 34–73, and Robert White, *White Mythologies: Writing History and the West* (London: Routledge, 1990), especially the chapter 'Disorienting Orientalism', 119–40. The problem of Said's reliance on binary oppositions is seized on by John MacKenzie, who remarks that 'Said is situated at the watershed of the modernist-postmodernist debate. ... In *Orientalism* he seems to be a monolithic modernist; in all his ideological statements since, a committed postmodernist'; see John M. MacKenzie, *Orientalism: History, Theory and the Arts* (Manchester: Manchester University Press, 1995), 6–7. For a critique of Said's thesis in relation to its possible application to the image of the Turk in early modern English literature, see A.J. Hoenselaars, 'The Elizabethans and the Turk at Constantinople', *Cahiers Elisabethains* 47 (1995), 29–42.

[16] It is revealing that *Orientalism* does not mention Lady Mary Wortley Montagu's letters, for these texts clearly do not demonise the Ottoman Empire, as Said's thesis demands, but instead are often positive responses to the experience of cultural difference.

[17] Said, 59–60.

[18] See for example N.I. Matar, 'The Renegade in English Seventeenth-Century Imagination', *Studies in English Literature* 33 (1993), 489–505, and '"Turning Turk": Conversion to Islam in English Renaissance Thought', *Durham University Journal* 55.1 (January 1994), 33–41; Roslyn L. Knutson, 'Elizabethan Documents, Captivity Narratives, and the Market for Foreign History Plays', *English Literary Renaissance* 26.3 (Winter 1996), 75–110; Lois Potter, 'Pirates and "Turning Turk" in Renaissance Drama', in Jean-Pierre Maquerlot and Michele Willems, eds, *Travel and Drama in Shakespeare's Time* (Cambridge: Cambridge University Press, 1996), 124–40; Ania Loomba, 'Shakespeare and Cultural Difference', in Terence Hawkes, ed., *Alternative Shakespeares: Volume 2* (London: Routledge, 1996), 164–98; Daniel J. Vitkus, 'Turning Turk in *Othello*: The Conversion and Damnation of the Moor', *Shakespeare Quarterly* 48.2 (Summer

1997), 145–76; Carolyn Prager, '"Turkish" and Turkish Slavery: English Renaissance Perceptions of Levantine Bondage', *Centrepoint* (Fall 1976), 57–64; Orhan Burian, 'Interest of the English in Turkey as Reflected in English Literature of the Renaissance', *Oriens* 5 (1952), 209–29; and Louis Wann, 'The Oriental in Elizabethan Drama', *Modern Philology* 12.7 (January 1915), 423–47.

[19] Huston Diehl, *Staging Reform, Reforming the Stage: Protestantism and Popular Theater in Early Modern England* (Ithaca and London: Cornell University Press, 1997), observes that 'even though revisionist historians emphasize the divisiveness of the Reformation, literary scholars have to a remarkable extent disregarded the contested nature of sixteenth-century Christianity. Many who examine the Christian elements of Renaissance drama ignore Reformation controversies altogether, instead choosing to treat Christianity as a single, unified religion and to focus on archetypes, myths, and biblical narratives that are shared by all Christian faiths' (3, 7n). Similarly, Deborah K. Shuger contends that 'contemporary [i.e. modern] critics of Shakespeare have ... tended to bypass or subvert any religious content of the plays in order to reclaim their authority for more radical, politicized, skeptical – and therefore more congenial – audiences'. See Shuger, 'Shakespeare and Christianity', in Donna B. Hamilton and Richard Strier, eds, *Religion, Literature, and Politics in Post-Reformation England, 1540–1688* (Cambridge: Cambridge University Press, 1996), 46–69, 47.

[20] Kevin Wilson and Jan van der Dussen, eds, *The History of the Idea of Europe*, rev. edn (London: Routledge and The Open University, 1995), 37.

[21] Vaughan for example asserts that 'in Shakespeare's day, the Eastern Other – the Turk – was not only transformed but demonized as well in a *European frenzy* of fear and hatred that indicated just how threatened *the West* really felt' (italics added), 23.

[22] An instance of this occurred in 1997 when a Dutch politician declared that Turkey would never become a full member of the European Community because the EC is a 'Christian Club'.

[23] For an early sixteenth-century account of the capture of the city which participates in the 1453 narrative's call to arms, see Theodore Spandounes, *On the Origin of the Ottoman Emperors* trans. and ed. Donald M. Nicol (Cambridge: Cambridge University Press, 1997). The text was first published in Italian in 1509 and translated into French in 1538. As Nicol observes, 'Spandounes repeatedly deplores the inability of the western Christian powers to sink their own petty

squabbles and collaborate in this nobler and more vital cause' – the war against the Turks; see his Introduction, viii.

24 For a survey of sixteenth- and seventeenth-century responses by English writers to the Turkish victory in 1453, see Kenneth Friedenreich, 'English Renaissance Accounts of the Fall of Constantinople', *English Miscellany* 26 (1977), 105–27.

25 See Hayden White, *Metahistory: The Historical Imagination in Nineteenth-Century Europe* (Baltimore and London: The Johns Hopkins University Press, 1973); *Tropics of Discourse: Essays in Cultural Criticism* (Baltimore and London: The Johns Hopkins University Press, 1978) and *The Content of the Form: Narrative Discourse and Historical Representation* (Baltimore and London: The Johns Hopkins University Press, 1987). For a discussion of White's work, see F.R. Ankersmit, 'Kantian Narrativism and Beyond', in Mieke Bal and Inge Boer, eds, *The Point of Theory: Practices of Cultural Analysis* (New York: Continuum, 1994), 155–60, 193–7. A relevant example of a historian's troping of history – whereby the text is no longer a study in historical method, but becomes a 'literary' text, since it relies on the use of a literary trope to illustrate its 'historical' project – is Steven Runciman's *The Fall of Constantinople, 1453* (Cambridge: Cambridge University Press, 1965). Runciman formulates the capture of the city in Biblical terms (the *Fall*) and tropes 1453 as a tragedy. His project is not merely 'historical', but sets out to portray the Turks as barbarians who threaten civilization. A secondary narrative, linked to this 'barbarity', is the text's plea for the study of Classics to be restored to the 'centre' of learning. Thus Runciman writes that 'the date of 29 May 1453 marks a turning point in history. It marks the end of an old story, the story of Byzantine civilization. For eleven hundred years there had stood on the Bosphorus a city where intellect was admired and the learning and the letters of the Classical past were studied and preserved' (189). He does make it clear at the outset, however: that 'in this story the Greek people is the tragic hero; and I have tried to tell it with that in mind' (xiii) – despite the fact that he acknowledges that 'even in the wide political field the fall of Constantinople altered very little', xi. Runciman does include a useful overview of 'Principle Sources for a History of the Fall of Constantinople' (192–8). See also in this respect Elizabeth Hallam, ed., *Chronicles of the Crusades: Eye-Witness Accounts of the Wars Between Christianity and Islam* (Godalming: Bramley Books, 1996).

26 Jacob Burckhardt, *The Civilization of the Renaissance in Italy*, trans. S.G.C. Middlemore (Oxford and London: Phaidon Press, 1945), 59.

27 As Christopher Tyerman remarks, 'the Crusade was a carefully defined weapon in the temporal and spiritual armoury of the western church, the particular prerogative of the papacy'; see Tyerman, *England and the Crusades, 1095–1588* (Chicago and London: Chicago University Press, 1988), 345.

28 See Edwin Pears, 'The Spanish Armada and the Ottoman Porte', *The English Historical Review* 8 (1893), 429–66.

29 John Sweetman, *The Oriental Obsession: Islamic Inspiration in British and American Art and Architecture, 1500–1920* (Cambridge: Cambridge University Press, 1988), 10–11; see especially 10–43. For a brief discussion of the Turkish carpet in Holbein's *The Ambassadors*, see Lisa Jardine, *Worldly Goods: A New History of the Renaissance* (London and Basingstoke: Macmillan, 1996), 429. John M. MacKenzie discusses the issue of influence in *Orientalism: History, Theory and the Arts*. See also the catalogue for the 1988 exhibition of Islamic art at the British Museum, J.M. Rogers and R.M. Ward, eds, *Suleiman the Magnificent* (London: British Museum Publications, 1988).

30 On Elizabeth's desire for economic and political co-operation with the Ottoman Empire, see Arthur Leon Horniker, 'William Harborne and the Beginning of Anglo-Turkish Diplomatic and Commercial Relations', *The Journal of Modern History* 14.3 (September 1942), 289–316. Harborne's desire to further England's relations with the Turks, and enlist their help against Spain, is evident in a memorial he wrote to the sultan in November 1587. Horniker writes that Harborne 'exhorts the sultan to unite his forces with those of the queen for the complete extermination of the common enemies of England and the Porte. Like his mistress, he completely dissociates the English people and their faith from the other Christians and establishes a definite religious identity between Protestantism and Islam' (309). See also Susan Skilliter, 'William Harborne, The First English Ambassador, 1583–1588', in William Hale and Ali Ihsan Bagis, eds, *Four Centuries of Turco-British Relations: Studies in Diplomatic, Economic, and Cultural Affairs* (Humberside: The Eothen Press, 1984), 10–25. Skilliter notes that 'perhaps the most important achievement of his embassy was the bringing about of the cancellation of the renewal of the Hispano-Ottoman armistice by land and sea in 1587, since the insecurity thus created on Spain's Mediterranean flank may have helped to prevent the sending of the Armada against England that year' (23). Skilliter explores the subject of Anglo-Turkish relations in greater depth in *William Harborne and the Trade with Turkey, 1578–1582: A Documentary Study of the First Anglo-Ottoman Relations*

(Oxford: Oxford University Press, 1977). See also Sarah Searight, *The British in the Middle East*, rev. edn (London and The Hague: East-West Publications, 1979), especially 16–41, and Mordecai Epstein, *The English Levant Company: Its Foundation and its History to 1640* (New York: Burt Franklin, 1968).

31 Elizabeth I was excommunicated by the Pope in February 1570, just before the Turkish attack on Cyprus; England began supplying military raw materials to the Ottoman Empire after 1570; see Jardine, 373–4.

32 Geoffrey Lewis, 'Turks and Britons Over Four Hundred Years', in Hale and Ihsan, eds, *Four Centuries of Turco-British Relations*, 125.

33 Richard Knolles published *The Generall Historie of the Turkes* in 1603, dedicating it to James I, and brought out a second edition in 1610. After his death in 1611 further editions were published (with 'collaborators'' editions) in 1621, 1631 and 1638, and throughout the seventeenth century. Most scholars believe Shakespeare consulted Knolles while writing *Othello*. Virginia Mason Vaughan rather absurdly remarks that Shakespeare 'would also have sensed – by the bulk of the volume if nothing else – Knolles' fear of Turkish threats to Christian civilization' (25). On Knolles's *Historie*, see Christine Woodhead, '"The Present Terrour of the World"?: Contemporary Views of the Ottoman Empire c.1600', *History* 72.234 (February 1987), 20–37.

34 See for example Bernard Harris, 'A Portrait of a Moor', *Shakespeare Survey* 11 (1958), 89–97 and G.K. Hunter, 'Elizabethans and Foreigners', *Shakespeare Survey* 17 (1964), 37–52.

35 See Simon Shepherd, *Marlowe and the Politics of Elizabethan Theatre* (Hemel Hempstead: Harvester Wheatsheaf, 1986), 'Turks and Fathers', 142–77.

36 Ann Williams remarks that 'both the relief of Malta [from Turkish siege, in 1565] and the success at Lepanto were greeted with public rejoicing and the ringing of bells in the west': Williams, 'Mediterranean Conflict', in Metin Kunt and Christine Woodhead, eds, *Suleyman the Magnificent and His Age: The Ottoman Empire in the Early Modern World* (London and New York: Longman, 1995), 53. On the battle of Lepanto, see Fernand Braudel, *The Mediterranean and the Mediterranean World in the Age of Philip II*, vol. 2, trans. Sian Reynolds (London: Fontana, 1987), 1088–1142; Andrew C. Hess, 'The Battle of Lepanto and its Place in Mediterranean History', *Past and Present* 57 (November 1972), 53–73; Bernard Lewis, *The Muslim Discovery of Europe* (London: Phoenix, 1994), 43–4; and R.C.

Anderson, *Naval Wars in the Levant, 1559–1857* (Liverpool: Liverpool University Press, 1952), 24–54.

37 Braudel, vol. 2, 1105.

38 The expression is employed here with Catherine Belsey's discussion in mind; see her 'Criticism and Common Sense', in *Critical Practice* (London: Methuen, 1980), 1–36.

39 James I ended England's sea war with Spain on 23 June 1603. See D.B. Quinn, 'Sailors and the Sea', *Shakespeare Survey* 17 (1964), 21–6, 35.

40 See Vaughan: 'During Elizabeth's reign relations had been poor, and only after her death did the Venetian Senate vote to send formal emissaries to the English monarch'; Venetian ambassadors arrived in Southampton on 17 November 1603 (15). Vaughan also discusses the 'myth of Venice' in England (15–21).

41 Horatio F. Brown, ed., *Calendar of State Papers and Manuscripts Relating to English Affairs, Existing in the Archives and Collections of Venice*, vol. 10 (London: Kraus Reprint, 1970), 125; cited in Vaughan, 27.

42 See Niall Ferguson, ed., *Virtual History: Alternatives and Counterfactuals* (London: Picador, 1997), especially his Introduction, 1–90.

43 According to Ferguson, 'counterfactuals should be those which contemporaries contemplated'; ibid., 87.

44 Emrys Jones, '*Othello*, Lepanto, and the Cyprus Wars', *Shakespeare Survey* 21 (1968), 47–52; reprinted in *Aspects of 'Othello': Articles Reprinted from 'Shakespeare Survey'* (Cambridge: Cambridge University Press, 1977), 61–6, to which reference is made here. Jones points out that Cyprus was attacked by the Turks only once. Alvin Kernan suggests a possible textual correspondence between the poem and Shakespeare's play – *Lepanto* refers to 'circumcised Turband Turkes'. Kernan's description of a number of Shakespeare plays performed at court, including *Othello*, as 'patronage art' further underlines the possibility that the play was designed to please the King's Men's new patron. If Shakespeare *did* quote *Lepanto*, then it is striking that this textual moment should occur at the play's close, when the play appears to resolve the question of Othello's identity in his suicide. See Alvin Kernan, *Shakespeare, the King's Playwright: Theater in the Stuart Court, 1603–1613* (New Haven and London: Yale University Press, 1995), 61, xxiii.

45 'It was written several years before, probably in 1585, when James was nineteen'; ibid., 61. Jones cites James Craigie's edition, *The Poems of James VI of Scotland*, vol. 1 (Edinburgh and London, 1955),

xlviii. If this date is correct then James wrote this 'European' poem when Elizabeth's isolationist, 'pro-Turkish' policy was being established. Kernan dates the poem to 1584 (61).

46 Most editors date the composition of the play to 1603–1604, but for an earlier date see E.A.J. Honigmann, 'The First Quarto of *Hamlet* and the Date of *Othello*', *Review of English Studies* 44.174 (1993), 211–19.

47 For a discussion of stage pirates as a *deus ex machina*, see Richard S. Ide, 'Shakespeare and the Pirates', *Iowa State Journal of Research* 58.3 (February 1984), 311–18. Ide quotes the comment of Georges de Scudery: 'You might think that God had given them [the playwrights] the winds done up in a bag as they are given to Ulysses, so freely do these gentlemen loose them to create a shipwreck' (311). Ide's conclusion is pertinent to the argument pursued here: the Shakespearean pirate, then, should be understood finally as a metaphor for the intervention of a just Providence in the affairs of men, indeed as a symbol of God's active government of the world stage (317). Much the same might be written about the storm in *Othello*, particularly in the sense of a device sent from God to destroy the Turks.

48 Jones, 63.

49 Braudel, vol. 2, 1103. It is somewhat ironic that in *Othello* the Turkish fleet *is* destroyed by the weather.

50 Yet Roslyn L. Knutson may be right to claim that 'playgoers had a more tangible knowledge of international commerce and diplomacy than some recent commentators imply ... London playgoers might have developed a theatrical sensibility influenced not only by titillation and prejudice but also by current events in international politics and trade' (78). Similarly, Jones remarks that the play 'could hardly have failed to arouse the memory of anyone in Shakespeare's audience who was at all aware of recent European history' (63).

51 Jones, 64.

52 The term is Stephen Greenblatt's; see his *Renaissance Self-Fashioning: From More to Shakespeare* (Chicago and London: University of Chicago Press, 1980).

53 I am indebted to A.A. Bromham for this suggestion.

54 In his introduction to *Othello* Walter Cohen refers to the Ottoman force as 'the Turkish *armada*', 2091 (italics added).

55 Jones, 64.

56 The fiction may well have pleased King James, of course.

57 Suhelya Artemel also notes this possibility; see Artemel, '"Turkish" Imagery in Elizabethan Drama', *Review of National Literatures*

[Special Issue: 'Turkey: From Empire to Nation'] 4.1 (Spring 1973), 82–95.
58 See Lee W. Eysturlid, '"Where Everything is Weighed in the Scales of Material Interest": Anglo-Turkish Trade, Piracy, and Diplomacy in the Mediterranean During the Jacobean Period', *Journal of European Economic History* 22.3 (Winter 1993), 613–25. Eysturlid observes that 'the death of Elizabeth in 1603 and the subsequent rise of James to the throne thereafter represented the end of any direct royal interest in the development of diplomatic relations with the Turks' (615).
59 Suheyla Artemel argues that 'the possibility of a fresh Turkish attack is present throughout and looms over the action like a menacing shadow', but this is at variance with the text, which offers no direct evidence to support Artemel's argument. Othello is to be replaced by Cassio, so presumably the Venetian senators perceived the Turkish threat to be somewhat diminished. It is of course a critical commonplace that Othello is a surrogate Turk in the play, becoming the very threat which the storm displaces. See Artemel, 87.
60 Compare Artemel's reading: 'it is known that the news of the victory [of Lepanto, when it reached England] caused great rejoicing in England and that bonfires were lit in the streets in celebration of the event. ... The destruction of the Turkish fleet by the storm in *Othello* may have evoked the mood of festivity experienced in England after the historic battle of Lepanto' (86).
61 Burckhardt, 43.
62 On the theatrical potential of such a scene, see Louis B. Wright, 'Elizabethan Sea Drama and its Staging', *Anglia* 39 (1927), 104–18. Wright makes the valid point that 'in representing sea fights, the players achieved more realistic effects than in the portrayal of land battles, for a stage more easily represented the deck of a ship than a far-flung battle' (111).
63 Patricia Parker, 'Shakespeare and Rhetoric: "Dilation" and "Delation" in *Othello*', in Patricia Parker and Geoffrey Hartman, eds, *Shakespeare and the Question of Theory* (New York and London: Routledge, 1985), 58.
64 Greenblatt, 234, 235, 237 (italics original).
65 See for example Gary Taylor, 'Forms of Opposition: Shakespeare and Middleton', *English Literary Renaissance* 24 (1994), 283–314.
66 Ibid., 288.
67 Braudel, vol. 2, 1088.
68 Ibid.

FROM TEXT
TO PERFORMANCE

CHAPTER 14

Don Pedro, Don John and Don ... who?– Noting a Stranger in *Much Adoodle-do*

Pamela Mason

In a letter to Ellen Terry on 3 June 1903 George Bernard Shaw wrote, 'I went to see Much Adoodle-do yesterday evening. It is a shocking bad play'.[1] He went on to express his belief that the play can only be saved by Dogberry 'picking it up at the end' but, 'Dogberry *cannot* pick it up unless he has his scene before the wedding'.[2] In an later review (11 February 1905) of another production Shaw developed his concern about the way in which Shakespeare's play is too often adapted, shaped and mutilated. Beerbohm Tree had

> erased Verges from the book of life ... The really exasperating stupidity of cutting out the scene of the visit of Dogberry and Verges has been made traditional on the London stage ever since Sir Henry Irving ... ingeniously discovered that means of reducing Dogberry to a minor part.[3]

Shaw's sharp ear was always attentive to Shakespeare's language and his reviews frequently comment upon the nature of the performed text. Crucially he was commenting upon what he judged to be inappropriate cutting which denies the play's structure and cripples its theatrical shape.

Much Ado is not a text that we might immediately associate with interpretative cutting and shaping but Shaw draws our attention to how they can be significant factors. In this article I shall explore how the consensus of editorial opinion and more recent productions of the play (details provided in Appendix A) have been influenced by a disregard for the integrity of the Quarto and Folio texts. In the last fifty years the number of lines cut in major productions of the play has generally varied between at least 200 and 400. An analysis of some of what have come to be regarded as the 'usual cuts' can reveal meddling far beyond ways in which the play might be made more accessible for modern audiences.

Kenneth Branagh's 1993 film of *Much Ado About Nothing* cuts half the play. Few people seem either to have noticed or to have cared very much. There is the argument that different rules apply to film, but with his *Hamlet* Branagh wanted to 'take the play into the cinema in its fullest form'[4] and he was rewarded with an Oscar nomination for his conflated screenplay.

However, he sought to justify his adaptation of *Much Ado* on the grounds that there is a need to give 'a strong sense of the interpretative line'. Branagh made a generic distinction, writing 'In the comedies this is crucial. They must be inflected'. They lack the 'strong narrative' of the histories. So he explained: 'We did cut lines and occasionally scenes where the plot (such as it is) was not advanced'. The overhearing scenes were integrated to take 'acting pressure off the women'. By enacting the scene in which Margaret is mistaken for Hero, Branagh claimed 'to add a new dimension to our understanding of Claudio',[5] but the effect of his various modifications was to let the men in general, and Claudio in particular, off the hook that Shakespeare has fashioned for them.

Although the 'wedding morning scene' (3.4) was shot and 'beautifully acted', it was cut 'on the grounds that the dramatic way in which the previous night-time sequence had played made the audience alive with expectation for the events of the wedding itself. The scene with the girls seemed finally to frustrate'.[6] It is not just an interest in Margaret's pivotal role or her structural and thematic importance that might prompt regret at this particular cut. In 1905 Shaw had commended Miss Winifred Emery's Beatrice as being 'clever enough to play Lady Disdain instead of playing for sentimental sympathy' and he was particularly pleased that 'she had the *carduus benedictus* scene restored, to the great benefit of the play'.[7]

The text is given priority at the beginning of Branagh's film when the words of '*Sigh no more ladies*' are reversed out on a black screen. This draws attention to the play's concern with 'the fraud of men' who 'are deceivers ever'. However, the promise of an interpretative seriousness is sadly unfulfilled. Rather than explore the play's emphasis upon 'misprision' the film merely offers, in Shaw's phrase, 'sentimental sympathy'. It embodies the view that 'the wit, irony and apparent lack of feeling cover only superficially two of the most romantic, generous and emotional of Shakespeare's characters'.[8] Unfortunately, the film's popularity is likely to reinforce the soggily romantic reading preferred by most editors.

This article has been prompted by the experience of 'noting' a passage in the text that I have no recollection of having heard spoken in the theatre. It perhaps suggests fresh thoughts about the play in general and Benedick's character and role in particular. Evidence from promptbooks reveals that modern audiences have had less than an evens chance of hearing the lines in question and certainly none of the first Benedicks I saw spoke them. They were cut in the Royal Shakespeare Theatre productions of 1971, 1976, 1979, 1982 and in the 1988 Renaissance Theatre production. The lines in question occur in Act 5, scene 2 and are reproduced in Quarto facsimile at the end of this article (Appendix B). Acknowledging their force makes that scene intensely serious. Benedick surrenders to Margaret and he reveals a self-awareness, a maturity of thought and reflective insight. However, before attempting detailed analysis of the passage I shall discuss what a reading of Shakespeare's full text might restore to Benedick.

An audience's first impression of him is shaped by Beatrice. Her mocking 'Signor Mountanto' cannot hide her interest but the emphasis in the play's opening moments is on Benedick as a soldier. While Beatrice ostentatiously doubts whether he will have killed any men in the battle, the Messenger assures us that he is a 'good soldier'; and within his male group he is 'a lord to a lord, a man to a man, stuffed with all honourable virtues' (1.1.52–3).[9] The main thrust of Beatrice's attack is not directed against misogyny but at inconstancy. Benedick is a good soldier 'to a lady', 'he wears his faith but as the fashion of his hat; it ever changes with the next block' and any new male companion of his 'will make a voyage with him to the devil'. Benedick is a bad influence, a corruptive force: if the 'noble' Claudio has 'caught the Benedick, it will cost him a thousand pound ere 'a be cured' (1.1.50, 69–71, 75–6, 81–3).

Within moments of the men entering we are given an insight into the dynamics of their group and perhaps Beatrice's judgment is confirmed. It is often argued that it is to Benedick's credit that he interrogates Leonato's joke about the legitimacy of Hero, 'Were you in doubt, sir, that you asked her?', but Leonato's riposte, 'Signor Benedick, no; for then were you a child', redirects the barb, and suggests that Benedick is a man with a reputation. Moments later, in his first exchange with Beatrice, Benedick apparently confirms the innuendo as he announces 'it is certain I am loved of all ladies, only you excepted' (1.1.116–17). The self-portrait that Benedick presents is of a man who knows that he is attractive to women but who is determined not to get involved. He seems proud of his 'hard heart' (1.1.118). These lines suggest more the image of a Don Juan rather than that of a confirmed bachelor. Indeed, they make clear the accuracy of describing Benedick as a forerunner of Mirabell, though critics who make this comparison generally prefer to ignore Mirabell's sexual appetite.

In conversation with Claudio, Benedick seems cynically experienced. 'Can the world buy such a jewel?' asks the romantic Claudio. Benedick replies with the voice of experience: 'Yea, and a case to put it into'

(1.1.169–70). He compares Beatrice and Hero fairly objectively in terms of their appearance. It is not women to whom he is antagonistic but the social institution of marriage: 'But I hope you have no intent to turn husband, have you?' (1.1.180–81). It is Claudio's wish to make Hero his 'wife' (1.1.183) that sparks Benedick's attack.

It is illuminating that Benedick's instinctive response to the notion of marriage is fear of being cuckolded. The image of wearing 'his cap with suspicion' comes before the 'yoke' and the boredom of 'sighing away Sundays' (1.1.184–8). He would have bachelors of threescore but it would be naive to think he means celibate bachelors. His later manifesto may send students to the notes to make sense of the 'recheat winded in my forehead' and hanging his bugle in an 'invisible baldrick', but he then clearly proclaims: 'Because I will not do them the wrong to mistrust any, I will do myself the right to trust none' (1.1.224–6). He is confident of the difference between wrong and right in relationships with women. His assured conclusion is he will 'go the finer' (1.1.226) unmarried.

A few lines later the 'sensible Benedick' again stoutly resists the 'yoke' of marriage. If he were a married man, 'bull's horns' should be set in his forehead (1.1.241–4). His parting shot seeks to alert his friends to an awareness of their vulnerability, from one who knows: 'Ere you flout old ends any further, examine your conscience' (1.1.267). His deference to Don Pedro has just been displayed. When charged 'on his allegiance' (1.1.193), he breaks faith with Claudio by revealing what he had been told in confidence and then is used as a messenger boy, sent to accept Leonato's invitation to supper. With Benedick's exit, the informality of prose gives way to verse and Claudio puts a distance between his own concerns and what has gone before: 'My liege, your highness now may do me good' (1.1.269).

The masked ball provides opportunities for deception and subversion which the men relish. Don Pedro's pursuit of Hero is at the very least ambivalent. Claudio had asked for advice, support and guidance. Don Pedro's plan to impersonate him and 'in her bosom ... unclasp his heart' (1.1.302) is met with silence. Even before the ball Don Pedro's plan has been misunderstood and uncertainty about his motives will be confirmed as he withdraws with Hero imploring her 'Speak low, if you speak love' (2.1.87). There then follows a piece of dialogue which is nowadays nearly always judged to require the editorial hand. I worry about the motives that lie behind the conviction that change is required.

The generally accepted view is that the 1600 Quarto text of *Much Ado* was set from Shakespeare's foul papers and as such provides, in Hinman's words, 'both an authoritative and a generally satisfactory text'.[10] However, the underlying manuscript is judged to be 'in need of a good deal of tidying up'[11] and the Quarto text is therefore 'somewhat imperfect'.[12] One imperfection which Hinman identifies (here agreeing with Theobald and Dyce) relates to the speech prefixes in the dialogue I mentioned (2.1.86–96). It is reproduced in the passage included in Appendix B. The Quarto gives three speeches to *Bene.*[dick] and two to *Balth.*[asar]. Hinman asserts that 'Margaret's interlocutor was certainly not Benedick' and he suggests that it 'may even have been' Borachio rather than Balthasar.[13] Sisson argues for Borachio on the grounds of his superior rank and in doing so he agrees with Dover Wilson that he is the 'obvious partner for Margaret'.[14] The Riverside edition (edited by Blakemore Evans) emends all five speech headings to Borachio.[15] Alan Brissenden makes 'The Case for Balthasar' on the grounds that the structure of the dialogue 'accords with the figures of the dance' and for Benedick to speak to Margaret would require a change 'half-way through the figure' which he declares 'an extremely improbable movement'.[16] The editors of the New Penguin (R.A. Foakes, 1968), the Arden (A.R. Humphreys, 1981) and the New Cambridge (F.H. Mares, 1988) all give all the speeches to Balthasar. Stanley Wells's decision for the Oxford text is that the speech headings of 'Benedick' are Shakespeare's first uncorrected thoughts and Wells fancifully suggests a 'conjectural reconstruction' of the crafting of the scene:

> Margaret could dance with Benedick. But no; a duologue between Benedick, masked, and Beatrice would make excellent comedy, and had to be reserved as a climax; so he replaced Benedick with Balthasar ... but forgot to make the prefixes consistent.[17]

Consequently, the Complete Oxford text also assigns all the lines to Balthasar. Sheldon P. Zitner in his single Oxford edition postulates that 'the Margaret-Balthasar dialogue might have been intended from the outset, and the male speech-prefixes misread'.[18] He firmly rejects the notion of assigning the lines to Borachio and follows the usual reading of giving the lines to Balthasar.

Modern editors are deviating here from Rowe, Pope, Capell, Malone and Collier among others who (unlike Theobald and Dyce) were happy to leave the Quarto (and Folio) reading intact. Capell added an interesting (and explanatory stage direction) *'turning off in Quest of another'*. Collier (1842) argued for Benedick as follows:

> The fact is that Margaret turns from Benedick with the words, 'God match me with a good dancer!' maliciously implying that

Benedick is a bad one; and then Balthasar takes up the dialogue with 'Amen', meaning that he is what Benedick is not.[19]

Alone amongst modern editors, David L. Stevenson allows Benedick to keep the lines in the Signet edition (1964). He adds a stage direction on Balthasar's first line (*'interposing'*) and offers the following note:

> Many editors emend the Quarto, and give this and Benedick's two subsequent speeches to Balthasar, but in V.ii Benedick and Margaret spar, and they may well do so here.[20]

Both Collier and Stevenson argue their case on the grounds of character and with reference to the play's structure. They do not identify an error or imperfection here and see no need for emendation. Arguments about staging, on the lines of Brissenden's choreographic points, can be met by Collier's and Stevenson's stage directions and were challenged on stage in the 1982 RSC production. Although the New Penguin edition was used for that production, the Quarto speech prefixes were restored and the promptbook records that the dance was organized to provide moments of 'interchange', 'walking' and 'changeover'.[21] The only RSC promptbook which has used the Signet edition is that for Howard Davies's 1979 touring production. However in this case the director did the editorial work Stevenson had rejected. The printed text was emended to give the lines to Balthasar.

In his New Cambridge edition F.H. Mares asserts 'It is hardly probable that the mask would have been managed like an "excuse me" foxtrot'.[22] However, Don Pedro's dialogue and actions have just characterized the dance in that way.[23] If Benedick is allowed to speak the lines to Margaret it shows a Benedick aware of his attraction to women and following his superior's lead in not respecting established alliances. Margaret is quick-witted and sure-footed as she moves from Benedick to Balthasar and marks the move, 'Answer, clerk', and Balthasar replies 'the clerk is answered'.

The almost universal editorial conviction that these are not Benedick's lines owes little to arguments about authorial inconsistency, matters of paleography or compositorial methods. It owes substantially more to convictions about character. Dyce in 1857 blazed the trail that others have readily followed:

> is not the effect of the scene considerably weakened if Benedick enters into conversation with any woman except Beatrice?[24]

Emendation here creates a constancy in Benedick which better suits editors' preconceptions and possibly their sense of masculine solidarity. It is, perhaps, another example in the play of what Terence Hawkes has described as 'editors engaging Dogberry-like in characteristic policing of the text'.[25] Once upon a time a confident case used to be made for giving Miranda's 'Abhorred slave' speech in *The Tempest* (1.2.353–64) to Prospero on the grounds that the language was 'too indelicate and too philosophical for Miranda'.[26] We might detect something of the same kind of argument in Hinman's assertion that the man who flirts with Margaret saying 'Well, I would you did like me' (2.1.88) 'was certainly not Benedick'.[27] If we allow that it was him, then the description which Beatrice offers just a few lines later might register more strongly:

> only his gift is in devising impossible slanders. None but libertines delight in him, and the commendation is not in his wit, but in his villainy; for he both pleases men and angers them, and then they laugh at him and beat him. (2.1.123–8)

These are serious accusations. But productions frequently soften them by removing 'and the commendation is not in his wit, but in his villainy'. The words were cut in 1961, 1971 and 1976 at Stratford-upon-Avon and in the 1988 Renaissance production; critics readily ignore them (or simply disbelieve Beatrice) and editors offer notes which seek to offer excuse or extenuation. In glossing Beatrice's use of 'libertines' editors consistently prefer the *OED* definitions of 'One who holds free or loose opinions about religion; a free-thinker' or 'One who follows his own inclinations or goes his own way; one who is not restricted or confined'[28] and ignore the possibility that Shakespeare had anticipated the use he makes of the word in *Hamlet* (1.3.49) which the *OED* cites as illustrating 'A man who is not restrained by moral law especially in his relations with the female sex; one who leads a dissolute, licentious life'.[29] Previous instances for this usage are cited in Harvey and Nashe (1593).

The 'libertines' that we see delighting in him are Don Pedro and Claudio and we do need to see Benedick as one of the group. When he believes that Don Pedro has wooed Hero for himself, Benedick shows no moral outrage or indeed surprise but rather briskly and abruptly tells Claudio 'the Prince hath got your Hero' (2.1.176). Later Benedick will use the fairly innocuous comparison of 'The flat transgression of a school boy' to discuss Don Pedro's action of stealing Claudio's 'bird's nest' (2.1.203–5). Benedick shares their attitudes, language and fallibility. He does not seem disconcerted that a man's sworn friend should betray him in this way.

Alone and with the opportunity for introspection Benedick shirks self-analysis. He edits Beatrice's words to muse upon her definition of him as 'The Prince's fool!' (2.1.187). This is then the basis for his complaint to Don Pedro that she 'misused' (2.1.219) him. He fails to mention in either of these accounts the main thrust of her attack. Her reported words really do not justify his metaphor – 'She speaks poniards, and every word stabs' (2.1.226–7) – but the physicality of his words reveals that whatever she said has struck home. The comedy of his desperate pleas for increasingly unlikely errands can provide a distraction but his exit-line reveals his attempt to console himself that the woman to whom he was talking was not Beatrice but a monstrous caricature: 'I cannot endure my Lady Tongue' (2.1.251–2).

Don Pedro's admonition, 'Come, lady, come; you have lost the heart of Signor Benedick' (2.1.253–4), is challenged by Beatrice's account of a previous relationship in which she was not just emotionally bruised but betrayed: 'he won it [i.e. her heart] of me with false dice' (2.1.257). Her metaphor of gambling reinforces the strength of her earlier attack on Benedick. Don Pedro himself will later acknowledge that Benedick 'hath twice or thrice cut Cupid's bow-string and the little hangman dare not shoot at him' (3.2.9–11). But crucially Beatrice's personal history is echoed in Balthasar's song. He implores ladies to '*Sigh no more, ladies, sigh no more*' as he sings that

> *Men were deceivers ever*
> *One foot in sea and one on shore,*
> *To one thing constant never:*
> *Then sigh not so, but let them go,*
> *And be you blithe and bonny,*
> *Converting all your sounds of woe*
> *Into Hey nonny, nonny.* (2.3.60–67)

And in the second verse he announces,

> *The fraud of men was ever so ...* (2.3.70)

Don Pedro commends the song: 'By my troth, a good song' (2.3.76) and in so doing endorses a pattern of male inconstancy.

Benedick's over-reaction to the song merits analysis. As Balthasar prepares to sing Benedick talks sarcastically of the 'divine air' and the notion of a ravished soul. He mocks and derides the power of music: 'Is it not strange that sheep's guts should hale souls out of men's bodies?' When he suggests 'A horn for my money, when all's done' (2.3.56–9), he is revealing more than his preference for a musical instrument. Benedick vigorously dismisses the song in language that in its intemperance recalls his opening exchange with Beatrice. Her reference to her dog barking at a crow [1.1.123-4) is paralleled here by his words about a dog howling and the night raven. The song seems to anger Benedick in a way that suggests a similar emotional investment.

Woven into the comic details of the men's fabricated account of Beatrice's expressions of love are critical comments upon Benedick which come from those who know him best. We might take them more seriously if we were to hear them more often, for again they are very often cut (at Stratford in 1949, 1958, 1961, 1971, 1976 and in the 1988 Renaissance production). Don Pedro describes him as a man with 'a contemptible spirit' whose wisdom can be seen 'in the managing of quarrels ... for either he avoids them with great discretion, or undertakes them with a most Christian-like fear' (2.3.181-203). Even when we are reading the play the editor's notes can encourage us to gloss over the implications. To describe Don Pedro's comments (as Humphreys does) as a 'witty slander' and suggest that the 'improbability' of his words risks revealing the trick seems like special pleading.[30]

In the soliloquy that follows, Benedick accepts the criticism of his friends, 'I hear how I am censured' (2.3.219), but he moves on rapidly to celebrate the revelation of Beatrice's love for him. His announcement that 'the world must be peopled' (2.3.234-5) is hailed as triumphantly life-assertive; yet it is conventional to regard Caliban's desire to people his island very differently. The 'good men and true' in *Much Ado*, the Watch, articulate a truth when they observe that 'Deformed ... goes up and down like a gentleman' (3.3.122-4).

Events in the church scene challenge Benedick in terms of his professional and private allegiance to his peer group. His early interjections (4. 1.19-20, 66) are generally found to be awkward and again are frequently cut, but Zitner's comment that Benedick's 'choice understatement *This looks not like a nuptial* ... always gets a preventive laugh'[31] is not true. In the 1988 Renaissance production Branagh's Benedick grabbed Claudio by the shoulders, shook him and played the line as angry accusation with the force of 'What on earth do you think you are you doing? Pull yourself together'. It worked and nobody laughed.

It is to his credit that Benedick's initial reaction to events is one of stunned silence as he confesses that, for the first time, 'I know not what to say' (4.1.143). He expresses to Leonato his divided disposition and affirms a spiritual commitment as he promises that he will

> deal in this
> As secretly and justly as your soul
> Should with your body. (4.1.245-7)

Alone with Beatrice he confesses his love, but his drift into conventional rhetoric in his declaration 'Come, bid me do anything for thee' is sharply challenged by Beatrice's imperative 'Kill Claudio' (4.1.284–5). If we have been allowed to hear and register Don Pedro's lines earlier, implying a Benedick who generally believes in discretion being the better part of valour, then we will not be surprised by Benedick's refusal 'Not for the wide world'. Beatrice feels betrayed, 'there is no love in you' (4.1.289–90), and she now does speak poniards and every word stabs. She effects a change of allegiance in him and shocks him into action which is deadly serious. His parting words are focused, brisk and concise:

> Enough, I am engaged; I will challenge him. I will kiss your hand, and so I leave you. By this hand, Claudio shall render me a dear account. As you hear of me, so think of me. Go, comfort your cousin; I must say she is dead; and so, farewell. (4.1.326–30)

The radical change in Benedick is clear as he confronts Don Pedro and challenges Claudio:

> You are a villain; I jest not. I will make it good how you dare, with what you dare, and when you dare. (5.1.142–4)

Benedick's new-found commitment is belatedly recognized with wonder by both Don Pedro, 'He is in earnest', and Claudio, 'In most profound earnest' (5.1.187–8).

That earnestness is not only sustained through the closing movement of the play but is indeed developed in 5.2. The scene has four movements beginning with Benedick's request that Margaret help him 'to the speech of Beatrice'. After Margaret's departure to 'call Beatrice' to him Benedick is alone. His attempts at song and verse fail. Beatrice arrives and their dialogue is taut and complex until Ursula enters to announce that Hero's innocence has been proved. Benedick is on stage throughout the scene and in the course of it he comes into contact with Margaret, Beatrice and Ursula and he asks about Hero. He is accommodated by the women and is accommodating to the women. At the heart of the scene Benedick reveals an intense introspection and inner calm. Benedick has changed.

At the ball Benedick had flirted with Margaret, but now he is courteous, 'Pray thee, sweet Mistress Margaret', and commendatory, 'thou deservest it'. He praises her wit for being 'as quick as the grey hound's mouth' while she notes the decline in his verbal prowess. She defeats him in much the same way as she defeated Beatrice earlier. Benedick has now forsaken 'the paper bullets of the brain' (2.3.233) to wield his sword in earnest. He does not confide in Margaret but her mention of 'fencer's foils' has a seriousness beyond what she might realize. His response does far more than continue her metaphor. He has acknowledged the force of Beatrice's attack and recognizes its truth:

> But manhood is melted into curtsies, valour into compliment, and men are only turned into tongue, and trim ones too. He is now as valiant as Hercules that only tells a lie and swears it. (4.1.313–17)

His words to Margaret here reveal the extent of the change. His is 'A most manly wit' in that 'it will not hurt a woman'. Memories of past events and the present situation revive the urgency in Benedick, 'And so, I pray thee, call Beatrice', and with his final phrase, 'I give thee the bucklers', he signals his surrender. He hands over his shield of wit, but Margaret, in extending the military metaphor, indicates that she is armed already. Her command 'Give us the swords' is admittedly sexual but in its context it echoes Beatrice's frustration at being confined in a patriarchal world, 'O that I were a man' (4.1.312), and is a demand for power.

As he waits Benedick attempts to sing. The banality of the lyrics *'The God of love, That sits above'* alerts us to the song's inappropriateness. The general assumption (of critic and actor) is that this is a wildly comic moment. It may seem like a reprise of Benedick's soliloquy at the end of the overhearing scene, but the serious context of this scene with Benedick still believing a duel is ahead of him is expressed in both text and subtext. The man who earlier had scorned Balthasar's music now seeks to provide his own. Popular love songs cannot challenge the appropriateness of *Sigh no more ladies* and Benedick's inept singing revives the memory of the power of the former.

Benedick's attempts to escape into song, verse or myth with his reference to Leander and Troilus will not work. He is struggling to find a voice for his love; inhibited by the pressure of events which threaten the possibility of any future relationship. His attempts at rhyme (lady/baby, scorn/horn, school/fool) are, as he recognizes, 'ominous endings'. They insistently invoke a disturbing reality of sexuality, fear of cuckoldry and indulgent fondness which disrupt his attempt to lose himself in a creative world. His announcement that he 'cannot woo in festival terms' reminds us of the solemnity of his situation.

Beatrice's arrival prompts

> [Benedick.] Sweet Beatrice, wouldst thou come when I called thee?
> Beatrice. Yea, signor, and depart when you bid me.
> (5.2.41–2)

In their opening exchange they match each other's commitment until 'then' is spoken. Beatrice's play on words allows us to see how the verbal flexing of muscles is a cover for her real anxiety: indeed the reason why she came. Her commitment to Hero has taken precedent over her own emotional concerns. Although an audience knows that Don John's plot has been discovered and that the proposed duel between Benedick and Claudio will not therefore need to take place, Beatrice and Benedick do not. Unfortunately in performance the mood of reconciliation is too often allowed to infect the playing of this scene. Beatrice will depart 'unkissed' because foul words between Benedick and Claudio are not enough. Benedick knows that. He reveals how he has sought to use wit as an euphemism, as a way of preventing reality from intruding upon their time together:

> Thou hast frighted the word out of his right sense, so forcible is thy wit. But I must tell thee plainly, Claudio undergoes my challenge; and either I must shortly hear from him, or I will subscribe him a coward. (5.2.51–4)

He and Claudio are professional soldiers so of course Claudio will fight. He wears his sword and had reached for it when challenged by Leonato and Antonio. In action against Don John Claudio had done 'in the figure of a lamb, the feats of a lion' (1.1.14–15). There can be no doubt of the serious implications of Benedick's words. So having confirmed the imminent duel and without waiting for a response from Beatrice, Benedick changes the subject. He reveals his determination not to waste these precious moments with her.

The shifting, fluctuating rhythms of prose in 5.2 also allow for silence to provide tense transitions or anxious pauses. Benedick's inquiry 'tell me for which of my bad parts didst thou first fall in love with me?' invites a foray into romantic past history which Beatrice accepts and she responds in kind. But they cannot sustain the façade; they cannot play the game because, as Benedick says, 'Thou and I are too wise to woo peaceably'. Beatrice suggests that such an assertion belies wisdom: 'there's not one wise man among twenty that will praise himself'. In rejecting her argument Benedick allows us to see the intense seriousness of his commitment. There was a time when Beatrice's point of view was valid, 'in the time of good neighbours' but now, in this time, in this place,

> if a man do not erect in this age his own tomb ere he dies, he shall live no longer in monument than the bell rings and the widow weeps. (5.2.69–72)

Benedick's words are an unconscious echo of Leonato's instruction to Claudio in the previous scene, 'Hang her an epitaph upon her tomb' (5.1.271), and they anticipate the opening line of the next scene, 'Is this the monument of Leonato?' (5.3.1). It is a connection that only the audience can make but the parallels reveal Benedick's state of mind. He is contemplating the possibility of his own death. 'If a man do not erect in this age his own tomb' has a personal subtext, as does the image of 'the widow'. Benedick's definition of his relationship with Beatrice, 'too wise to woo peaceably', has the force of epigram and the weight of epitaph.

Benedick acknowledges man's transience and in doing so anticipates the solemnity of Hamlet's recognition: 'And a man's life's no more than to say "one"' (5.2.74). This is serious debate and Benedick engages with Beatrice's argument. 'Therefore', he explains, 'it is most expedient for the wise ... to be the trumpet of his own virtues'. That is his conclusion and the form of words reproduced in the previous sentence does what the majority of Benedicks do, that is remove the intervening conditional clause. Delivered in this cut version Benedick sounds confident, even arrogant, and certainly robust in his self-confidence. But the words which were omitted, words which are rarely spoken in performance, reveal the inner man. Benedick makes it clear that in order to offer an objective self-assessment it is necessary to have a clear conscience. The full text of the Quarto edition identifies the 'stranger' to whom I alluded in my title:

> Therefore it is most expedient for the wise, if Don Worm, his conscience find no impediment to the contrary, to be the trumpet of his own virtues.

In a play with characters called Don Pedro and Don John the introduction at this late stage of Don Worm can read strongly. Benedick has severed both bonds of allegiance and friendship with Don Pedro, a man who has been 'reconciled' (1.1.146) to his brother Don John. Benedick's 'companion now', his 'new sworn brother' (1.1.66–7), is Don Worm, his conscience.

A possible justification for cutting the line might be that it is obscure. Readers might well consult their notes. If they do they will find remarkably similar annotation whatever edition they use. Editors give the Biblical reference (Mark 11.46) and readers are urged to make a comparison with 'the worm of conscience' in *Richard III*. The editorial glosses read: 'the common image' (New Penguin); 'A traditional idea' (Arden); 'the image is traditional' (New Cambridge); and 'a traditional image' (Oxford). I doubt whether such notes provide much help or insight.

It may be more illuminating to note the single other references to 'conscience' and 'worm' in this play. In the first scene Benedick, under attack from Don Pedro and Claudio fends off his friends and urges them to 'examine your conscience' as he leaves the stage (1.1.264–8). But later he has moved from 'dispensing preceptial medicine' to others to examine his own conscience. The earlier reference to 'worm' also occurs in a scene of Benedick-baiting. He attempts to hide his freshly shaven face by swathing his jaw as he unconvincingly feigns 'the toothache' (3.2.20). 'What, sigh for the toothache', mocks Don Pedro and Leonato teases, 'Where is but a humour or a worm'. Benedick's reply that 'everyone can master a grief but he that has it' is insincere and self-pitying (2.2.26–7). By Act 5 he has suffered real pain and has developed a self-reliance that enables him to 'master' his grief. Hamlet's words to reassure Horatio might provide a parallel for Benedick's words about Don Worm:

> There is special providence in the fall of a sparrow. If it be now, 'tis not to come; if it be not to come, it will be now; if it be not now, yet it will come. The readiness is all. Let be. (5.2.213–18)

Benedick has reached a similar point of recognition to that attained by Hamlet in the same-numbered scene of his play. Both men are ready to face death when 'tis to come.

Benedick rounds off his reflection with a balanced, well-turned sentence: 'So much for praising myself, who, I myself will bear witness, is praiseworthy' (5.2.78–9). He has found a voice, one that is distinct and personal. The earlier repartee, the innuendo, the song, the verse, the report and the request have all been underpinned by the sincerity and sadness of this moment. The language then is laid bare to reveal the emotional core of the scene:

> Benedick. And now tell me, how doth your cousin?
> Beatrice. Very ill.
> Benedick. And how do you?
> Beatrice. Very ill too.
> Benedick. Serve God, love me, and mend. (5.2.79–83)

Beatrice and Benedick share an emotional concern for Hero and an integrity which subjugates their quest for private happiness. The play's precarious balance between joy and weeping is held poised here until the news that Ursula brings relieves the tension. But it is only at this point that Beatrice and Benedick can relax. Too often the resolution is anticipated and a complacent anticipation of a happy ending invades the play to destroy the moment-by-moment subtlety, complexity and emotion of the scene. Branagh's film destroyed the function of the encounter between Beatrice and Benedick by playing the monument scene first.

The maturity of Beatrice and Benedick will enable them to replay their public roles, offer a revival of the 'merry war', entertain the crowd with 'a skirmish of wit' and thereby effect peace. But tensions remain as do the rifts in the male world. Once again editorial meddling prefers to effect a more conventionally acceptable romantic tableau. Once again it is brought about by changing a speech prefix. Both the Quarto and Folio texts give 'Peace, I will stop your mouth' (5.4.98) to Leonato. But the sentimental pleasure gained by allowing Benedick to say the line as preface to stopping Beatrice's mouth with a kiss has proved seductive for editors since Theobald. Collier initially resisted the emendation but relented in his second edition. Not only is the line now always assigned to Benedick but the insertion of a stage direction secures the romantic imperative: most editors add *'kissing her'* or *'kisses her'*.[32] Branagh's screenplay states 'Kisses her, with the greatest tenderness. Great applause, ah's and ooo's'.[33] So secure is the consensus of editorial opinion upon the emendation that Foakes baldly states that the line is 'wrongly assigned to Leonato in Q and F'.[34] Mares is similarly assured:

> It is necessary to accept Theobald's emendation here: it is hard to think of any argument that could justify this speech in Leonato's mouth, while there are many parallels for Benedick.[35]

There are 'many parallels' for the Benedick who is firmly enshrined in the popular sentimental consciousness but trusting the text and allowing the line to be spoken by Leonato permits other possibilities to emerge. Spoken by Leonato the effect could be to reveal his determination to relinquish care and control of Beatrice to Benedick. The words might warn Beatrice to concede the debate and not risk (perhaps for a second time) wrecking her prospect of marriage. Don Pedro's question, 'How dost thou, Benedick the married man?' (5.4.98), carries a sharper edge coming after the prospective wife has been castigated than after the sentimentality of a kiss. Benedick's sustained reply (ten lines) is directed explicitly to Don Pedro and Claudio and is a vigorous rebuttal of their attempt to provoke him by reviving earlier attitudes. Benedick has changed: 'since I do purpose to marry, I will think nothing to any purpose that the world can say against it' (5.4.103-5). But Don Pedro has not changed. To Benedick's imperative 'get thee a wife' (5.4.120) Don Pedro remains silent.

It can be instructive to follow Sir William Davenant's lead in *The Law Against Lovers* (1662) and yoke *Much Ado* with *Measure for Measure*. Shakespeare's Vienna feels the need to revive some pretty fierce laws for lovers to deal with a world in which there are no more marriages. With sexual promiscuity rampant an alternative society is presided over by the aptly named Mistress Overdone. In that world Claudio has anticipated his wedding night and his Juliet has a child for her cradle 'ere she has a husband for her bed. And she is not the only one. There is Kate Keepdown to whom Vienna's elegant, witty man 'turned into tongue' 'had promised ... marriage'. At that end of the play we learn her 'child is a year and a quarter old come Philip and Jacob' (3.1.45–8) and that Mistress Overdone has been combining her role as bawd with that of child-minder. Lucio scorns marriage to the mother of his child: 'do not marry me to a whore ... do not recompense me in making me a cuckold' (5.1.511–14). Angelo, too, had broken his contract to marry Mariana, but arranged to give his 'sensual race the rein' (2.4.160) and bed Isabella. The Duke is forced belatedly to recognize that while the law cannot legislate for sexual behaviour it is vital that social order is established and preserved. He sentences characters to life and a condition of that sentence is marriage.

I would suggest that the writing is on the wall in *Much Ado*. Of the men it is only Benedick who has made the acquaintance of Don Worm. Those who did offer evidence of a caring community, the genuine but undervalued 'good men and true' who are the 'Watch', do not appear in the last scene. The men on stage include a Count who has behaved appallingly in the way he has used and abused the woman who loves him. At the centre of the male group is a man who has claimed for himself a god-like status (2.1.357–8) to control, manipulate and interfere in the lives of others. The play's final moments reaffirm the fraternal links of Don Pedro and Don John. The latter is the embodiment of the cuckoldry that has been a mainstay of the play's verbal energy and its plot. Shaw was right. It is, though in moral not artistic terms, a 'shocking, bad play'.

Appendix A

Much Ado About Nothing was the opening production at The Shakespeare Memorial Theatre in 1879. Since then there have been over forty productions in Stratford-upon-Avon.

1949   dir. John Gielgud; des. Mariano Andreu
Diana Wynyard, Anthony Quayle, Harry Andrews
(in subsequent years: Peggy Ashcroft, John Gielgud,
Leon Quartermaine/Paul Scofield/Anthony Ireland)

1958   dir. Douglas Seale; des. Tanya Moiseiwitsch, Motley
Googie Withers, Michael Redgrave, Anthony Nicholls

1961   dir. Michael Langham; des. Desmond Heeley
Geraldine McEwan, Christopher Plummer, Noel Willman

1965   The National Theatre, The Old Vic and on tour
dir. Franco Zeffirelli; des. Franco Zeffirelli, Peter J. Hall
Maggie Smith, Robert Stephens, Albert Finney

1968   dir. Trevor Nunn; des. Christopher Morley
Janet Suzman, Alan Howard, Norman Rodway

1971   dir. Ronald Eyre; des. Voytek
Elizabeth Spriggs, Derek Godfrey, Jeffrey Dench

1976   dir. John Barton; des. John Napier
Judi Dench, Donald Sinden, Robin Ellis

1982   dir. Terry Hands; des. Ralph Koltai
Sinead Cusack, Derek Jacobi, Derek Godfrey

1988   dir. Di Trevis; des. Mark Thompson
Maggie Steed, Clive Merrison, David Lyon

1988   Renaissance Theatre Company, Birmingham Repertory Studio
dir. Judi Dench; des. Jenny Tiramani
Samantha Bond, Kenneth Branagh, Richard Clifford

1990   dir. Bill Alexander; des. Kit Surrey
Susan Fleetwood, Roger Allam, John Carlisle

1996   dir. Michael Boyd; des. Tom Piper
Siobhan Redmond, Alex Jennings, Peter Wight

Appendix B

Extracts from the Quarto of 1600

    Pedro My visor is Philemons roofe, within the house is Ioue.
    Hero Why then your visor should be thatcht.
    Pedro Speake low if you speake loue.
    Bene. Well, I would you did like me.
    Mar. So would not I for your owne sake, for I haue many ill qualities.
    Bene. Which is one?
    Mar. I say my praiers alowd.

                                      Bene.

    Bene. I loue you the better, the hearers may cry Amen.
    Marg. God match me with a good dauncer.
    Balth. Amen.
    Marg. And God keepe him out of my sight when the daunce is done : answer Clarke.
    Balth. No more words, the Clarke is answered.

    Bene. Thou and I are too wise to wooe peaceably.
    Beat. It appeares not in this confession, theres not one wise man among twentie that will praise himselfe.
    Bene. An old, an old instance Beatrice, that liu'd in the time of good neighbours, if a man do not erect in this age his owne toomb ere he dies, he shall liue no longer in monument, then the bell rings, and the widow weepes.
    Beat. And how long is that thinke you?
    Bene. Question, why an hower in clamour and a quarter in rhewme, therefore is it most expedient for the wise, if Don worme (his conscience) find no impediment to the contrary, to be the trumpet of his owne vertues, as I am to my selfe so much for praising my selfe, who I my selfe will beare witnes is praise worthie, and now tell me, how doth your cosin?
    Beat. Verie ill.
    Bene. And how do you?
    Beat. Verie ill too.
    Bene. Serue God, loue me, and mend, there wil I leaue you too, for here comes one in haste.   *Enter Vrsula.*

Notes

1. Edwin Wilson, ed., *Shaw on Shakespeare* (Harmondsworth: Penguin, 1969), 169.
2. Wilson, 169.
3. Wilson, 167.
4. Kenneth Branagh, *Hamlet* Screenplay (London: Chatto and Windus, 1996), vii.
5. Kenneth Branagh, *Much Ado About Nothing* Screenplay (London: Chatto and Windus, 1993), xiv–xv.
6. Branagh, *Much Ado* Screenplay, xv–xvi.
7. Wilson, 168.
8. Branagh, *Much Ado* Screenplay, xi.
9. All references have been standardized to the New Penguin edition of *Much Ado About Nothing*, ed. R.A. Foakes (Harmondsworth: Penguin, 1968).
10. *Much Ado About Nothing*, Shakespeare Quarto Facsimiles, Number 15, eds Walter Greg and Charlton Hinman (Oxford: Clarendon Press, 1971), xvii.
11. Greg and Hinman, xvi.
12. Greg and Hinman, xvii.
13. Greg and Hinman, xvi.
14. C.J. Sisson, *New Readings in Shakespeare*, vol. 1 (Cambridge, Cambridge University Press, 1956), 100.
15. G. Blakemore Evans, ed., *The Riverside Shakespeare* (Boston, Mass.: Houghton Mifflin Company, 1974).
16. *Notes and Queries* (April 1979), 117.
17. Stanley Wells, 'Editorial Treatment of Foul-Paper Texts; *Much Ado About Nothing* as Test Case', *Review of English Studies* 31 (February 1980), 10.
18. Sheldon P. Zitner, ed., William Shakespeare, *Much Ado About Nothing* [Oxford Shakespeare] (Oxford: Oxford University Press, 1993), 84.
19. Horace Furness, ed., William Shakespeare, *Much Ado About Nothing* [New Variorum Shakespeare] (London, 1899), 70.
20. David L. Stevenson, ed., William Shakespeare, *Much Ado About Nothing* [Signet Classic Shakespeare] (New York: The New American Library, 1964), 51.
21. Promptbook consulted at the Shakespeare Birthplace Trust Library.
22. F.H. Mares, ed., William Shakespeare, *Much Ado About Nothing* [New Cambridge Shakespeare] (Cambridge: Cambridge University Press, 1988), 150.

23 See also C.L. Prouty, 'A Lost Piece of Stage Business in *Much Ado about Nothing*', *Modern Language Notes* 65 (1950), 207–8.
24 Furness, 70.
25 Terence Hawkes, 'Shakespeare's Spooks, or Someone to Watch over Me', in *Shakespeare in the New Europe*, eds Michael Hattaway, Boika Sokolova and Derek Roper (Sheffield: Sheffield Academic Press, 1994), 205.
26 Frank Kermode, ed., William Shakespeare, *The Tempest* [Arden Shakespeare, 2nd edn] (London: Methuen, 1954), 32.
27 Greg and Hinman, xvi.
28 *The Oxford English Dictionary*, Second Edition on CD-ROM.
29 Ibid.
30 A.R. Humphreys, ed., William Shakespeare, *Much Ado About Nothing* [Arden Shakespeare, 2nd edn] (London: Methuen, 1981), 139.
31 Zitner, 57.
32 Although Stevenson reassigns the line to Benedick he offers an interesting note: 'Both Quarto and Folio assign this line to Leonato; possibly the original reading is correct and Leonato forces Benedick to kiss Beatrice', 130.
33 Branagh, *Much Ado* Screenplay, 82.
34 Foakes, 165.
35 Mares, 144.

CHAPTER 15

'The Silent Griefs Which Cut the Heart Strings': John Ford's *The Broken Heart* in Performance

Kristin Crouch

> All pleasures are but mere imagination
> Feeding the hungry appetite with steam
> And sight of banquet, whilst the body pines
> Not relishing the real taste of food. (2.3.34–7)

In Michael Boyd's 1994 production of *The Broken Heart* for the Royal Shakespeare Company, this strong, specific image is pulled out of the text and underlined for the audience through the use of frozen tableaux. The upstage shutters are raised to reveal an elaborate banquet table – a celebratory wedding feast (fig. 1). Crowning the centre-piece of the table is the delicate figure of a swan. Later in the performance, the shutters are again raised to reveal the same banquet, but with a crucial difference – the food is rotting and decaying, the sound of buzzing flies fills the air, and the swan is hung by the neck, dripping blood from its disembowelled body onto the wasted scene (fig. 2).[1]

These tableaux are concrete 'visual signifiers' of the suffering that is indicated in the speech. Ironically, the use of the physical, tangible banquet reinforces the understanding of the spiritual petrification and starvation. Though not literally required by the stage directions of Ford's quarto, these tableaux encapsulate the social situation of the text, and the resulting emotional oppression. They are included in Boyd's production as subtextual expressions of the socially ineffable and allow the spectator to participate with the characters in their precise moments of deepest emotional anguish.[2]

Boyd makes use of this device to solve a challenging theatrical problem, namely, the problem of taking a relatively unknown seventeenth-century text and making it relevant and accessible, giving it 'life', for contemporary theatre-goers. What decisions are to be made in response to the formality of speech and the restrained events of the text as it stands on the page? It was difficult in the twentieth century, an age of comparatively liberated sexual beliefs, to identify with the strict seventeenth-century moral climate. The director, choreographer, designer and musical composer have to provide a way for contemporary spectators to sympathize with the play's characters from our current perspective.

This difficulty is exacerbated by certain problems of performance. In *The Broken Heart* there is no 'direct' utterance of inner experience. Characters either remain silent, self-reference their own inability to speak effectively and truthfully, or speak periphrastically through irony and clouded metaphor. Lisa Hopkins points out characters' attempts to articulate personal pain *indirectly* through reference to other parts of the body. The blood, heart, tears and sweat are appealed to as more reliable indicators of true feeling and emotion:[3] 'Heaven / Does look into the secrets of all hearts' (1.1.51–2); 'Since cruelty enforced / Divorce betwixt my body and my heart' (2.3.56–7); 'Could my tears speak, / My Griefs were slight' (5.2.73–4); 'Whiles I / Quench my hot sighs with fleetings of my tears' (3.2.57–8). The reluctance of characters directly to articulate personal and emotional pain within the restrictive world of the play suggests that Ford's dramaturgy will necessarily present difficulties for the spectator. According to Hopkins,

> In dramatic terms, it is an obvious menace – if the only thoughts of value are to remain shrouded in silence, because to give them verbal expression would be to pollute them, and only what is unimportant can be voiced, then that will lead to a peculiarly frustrating experience for the audience.[4]

She does, however, suggest that the performative aspects of the drama, the staging of 'visual signifying systems such as the use of gesture, ritual, emblem and tableau', possess potential for a satisfactory dramatic communication.[5] She asserts that, 'it is then, only on the stage that Ford's plays can fully come to life'.[6]

Michael Boyd successfully tackles and overcomes these difficulties, by making full theatrical use of these 'visual signifying systems'. Boyd does not impose spectacle upon the text, but rather illuminates and extends images and experiences found directly within it. The formal and dignified nature of this court is conveyed through constricting and corseted Caroline costumes, impeding travel across the stage through the sheer weight of the material. Movement is further restricted through the slow pace of actors' movements and carefully calculated gestures, bows and curtsies. The audience is directly confronted by the impossibility of directness, or casual movement, or even casual asides in a claustrophobic court where 'walls have eyes'.[7]

The situations of the *dramatis personae* show us that the tension of the tragedy derives from the interaction of characters in response to an unalterable set of social circumstances. The action revolves around three pairs of lovers: Orgilus and Penthea, Prophilus and Euphrania, and Calantha and Ithocles. The main cause for grief is enforced marriage.

Prior to the opening of the play, Orgilus and Penthea had been betrothed in a vow of 'holy and chaste love' (1.1.30), until Penthea's brother, Ithocles, disrupted the union by forcing her to marry the older, jealous Bassanes. She escapes her situation by deliberately starving herself to death. Orgilus, on the other hand, releases his frustration through the ritual execution of the offending brother, before Ithocles can consummate the marriage to his own secret love, the princess Calantha. Calantha's eventual response to the news of the deaths of those dear to her is the literal breaking of her heart on stage, leaving the kingdom to the able rule of the neighbouring prince Nearchus of Argos.

I would now like to focus on the 'visual signifying systems' in Michael Boyd's 1994 production for the Royal Shakespeare Company. I will examine the specific decisions of the production team (the director, the designer and the choreographer) that are employed to solve the problems and complexities involved in a staging of *The Broken Heart*.[8]

Tableaux

In Act 4, scene 2, the 'mad' scene, Penthea finds release from the silence of stoicism in her own self-destruction. Deprived of any spiritual source to sustain her soul, Penthea refuses all physical sustenance, and, according to the other characters, is left 'a prey to words' (4.2.44). In this scene, the tableau device emphasizes Penthea's awareness of the oppressive capacity of her surrounding community. Penthea recognizes the sharp distinction between the happy union of Prophilus and Euphrania and her own obstructed union. Upstage, at the opening of the scene, Boyd has placed the well-lit 'perfect' wedding feast. At line 110, the happy couple enter the space at the table, joyously enjoying the fruits of their wedding banquet. This disconnected display, through its mere presence, ironically comments upon the main action of the scene. Penthea takes hold of Orgilus's hand and points his attention to the newly married couple: 'Hark in thine ear: / Like whom do I look, prithee?' (113–14). As soft, private laughter is heard from the upstage couple, Penthea circles upstage to hush them, 'Nay, no whispering. / Goodness! We had been happy' (114–15). She is the married-maid, the virgin-wife, the bride that never was (fig. 3). Janet Smith rehearsed with the actors to present a 'lack of form', loose patterns of circling and weaving in and around her tormentors and her desire.[9] The director has used the upstage tableau to magnify this moment of Penthea's greatest emotional pain. The audience is, therefore, allowed to feel the violence with her and to see the effect on Penthea of the loss of this perfect happiness (fig. 4).[10]

In Act 4, scene 4, the second tableau occurs during Orgilus's execution of the offending brother, Ithocles. Three seated characters are presented in front of the 'wasted' banquet: Ithocles trapped in a trick chair, the betrayed Orgilus in the middle and the dead (from starvation) figure of Penthea at his side. The disembowelled and bloody swan of this wasted feast, here, underlines the destruction wrought by Ithocles: three souls confined and destroyed by an unalterable, unbearable, social situation.

'Imaginings'[11]

Another way of exploring the psychological subtext of a scene is developed through the use of 'imagined' prologues, as termed by Janet Smith. The staging attempts to explore and amplify the emotional life *beyond the text,* and allows the spectators to experience characters' pain in specific moments of impossible, possible and imagined social situations. These opening sequences in the first and second halves of the performance are not spoken, but imaginary extensions of images found in the text. They function as a means of allowing the audience to see a particular situation or moment in the same way that the character sees it. For instance, Boyd's opening prologue quietly indicated the inexplicable loss of 'troth-contracted loves' (2.3.34). Sitting alone on stage, Iain Glen as Orgilus sombrely sings, accompanied by his own guitar, as the veiled figure of Penthea slowly walks forward to meet his position on stage at the close of the song (fig. 5). Both characters stand facing front for a moment of silence and stillness. Orgilus then lifts Penthea's veil; she slowly walks around the upstage and off as Crotolon comes on for the textual beginning of 1.1 to question his son's reasons for leaving Sparta. The intermingling of scenes allows us to witness her departure at the same time that we hear of Orgilus's 'violent' griefs, and so we are left to sympathize with his professed need to 'lose the memory of something / Her presence makes to live in me afresh' (1.1.81–2). Further, transposed from 3.4, the song that was meant to celebrate the coming wedding of Prophilus and Euphrania (the only couple allowed a fulfilling union), here, in combination with the subsequent silent moment, also points out the 'comforts lasting, loves increasing' (3.4.70) that has been irrevocably lost. It is the briefly glimpsed joy that could have been, had Orgilus and Penthea's union not been destroyed.

In Act 1, scene 3, Orgilus remains behind in Sparta under disguise as the scholar, Aplotes, to observe secretly the society from which he has been denied a public place as husband to Penthea. In performance, the veiled figure of Penthea re-appears upstage behind Orgilus (fig. 6), to underline his loss as he 'alone' on stage complains:

> The secrets of those flames which, hidden, waste
> A breast made tributary to the laws
> Of beauty, physic yet hath never found
> A remedy to cure a lover's wound. (1.3.38–41)

The actress again disappears off stage by line 44, when Euphrania, Orgilus's sister, is courted by Prophilus, Ithocles' best friend. Penthea's presence, though, will remain in the spectators' minds (as in Orgilus's) as we watch the private scene, and listen to Orgilus's painful asides: 'So was ... [my love] / To my Penthea, chastely honourable' (58–9); 'But a brother / More cruel than a grave' (63–4); 'I have a pretty memory. / It must prove my best friend' (164–5). As a way of dramatizing Orgilus's inability to speak directly, Boyd places him on stage in the shadows. We in the audience, realize that observing this lovers' scene must be an intolerable strain for him.

Additionally, in 1.2, 3.4 and 4.1, Penthea and Orgilus variously appear, observing the main action through a window. Again, the presence of these characters is not literally required by the text, but is a performance adaptation. It is impossible to know for certain the intent of this particular staging decision, but their presence could perhaps be read in three ways. The appearances *outside* of the major playing space may emphasize their exclusion from the main action, or it may further develop the idea that nothing is secret in this court of intrigue – no action, no movement, no word is ever casual, informal or relaxed. Finally, their observance of the scenes may heighten, or ironically comment upon, their original cause for grief.

Chairs

Ford devises specific visual spectacle to reinforce physically the stillness looked for in the language, and the slow silence of the bodies' progress towards death.[12] One important image recurring throughout *The Broken Heart* is that of the 'seated' character. Ford's stage directions explicitly call for the presence of chairs. These directions suggest the very visual elements that Boyd develops and extends in his productions. Here the staging does not involve adaptation, but brings out the power already present in the literal text. First, the seated character suggests the initial stages of emotional entrapment. Desires are held down, trapped within the passive posture. Further, this emotional isolation is more extremely projected by the placing of multiple chairs on-stage.

During the period two was represented as the number of division.[13] In the text, Ford makes use of this idea during several scenes in which the stage directions call for chairs. During Ithocles's interview with Penthea, the characters are both revealed seated upstage, facing front.[14] Boyd exacerbates this division, and the implied frustrated communication, by having his performers avoid all eye contact during the scene until Penthea's plea for death: 'Pray, kill me: nay, will 'ee?' (3.2.67).[15] The image of isolation is again repeated in Act 4, scene 4, during Orgilus's execution of Ithocles. Featured in the seated position also are Ithocles, the veiled figure of the dead Penthea and Orgilus. Penthea, ironically, is seated between her lost, inaccessible love, and the perpetrator of the obstructed love. All perish by participation in the rigid social imperatives of their society, sharing the same trapped, lifeless fate.[16] Hopkins has critically observed the 'impending doom' of this seated position: 'Every character whom we see sitting will die'.[17]

Dance

Paradoxically, Ford's drama even further suggests the silencing of the body through the use of music and movement. Renaissance belief in order and harmony applies to the activity of dance as well, linking it to 'the maintenance of moral order'.[18] Circling spheres were indicative images of peace and stability.[19] However, in performance, these orderly patterns can be effectively subverted and undercut. They may become expressive, rather, of the *lack* of harmony in these characters' lives, pointing out the tumult and chaos churning very closely below their cool surface exteriors.

Though Ford's text indicates only one dance, Boyd has developed two major dance sequences within his production.[20] The first is included in Act 3, scene 4 at Orgilus's blessing of the union of Prophilus and Euphrania. There is no dance specifically required by the stage directions for this scene. Boyd's addition here extends images found within the language and action, and amplifies them through the use of dance. The second dance takes place in Act 5, scene 1 during the actual 'revels' for the new bride and bridegroom. The choreography and structure of the dances and the contrast of the accompanying music serve as visual and aural commentators on the inner and outer states of the participants. They explore two contrasting ideas. First, the court's emphasis on outer form, the 'corseting of behaviour' is suggested through constrained and formal posture, bows and curtsies, and the musical restrictions of time and tempo. Second, the emotional subtext of unbearable social situations is investigated. I would like to concentrate my discussion on this emotional / psychological subtext.

The first major dance sequence, Act 3, scene 4, contains Orgilus's consent to the union of his sister, Euphrania, and Prophilus, Ithocles's best friend. The scene was edited to produce a performance that indicated a clear division between character speech and inner desire. On the surface, it is a wedding celebration and an affirmation of a renewed friendship between Orgilus and Ithocles, but is totally at odds with the subtext of Orgilus's real feeling. The choreographer's title revealingly indicates the dramatic function of this dance: 'Orgilus's Nightmare'.[21]

Boyd cut and tightened the dialogue to focus on Orgilus's spoken blessing: 'My sister's marriage / With Prophilus is from my heart confirmed' (3.4.49–50). Between lines 53 and 95, all dialogue has been cut except for that exchanged between Orgilus and Ithocles. The resulting dialogue, brought forward to be spoken before the song, runs as follows:

> Orgilus. Most honoured, ever famous!
> Ithocles.   Your true friend;
>   On earth not any truer. (57–8)

> Orgilus.   take her, Prophilus
>   Live long a happy man and wife (66–7)

Here the line is interrupted:

> Ithocles.   I but exchange
>   One good friend for another. (83–4)

> Orgilus. O my good lord, your favours flow towards
>   A too unworthy worm. But as you please;
>   I am what you will shape me. (92–4)

And the speech returns to complete line 67:

>   and further,
>   That these in presence may conclude an omen,
>   Thus for a bridal song I close my wishes. (67–9)

Orgilus's lack of participation in the marriage revels is emphasized by a telling placement on stage. Deprived of his rightful partner, he stands alone, centre-stage, as the couples dance around him. Orgilus offers his song of 'comforts lasting, loves increasing' (3.4.70). The repetition from the adapted prologue may trigger an impression in the spectators' minds of the 'holy union' (74) that should have belonged to Orgilus and Penthea. The driving and menacing musical accompaniment to Orgilus's song is in direct contrast to the graceful, stylized movement of the couples. The music aligns, rather, with the frenetic activity of Orgilus's vengeful mind, dramatically emphasized by the smiling exterior projected in counterfeit friendship to Ithocles. As he speaks, his eyes do not focus on any other character on stage, but instead look straight ahead to the audience – existing, but not within the structure of the joyous marriage revels. It is a moment of Orgilus's deepest agony that the audience is allowed to experience with him. The dance ends, and his father thanks him for his 'acknowledgment' (95). By this time, the audience is well able to read the heavy syllables of his answer, 'But my duty' (96), with the intended irony.

The ultimate rejection of expression takes place in the final dance of Act 5, scene 2. I will deal first with the situation as presented by Ford's text. The dance is hosted by the princess Calantha and is meant to be a court celebration of marriage, life, unity and new beginnings. But three times the dance is interrupted by news of the death of someone close to the princess – a father, a friend and a lover. Three times Calantha rejects the opportunity for emotional response:

> To the other change ...
> Lead to the next ...
> How dull this music sounds! Strike up more sprightly;
> Our footings are not active like our heart,
> Which treads the nimbler measure. (5.2.13, 15,17–19)

Calantha does her public duty as a Spartan ruler and does not let any feeling show that might disturb the 'clear mirror of absolute perfection' – the symmetry of celebration.

In Boyd's production the dance is choreographed by Janet Smith in sets of partners and circular patterns. The circles may initially seem to express peace and harmony, but this is soon subverted and overturned through the essential contradictions of its participating elements.[22] Boyd directly supports and extends the images of the text through Craig Armstrong's musical score. The music chosen for the dance is slow and sombre, heavily evocative of doom. It is in direct opposition to the quick skipping steps of the dancers' feet. Smith also incorporated weaving and intermingling into the dance. The entanglement of the characters, together with the disjunctive music creates forms that appear to be eroding even as they try to hold it all together – a physical expression of the turbulence inside that Calantha must be struggling to keep in check.

A question comes to mind: just how much mastery of will does it take to control grief? As it has been shown earlier, 'Griefs will have their vent'. In what way will the destructive energies of these denied griefs manifest themselves? What will be the ultimate cost to the health of Calantha's soul, and therefore the State to which she is now Queen? Calantha holds all her grief in until the final scene, in which both Ithocles's funeral and her wedding to her dead lover takes place. Olivia Williams, as Calantha, remains perfectly poised and in control until she confesses the truth of her inner pain:

> O my lords,
> I but deceived your eyes with antic gesture,
> When one news straight came huddling on another,
> Of death, and death, and death. Still I danced forward;
> But it struck home, and here, and in an instant. ...
> They are silent griefs which cut the heartstrings.
> Let me die smiling. (5.3.67–76)

She expresses the contents of her heart, and so destroys herself; Calantha's heart breaks on stage: 'Crack, crack!' (78). According to Peter Holland's review in The *Times Literary Supplement*,

> Olivia Williams's voice has never wavered, only her eyes and lips fleetingly suggesting what might be happening within. Now the voice lets go its restraints, achieving a volume and power unprecedented and unpredicted. Her awesome shout of those two words is one of the most extraordinary and appalling sounds I have ever heard in the theatre. The audience knows, even before Bassanes tells us, that 'her heart is broke indeed'.[23]

Conclusions

I have explored, in detail, Michael Boyd's efforts to create a relevant piece for contemporary theatre-goers. So why has this text attracted no more response from the theatrical community? The last major production of *The Broken Heart* was performed over thirty years ago. Certainly the lack of performance history has limited our critical reception of Ford in the past. Performance commentary has been largely confined to hypothesizing on imagined theatrical effects – stagings of the mind. Our reception of Ford may be more fully informed if we take into account Boyd's recent staging and the possibilities suggested by this record of the living presence of the actor.

With the aid of tableaux, 'imaginings', music and dance, Boyd has presented and extended images found directly within the text, and effectively communicated the raw power, passion and intensity of drama. Further consideration of these tools and techniques may also raise new questions and invite further critical re-evaluations of the text, newly attuned to dramatic and theatrical potentialities. After all, the presentation of frustration, social deadening and internalization of desire unite Ford with many twentieth-century dramatists as well. I would suggest that the intensity of this production certainly leaves room for further professional productions of *The Broken Heart*, not just in England, but everywhere, and for anyone not yet acquainted with the 'silent griefs which cut the heartstrings'.

I would also argue that in light of Boyd's production, it is appropriate to consider *The Broken Heart* not as an affirmation of the 'traditional moral order', but, rather, as an indictment against a society that has lost its soul. Tragedy here does not result from some great transgression of moral norms. On the contrary, it is those most strictly adhering to society's expectations for correct behaviour who are ultimately destroyed. Through the exhibition of perfection and control, Ford's characters neglect all inner, spiritual nourishment of the soul, and bury all unacceptable human experience, inner desire and emotional impulse under the weight of silence, stillness and death.

Notes

[1] Figures 1 and 2 courtesy of The Shakespeare Birthplace Trust.
[2] The only available early edition of *The Broken Heart* is the Quarto of 1633.
[3] Lisa Hopkins, 'Silence and the Language of the Body: Women in the Plays of John Ford', unpublished article, 5.
[4] Hopkins, 5. Lisa Hopkins, *John Ford's Political Theatre* (Manchester: Manchester University Press) was published in 1994, the same year as Boyd's production, and was likely written before the production. 'Silence and the Language of the Body' is unpublished, and may have been written after the production.
[5] Hopkins, *John Ford's Political Theatre*, 162.
[6] Ibid., 162.
[7] Interview with Janet Smith (21 January 1997); 'walls have eyes' is a phrase she repeatedly used in reference to ways of thinking about movement, posture, and character relationships during the rehearsals. I am indebted to Janet Smith for her perspective on the production

team's approach, especially the movement, to the staging of the text in rehearsal and performance.
8. Director, Michael Boyd; Movement, Janet Smith; Design, Tom Piper; Music, Craig Armstrong.
9. 'Lack of form' is the chief phrase used by Smith in her explanation of the movement for this scene.
10. Figures 3–6 are courtesy of Sean Hudson Photography.
11. This word 'imagining' was used both by Janet Smith and by several reviewers in description of the production.
12. Also note that the movement is further represented as restricted through slow pace of the actors' movement across the stage space.
13. Hopkins, *John Ford's Political Theatre*, 165. This image of the divided two also occurs on the publicity poster, in the staging of the prologue, the interview between Penthea and Ithocles, and the eavesdropping of Bassanes and Grausis, etc.
14. The characters would likely to have been revealed by drawing back the curtain on the 'discovery space' at the Blackfriar's Theatre.
15. Boyd has re-arranged the order of this line for performance. The New Mermaids edition reads: 'Kill me, pray: Nay, will 'ee?'
16. See also Keith Sturgess, *Jacobean Private Theatre* (London: Routledge and Kegan Paul), 126: 'The chair is a sick bed, a throne or a trap, and it emphasises those key moments of the play when characters reach their nadirs of physical or mental exhaustion, or death itself.'
17. Hopkins, *John Ford's Political Theatre*, 166.
18. Ibid., 167.
19. Ibid., 167.
20. Janet Smith's promptbook notes for the dances includes 7 'Dancey scenes': 1.3. – Prophilus, Euphrania, and Orgilus; 1.2. – (Courtiers) Lemophil, Groneas, Christalla, Philema; 2.2. – Calantha 'ambition'; 3.4. – engagement; 3.5. – Prologue: Calantha and Nearchus; 4.3. – Court strut; 5.2. – Wedding Dance.
21. See the Michael Boyd's promptbook and Janet Smith's dance notes, *The Broken Heart*, Royal Shakespeare Company (1994), The Shakespeare Birthplace Trust, Stratford-upon Avon.
22. Also allusive of the medieval Dance of Death – patterns of eight circling dancers (Hopkins, *John Ford's Political Theatre*, 167).
23. Peter Holland, *TLS* (28 October 1994).

272 CROUCH

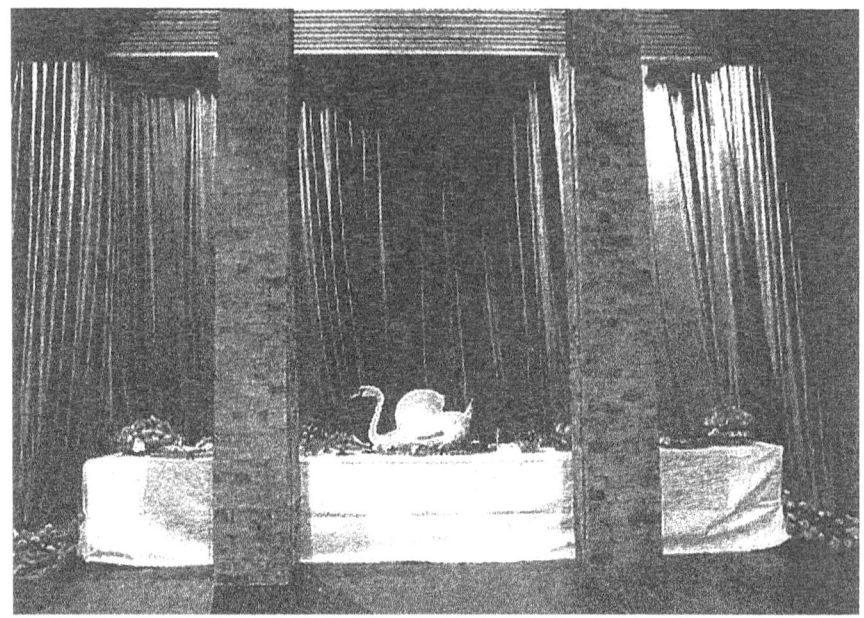

15.1 Perfect feast

15.2 Wasted table

JOHN FORD'S *THE BROKEN HEART* IN PERFORMANCE 273

15.3 Penthea in perfect stoic reserve

15.4 Emotional release allowed only in 'madness'

15.5 Orgilus and the veiled Penthea

15.6 Orgilus/Aplotes and the re-appearance of the veiled Penthea

CHAPTER 16

Cunning with Pistols: Observations on Gale Edwards's 1996–7 RSC Production of John Webster's *The White Devil*

Nick Tippler

Critical interpretation of the text of *The White Devil* often tends to the theory that the titular character is Vittoria. This derives from several sources, not the least of which is the reference to her on the title page of the 1612 quarto as 'the famous Venetian Curtizan'. Her early desire to be rid of Camillo and Isabella, and institute her affair with and marriage to Bracciano may be taken as evidence enough to point to her as the obvious character for the title role. Even analysis which recognizes that devilry within the play is multifaceted still refers to Vittoria as 'The White Devil herself'.[1] Attribution of title to character depends frequently on figurative aspects of the play, such as the references by other characters to woman as wolf or devil, the association of whore with cold Russian winter, and both Vittoria's and Bracciano's use of crystalline mirror/light imagery at critical points of flux. However, this ignores the dramatic action, within which she is only one amongst many characters prosecuting an ambition to higher status, from Zanche's attempt to seduce Mulinassar to Monticelso's elevation from cardinal to Pope. If so many display such a tendency, any distinction becomes tenuous. As A.J. Smith's discussion of Lodvico's and Flamineo's meeting during 3.3 suggests, 'Webster aims ... to play off the adversaries in the audience's judgement so that one doesn't commit oneself to either but is forced to take a relative view of them'.[2] And this relativism applies throughout the play to all characters, including Vittoria. I will propose the alternative case that, rather than attribution to one character, the White Devil is a definable element of almost all the characters. Webster, then, builds an interplay that produces the social circumstance of life within the court at Rome as requiring such Machiavellian behaviour for survival, and presents it as a sequence of emblematic devices.

Gail Edwards's 1996–7 RSC production, played first at the Swan theatre at Stratford and later at the Barbican Pit,[3] demonstrates clearly in the translation from text to performance that ethic which clarifies the latent evil in all the main players. Particularly in the Pit version, which I will discuss in this essay, it incorporates the audience as a supplementary character. The depth below the London streets of the playing space, the immediacy of the relationship between the small thrust stage and audience seating, and a claustrophobic confinement imposed by the proximity of the lighting gantry all signify Hell. Within the dramatic space, there is no access to the vertical dimension of the full stage that the Swan production allowed, and was similarly available at the play's original venue, the Red Bull. Instead, representation of depth and elevation must be by action, or signifiers encoded in the set and properties. It is as if, having descended from the normality of the street, one enters a place from which there can be no return. The semiotic potential of the Pit as a playing space ties it closely to Renaissance art such as Ring's *The Last Judgement* (fig. 1), or Breugel's *The Fall of the Rebel Angels*. It is perhaps the best of all theatres in which to stage *The White Devil*.

There are remarkable consistencies between the Pit and Red Bull stages, particularly between specific areas of the stage, which offer a continuity of effect between this and Jacobean productions. Though the Red Bull was an open theatre, and considerably larger than the Pit, the stage foci coincide. Each has (or had) a partitioned tiring-house wall or back cloth resembling a stone wall, a floor resembling flagstones, and a configuration within this of traps or indices to a lower location. The Pit offers a quincunx of gratings – smaller ones at the front and rear corners of the stage, and a large, central one. By comparison, Fullmer Reynolds cites evidence from contemporary plays that suggests the Red Bull had a large central trap, and others at the front corners.[4] As figure 2 shows, the central area provides a focus for stage activity, and appears to create in the performance space a defined area within which not just the audience but the cast too become observers of the dramatic action, which therefore intensifies. Blocking in the Pit production makes heavy use of all these areas and particularly concentrates on the central grating as a common anchor for the action. Though it is not in reality a trapdoor, there is clearly access to the 'below' of the stage through the piercing, therefore it functions as an index to undiscoverable depth – the fatal pivot between this limbo and ultimate damnation. It is important to note here that there are two characters whose blocking dissociates them from the central grating. Both Franscisco and Monticelso, the prime movers of this production, avoid objective collocation with it. Though Monticelso encroaches briefly on the space several times during Vittoria's arraignment (3.2),[5] his rapid spiralling and circular movement is redolent of the predator working its prey – wearing it down while remaining without the range of retaliatory strikes. Francisco remains clearly on the periphery, controlling the actions of others.

Edwards's modifications to the structure of the play, though few, reflect this spatial pivot by placing the arraignment between the murders of Camillo and Isabella, and by making several small changes to the text which point clearly to Bracciano's motivation to be rid of Isabella, before Vittoria suggests the possibility in her dream recollection at 1.2.231–55. When Lodovico links his banishment with Bracciano at 1.1.38–44 and indicates that they are both guilty of adultery, that the injustice of his punishment is reflected in Bracciano's continued freedom to 'prostitute / The honour of Vittoria Corombona', there is suggestion, but no specific evidence within the text, that Bracciano is responsible for his fate. This production promotes suggestion to fact by giving Francisco an extra line after 2.1.142:

> Francisco: [to Attendant off-stage] Call Camillo hither –
> You have received the rumour, how Count Lodowick
> **Who you yourself have banished from our sight**
> Is turn'd a pirate.
> Bracciano: Yes.
> Francisco: We are now preparing
> Some ships to fetch him in. (2.1.141–4)

Immediately Bracciano's justification for divorcing Isabella alters. No longer is his action a development of Vittoria's dream, the first stage of which is to remove Isabella to allow his continued dalliance with Vittoria. Rather, it is Isabella's punishment for her supposed transgression with Lodovico.

Now the structural changes allow a cohesive development of Bracciano's machinery as an issue unrelated to his desire for Vittoria, or her own ambition. Edwards removes the dumb show presentation and its related dialogue as a framing device, and creates instead two separate episodes of direct action, during which Bracciano is absent from the stage. In each, he arrives immediately after the event to receive report from Hortensio (who replaces the conjurer). During Camillo's murder, Hortensio is on-stage, and remains there while it clears. Bracciano enters, as if from Vittoria's house, and they engage in the dialogue adapted from 2.2.38–52:

> Bracciano: 'Twas quaintly done, but yet each circumstance
> I taste not fully.
> Page: They fixed this merrily, my lord.
> Hortensio: Charged with their deep healths
> To their boon voyage, and to second that,
> Flamineo calls forth a vaulting horse to

> Maintain their sport. The virtuous Marcello
> Is innocently plotted forth the room,
> **And thus Camillo meets his politic fate.**
> Bracciano: It seems Marcello, and Flamineo
>   Are both committed.
> Hortensio: And now they are come with purpose to apprehend
>   Your mistress, fair Vittoria.
> Bracciano: We are now beneath that roof –
> Hortensio: Twere fit we instantly
>   make out by some back postern.   Exeunt

Again the insertion of an extra line, after 44, reinforces the Bracciano/Isabella/Lodovico triangular relationship. Removal of Camillo here thwarts Francisco's plan to send ships after Lodovico, who is bound for Padua. We must presume that, having not appeared on stage since 1.1, he is unaware of Isabella's journey to Rome. However, Bracciano correctly assumes that banishment from Rome will naturally lead to Padua, so divorcing Isabella will also guarantee her return and their subsequent meeting.

Now, by placing Isabella's death after the arraignment, Edwards's modified plot removes any possibility of Vittoria's complicity, beyond the suggestions of dream relation, and makes more credible the contrition she displays during 1.2 when Cornelia vents her moral passion. Bracciano's motive to murder becomes contingent on his relationships with Monticelso and Francisco during the trial, in which his added final couplet reinforces the argument. His exit speech becomes:

> Bracciano: Thou liest – 'twas my stool.
>   Bestow't upon thy master that will challenge
>   The rest a'th'household stuff – for Bracciano
>   Was ne'er so beggarly, to take a stool
>   Out of another's lodging: let him make
>   Valance for his bed on't, or a demi-foot-cloth
>   For his most reverend moil, – Monticelso,
>   **Who slanders me must answer to the shame.**
>   **I shall requite the wrongs you do my name.** (3.2.172–9)

This highly dramatized translation of Webster's Latin is the stuff of vendetta, the result of provocation of the upstart Bracciano by his wiser and more calculating peers apparently to commit action that subsequently justifies his own murder. However, the meeting with Doctor Julio has already taken place, so this is public opportunity to give portent for a previously conceived plot, and to align it with the Machiavellian power play between Bracciano and Francisco. Hortensio's report of the poisoning (relocated between 3.2.294 and 295) now brings forth from Bracciano the question 'Was Count Lodowick there?', as a replacement for Webster's 'Methought I saw | Count Lodowick there' (2.2.31–2). The register changes from musing to interrogative – of course, he expects Lodovico to be with Isabella, after all Camillo's pursuit did not take place, there was no-one to interrupt the predicted voyage.

The play text with these alterations irons out some of the convolution of the original, and makes it more accessible to a modern audience. It discovers, rather than one white devil, who may or may not be Vittoria, a conflict between the established dynasties of Francisco and Monticelso, and Bracciano – the young pretender. There is some textual substantiation in this; during the reworked dialogue of 3.2 Bracciano forfeits his line of Latin *'Nemo me impune lacessit'* (178) to Edwards's blue pencil, and acquires the English couplet discussed above. His lack of Latin makes him of the new order, whereas the lawyer who pleads against Vittoria stands as a symbol of the establishment, enshrined in legal double talk.

We now no longer have a case that demands either support or denouncement of Vittoria as the titular character. Bracciano has displaced her (and he, after all, merits a higher position on the title page), but neither is there an absolute case to identify him. As Robert Hanks observes of the production, 'here, powerful men use morality as a cover for merciless pragmatism ... for women the only lever to use ... is sex'.[6] Exactly the same case is true of the original text, except that Webster's subtle foldings direct the attribution of sin towards expressions of sexuality rather than towards the ruthless political machine. Brown proposes that 'Webster closely followed the outline of events given in his source, save only that he made Vittoria wholly responsible for instigating the murder of Isabella and Camillo',[7] which is satisfactory insofar as it identifies one of several incitements to murder, but makes no comparison with others' motives, beginning with Lodovico, whose habits are relayed through the discourse of Antonelli and Gasparo at the opening of the play. Edwards's alterations to the play bring it closer to the events reported in the *Fugger News Letter*, *'A Letter lately written from Rome'*, and other contemporary sources available to Webster, and bias the plot towards suppression of Bracciano and victimization of Vittoria.[8] Her structural changes offer us the trial as a contrived proceeding to forestall Vittoria's already dissipated gambit for power by those who are unprepared to relinquish theirs. In this arena there is no one devil, they have all fallen from grace, and contend for position with the audience at the bottom of the Pit. Life as it is represented is precarious. To keep even a tenuous grasp on it requires practice of *realpolitik*, whether that be the discourse of the sexual game played openly, or a merciless abuse of the power of state which does not quite manage to disguise that it is rooted in the same.

Here then is a series of actions and reactions which Peter Smith considers a 'brilliant capitalisation on Webster's monstrous scenarios, rather than [an] elucidation of the whole'.[9] The governing force is sexual obsession, which precipitates disaster upon disaster for those who succumb to its power. However, these are the powerless, misled by the chiaroscuro that sexuality casts over the real source of power – believing, as Lodovico does, that by appealing to a higher order of desire, they can receive absolution, or as Flamineo, whose pandering seeks the fulfilment of status that his father had foregone.

Representations of sexuality cannon off each other in this production, even before the cast appears on stage. Set in the recess between the central tiring-house pillars is a large portrait of Bracciano, which smoulders with ire in its portal, illuminated by concealed floodlights. The overture, which begins while the audience is still finding its seats, reflects the menace in a discordant clarinet solo, supported by double bass whose repetitive beating note both stands for the collective heart of the assembly and as a symbol of the repression to come. Here Edwards makes her only addition to the structure. As the lights dim, Isabella, costumed in a turquoise gown, walks between the pillars and the backdrop to the picture, kisses it passionately and leaves by the opposite entrance, as a parallel to her poisoning, but without the later entourage of Lodovico and Giovanni. Spots at the rear of the house come up to pick out the portrait as it thrusts forward to fill the central embrasure momentarily, then retreats to its original position, an icon of youthful insurgence constrained between the dual phalli of authority. Immediately, Lodovico enters and stands on the central grating to deliver the opening verse. Now only one light illuminates the stage – a steel blue spot immediately above, which is directed down to cast a weak light and little shadow. At the end of the performance, this light appears for a second time. It is specifically Lodovico's index, and a clear indicator that he is a force of little consequence. Thus he and Bracciano's image are immediately cast into opposition by both spatial and visual signification. Weak blue light contests with the strong, cold illumination of the picture. Bracciano's depicted facial beauty and rich apparel overpower the functional black leather coat and scarred eye that Lodovico bears. The forward gesture of the picture is also an act of aggression directed at the central grating. This begins to establish the hierarchy of stage spaces that complements the hierarchy of power within the text. Schematically the parallel looks like this:

Tiring-house wall and pillars, and stage periphery (including the two fore stage gratings)	==>	Francisco and Monticelso – established power of state and church
Central discovery area	==>	Bracciano and Flamineo – usurpation and instability
Central grating	==>	Vittoria, Camillo, Isabella – death, persecution and vulnerability

Isabella's walk becomes one of particular danger – a treacherous passage between loci of destructive forces, which neither she nor Vittoria ever transcend.

Against the sinister, highly structured opening, Vittoria's entrance with her entourage at 1.2 is a carnivalesque wave of disorder and noise, a spontaneous outflow from the discovery area and wings, unmeasured, unconstrained and threatening to the boundaries of state. Here, the lights are bright – banks of orange and yellow illuminate the whole stage, and when Vittoria announces 'Unto my lord the duke, / The best of welcome. More lights, attend the duke' (1–2), extra banks of tungsten floods increase the intensity and heat of the moment.[10] There is a spectacular transience present. All the cast except Camillo and Flamineo wear clothes of taffeta and shot silk. The flowing gowns of the women shift from green to blue and black, Bracciano's jacket reflects blue and green and the male courtiers' jackets have several kinds of metallic finish. Camillo stands apart immediately in his robe and cap, which predicate the second lawyer's garments. He is a symbol of state, fixed in his relationship to Monticelso (as nephew, rather than cousin, here), neither able nor wanting to break that boundary, and standing paradoxically as an emblem of virtue among the manifold arms of vice.[11] The matt black cloth allows no reflexion – his space is always a point of darkness, absorbing and destroying cast light from the other costumes as the totalitarian state will absorb and destroy Bracciano.

Vittoria stands in contrast both against the courtiers and Isabella. Her gown is scarlet and her bodice split, beneath which she wears nothing. An immediate conclusion might be that she is an icon of the women Joseph Swetnam vilified in his 1615 pamphlet *The Arraignment of Lewde, idle, froward, and unconstant women*, which portrays the objectified women as 'in shapes angels but in qualities devils, painted coffins with rotten bones'.[12] Yet the red does not signify harlotry or depravity in this instance, rather it contextualizes Vittoria's lines at 5.6.240–41, after Lodovico strikes the mortal blow:

> O My greatest sin lay in my blood.
> Now my blood pays for it.

Brown glosses the blood as passion, but it also carries implications of lineage and death, and with the sequence of costume colour changes that develops, certainly does not depict Vittoria as the scarlet woman that Cave found so disorientating in Frank Dunlop's 1969 National Theatre production.[13] However, while Ferris considers that the Duchess of Malfi, constrained by her brothers to wear her widow's weeds, is in a 'safe, inert social position',[14] Vittoria in her open, red gown is certainly the opposite: volatile, unsafe and a potential threat to the unbroken absolutism of state. And this threat takes greater symbolic form as Flamineo's proxy wooing at 1.2.130ff develops Camillo's 'Now he begins to tickle her' (134) into patently incestuous foreplay. Vittoria leans against the left tiring-house pillar, threatening the authority it symbolizes both by her proximity and her wanton abandon with Flamineo, simultaneously transgressing the politics of sexual behaviour and the divisions of social position.

However, here appears the first identifiable thematic threat to women. Flamineo thrusts his hand several times into her skirt, and reports to Camillo 'I am opening your case hard' (150), and 'I find her coming' (164), both visual as well as literary puns. But their tone of objectification and inspection identifies the action as a signifier of patriarchal power, in this case with Flamineo as agent. The location is therefore as threatening to Vittoria as she to it. During 2.2, Bracciano replicates the action with Isabella. On her arrival from Padua, they have the stage to themselves from 146–225. Here, according to Edwards's textual modifications, Bracciano prosecutes for divorce because of his suspicion of Isabella's disposition toward Lodovico. We may take his 'What amorous whirlwind hurried you to Rome?' (148) as substantiation of this, and his subsequent questioning and vocal abuse as grievance rather than dissembling. Their discourse takes place entirely within the central stage space, and primarily on the grating – the locus of persecution. Bracciano first threatens Isabella at sword point, but she resists. He then forces her to the ground and replicates Flamineo's action, thrusting his hand into her skirt, at 174–5 – 'was't your trick / to meet some amorous gallant here in Rome...?' then stands back from her as she prostrates herself across the grating, utterly abject. There are two further examples of this action, both committed against Vittoria: the first as part of Bracciano's rather inappropriate reconciliation action in the house of convertites (which borders on rape), and Lodovico's stab, with which I shall deal later.

Each instance is a display of power over powerlessness represented at the level of microcosm – a small, apparently insignificant action which by its repetition becomes part of the thematic structure of the whole, both contributing to and defining the overarching theme that if anything is the White Devil, it is the motive and ability to abuse power. At its ultimate construction this becomes abuse by proxy to maintain rigid order and ensure that there is no threat to the *status quo* from the Pandora's Box unleashed by Bracciano's lust for Vittoria. Edwards develops on Webster and makes the case that, though she breaks the bounds of Jacobean concepts of female behaviour, Vittoria's circumstance proscribes any notion she might have of existing either in opposition to or independent of the cast iron patriarchy, represented here both by the set and within the structures of symbolic action. The danger posed by both Vittoria and Isabella is that they have the textual opportunity to personate masculine behaviour, thus 'Webster's male impersonators seem to show women becoming "masculine", and yet the sense of released power in their acting suggests that these women have broken out of a merely imitative role'.[15] But their male respondents remorselessly defend against the incursion. However, we know from contemporary records that women behaving in a masculine fashion were tolerated in Renaissance society. Orgel gives several cases, notably of Penelope Rich, an approximate contemporary of Vittoria Accaramboni, and of Mary Markham (Moll Cutpurse), whose public personas differed considerably from recognized feminine behaviour, and who both made great successes of their lives.[16] Each negotiated an existence forbidden to Isabella and Vittoria. In which case we should view Webster's portrayal of the patriarchal hegemony as one aspect in the public discourse which included both the White Devil, Swetnam's pamphlet and later, the play *Swetnam the Woman Hater*.

If the locus for the debate is the public arena, then both the frontispiece of *Swetnam* (fig. 2) and the thematic blocking within Edwards's *The White Devil* represent that arena. As Swetnam the stage figure and pamphleteer is exposed as a hypocrite, so are the machinery of court and state represented by Monticelso, Francisco, Bracciano and indeed Flamineo. Isabella is therefore on trial when she dissembles her divorce. Her position on the centre grating (fig. 3), pinioned by her interlocutors, prefigures Vittoria's during her arraignment. Isabella has no range of mobility, but both Francisco and Monticelso are free to move in the same circular and spiral movements that later constrain Vittoria. She is portrayed here as 'strong-willed, victimised and … unusually vehement',[17] and manifests the 'power / To execute my apprehended wishes' (2.1.243–4), because she has authority even in her state of immobility, accorded by symbolic manipulation of her wedding ring. Its public removal, though mimicking Bracciano's earlier action, rejects any constraint imposed by the circling male characters, in a manner inaccessible to Vittoria. There is here an exchange of position in which Isabella rises from her previously debased and abused status to hold in complete control the ring as a symbol of the closed and possessive patriarchy. Rather than offering a strong opposition, she dominates the patriarchal order, and proposes its failure by dropping the ring through the grating into its indexed 'below'.

A comparison with *The Last Judgement* here (fig. 1) is apposite to display the planes of symbolism accorded by the moment to the audience-as-jury watching the iconoclastic judgement of hypocrisy. The circumspect order of the theatre sits on the brink of the chaos of the pit in a moment of instability as the ring falls. 'Below' is separated from the 'here' of the auditorium only by the grating, on which Isabella stands or sits. If the symbol of hypocrisy passes through and she does not, then as does the figure seated on the orb, she passes visual sentence on those who will follow. Bracciano attempts to stop the fall, but here he is the victim of abuse rather than its progenitor engaging a patently weak action and thus presaging his demise.

If Isabella gains power by disposing of her ring, Vittoria conversely loses hers during the trial. The blocking of the scene is consistent with that of 2.1 in that it immobilizes Vittoria on the grating and allows Monticelso and Francisco free movement about the stage. As the scene opens, both take up positions on the fore-stage corner gratings. Here, they symbolize the pillars of state, an invisible proscenium forcing the spectacle into a more rigid mode of representation and mirroring the pillars of the tiring-house. Yet simultaneously they stand suspended above the imagined void, so their locus reinforces the duality of power and corruption proposed by the ring. Within this image, Vittoria is trapped. In spite of her spirited response to Monticelso's remorselessly corrupt prosecution, she has already lost the case. Her gown, diluted from its earlier scarlet (perhaps by the tungsten lights of Bracciano's first entrance), now has an orange hue. Its previous association with blood therefore suggests an aural/visual metaphor whose tenor is the letting process evident in Monticelso's lustful vitriol. It is as though in 'paint[ing] out / Your follies in more natural red and white' (3.2.51–2), he absorbs into his crimson soutane her very existence by transfusing the passion of her blood to himself.

If, as Bromley suggests of the play, 'all women, including the "good" ones, are perceived and addressed without distinction [and] reduced to the status of generic "woman"',[18] Monticelso's stage behaviour here displays the social difference and portrays vividly 'a great sickness in him[self], which is the sickness of the state'.[19] His manifest lust for Vittoria and his leering at her cleavage bring out the *Crucible*-like logic of the text such that it subsumes the accusation of whoredom directed at Vittoria as an icon of woman. Her guilt is predetermined by her failure to arrive in mourning and compounded by her innocence of Camillo's death (3.2.119–29), then proven by, among other things, the deliberately false interpretation of Bracciano's love-letter (192–8). Monticelso's unconcealed desire for what he wishes to destroy redirects his charge so that the audience perception of Monticelso-as-state/church and his perception of Vittoria-as-woman/whore are identical – both centred on the lust for what must not be had. However, she stands alone on the central grating, and he wields authority, empowered by mobility, to constrain her. She therefore represents Stevenson's proposition that 'Renaissance discourses concerning the nature and roles of women ... restrict[ed] the proper sphere of women's speech.'[20] Vittoria gives power to the voice as Penelope Rich or Mary Markham might have, but Monticelso's greater authority negates it.

When next she appears, after the trial, at the house of convertites, Vittoria displays the attributes of a woman entirely at the mercy of a power against which she has no recourse. Even her previous weapon of speech is diminished. Her dress is no longer a vibrant gown, rather it reflects the social standing from which she has tried to escape. It is of the same grey/brown hue as the material of the stage and set. We may presume for an instant that Barthes' inoculation theory has worked its course by absorbing and normalizing what has transgressed the boundary of hegemonic control. From this point she ceases to display the freedom of movement which characterized her earlier: her status is now that of victim, rather than threat. The changes in lighting for this scene emphasize the transformation. During her reunion with Bracciano, there is no illumination from the gantry above. From below the gratings brilliant white light floods the centre stage, casting long character shadows and the pattern of a grille that matches the barred gates which now divide the stage apron from the tiring-house. The full effect of 'below' complements Webster's own ghosts. This is the light from Isabella's ring, both exposing her husband's dire folly and reinforcing its index to the imagined pit, congruent with that of figure 1, and rendering ironic Bracciano's 'O my sweet duchess / how lovely art thou now' (4.2.99–100) long before Vittoria's response. Bracciano is on the point of escaping to Padua, repeating the earlier journey made by Lodovico, and the irony should not go unremarked that in both cases Isabella is a governing influence. In the first, Lodovico travels towards her; in the second, Bracciano escapes her posthumous sphere of representation, and moves towards her recently wound corpse. That the end of his own influence is imminent we may discern in the visual reconfiguration of the stage created by the brilliance of the lighting. The perimeter dissolves into shadow and the tiring-house wall becomes a screen to recreate in shadow-play the action of the centre. The closure constrains all three characters within the 'murky territory where psychology, ethics, metaphysics and religion shade imperceptibly into each other'.[21] Bracciano has now only one interest – to possess Vittoria; therefore his actions resemble rape and not those of a lover. She has become merely an object, entirely without influence.

It is appropriate for Edwards's final scene to resolve the threads of the argument. Solid doors here divide the discovery area from the stage apron, which is now sanctuary, isolating the players and audience from the court. Vittoria is by now bled of all resistance and absolutely vulnerable – her dress is a white linen smock with a small bodice and she wears no shoes. Zanche, in contrast, still has her green taffeta gown, whose colour switches as rapidly as her loyalty. Flamineo's coat, discarded on the apron and transformed from grey to faded red soon after he murdered Marcello, symbolizes both bloodshed by his own hand and the now impossible task of daily renewing his lease of life. Vittoria aligns specifically with Cornelia and her attendants during their mourning for Marcello – represented at 5.4.66–112 in this production as a pieta – the white smock does not signify 'devil'. Together, she and Flamineo have almost completed their move towards a final unity as corpse and winding sheet. The arrival of Lodovico at 5.6.167 therefore balances and inverts the opening. Bracciano's agent and wife are blocked in the locus of vulnerability when he appears through the central discovery area, taking the same course as Bracciano's portrait. This follows precisely the changes in the structure of power propagated by Bracciano's ceaseless folly. When Lodovico removes his disguise (of Capuchin monk), the steel blue spot again illuminates the central grating, reiterating his promise to 'make Italian cut-works in their guts / If ever I return' (1.1.51–2). Within this structure, the absolute powerlessness of Vittoria becomes apparent. Lodovico's stab, unlike the previous thrusting of Flamineo and Bracciano is extended and violating. Such is his strength that he lifts Vittoria clear of the ground on the point of the knife, so when she falls, there is a large bloodstain from her vagina, spreading across the smock. The sin for which she is punished finally is that she is woman. At the last, Flamineo recognizes that, and his 'if woman do breed man / she ought to teach him manhood' (5.6.242–3) counterpoints the earlier taunting of Cornelia at 1.2.308–45. They both die on the central grating, he lying across her.

John Brown prudently suggests that the play is 'not the instrument to present, with massive assurances, types of good and evil; if a critic sees that in *The White Devil* the assurance must come from him and not from the play'.[22] However, if we consider its moment of production as being consistent with the Jacobean public debate on the nature of woman, alongside Swetnam and others, and that 'the controversy over women is an issue fundamental to the very nature of theatre',[23] we may argue quite reasonably that the portrayal of power is one in which a patriarchal system proscribes in quite hypocritical manner the inclusion of women within its structure. Edwards's production clarifies this as one facet of the debate, and demonstrates that the devil in crystal is actually the possession and misuse of that power, rather than any individual character in the play.

Notes

[1] Inga-Stina Ewbank's ascription in 'Webster's Realism, or, "A Cunning Piece Wrought Perspective"', in *John Webster*, ed. Brian Morris (London: Ernest Benn, 1970), 166. Also see the analysis of Vittoria as 'an ambitious "strumpet" with her lustful victim' in Charles R. Forker, *Skull Beneath the Skin: The Achievement of John Webster* (Carbondale and Edwardsville: Southern Illinois University Press, 1986), 254.

[2] A.J. Smith 'The Power of *The White Devil*', in *John Webster*, ed. Brian Morris (London: Ernest Benn, 1970), 73.

[3] This production of *The White Devil* ran during 1996 at The Swan in Stratford-upon-Avon, and transferred to the Barbican Pit for a subsequent four-month season. It was the RSC's first production of the play, and the result of a new directorial relationship with Gale Edwards (in tandem with *The Taming of the Shrew)*. The principal players were:

Vittoria Corombona	Jane Gurnet
Flamineo	Richard McCabe
Marcello	Alisdair Simpson
Cornelia	Caroline Blakiston
Camillo	Adam Godley
Zanche	Martina Laird
Brachiano	Ray Fearon
Isabella	Teresa Banham
Giovanni	Devin Griffin/Omar Nawaz
Hortensio	David Fahm
Francisco de Medici	Stephen Boxer
Monticelso	Philip Voss
Jaques (not silent)	Paul Ritter
Lodovico	Philip Quast
Gasparo	Andrew Hesker
Antonelli	Stephen Billington

[4] George Fullmer Reynolds, 'The Staging of Elizabethan Plays at the Red Bull Theater 1605–1625', *PMLA* 9 (1940), 88–92.

⁵ All textual references are to the John Russell Brown edition of *The White Devil* (London: Methuen, 1960; Manchester: Manchester University Press, 1977).
⁶ *Independent* (29 April 1996), reprinted in *Theatre Record* 22 April – 5 May 1996, 564.
⁷ Brown, xxix.
⁸ See Brown, 189–97.
⁹ Peter J. Smith, '1996 RSC Spring/Summer Season, Stratford-upon-Avon', *Cahiers Elizabéthains* (October 1996), 73–5, 73.
¹⁰ There is ironic reference here to the Creation, particularly the oratorio by Haydn with its sudden fortissimo chord on 'and there was LIGHT'. Though in this case the sequence is the transformation of order into chaos.
¹¹ See Rosemary Freeman, *English Emblem Books* (London: Chatto and Windus, 1948), 10–13 for a discussion on emblems of Virtue and Vice, which refers to Bracciano's ghost carrying its pot of lilies. Though the lilies are not used in this production, there is a parallel image in the juxtaposition of the costuming in this scene.
¹² Quoted in Lesley Ferris, *Acting Women* (Basingstoke and London: Macmillan, 1988), 11.
¹³ Richard Allen Cave, *The White Devil and the Duchess of Malfi: Text and Performance* (Basingstoke and London: MacMillan, 1988), 44.
¹⁴ Ferris, 117.
¹⁵ Sheryl Stevenson, '"As Differing as Two Adamants": Sexual Difference in *The White Devil*', in *Sexuality and Politics in Renaissance Drama*, eds Carole Levin and Karen Robertson (New York: Edwin Mellen Press, 1991), 166.
¹⁶ Steven Orgel, *Impersonations* (Cambridge: Cambridge University Press, 1996), 129–53.
¹⁷ Michael Billington, 'The White Devil', *Guardian* (24 April 1996), reprinted in *Theatre Record* (22 April – 5 May 1996), 565.
¹⁸ Laura J. Bromley, 'The Rhetoric of Feminine Identity in *The White Devil*', in *In Another Country: Feminist Perspectives on Renaissance Drama*, eds Dorothea Kehler and Susan Baker (Metuchen and London: The Scarecrow Press, 1991), 51.
¹⁹ Rod Dungate, 'Rod Dungate at the Swan (RSC): The White Devil', *Plays and Players* (June 1996), 43.
²⁰ Stevenson, 163.
²¹ Forker, 252.
²² Brown, xlix.
²³ Ferris, 19.

EDWARDS'S RSC PRODUCTION OF WEBSTER'S *THE WHITE DEVIL* 289

16.1 *The Last Judgement*, Herman Tom Ring (1555)

16.2 Frontispiece from *Swetnam the Woman Hater*: the Red Bull Stage

290 TIPPLER

16.3 Isabella: 'Henceforth I'll never lie with you, by this wedding ring' (2.1.254–5)

16.4 Vittoria's arraignment

16.5 Vittoria and Flamineo: 'Strike thunder, and strike loud to my farewell' (5.5.276)

CHAPTER 17

The Nineteenth-Century Productions of *A Yorkshire Tragedy* (1608)

Barry Gaines

A Yorkshire Tragedy is a short but intense domestic tragedy published in London in 1608. It was entered that year in the Stationers' Register as 'written by WYLLIAM SHAKESPERE', and the title pages of the 1608 and 1619 quarto editions both state that it was 'Written by W. Shakspeare'.[1] Indeed, *A Yorkshire Tragedy* has more bits of external evidence connecting it to Shakespeare than do several of his genuine plays, and this connection with Shakespeare has lead to most of the attention that the play has received. On the stage, *A Yorkshire Tragedy* was apparently first performed by Shakespeare's company and later adapted for performance in the eighteenth century. In the nineteenth century, however, two productions – in two unexpected places – returned to the original text for brief revivals of the play.

A Yorkshire Tragedy is based upon actual historical characters and events. On 23 April 1605 Walter Calverley of Calverley, who had gambled away his estate in the West Riding of Yorkshire, killed his older sons, one not yet five years old and the other but a year and a half. He also seriously wounded his wife Philippa, but he was apprehended before he could harm his remaining infant son. At his trial Walter stood mute and was, therefore, forced to undergo *la peine forte et dure* (the placing of heavy weights upon the accused's chest until he entered a plea of guilty or not guilty or died).[2] Walter Calverley remained silent and on 5 August 1605 he was pressed to death.[3] This sensational murder attracted considerable attention in London where two pamphlets, two ballads and two plays were written both to establish and to take advantage of public interest. *A Yorkshire Tragedy* closely follows the pamphlet *Two most vnnaturall and bloodie Murthers: The one by Maister Cauverley* ... (1605).

The composition of *A Yorkshire Tragedy* is easily bracketed between June 1605 and May 1606.[4] A comparison of the text of *A Yorkshire Tragedy* with the plays that Shakespeare was composing around that time does not suggest that he was the author. Moreover, the play was not included in the First Shakespeare Folio of 1623 which included all of the canonical plays except *Pericles*. An editor of the play sums up the argument this way: 'Neither in characterization, nor in plot, nor in metrical peculiarities have the most ardent defenders of the *Yorkshire Tragedy's* authenticity pretended that there is any approach to Shakespeare's manner subsequent to 1605'.[5] While the question of authorship is beyond the scope of this paper, there is strong evidence that points to Thomas Middleton as the author.[6] Yet the play seems to have been performed by Shakespeare's theatrical company, and there is always the possibility that Shakespeare himself might have had a hand in some of the situations or dialogue of the play. Algernon Charles Swinburne has expressed the frustration inherent in the authorship quest:

> *A Yorkshire Tragedy* does not at any rate belong to the class of obviously spurious plays which it is impossible for any Englishman other than an incurable dunce to associate even in thought with the incomparable name of Shakespeare. ... This is not to say that I believe it to be Shakespeare's: indeed I would rather think that impossible: but impossible I cannot quite bring myself to feel comfortably assured that it is.[7]

A Yorkshire Tragedy is a charter member of the 'Shakespeare apocrypha', the group of plays at one time or another attributed to Shakespeare. It was included in the revised impression of the Third Shakespeare Folio, in the Fourth Shakespeare Folio, and in the collections of Shakespeare's plays edited by Nicholas Rowe, Alexander Pope, Jacob Tonson and Robert Walker in the seventeenth and eighteenth centuries. *A Yorkshire Tragedy* may have been considered by many to be Shakespeare's work, but what of its stage history? In preparing the Revels Plays edition of *A Yorkshire Tragedy* with the late Arthur Cawley, this was the question I attempted to answer. The title page of the first quarto states that the play was 'Acted by his Maiesties Players at the Globe', which would suggest a seventeenth-century performance by the King's Men. In more recent times, since the nineteen fifties, there have been at least ten revivals of the play, both professional and amateur,[8] the latest of which I am aware occurred ten years ago in Los Angeles.[9] When I went looking for productions between the seventeenth and twentieth centuries, I found no record of any professional staging of the play in Great Britain. I did, however, stumble upon two nineteenth-century productions in two unlikely places. Indeed, these are the only performances of *A Yorkshire Tragedy* I have found between Shakespeare's time and the second half of the twentieth century.

Our play appears to have been known up until the closing of the theatres. Playwright Thomas Heywood makes this reference to it in *Philocothonista*, published in London in 1635:

> One Master *Coverlee*, a gentleman of quality and good descent, in the like distemper wounded his Wife and slew his owne Children; whom I am the bolder to nominate, because the facinerous act hath by authority bin licensed to be acted on the publike Stage.[10]

We have, however, no records of performances during the seventeenth century beyond the title page reference.

In the next century, *A Yorkshire Tragedy* was sentimentalized into *The Fatal Extravagance*, a one-act play published under Joseph Mitchell's name but often attributed to Aaron Hill.[11] In the Preface to *The Fatal Extravagance*, Mitchell states, 'I took the Hint (and only the Hint, as the Reader may see) ... from SHAKESPEAR's Yorkshire Tragedy, which was put into my Hands, on purpose, by my good friend, Mr. Hill, to whom I take this Occasion of expressing my Gratitude, in the most publick manner I can'.[12] This adaptation of *A Yorkshire Tragedy* was performed at the Theatre Royal, Lincoln's Inn Fields, on 21 April 1721, and it became so popular that Mitchell was moved to expand it to a five-act version which was published in 1726.[13] In the Dedication he tells us that his aim was to make the 'little Tragedy more fashionable ... with the Help of some new Characters, which I have leisurely drawn, and connected in the old Fable'. Allardyce Nicoll believes that Hill is responsible for *The Fatal Extravagance*, and that he 'deserves the credit, normally given to Lillo, of having been the first to introduce to his age the tragedy of contemporary English types and to provide the definite basis for the popular *Schicksalstragöde* of later years'. Finally, toward the end of the century, *The Fatal Extravagance* itself was reworked by Francis Godolphin Waldron as *The Prodigal* (1793). That play was acted at the Little Theatre in the Haymarket on 2 December 1793, and may have prompted a revival of *The Fatal Extravagance* in May 1794. That brings us to the nineteenth century, the focus of this study.

Before considering the two nineteenth-century productions of *A Yorkshire Tragedy*, let me provide a synopsis of the play to demonstrate how it may have appealed to the theatre people who staged it. *A Yorkshire Tragedy* presents the story of an unnamed Yorkshire family. The husband inherited an unblemished name and a wealthy Yorkshire estate, but through gambling and dissolute living he managed to lose it all. He sends his long-suffering wife to her uncle to obtain funds, but her uncle, aware of the husband's treatment of his wife, offers instead a place at court through which the husband can redeem himself. When the wife returns and delivers this message, her husband flies into a rage and draws a dagger. A servant intervenes, but as the husband contemplates his situation, he is convinced that the only way to save his wife and three sons from penury is to kill them himself. He kills two of his sons and wounds his wife on stage, but as he goes off on horseback to dispatch his infant son who is away at nurse he is thrown off his horse and is captured. When he confronts his forgiving wife, he repents his actions and accepts his fate. The play is very short, barely 700 lines, and the head-title at the beginning of the play, 'All's One, or, One of the foure Plaies in one', suggests that the play may have been one of four plays acted at the same performance. We have no indication of the existence or nature of these three other plays, but *A Yorkshire Tragedy* has a powerful impact on its own.

My research uncovered productions of *A Yorkshire Tragedy* in Boston in 1847 and in St Petersburg in 1895. Similar considerations seem to have motivated both productions: the connection with Shakespeare's name, the brevity of the play, the relatively small cast required, and the presence of an attractive role for the star – the long-suffering Wife in the case of the Boston production and the crazed Husband in the case of the St Petersburg staging. Let us examine these productions in turn.

On the first of March 1847 *A Yorkshire Tragedy* was performed as the first part of a triple bill at the Boston Theatre, Federal Street. The performance was a benefit for Mrs Harriet Bland, and the final piece on the bill was the operatic drama *Clari, the Maid of Milan* in which Mrs Bland played the title role and sang the very popular songs 'Bid me discourse' and 'Home, sweet home'. Looking for something else to attract an audience, Mrs Bland included *A Yorkshire Tragedy*, and the playbill for that evening attributes the play to Shakespeare and proclaims that it will be acted for the 'first time in America'. The playbill also trumpets that the play was 'not acted for 200 years'. Harriet Bland was the elder sister of the popular English actress Helen Faucit. She had made her American debut in New York City on 30 August 1845, and, with her husband actor Humphrey Bland, had moved to the Boston theatre a year later. She is credited with being the first actress to play the role of Shakespeare's Cleopatra in the United States, and she was warmly appreciated by critics on both sides of the Atlantic. As the 1846–7 season was coming to a close, the Boston newspapers were most complimentary of Mrs Bland, and they encouraged theatre-goers to attend her benefit. The *Boston Daily Times* described her as 'an elegant woman and accomplished actress',[14] and the *Boston Courier* wrote,

Mrs. Bland moves in the higher walks of her profession, and her claims are equal or superior to many who appear upon the stage only in the quality of stars. It is to be hoped that she may have a full house.[15]

The *Evening Transcript* wrote, 'During her short sojourn in this city, Mrs. Bland has acquired an enviable reputation in her profession, and has secured to herself numerous friends. ... Universally correct in everything she has undertaken, and her range has been most extensive, in very many of the characters in the higher walks of the drama she is excelled by no actress on the stage'.[16] The *Boston Post* added, 'we hope Bostonians will seize the opportunity of bestowing a *solid* compliment to a worthy and talented actress'.[17]

Carol Carlisle has written an excellent overview of Harriet Bland and provided information to help us understand why she might have chosen to perform *A Yorkshire Tragedy* for her final benefit of the season.[18] While unaware that she had played the Wife in the *Tragedy*, Carlisle describes Mrs Bland as 'an unusually fine actress in domestic melodrama (arousing pathos by natural rather than exaggerated means)'.[19] In the suffering yet forgiving wife of *A Yorkshire Tragedy*, Mrs Bland found the ideal character for her acting skills and a moving performance to arouse a responsive benefit audience. She may also have been influenced by the success of Mr and Mrs Charles Kean in *The Gamester* at the Boston Theatre four months earlier.[20] Mrs Bland would also be performing with her husband in a similar melodrama which had the added attraction of being 'by Shakespeare' and never performed anywhere since the seventeenth century.

A Yorkshire Tragedy had not yet been published in the United States,[21] but it is clear that the Boston Theatre production used for its text the final volume of *The Pictorial Edition of the Works of Shakspere* edited by Charles Knight in London in 1843. The playbill contains two quotations under the bold assertion 'Not Acted for 200 years'. The first is background material about the play and its historical basis, and the second is Schlegel's contention that the *Tragedy* 'is not only unquestionably Shakspere's, but in my opinion deserves to [be] classed among his best and maturest works'. Both of these quotations are to be found in Knight's edition.[22] This background was taken by Knight from Edmund Malone's edition of the apocryphal plays [23] and reproduces Malone's error in dating the events in 1604 instead of 1605 (an error Malone corrects in his list of errata).[24] The Boston playbill introduces another error by changing Stow's Chronicle to 'How's Chronicle'. Schlegel's effusive evaluation is from John Black's translation *A Course of Lectures on Dramatic Art and Literature* and is found in Knight's introduction to *Sir John Oldcastle*.[25] These, and the peculiar spelling of 'Shakspere' confirm Knight's edition as the source of the play. Harriet Bland may have heard of our play, or even received a copy of Knight's edition, from the celebrated Helen Faucit, who was very attached to her elder sister. William Charles Macready owned a copy of Knight's edition of Shakespeare,[26] and he may have shared it with his leading lady Helen Faucit who may, in turn, have passed it on to Harriet Bland. The poet Robert Browning, a friend of Miss Faucit, also knew the play[27] and may have spoken of it. In any case *A Yorkshire Tragedy* was performed in Boston on 1 March 1847 with Harriet Bland in the leading role.

I have not found any contemporary reviews of that production. Mrs Bland might have wished to perform the play again if it were successful, but she never had the opportunity. She and her husband Humphrey left the Boston Theatre company at the end of the season in mid-March. He joined with John Brougham to manage Brougham and Bland's Boston Adelphi, the programme of which 'consisted entirely of vaudevilles, farces, and burlesques'.[28] Harriet played some parts in these productions, but she never again acted serious roles because she died unexpectedly on 5 November 1847 of typhus fever. She was thirty-eight years old.[29] She was, however, responsible for introducing *A Yorkshire Tragedy* to America and for performing the play for the first time in over two hundred years.

The other nineteenth-century production of *A Yorkshire Tragedy* took place in St Petersburg, Russia, in January 1895. Just as Harriet Bland saw the *Tragedy* as a vehicle for her talents as well as a curiosity associated with Shakespeare, Vasilii Panteleimonovich Dalmatov found the Husband's role as worthy of his theatrical skills. V.P. Dalmatov was the featured actor in the production of *A Yorkshire Tragedy* by the Theatre of the Literary and Artistic Club of St Petersburg. The play was again part of a triple-bill: it was followed by the one act comic opera *Le Passant* by Emile Paladilhe and scenes from Shakespeare's *1 Henry IV* (with Dalmatov playing Falstaff). The event was first scheduled for 30 December 1894, but one of the women in the opera fell ill and the performances were rescheduled for 13 January 1895. They were repeated 30 January.

A Yorkshire Tragedy had been translated into Russian several times: N.D. Zaionchkovskaya published a verse and prose translation in 1887, and the play was included in P.A. Kanshin's complete Shakespeare in 1893.[30] The play had also received some scholarly attention in the columns of the literary magazines such as *Dielo*, and N. Storozhenko, the dean of Russian Shakespeare scholars, wrote about the play in the magazine *Artist*.[31] The production of the play by the Literary and Artistic Club was, I believe, the first time it was performed in Russia.

The production of *A Yorkshire Tragedy* in St Petersburg was accomplished by Petr Petrovich Gnedich, the chairman of the Literary and Artistic Club, and later a producer at the Aleksandrinskii Theatre, the leading theatre in the Imperial capital. The actor V.P. Dalmatov had arrived at the Aleksandrinskii in St Petersburg in 1884 after acting in the provinces and in Moscow. He was born V.P. Luchich in 1852 in Serbian Dalmatia, and he took his stage name from the region of his birth. Shortly after he arrived in St Petersburg, he quarrelled with the management over the roles he would play and stayed away from the Aleksandrinskii Theatre for about a year. P.P. Gnedich took advantage of this estrangement to employ Dalmatov in the Literary and Artistic Club productions. Gnedich was himself a writer as well as a man of the theatre. The masterful Russian playwright Anton Pavlovich Chekhov provides this assessment of Gnedich:

> This man is a real writer. There is one thing he cannot do: *not* write. Whatever conditions you surround him with, he'll take a gnawed pencil if he can't find a pen, and he'll take a piece of paper, and he'll write – a sketch, a story, a comedy, a collection of anecdotes. He married a wealthy woman, he has no need of earning a livelihood, and he goes on writing more than ever. When he's short of an original theme, then he takes to translating.[32]

So it was that Gnedich, with the assistance of Y.P. Bachmetev, prepared the Russian translation of *A Yorkshire Tragedy*.

The production itself received little notice. In *Novoye Vremya* (New Times) critic A. Suvorin noted that everyone had worked without pay, and he charitably wrote,

> The stage direction was done masterly by P.D. Lensky. The stage, both the decorations and the costumes, were nice. So was the acting. I am speaking only about the dramatic performance. Whoever wrote *The Yorkshire Tragedy* does not matter since the performance creates a deep impression. There is now as then plenty of such gamesters, like the husband, rude, greedy, who under the influence of passion forget both their family and children as well as honor. Mr. Dalmatov and Mrs. Pavlov [who played the Wife] have played very expressively.[33]

But Suvorin's son-in-law A.P. Kolomin was involved with the Literary and Artistic Club, another reason that his review may have been gentle. Gnedich himself later called Dalmatov 'a terrible tragedian',[34] and

Aleksandr Rafailovich Kugel provides another reminiscence of the production in his memoirs.

> The first performance was unsuccessful. I could say more. Dalmatov insinuated himself into the first play because he had nothing better to do. He bleated in Yorkshire style. ... The play turned out to be a very uninteresting sample of pre-Shakespearean writing in the spirit of Greene, Marlowe and others. The stage setting was extremely primitive and, in general, everything was unnecessary. Gnedich pursed his lips and argued that without doubt the Shakespeare Society would devote special attention to this production. But this did not reassure anyone.[35]

Russian theatre historian B.V. Varneke considers Dalmatov excellent at playing stage dandies, but 'by a fatal misunderstanding, he believed himself a tragedian and mutilated the parts of Hamlet and Macbeth'.[36] I suspect that we can add the role of the Husband in *A Yorkshire Tragedy* to the list of mutilations.

We have precious little information about either the Boston or the St Petersburg productions of *A Yorkshire Tragedy*, but they appear to be the only ones during the nineteenth century. In both cases, the play was presented as a Shakespearean novelty, and in both cases the run was short. The brevity of the play and its dependence on only two central characters gave it a practical appeal and allowed for other plays on the same bill as was often the practice in the nineteenth century. Neither Harriet Bland nor Vasilii Dalmatov enhanced their careers by playing in *A Yorkshire Tragedy*, and the performances were almost lost. It is not until the twentieth century that the play was given a successful, or at least satisfying, production.

One final note. P.P. Gnedich's translation of *A Yorkshire Tragedy* may have been staged another time in Russia. In the journal *Teatral* Gnedich published his translation of the play. He added stage directions and condensed or omitted minor characters and speeches to make the play better suited to performance. He even included a list of properties needed by any company performing the play. It is possible that another company did just that and staged the play yet again although I have not found direct evidence of such a performance. In the *Athenaeum* of 16 July 1904, W.R. Morfill writes, 'a short time ago we saw by the Russian newspapers that *A Yorkshire Tragedy* was being performed at St Petersburg. We hope that this indubitably spurious piece will not be included in the new Shakespeariana' (91). If he is not referring to the 1895 production, which was hardly 'a short time ago' in 1904, then he knew of a more recent Russian production of which I remain unaware. His tantalizing reference takes us, however, safely into the twentieth century – and beyond the scope of this paper.

Notes

1. A.C. Cawley and Barry Gaines, eds, *A Yorkshire Tragedy* (Manchester: Manchester University Press, 1986), 26–7; Samuel Schoenbaum, *William Shakespeare: Records and Images* (New York: Oxford University Press, 1981), 218.
2. See Cliffford Dobb, 'London's Prisons', *Shakespeare Survey* 17 (1964), 91–2.
3. Gaines and Cawley, 10–11; Edward Garnett, *The Story of The Calverley Murders* (Calverley, West Yorkshire: Edward Garnett, 1991).
4. Gaines and Cawley, 1–2.
5. C.F. Tucker Brooke, ed., *The Shakespeare Apocrypha* (Oxford: Clarendon Press, 1908), xxxiv.
6. Cawley and Gaines, 2–6; David J. Lake, *The Canon of Thomas Middleton's Plays* (Cambridge: Cambridge University Press, 1975), 163–74; MacDonald P. Jackson, *Studies in Attribution: Middleton and Shakespeare* (Salzburg: Institut für Anglistik und Amerikanistik Universität Salzburg, 1979), 43–53.
7. Algernon Charles Swinburne, *Shakespeare* (London: Frowde, 1909), 42–3.
8. Gaines and Cawley, 24–6.
9. Joseph H. Stodder, 'Apocryphal Plays in Los Angeles: Continued', *Shakespeare Quarterly* 39 (1988), 237–8.
10. Thomas Heywood, *Philocothonista* (London, 1635), sig. L4r.
11. Joseph Mitchell, *The Fatal Extravagance* (London: 1727); for questions of authorship of *The Fatal Extravagance*, see Paul S. Dunkin, 'The Authorship of *The Fatal Extravagance*', *Modern Language Notes* 60 (1945), 328–30, Paul P. Kies, 'The Authorship of *The Fatal Extravagance*', *Research Studies of the State College of Washington* 13 (1945), 155–58 and Calhoun, Winton, 'Authorship of *The Fatal Extravagance*, Once Again', *Theatre Survey* 24 (1983), 130–33. I would like to acknowledge the assistance of the staff of the Harvard Theater Collection and the Boston Athenaeum during my research in Boston. I would also like to thank Professor Richard Marius of Harvard University.
12. Mitchell, sig. A2r.
13. See Dorothy Brewster, *Aaron Hill: Poet, Dramatist, Projector* (New York: Columbia University Press, 1913), 98 and Allardyce Nicoll, *A*

History of Early Eighteenth Century Drama 1700–1750 (Cambridge: Cambridge University Press, 1929), 336.
14. *Boston Daily Times* (1 March 1847), 2.
15. *Boston Courier* (1 March 1847), 2.
16. *Evening Transcript* (27 Februay 1847), 2.
17. *Boston Post* (27 February 1847), 2.
18. I would like to thank Professor Carol Carlisle for answering my questions with her encyclopedic knowledge and customary graciousness.
19. Carol J. Carlisle, 'The Other Miss Faucit', *Nineteenth Century Theatre Research* 6 (1978), 86.
20. William W. Clapp, Jr, *A Record of the Boston Stage* (Boston: J. Munroe, 1853), 390.
21. The first American publication was edited by William Gilmore Simms in 1848 (see William Gilmore Simms, ed., *A Supplement to the Plays of William Shakspeare* (New York: Cooledge, 1848) and Edd Winfield Parks 'Simms's Edition of the Shakespeare Apocrypha', *Studies in Shakespeare*, eds Arthur D. Matthews and Clark M. Emery (Coral Gables: University of Miami Press, 1953), 30–39).
22. Charles Knight, ed., *The Pictorial Edition of the Works of Shakspere*, vol. 8 (London: Knight, 1839–43), 241.
23. Edmond Malone, ed., *Supplement to the Edition of Shakspeare's Plays Published by Samuel Johnson and George Steevens*, vol. 2 (London: 1780), 426.
24. Malone, vol. 2, ix.
25. Knight, vol. 8, 209; Augustus William Schlegel, *A Course of Lectures on Dramatic Art and Literature*, trans. John Black, rev. A.J.W. Morrison (London: Bohn, 1846).
26. *Catalogue of the Library of William Charles Macready* (London: Christie, 1873), #191.
27. Cawley and Gaines, 142n.
28. Carlisle, 84.
29. Carlisle, 85.
30. P.P. Kanshina, trans., *Yorkshire Tragedy. Dielo* 20 (1887), 9–40.
31. N. Storozhenko, '[The Plays Ascribed to Shakespeare]', *Artist* 45 (1895), 14–19.
32. Quoted in Vladimir, Nemirovitch-Dantchenko, *My Life in Russian Theatre*, trans. John Cournos (London: Geoffrey Bles, 1937), 32.
33. I would like to express my appreciation to the late Professor Alexander Anikst who provided and translated this review and gave me a great deal of assistance in working with the Russian production. I would also like to thank the staff of the Research Institute on Russia and Eastern

European at the University of Illinois and the Soviet Section of the Library of Congress for assistance. I also received help in translating from my colleagues at the University of New Mexico, Professors Natasha Kolchevska and Byron Lindsay.

[34] P.P. Gnedich, *Kniga Zhizni: Vospominaniya [Book of Life: Reminiscences]* (Leningrad: Priboi, 1929), 224.

[35] A.R. Kugel, *Literaturnie Vospominaniia [Literary Reminiscences]* (Petrograd: Izdatelstvo 'Petrograd', 1923), 162–3.

[36] B.V. Varneke, *History of the Russian Theatre*, trans. Boris Brasol, rev. and ed. Belle Martin (New York: Macmillan, 1951), 390.

CHAPTER 18

The Magnetick Lady: Is the Unperformed Performable?

Peter Happé

To begin with I should like to raise some issues about dealing with the performance values of a text which has virtually no stage history. In the second part of this piece I shall try to read or identify some of the performance characteristics of *The Magnetick Lady*.

The absence of stage history may well be accidental: there are many dramatists who feel that their play did not have a fair run first time out. When Jonson wrote *The Magnetick Lady*, presumably in 1632, he had been confined by illness to his chamber for about four years and the Induction, making direct reference to his absence, shows that he was all too conscious of not being able to influence the performance by being in the theatre personally. What seems to have happened at the initial performance at the Blackfriars in November 1632 is that a number of Jonson's enemies, amongst whom we must number Inigo Jones, Nathaniel Butter and Alexander Gill, ridiculed what was going on. Moreover there was subsequently a legal problem in that the actors seem to have embroidered the dialogue with unacceptable oaths, drawing the attention of the Court of High Commission at Lambeth.[1] If we add to this a sense that Jonson had never been quite as successful with King Charles as he had been with his father, we get the impression that the odds were against the play. There is admittedly a mocking reference to Arminians and Precisians which might have attracted the attention of Archbishop Laud.[2] Perhaps Jonson contributed to his uncertain fortunes by his *Ode to Himself* which was printed with the first edition of *The New Inn* in 1631. This was two years after the first performance during which time the *Ode* had been widely circulated.[3] He wrote,

> Come, leave the loathèd stage,
>   And the more loathsome age,
> Where pride and impudence, in faction knit,
>   Usurp the chair of wit. (1–4)

There was also the contemporary view, sustained by Dryden's later comment about 'dotages', which held that Jonson's powers faded after 1616 though it is now very difficult to decide what this view is based upon.

It is apparent that none of these items has much to do with the quality of *The Magnetick Lady* or with the characteristics of the first performance. Even though any of them may have been sufficient to prevent further exposure to the public there is nothing in them to show that the play was so bad that no-one ever wanted to do it again. Subsequently because it was apparently not performed it has lacked that complex of attention which some of Jonson's other plays received, particularly after the Restoration when his reputation as a successful playwright, his connection with the King's Men, the publication of the Second and Third volumes of his *Works* in 1640, and his political position as one who had supported King Charles I might all have weighed in the new society. The handsome reprint of his *Works* for Herringman and others in 1692 is evidence of high esteem.[4] There is little doubt that the strength of Jonson's satire and his skill in using 'humours' characters fed into Restoration Comedy. That this play did not then take root is hard indeed to explain, but I think this failure is crucial in accounting for its later obscurity. It meant that no performance culture was evolved around the play, and that its dramatic or theatrical qualities were never explored by actors and directors, as well as by reviewers or indeed by scholars. Because the play was not performed and its values not revealed it inevitably came to be seen as unsuccessful. The Jonsonian canon dominated by *Epicoene, Bartholomew Fair, The Alchemist* and *Volpone* developed without it.[5]

This is an unprepossessing scenario, but it cannot be doubted that the earning of public interest and acclaim is not an objective process. Plays need performance to reveal their true nature, even if the performance is somewhat questionable. *Hamlet on Ice* may tell us something about *Hamlet*, negatively or positively. The essence of the position seems to be that *The Magnetick Lady* lacked enthusiastic support at its inception, and very little has happened since to put this right. Indeed the position is such that few read the play, on the assumption that it is not up to much compared with plays more well known. It seems little use to suggest that true worth will out if no one reads the play, let alone brings it to performance. If one looks at the spate of books on Jonson in the last twenty years one finds that very few critics have sought to fit the play in with their theories, and this surely cannot be because it will not fit in somewhere.[6]

The recent RSC production of *The Devil is an Ass* brings out some of the issues mentioned here. Its stage history in some ways resembles that of *The Magnetick Lady* in that it disappeared into obscurity after its first few performances, perhaps because Jonson included some satirical thrusts not welcomed by someone with influence with King James. Jonson's remarks in *Conversations with Drummond* refer to unspecified intervention by him.[7] The production revealed extraordinary strength in the characterization, especially that of Fitzdottrel and Wittipol, and showed that many of the set pieces in the action such as the cloak scene, the wooing of Mistress Fitzdottrel at her window, and Wittipol's disguise as a voluble Spanish Lady who catalogues the extravagances of cosmetics and face painting were conceived with theatrical skill. Moreover the experience of the production as a whole yielded exactly that uncertainty about the nature of the Fitzdottrel marriage and Wittipol's assault upon it which is discernible in the text, and which exemplifies Jonson's almost Brechtian concern with the thought-provoking ambiguity of his exposition backed up by the whirlwind concatenation of events in Act 5.[8]

What seems to have happened to *The Magnetick Lady*, then, is that an accumulation of anecdote and circumstantial detail has prevented an adequate reading of the play. It must also be admitted that there must be dozens of other plays, some of them also by Jonson, in which the build up of such anecdotal detail has prevented them from becoming known and thought about. This is in line with George Parfitt's suggestion that in order to appreciate the theatrical qualities of *Poetaster* it is useful to ignore the fact that it was partly conceived as part of the so-called War of the Theatres.[9] In Jonson's case it seems that the success of *Volpone*, *The Alchemist* and latterly of *Bartholomew Fair* has stood in the way of an appreciation of his other works. It cannot be doubted, too, that however the historical circumstances noted above may have helped to form this reputation, our institutionalized teaching of certain plays, supported by the decisions of publishers, who are our servants or our masters, reinforces the prejudice. In saying this I want to sidestep the attractive idea that this process is primarily political by suggesting that the evolution of reputation seems far more arbitrary and inconsequential. If Jonson had not upset Inigo Jones over the title-page of *Love's Triumph through Callipolis* in 1630, things might have got off to a different start.[10]

So, finally, it seems that one has to overcome a dead weight of assumptions in arriving at a new performance. But on the other hand, perhaps we should cheer up and see this as an opportunity for a new encounter with an unread and unperformed play by a gifted and experienced playwright.

Most of what I should like to say about *The Magnetick Lady* can be derived from the play itself, but the nature of Jonson's dramatization in most of his plays leads inevitably to comparison since he uses cross-reference. This can be quite specific – here he mentions that in writing a 'humours' comedy he has *Every Man in His Humour* in mind and is closing or shutting up his circle (Induction, 99–106) – but we also find ourselves making our own comparisons. I think it would be untrue to Jonson's mode of playwriting therefore to leave out any reference to his other plays, even though my main purpose is to ask for a consideration *ab initio*, as it were, of this particular play in order to avoid its being overshadowed by the more famous earlier ones.

Underlying the play, it seems to me is Jonson's Janus-like approach to theatre. Putting this at its most extreme it could be said that he both loved and hated the art of theatre. The hatred is evidenced by his continuous pressure upon audiences to react in ways he wanted. His perception is undoubtedly that audiences demanded his closest attention, because if he did not see to them circumspectly they would take away from his plays things he did not intend. That they actually did this is the cause of much of his castigation and his expressed contempt for the 'loathèd stage'. Beyond this there is also his own concept of himself as a poet, and as such the utmost achievement is the printed page rather than the performance. Hence his meticulous attention, extending to the details of punctuation, spelling and italic type in the preparation of his printed *Works* in 1616 and in the abortive attempt at the *Second Volume* in 1630. However it is important not to see this as mere pedantry for it is a part of Jonson's concern with the authority of his texts. There is also the question of how far such detailed concern is actually a discrimination of difference. Jonson repeatedly, by these methods, draws attention to unlikely parallels.[11]

In deducing his love for the stage we can only proceed obliquely, using circumstantial evidence. This is primarily that he did spend so much of his life on plays – he acted, revised the work of others and collaborated, besides writing his own work. Moreover the very tendency already noted to bring the plays together by implicit and explicit cross-reference is an indication that what he wrote mattered to him very much. There is also the question of the skill in creating theatrical material which he must have been aware of, and which for a large part of his life he exploited repeatedly. But it would perhaps be unwise to attempt to polarize his attitudes to the stage: we must turn instead to the actualities of *The Magnetick Lady*. In doing so, in order to illustrate the theatrical nature of the play, I propose to consider structure and plot, the location of the play and some features of dialogue, scene and character.

The structure shows Jonson's close attention to the manipulation of his audience. He introduces a number of metatheatrical devices which sharpen the sense that this is a performance which follows clearly laid out purposes. Hence the framing device of the Induction and the inter-Act Choruses in which the two spectators, sent by 'the people', comment upon the author's intention and the way the play is developed. Mr Probee and Mr Damplay discuss with the Boy of the house – avowedly Jonson's proxy – the principles of construction deriving from classical theories as mediated through the education system by Donatus: the third form of Westminster School is specifically mentioned. There is emphasis more than once on the need to grasp the right thread of the narrative as well as a questioning of the undesirable process whereby the play might be seen too topically as an allegory for contemporary events. Needless to say Jonson has classical precedents for these, but the question of getting hold of the right thread is demonstrably important because of the way the pace of the plot is developed. The Boy says,

> For, I must tell you, not out of mine own dictamen but the author's, a good play is like a skein of silk: which, if you take by the right end, you may wind off, at pleasure on the bottom or card of your discourse in a tale or so, how you will: but if you light on the wrong end, you will pull all into a knot, or elf-lock, which nothing but the shears or a candle will undo or separate. (Induction, 138–44)

Jonson's exposition, through the Boy, of classical structure for comedy is more than a theoretical joke: it is clearly exemplified in the dramatic movements of the play. There is a marked contrast between the *protasis*, the opening of the play, and the *epitasis*, the making complex. In this the play shares a significant increase of complexity with other Jonson plays, such as *The Devil is an Ass* where the intrigue over the fate and destination of Fitzdottrel's ring has been a concern for one of the modern adapters. In *The Magnetick Lady* the initial exposition is a leisurely affair in which the suitors for the hand of Placentia, the heiress, are reviewed and characterized. In fact their arrivals and their descriptions by Compass, the manipulator and hero, follow a Chaucerian model, and once his view is established we see them again from the point of view of some of the women characters. In fact these sequences are really a procession of 'humours' which, according to Jonson's subtitle, it is the ultimate business of the play to 'reconcile'. The acceleration of the plot from Act 3 onwards depends upon a skilful interweaving of two lines of narrative. On the one hand Placentia is delivered of a child, as the audience is clearly shown, not least by the fact that the pretentious Dr Rut is egregiously and ridiculously wrong in failing to spot the pregnancy. It becomes a factor that this birth has to be concealed in order to sustain the issue of Placentia's marriage portion which is in the possession of her uncle.

But the second plot line is the revelation in Act 4, scene 4, a very effective *late* moment in the play, to the audience and to Compass, who is quick to seize upon the advantage of this knowledge, that Placentia was exchanged in her cradle by Mistress Polish, her true mother, for financial benefit with the real niece, Pleasance. This piece of information is carefully managed by Jonson so that the audience know it instantly, but some other characters are kept either in complete ignorance or at least in some doubt as to whether the exchange really did occur. Compass proceeds to manipulate the circumstances so that he marries Pleasance, the real heiress, while he frustrates Sir Moth Interest, the avaricious uncle who seeks to keep the portion for himself. But there is no doubt that the unfolding of these events is deliberately made hard to follow by Jonson, not only to the characters but also to the audience. The resolution is only achieved by a clever interaction of the two narrative elements whereby the search for the very real baby is made the means by which the cradle exchange a generation ago is acknowledged by all, and justice is done universally. It is significant that when Pleasance says she definitely held the baby in her arms and that it was alive, Compass comments 'I ha' the right thread now and I will keep it' (5.10.81). In this way Jonson forces the audience not to take things for granted and the unexpected turn of events before the catastrophe, characterized in neo-classical terms as the *catastasis*, is clearly meant to make the audience alert in order to catch hold of the right thread which we have seen is a declared intention in the Induction through the Boy.

The locations used in the play show how clearly Jonson envisaged a space for the intellectual interaction essential to his drama. He follows the precedent of classical comedy in making the action virtually independent of a particular stage set. There are actually three locations. One is the theatre itself, the Blackfriars, in which the framing dialogues take place. The fictional events occur in the street outside Lady Loadstone's house for the initial sequence, and the whole of the rest of the action occurs in an unspecified place within her house. Her house functions like the centralizing, concentrating locations of other plays such as Volpone's chamber, the Alchemist's shop and Bartholomew Fair itself. Within these fictional places the characteristics are exposed by their own follies.[12] Jonson's approach here has marked significance in that the effect of this rather simple localization is to foreground the dialogue itself and to make more urgent the intellectual process by which the audience follow the plot. In short it is in line with Jonson's preoccupation exhibited in his quarrel with Inigo Jones over the relative importance of spectacle and words in their masques. This quarrel was at its height during the period in which Jonson was writing this play.

In approaching the dialogue of this play I should like to look at the kinds of scene the play offers. There is, for example, very little in the way of monologue or soliloquy: just the briefest aside by Compass as he thinks how to make the most of his chance discovery about the child-changing. But much of the play is conversation, and a good deal of that is about the exposition of character. This occurs directly, so to speak when Compass gives a 'character' to Parson Palate in couplets and another to Doctor Rut in blank verse. He draws attention to the verse form in the dialogue, and acknowledges that the verses were written by 'a great clerk' called Ben Jonson (1.2.33–4). This strikes me as deliberately unrealistic speech in which Jonson is relying for its theatrical effect upon the skill and flair with which it is delivered: in this way the dialogue is also a contribution to the characterization of Compass, who as we have seen has a special function as a kind of congenial presenter and manipulator of the action. There is also here an example of the self-deprecating joke for Jonson's 'great' refers to his twenty stones. It is a technique he shares with the bashful Chaucer of *The Canterbury Tales*.[13]

On the other hand Jonson sets out at times to write dialogue in which a large number of characters participate on quasi-realistic terms so that the changes in emotion which accompany changes in circumstances and fortune are portrayed, and we find ourselves carried forward by the momentum of the speech. This can best be seen at the beginning of Act 3 in a sequence of short scenes. Offstage, dinner is being served in Lady Loadstone's house. In the first scene Needle welcomes Item, the apothecary, who comes with news for Rut who is seated within at the dinner table. He is encouraged to go in by Needle who gives a description of the assembled diners, but this is interrupted by a noise within and the panicky entrance of Pleasance who needs help for Placentia now frightened because weapons have been drawn at table. The entrance of Compass, seeking to calm down the enraged and indignant Ironside is marked in the text, in Jonson's classical mode, as a new scene, but the action is clearly continuous. It turns out that Ironside took offence because Sir Diaphanous Silkworm, a courtier, insisted on drinking his wine 'with three parts water', a proceeding so effeminate that the aggressive Ironside thrust a glass in his face. The dialogue reaches a higher pitch of excitement however when Placentia, overwhelmed by the shock at the dinner table, which, it turns out, brings on her labour, is carried over the stage by Dr Rut, Mistress Polish, Nurse Keep, Pleasance and Lady Loadstone accompanied by the following:

    Lady: Good Gossip, look to her.
    Polish: How do you, sweet charge?

> Keep: She's in a sweat.
> Polish: Ay, and a faint sweat, marry.
> Rut: Let her alone to Tim: he has directions.
> I'll hear your news, Tim Item, when you ha' done.
> Lady: Was ever such a guest brought to my table?
> Rut: These boisterous soldiers ha' no better breeding.
> Here Mr Compass comes. Where's your captain,
> Rudhudibras de Ironside?
> Compass: Gone out of doors.
> Lady: Would he had ne'er come in them, I may wish ... (2.3.4–12)

Even in this short passage of rapid exchanges from different points in the stage space, we can see glimpses of character in Rut's bossiness, and Lady Loadstone's tentative sense of propriety. The irony is that it is she who marries Ironside in the end.

This discussion of some of the varieties of dialogue also points to the versatility in the construction of individual scenes. For example the crisis noted above leads directly to a sequence in Act 3 concerning duelling. Diaphanous is so offended by Ironside's action that he decides to challenge Ironside; but he is so incompetent that Compass has to intervene to manage the situation. When Ironside proves much fiercer than is comfortable – Jonson was always interested in the stage possibilities of physical violence and rage – Compass has to intervene to stiffen up the challenge. His contribution however leads in several different directions. One is to reveal the lack of true valour in Diaphanous; another is to show how the crafty, court-based self-interest of Mr Bias, the 'politique', is unwilling to carry the challenge for fear of his political masters: 'I will not hazard my Lord's favour so ... I have to commend me / Nought but his Lordship's good opinion' (3.6.8–11).

We should put this exploitation of the frightened duellist motif alongside a variety of other types of scenes. There is Rut's duff diagnosis of Placentia's fainting fit in which he gives a learned disquisition on several kinds of 'tympanies' (swellings), except the correct one. Here Jonson is pursuing another satirical theme in his exposure of medical incompetence. He also pursues avarice in another kind of scene in which Sir Moth Interest, the greedy uncle, gives eight reasons to justify his view that the love of money is not the root of all evil – or at least as far as princes are concerned with whom it may be a positive benefit (2.6.41–101). In contrast to these two scenes where there is a sense that the verbal and rhetorical devices dominate the action we have the instant improvisation of Compass who moves events along at a breakneck pace in the second half of the play – first he orders the coach to go to the church and wait; then as his own marriage plan develops rapidly he has it brought back. He manages also to give an amorous hint or two to Pleasance on the way. This process is undoubtedly stepped up by Jonson's decision to follow the classical precedent of confining events of the plot to the extent of one (somewhat overcrowded) day.

The range of scenes is enhanced by Needle's performance of demonic possession in Act 5. Prompted by Item's desire to restore Rut's reputation by giving him something that he *can* cure, Item suggests that Needle pretend to have a fit in which he reveals hidden treasure in the garden. This takes in Sir Moth who ends up falling into the well and having to be pulled out by rope. This result of Item's scheme is reported from offstage, with much confusion. Jonson used a similar possession device for Fitzdottrel in *The Devil is an Ass*, but here it works successfully because it acts as a distraction as Sir Moth tries to evade paying up the marriage portion which is due on the recognition of the child-changing and the marriage of Compass and Pleasance. In short the plot management and the establishment of a variety of scene presentations are carefully integrated. One of the effects of this deliberate variation is that our sense of the artificiality of the events portrayed is enlarged. Though Jonson hardly had a comparable ideological programme, there is no doubt that like Brecht he was prepared to exploit and juxtapose different processes of engaging the audience. That in itself increases that ways the audience can be induced to enjoy what they see, provided that they are not tied to 'realism': but it also means that the performance can be used to point up the evaluation of the moral issues which are at the heart of Jonson's poetic art. Performance is thus a servant of his intentions, and the text of this play gives us plenty of material which is entertaining, depending upon acting skills, and yet modulated in different ways. As to the ideological aspect, *The Magnetick Lady* is rather reticent, though we know from the poetry that problems of support and patronage were important for Jonson at this time.[14]

In turning to character I should first note that the treatment of Mistress Polish, the mother of Placentia, works quite differently from the 'Chaucerian' character noted above. She is self-opinionated and over-solicitous, and when it suits her, shows an excessive complaisance to her betters. But her main characteristic is her garrulousness, extending to malapropisms. These are carefully pointed up by Rut who scorns them and by Compass who exploits them by deliberately misunderstanding. Such features come close to Jonson's fundamental interest in the purity of language, and it noticeable that this is demonstrated dynamically and not by description. Indeed the hyperactivity of language is an effective performance feature. Experience showed Jonson, and should tell us, that bristlingly complicated language works well on stage.

The characterization in general shows a similar distancing to that noted in the plot. We are not really invited here to enter the emotional lives of the characters. Intimacy with the audience is not about emotions but about moral judgements and about the theatrical intentions which are necessary to mould the plot and direct the argument. In the marriage of Compass and Pleasance there are a few hints which give us the developing courtship, but really no sense that Compass, who on the whole is one of Jonson's admirable so-called 'gallants', is really in love with Pleasance. The contrast with Wittipol in *The Devil is an Ass* is striking. There the gallant sets out to seduce Mrs Fitzdottrel, but when it comes to the point he is moved more by compassion than lust and sets about giving her practical help – through plotting which is not unlike the dénouement of *The Magnetick Lady* in its complexity. In general the play follows a discernible trend in Jonson's characterization: that characters like Compass may be very active and ingenious, but we are not exactly being asked to like them. Nevertheless the performance opportunities are enormous because such characters have immense power and authority over the audience.[15]

But if the characters are not given emotional depth their treatment in moral terms is purposeful. The follies of the professionals – the lawyer, the courtier, the doctor, the priest and the 'politique' – are ruthlessly exposed, and it is done, as I hope I have shown, using a variety of techniques. These humours characters exist only in terms of their professional postures and posturing. Hence it does not really matter if they are not punished. Indeed what happens to them at the end is not about retribution but exposure. Such an emphasis is in line with the ending of several other of his plays including *Volpone* and *The Devil is an Ass*. Giving the characters signifying names is a further elaboration of this. The central attraction of the play, noted in the Induction, is Lady Loadstone who draws characters around her. She is guided by Compass and is eventually married to (capped by) Ironside whom she trusts. Such metaphorical manipulation which is both verbal and performative is paralleled by a wealth of other detail such as the play on the child-changed girls' names, Pleasance/Placentia, and the exposure of humours as in the gluttonous Parson Palate. Virtually all the names in *The Magnetick Lady* carry a symbolic or metaphorical reference.

It is desirable that a performance of *The Magnetick Lady* take account of the non-realistic elements identified here. The text reveals, explicitly and implicitly, a very active consideration of how the structure and design of the play can operate to make of the audience 'true understanders'. In this way Jonson is firmly in line with the humanist blend of pleasure and instruction – an objective he always set himself, even at the risk of alienating the courtly audience and participants of the masques. But there is a creative uncertainty which is generated in performance, and the performance culture which has built up around a number of famous plays is a valuable resource. One specially interesting feature is that performance allows one to perceive the relative importance of different elements within a given play, and indeed it is a way of adjusting such emphases.

Notes

1. For Gill's verses see C.H. Herford and Percy and Evelyn Simpson, eds, *Ben Jonson*, vol. 11 (Oxford: Oxford University Press, 1925–53), 346–8, and for the enquiry, vol. 9, 253. Play references are to this edition.
2. Martin Butler, 'Ecclesiastical Censorship of Early Stuart Drama: The Case of Jonson's *The Magnetick Lady*', *Modern Philology* 89 (1992), 469–81.
3. Michael Hattaway, ed., Ben Jonson, *The New Inn* (Manchester: Manchester University Press, 1984), 8.
4. See W.W. Greg, *A Bibliography of the English Printed Drama to the Restoration*, vol. 3 (London: The Bibliographical Society, 1939–59), 1082–4.
5. R.G. Noyes, *Ben Jonson on the English Stage, 1660–1776* (New York: B. Blom, 1935). The Appendix shows that in addition to frequent performances of these plays at several London theatres, only *Catiline*, *Every Man in His Humour*, and *Every Man out of His Humour* were performed, and that but rarely, 319–33.
6. Exceptions to this may be found in general surveys of Jonson's work: Anne Barton, *Ben Jonson: Dramatist* (Cambridge: Cambridge University Press, 1984) and R.A. Cave, *Ben Jonson* (Basingstoke: Macmillan, 1991).
7. For this and the seventeenth-century echoes of the play, see my edition of *The Devil is an Ass* (Manchester: Manchester University Press, 1994), 3, 22–5.
8. See my 'Staging *The Devil is an Ass* in 1995', *Ben Jonson Journal* 2 (1995), 239–46 and my programme note for *Volpone*, Olivier Theatre (17 July 1995), 'This is called the Fox-Trap'.
9. George Parfitt, *Ben Jonson: Public Poet and Private Man* (London:, Dent, 1976), 137.
10. Herford and Simpson, vol. 7, 733.

[11] M. McCanles, *Jonsonian Discriminations: The Humanist Poet and the Praise of True Nobility* (Toronto: University of Toronto Press, 1992), 4–7.

[12] Judd Arnold, *A Grace Peculiar: Ben Jonson's Cavalier Heroes* (University Park, PA: Pennsylvania State University, 1972), 9. For discussion of a recent set for *The Alchemist* see my '*The Alchemist* and *Le Bourgeois Gentilhomme*: Folly and Theatrical Illusion', *Ben Jonson Journal* 4 (1997), 181–6.

[13] G.C. Thayer, *Ben Jonson: Studies in the Plays* (Norman, OK: University of Oklahoma Press, 1963), 235.

[14] R.C. Evans, *Ben Jonson and the Poetics of Patronage* (Lewisburg: Bucknell University Press, 1989), 248.

[15] For a feeling of unease over certain characters like Surly in *The Alchemist* see Parfitt, 141.

A Postscript

I am much indebted to Brian Woolland for getting in touch to tell me about his production of *The Magnetick Lady* at Reading University on 4–7 December 1996. Unaware that this had occurred, I warmly welcome his account which endorses much of what I have said here, and, as might have been anticipated, adds a number of things which I had not foreseen. I can only refer briefly to some of the points which have arisen, and do so with some temerity since I speak of the living production secondhand. As to the endorsements, it is worth noting that the director was entirely pleased by the pace which the play generated and by the variety of effects which it offered. He found that both the Choric framework and the opening sequence were effective in attracting the attention of the audience, and this in spite of the fact that on the page they may look rather wordy. Indeed one of the surprises was that both quickly established a comic tone as the audience found much to laugh at, especially in the discussion of characters in Act 1, and in the metatheatrical introduction of Ben Jonson himself into the dialogue. The use of a plain unlocated stage with drapes and only one chair enabled the action to develop and allowed a fluent interaction between episodes.

Perhaps of greater interest were some things I had not anticipated. The part of Polish turned out to be very strong, and he found some interesting and perfectly plausible links between this character and Compass on the one hand and the conventional Harlequin of the *commedia dell'arte*. In general much of the energy of the play seemed to be generated by the women characters, and he was especially interested by the very small number of lines spoken by Placentia, a silence which he developed in performance. He also found that various inconsistencies of character as well as the apparent tendency to shift the tone and the dramatic initiative were not a difficulty as many of the scenes had a dynamism of their own.

FEMALE ROLES

CHAPTER 19

'A Woman's generall: what should we feare?': Queen Margaret Thatcherized in Recent Productions of *3 Henry VI*

Randall Martin

Theatre historians often credit John Barton and Peter Halls's *The Wars of the Roses* (1963–4) with helping to define the modern performance values of the Royal Shakespeare Company. Perhaps the most important way it did so was to normalize the practice of relating Shakespeare's history plays to contemporary political issues. Taking up the Kottian imperative to make Shakespeare relevant and modern, Hall and Barton dismissed the stained-glass attitudes of traditional productions to reclaim the histories as forums for cultural debate – in their case the protest of an anti-paternalistic, nihilistically minded younger generation towards the political sclerosis and social malaise of post-war Britain, mingled with a paradoxical nostalgia for lost heroic authority. Hall and Barton likewise confirmed the practice of presenting the histories as cycles, so that patterns of action, theme and character could be seen to relate and evolve intricately, yet coherently, over the course of several plays. Dame Peggy Ashcroft's much-lauded performance as Margaret of Anjou was one of the main beneficiaries of this approach, since she appears in each play of the First Tetralogy. Reviewers praised her for rediscovering a 'new' tragic heroine and one of the great Shakespearean female roles because of her convincing growth in psychological complexity, emotional range and rhetorical power over the course of Hall and Barton's condensed and rewritten versions of *Henry VI* and *Richard III*. Moreover, realizing the full stage potential of Margaret's multi-play personality also encouraged a critical reappraisal of the First Tetralogy, with feminist scholars in particular bringing gender-specific analyses to bear on the women characters who participate in, and struggle against, the masculine power structures of their political worlds.[1] After Ashcroft's searching re-interpretation and the critical legacy it helped to inspire, there appeared to be no going back to the older stage tradition – what Lynda Boose has termed the 'dramatic Salic Law'[2] – in which

Margaret's role, like those of other women in the histories, was marginalized, and her story troped according to familiar stereotypes such as sexually and political dangerous foreigner, and hysterical crone.[3]

Given *The Wars of the Roses*'s opening-up of self-consciously modern social perspectives, it is surprising to discover how many productions of the *Henry VI* plays since 1963 have reverted in varying degrees to earlier presentational traditions by shrinking Margaret's part and diminishing her motives for action. The result has been to restrict the potential diversity of audience reactions to her role, as well as a failure to respect, let alone expand, modern spectators' awareness of Shakespeare's dual tendencies to anatomize and endorse patriarchal values, and of his characteristic probing of historical representation to reveal its mediation by specific cultural interests. The interpretive reversion signalled by these productions has also occurred despite the fact that every major professional British production of *Henry VI* since Hall and Barton, whether in condensed or full form, has achieved conspicuous commercial, and often critical, success.[4] Though the reputation of the *Henry VI* plays continues to remain relatively low in popular esteem and academic criticism, with questions of authorship, chronology and textual revision continuing to dominate scholars' attention at the expense of higher aesthetic regard, in the theatre these plays have successfully challenged older notions judging them to be callow drum and trumpet stuff. Stage productions since Hall and Barton have shown how different in conception and effect these plays are from Shakespeare's later histories, and that their differences, if properly understood as alternative dramatic modes, have the potential to pay dividends in terms of challenging players and audiences alike. Women actors have especially come to appreciate the greater expressive scope afforded them in the First as opposed to the Second Tetralogy, in which no roles exist comparable to those of Joan La Pucelle, Queen Elizabeth or Margaret of Anjou.

In this paper I wish to examine the ways in which five recent stage and television versions of *3 Henry VI* have represented Queen Margaret. The directors and productions are: Terry Hands, Royal Shakespeare Company (RSC) 1977, Jane Howell, BBC 1982, Adrian Noble, *The Plantagenets*, RSC 1988, Michael Bogdanov and Michael Pennington, *The Wars of the Roses*, English Shakespeare Company (ESC) 1986–9, and Katie Mitchell, RSC 1994.[5] The first of these was billed not only as an artistic riposte to Hall and Barton, since it claimed to present all three parts of *Henry VI* uncut, but also as a political response to the alleged pessimism of their interpretation. Yet in terms of text, as we shall see, Hands's script did not go unedited, at least as far as the role of Margaret was concerned. Jane Howell was also committed to presenting the cycle with minimal cuts and with women characters given the fullest possibilities for self-expression. But in her case the playful, neo-Brechtian BBC version better lives up to these intentions. By staging *3 Henry VI* on its own, Katie Mitchell wished to demonstrate the integrity and stage-worthiness of this particular play, and also to reveal its mature capacity for commenting on modern political parallels such as the civil-war agonies taking place in Bosnia and Rwanda. The other two productions, Noble 1988 and ESC 1986-9, used condensed scripts, and thus their changes in presenting Margaret occurred within a wider context of total reductions of about one third of each play. Even though each one's approach differed (the RSC's being more character-centred and politically reticent and the ESC's more ensemble-driven and ideologically combative), both productions remained aware of their debt to what 1963 had begun: Noble called Margaret's role 'A King Lear for women'[6] (even if his own Margaret, Penny Downie, was not allowed such tragic scope), while Bogdanov and Pennington recycled Hall and Barton's title as well as their anti-traditional approach.

Before we go further, we need briefly to take account of the overall context of Margaret's appearances and of the total number of lines cut by each production. Margaret appears in seven of Part Three's 28 scenes (1.1, 1.4, 2.2, 2.5, 3.3, 5.4, 5.5) and is referred to in nine more. In terms of lines cut, I have tabulated the numbers and percentages for each production we shall be considering, with the exception of Noble 1988 which was too freely adapted and rearranged to gauge (in practice, however, the extent of its abridgments approximated ESC's). The *first* column identifies the production, the *second* the total number of all lines cut (out of the Folio total of 2915), the *third* cuts to Margaret's lines, the *fourth* cuts to lines that refer to Margaret, and the *fifth* the percentages of the combined cuts *to and about Margaret* in relation to the *total*:

PRODUCTION	TOTAL cuts	MARGARET	about MARGARET	of TOTAL
Hands 1977	164 / 6%	56 / 34%	17 / 17%	44%
ESC	1058 / 36%	104 / 10%	123 / 11%	21%
BBC 1983	155 / 5%	12 / 7%	10 / 6%	14%
Mitchell 1994	503 / 17%	39 / 7%	50 / 10%	17%

It will be seen that although Hands 1977 cut relatively few lines overall, in keeping with its advertised intention of presenting the plays whole, Margaret's role bore a disproportionately high percentage of those that were cut. The loss of these lines was all the more significant given that Margaret ranks fifth in terms of total words spoken, behind Edward, Richard, Henry and Warwick. Within the context of their more extensive conflation and re-ordering, cuts to Margaret's role were also extensive in the ESC (and by extrapolation Noble's 1988) production. Mitchell 1994 was more equitable, while the BBC version made the fewest reductions in any category, with the opening speech in 1.1 discussed below representing the most prominent instance.

Overall these figures stand in relation to Hall and Barton's script, which in the *Henry VI Part Three* section of *Edward IV* cut 98 lines by Margaret and 69 about her (I shall say more about Hall and Barton's cuts a bit later).[7] But it also added 4.5 and 6 lines respectively. While this may seem numerically insignificant, these additions carried a disproportionate impact because of their strategic emphasis on Margaret's political vision, military leadership and personal courage. And in the opening scenes (26 and 30) of *Edward IV*, in which speeches written by Barton outweighed the Shakespearean material taken from acts 4 and 5 of *Henry VI Part Two*, Barton also provided Margaret with further invented lines highlighting her authoritative sense of command; for example,

> What needs this question? March to London straight,
> And make demand of these insulting peers
> That they dismiss their dangerous mercenaries.
> [to Henry] Which done, make study how to govern better;
> Turn you your holy books and hold the sway.
> To London, lords, with all expedient wing,
> And bid York bow to his lawful king. (Barton and Hall, 95)

I am focusing on *Henry VI Part Three* because it introduces a crucial new aspect of Margaret's characterization – her role as mother and parent – that stands apart from the sexually defined continuum of her roles as French maiden-princess in Part One, ambitious and sorrowful lover in Part Two, avenging she-wolf in Part Three. From the perspective of traditional social mores, defending Prince Edward's legal inheritance ought to re-position Margaret in a more approved light. She ought also to benefit from comparisons with the sons of York, who, whatever their other shortcomings, are usually admired for pride in the value of their paternal heritage, which in turn is seen partly to justify their factional ambitions. Yet because maternal power is conventionally viewed as incompatible with martial pursuits, and elsewhere in Shakespeare's histories is delimited by masculine authority anxious to make use only of its reproductive and dynastically legitimizing functions, this new role serves to undermine Margaret's emerging political leadership, to say nothing of her seizure of sovereignty in the wake of Henry's less-than-grand refusal. One of the notable successes of Ashcroft's 1963 performance was that she managed to convey a sense of these conflicting dimensions, even though *The Wars of the Roses* abbreviated *Henry VI* to two plays. As Barton explained, he wished to give greater 'humanity and background to [Margaret's] scolding' by clarifying the sublimation of her failed marriage to a weak and sexually unsatisfying husband in her public role as field commander while also conveying a deeper sense of her personal inner life.[8] The latter is most evident in the new maternal identity which Margaret declares forcefully in the opening scene of Part Three and draws strength from throughout the remainder of the play. It is this same intimate and maternal self, however, that the productions I am concerned with in this paper seemed reluctant to acknowledge or accommodate.

To outline the matter in more historical terms, as the English warrior queen who displaces King Henry, Margaret becomes stereotyped as an amazon. Renaissance authorities conventionally described amazons as either sexually voracious or chastely reclusive (sometimes both under alternating conditions). Their monstrous otherness was defined largely in sexual terms insofar as they deviated from a 'natural' maternal destiny, defied patriarchal control, and usurped the male privilege of acting rather than being acted upon. This is the way Holinshed and Hall habitually frame Margaret's political ambitions. One way in which Shakespeare wrests a degree of artistic independence from the chronicles, however, is to complicate this traditional equation by fashioning Margaret in Part Three as fierce amazon *and* aggrieved mother, as a woman who savagely repudiates her political marginalization *and* champions the dynastic rights of her child.

The apparent unwillingness of certain productions to recognize this hybrid role combining aggressive public leadership with feminine solicitude may be related to the fact that all but one dates from the 1980s and 90s, and that these tend to present Henry's queen in ways distinctly recalling another contemporary politician named Margaret. This seems to have created a ideological conflict of interest. For in terms of the media-constructed image of the Conservative prime minister, whenever unsympathetic journalists drew attention to her status as a mother, it was virtually always within the context of her dysfunctional family – crack-head Mark and drunken emasculated Dennis. As for her womanhood, if the modern Boadicea ever wept, they must have been crocodile tears. Of course, Mrs Thatcher herself contributed to this image of dysfunction with biologically confused pronouncements such as 'We are become a grandmother'. Moreover, owing to the opposition-minded politics of most English theatre companies in an era of government funding cuts, stage allusions to Mrs Thatcher were universally negative. Thus the cultural domination of a bellicose amazonian PM who dismissed the social value of all the arts seems to have made it difficult for English theatre companies to imagine presenting Shakespeare's warrior queen with any convincing degree of integrity as a mother, or even a woman. Seduced by the opportunity to stage political satire, they consciously or unconsciously suppressed the maternal authenticity and political activism by which Shakespeare dignifies his Iron of Naples, since such qualities might inadvertently disturb the prevailing Spitting Image of the modern Iron Lady. One has to go back to pre-Thatcher Peggy Ashcroft for clear evidence of this composite portrait in Part Three or its equivalent, or (albeit to a lesser degree) to Katie Mitchell's post-Thatcher stand-alone production in 1994.

The evidence for these politically inscribed performances lies partly in the responses of spectators and reviewers, the anticipation of whose gender and political preconceptions undoubtedly worked to shape the ideological inflections of those same performances from the very beginning.[9] Their presentational decisions are also materially traceable, however, to the reductions in Margaret's role indicated by documented cuts and alterations to the theatrical scripts. There is also the impact on her full role in Part Three resulting from condensing *Henry VI* into two plays in the case of the ESC and 1988 RSC productions. I shall therefore consider a number of Margaret's speeches cut or abridged by virtually all these productions. These passages exemplify a variety of actions and responses related to Margaret's multiple selves and evolving subjectivity, but above all they bear on her heroically oriented role as militant mother. While Shakespeare's texts reveal Margaret expanding the dramatic frontiers of conventional female agency, as Ashcroft's performance in 1963 demonstrated so strikingly, the changes made by these later productions tended overall to reduce her transgressive hybridity.

Whereas the first two Parts of *Henry VI* portray Margaret as maid, newly-married consort and adulterous lover, and therefore regard her political interventions chiefly through the lens of illicit and subversive sexuality, Part Three shows her growing into the new role of 'invincible and ruthless mother'[10] protecting her child's personal safety and upholding his lineal inheritance. Margaret discovers a new sanctified outrage in this merging of domestic and political imperatives, impelled by the failure of Henry to defend Prince Edward's rights. This sets her apart from the play's other royal consort, Lady Grey, who refuses to risk her personal reputation for the sake of her children's birthright when propositioned by Edward in 3.2. Yet like Portia in *The Merchant of Venice*, Margaret seeks to raise her moral authority by embracing marital celibacy, a traditional prerequisite for heroic action (*Merchant* 3.3.56–7, *3 Henry VI* 1.1.247–8). Moreover, whereas in Part Two her relationship with Suffolk belies her professed loyalty to Henry, and perhaps neutralizes an audience's sympathy, in Part Three her angry protests gain legitimacy because virtually all social obligations and public protocols have been shattered, and defending family bonds becomes universally urgent.[11] Margaret's protective reactions and the primacy of kinship relations are also normatively validated by Shakespeare's recurring verbal images drawn from the animal world. Thus in 1.1 immediately following King Henry's disinheritance of Prince Edward his son, Margaret enters to deliver the first of two speeches which not only protest his submission to the Yorkists but also redefine her character along new lines:

> Who can be patient in such extremes?
> Ah, wretched man! Would I had died a maid
> And never seen thee, never borne thee son,
> Seeing thou hast proved so unnatural a father.
> Hath he deserved to lose his birthright thus?
> Hadst thou but loved him half so well as I,
> Or felt that pain which I did for him once,
> Or nourished him as I did with my blood,
> Thou wouldst have left thy dearest heart-blood there
> Rather than have made that savage duke thine heir
> And disinherited thine only son. (1.1.215–25)

This speech emphasizes the intense intimacy of the bond between mother and child as well as the fact that 'Edward has become *Margaret*'s son' rather than Henry's. He appears with his mother throughout the play and gradually begins to echo her warlike words and manner.[12] Of the five productions that concern us, only one kept this whole speech: Mitchell 1994. Foregrounding this dimension, combined with the fact that her production was not following a performance of Part Two and thus not explicitly linking Suffolk's death as a sexually related motive, shifted the rationale for Margaret's actions: 'Ruth Mitchell's powerful Margaret seem[s] a woman more sinned against than sinning, a mother who rightly wants to see her disinherited son reinstated but who instead [ultimately] sees him hacked down'.[13] Of the other productions, Hands 1977 cut three lines (221–3), as did Noble 1988 (215, 219, and 222), while BBC 1982 and ESC cut six lines (220–25). Though the effect of Hand's and Noble's cuts was more semantically neutral – like Hall and Barton, which selectively cut four lines (215, 217, 221, 224), they retained the central image but streamlined its expression – the effect of the BBC and the ESC productions, because of their more wholesale cutting, was to reduce or erase it. This devalued the social capital Margaret implies she has built up through pregnancy and childbirth, and cancelled the moral impetus for her new radicalized defiance, represented here as tantamount to violation of her physical integrity. The cuts made by both these productions, and to a lesser extent Hands 1977 and Noble 1988, reinforced traditional patriarchal ideology deeming maternal experience to be incompatible with political activism.

Thematically, Margaret's opening speech in 1.1 is related to her final lines in 5.5 when she reacts to the murder of her son:

> O Ned, sweet Ned, speak to thy mother, boy!
> Can'st thou not speak? Caesar shed no blood at all,
> Did not offend, nor were not worthy blame,
> If this foul deed were by to equal it:
> He was a man; this, in respect, a child;
> And men ne'er spend their fury on a child.
> What's worse than a murderer that I may name it?
> No, no, my heart will burst and if I speak –
> And I will speak that so my heart may burst.
> Butchers and villains, bloody cannibals,
> How sweet a plant you have untimely cropped!
> You have no children, butchers! If you had,
> The thought of them would have stirred up remorse;
> But if you ever chance to have a child
> Look in his youth to have him so cut off
> As, deathsman, you have rid this sweet young prince. (51–67)

In this case the only complete version was the BBC, as it moved towards anticipating her role as antique nemesis in *Richard III*. All other productions made cuts from Margaret's comparison to Caesar's assassination onwards: Hands 1977 five lines (53–7, 66), Noble 1988 nine lines (53–60, 67), ESC seven lines (in 53–67, 59–60), and Mitchell four lines (in 53–60). Except for the BBC, therefore, these productions not only muted Margaret's cries of grief and moral outrage at this climactic moment, but they also decoupled her identification with an historical event carrying powerful associations of epic tragedy and personal betrayal. Cutting the passage suggests that as a woman and mother she is ineligible to claim any affinity with Caesar's legacy because the bonds violated by his assassination were public and male, whereas her loss occurs within a domestic realm of merely private feelings and values. In short, she is denied the heroic magnitude to which her comparison to Caesar aspires, as well as full tragic validation through rhetorically heightened suffering, conditions which represent her final stand against being placed in 'the feminine subject position … she has so long rejected'.[14]

Similar kinds of reductions affect Margaret's appearances as leader of the Lancastrian forces. In the second major speech she makes towards the end of 1.1 after Prince Edward's disinheritance (230–56), all productions except Mitchell 1994 deleted lines referring to historical details which, although of minor significance to the plot, nonetheless convey the impression that she is well-informed about political developments taking place as the country's civil wars deepen. For example Hands 1977, ESC and Noble 1988 all cut the lines:

> Warwick is chancellor and the Lord of Calais,
> Stern Falconbridge commands the narrow seas,
> The Duke is made protector of the realm ... (240–42)

The absence of such small remarks suggests that Margaret acts less on good intelligence and rational calculation and more on instinct and passion, since all productions retain the comically frightened lines spoken by Exeter and Henry upon her entry, in which she conveys righteous indignation (or as the men would have it, shrewish rage) in her fierce expression and gestures:

> Exeter. Here comes the Queen, whose looks bewray her anger.
>   I'll steal away.
> Henry.   Exeter, so will I.
> Queen Margaret. Nay, go not from me. I will follow thee.
> (211–13)

Both ESC and Noble 1988 went on in this speech to cut a further eleven and three lines respectively, which further diminished Shakespeare's sense of Margaret's overbearing yet clear-sighted recognition of what needs to be done to reverse Lancastrian misfortunes. By contrast, in 1963 Hall and Barton did not remove a single line from this speech.

The results of these and succeeding cuts seemed to tell in performance. In the case of the Hands 1977 RSC production they led to a case of arrested character development. Most reviewers felt Helen Mirren's sexually driven Margaret, while intermittently thrilling, lacked 'conviction', 'nobility of mein' and 'emotional variety' in Part Three because she remained stuck in the mode established by Parts One and Two: what Irving Wardle called the 'fatal erotic approach' and B.A. Young 'the destructive female theme'.[15] When assessing these accounts we are now more aware of the possibility that the interpretation of Mirren's physical gestures, and especially the sexually defined reception of her performance, may have been affected by the gendered perceptions of her male reviewers (for example, Irving Wardle's observation that Mirren even played 'pleading for her own death [in 5.5] in the style of a bedroom invitation').[16] On the other hand as the diverse reactions to Peggy Ashcroft also suggested, the same reviews imply that Mirren's bodily expressions, through their affective presence in the theatre, functioned both to confirm and resist both the 'character' of Shakespeare's Margaret, constituted as a pre-existing discourse of critical, theatrical and social texts,[17] and the re-versioned figure represented by the abridged production-scripts we are considering. Nonetheless, while Mirren seemed to gain greater maturity and range by the time Hands's production transferred to the Aldwych in 1978, scenes such as the death of York in 1.4 suggested that frustrated sexual desire continued to animate her violence more than parental wrath or political survival, and that her savagery was a form of displaced revenge for her murdered lover Suffolk.

While this reduction of Margaret to *femme fatale* cannot be linked in 1977 to the presence of a Conservative government – although Mrs Thatcher had become Tory leader two years earlier and the Iron Lady image had already become popularized[18] – politically inspired caricature, operating together with textual cuts, was certainly visible in Michael Bogdanov and Michael Pennington's 1986–9 ESC productions. These were self-consciously post-Falklands radical Shakespeare. As Queen Margaret, June Watson's hairdo and manner unmistakably recalled her modern political namesake. Given this troping, it was not surprising that Watson seemed to subsume *both* erotic and maternal dimensions in a fierce, at times jubilant, drive to dominate. Her colder, harder Margaret was utterly free of self-doubt. In 1.4 Watson did not flinch through York's impassioned invective, expressed impatient contempt for Northumberland's weakened resolve, and at the end of the scene 'stabbed York in a business-like manner and continued on her way'.[19] In later scenes, she appeared rumpled in a Second World War uniform, bedizened in medals with her cap jauntily askew, and rhetorically stentorian, thereby conveying the kind of Churchillian simulacrum some people believed Mrs Thatcher was always trying to ape.

Penny Downie's performance in Noble's 1988 RSC production, while more varied than Mirren's or Watson's, nonetheless remained representationally polarized: ambitious seductress in Parts One and Two, psychotic warrior queen in Part Three.[20] Her moment of unhinging was Suffolk's death, which in this case gained prominence by coming at the end of the re-ordered first part of the two-play *Plantagenets*. As a 'Goneril of the Middle Ages',[21] Downey was magnificently cruel, even sadistic, but others felt she lacked imagination and inventiveness in *Edward IV* for finding other aspects of the role, instead remaining within the expressive compass of a 'cracked mind'. As we have seen, however, the varying limitations of all these performances cannot be attributed solely, nor perhaps even mainly, to the actors, but to the directors whose abridgements cut off the possibilities Shakespeare provides for suggesting more diverse and/or subtle motives for Margaret's actions.

Another change tending to undermine the heroic or tragic potential of Margaret's leadership occurs in Warwick's report of Lancastrian military preparations in 2.1. All versions except the BBC deleted the following lines testifying to her capacity for independent policy:

> For by my scouts I was advertised
> That [Margaret] was coming with a full intent
> To dash our late decree in parliament
> Touching King Henry's oath and your succession. (116–19)

ESC and Noble 1988 likewise cut the brief report brought by a messenger at the end of this scene:

> Warwick. How now? What news?
> Messenger. The Duke of Norfolk sends you word by me
>   The queen is coming with a puissant host
>   And craves your company for speedy counsel.
> Warwick. Why then it sorts. Brave warriors, let's away. (205–9)

These passages characterize Margaret as a virago, or masculine-spirited women. Because she internalizes a traditionally male sense of aggression, Margaret is open to charges of unwomanliness,[22] and this is how the male characters habitually attack her, most notably in 2.2 when the Yorkists' ferocious personal abuse succeeds momentarily in shaking her confidence ('Stay Edward'. / 'No wrangling woman' 175–6). But *3 Henry VI* does not stage Margaret as a virago simply to endorse the reductive stereotype but also to challenge it, thereby redrawing the received historical image. For while Hall and to a lesser extent Holinshed habitually use the word virago, or related terms such as amazon, to stress Margaret's transgressive behaviour, Shakespeare's full text suggests she appears both vicious and resilient. That Shakespeare's play managed to change historical perceptions in this regard is demonstrated by Thomas Heywood's *Exemplary Lives and Memorable Acts of Nine of the Most Worthy Women of the World* (1640), in which Margaret appears as one of the three Christian worthies. Heywood's account celebrates Margaret's magnanimity, military prowess and courageous defiance of Edward IV as virtues unconstrained by gender biases, perhaps harking back, as Eugene Waith suggests, to a more classical sense of heroic action operating beyond everyday moral or gender categories.[23] This is precisely the paradoxically ennobling dimension – inconsistent with the uniformly degenerate profile of a pathological she-devil – which these productions tended to diminish, especially when praise or grudging respect was taken from the mouths of Margaret's adversaries. In 2.6, for instance, all productions except Mitchell 1994 dropped

Edward's vivid report that she 'led calm Henry, though he were a king, / As doth a sail filled with a fretting gust, / Command an argosy to stem the waves' (234–6). A modern director may defend cutting such passages by arguing that they are part of the play's rhetorical amplification and merely reflect Elizabethan tastes for verbal ornament. But as these and other instances reveal, they also construct a polyvalent figure whose public behaviour is arguably justified in terms of diverse reactions to extreme challenges. Such cuts come as a particular surprise in Hands 1977 and BBC, both of which claimed to allow Shakespeare's plays to 'speak for themselves'. But clearly some characters were more privileged to speak than others.

The last passage representing Margaret as an inspirational military leader is the battlefield oration she delivers at the beginning of 5.4 before Tewkesbury. Her intervention has a notable impact because it marks her first reappearance since 3.3, during which time we are told she has independently led a 'great power' from France that now assumes cardinal importance because of Warwick's defeat and death at Barnet. Speaking in a genre conventionally associated with epic historical discourse, Margaret exhorts her men to action by allegorizing Lancastrian fortunes as a storm-battered but still courageously-manned ship (1–38). The galvanizing effect and transgendering implications of her words is immediately summed up by Prince Edward:

> Methinks a woman of this valiant spirit
> Should, if a coward heard her speak these words,
> Infuse his breast with magnanimity
> And make him, naked, foil a man-at-arms. (39–42)

In this case all productions except the BBC made extensive cuts to Margaret's speech. Hands 1977 cut 6 lines, Noble 14 lines, and ESC 17 lines. Even Mitchell 1994 cut 14 lines here. The last three productions, moreover, omitted passages stressing that Margaret is leading the Lancastrian forces not for personal glory but to uphold the legal rights of her husband and son, and as part of a collaborative national campaign:

> Yet lives our pilot still. Is't meet that he
> Should leave the helm and, like a fearful lad,
> With tearful eyes add water to the sea
> And give more strength to that which hath too much,
> Whiles, in his moan, the ship splits on the rock,
> Which industry and courage might have saved?
> Ah, what a shame, ah, what a fault were this. (6–12)

In the absence of these and other lines in this speech, Margaret's actions tend to appear more personally ambitious, a throwback to the anti-female characterization of Parts One and Two. Yet redefining this image is one of Part Three's crucial contributions to the tetralogy's fashioning of multiple selves for Margaret. Her motives are not purely self-seeking, though like everybody else except Henry they are personally vengeful. Without these Margaret is prevented from fully 'operating in terms of [Part Three's] different range of relationships and effects';[24] she remains frozen within an earlier, less complex profile. This refusal to recognize a change in Margaret's position in Part Three parallels the tendency of editors to view the relationship between the Folio text and *The True Tragedy of Richard Duke of York* as similar to that of Part Two and *The First Part of the Contention*, when in fact the nature of each pairing is unique and demands to be treated separately. Editors of *Henry VI*, who typically have been assigned the burden of preparing all three plays, have been reluctant to shift initial observations and textual assumptions by the time they reach Part Three, just as the stage productions we are examining seem hesitant to acknowledge differences to its depiction of Margaret. Perhaps this also explains why these same productions cut very little of her full-volume confrontation with York in 1.4: the 'tiger's heart wrapped in a woman's hide' colludes easily with popular perceptions of the modern Iron Lady, and 'naturally' confirms the preferred critical reading of a psycho-sexually damaged lover.

During Margaret's appearance in 3.3 at the French Court, Shakespeare's focus on the nexus of rhetorical and political initiative – one of the most fundamental relationships explored by the history plays – serves as another defining moment of her overall representation. Here Shakespeare draws together several themes from the chronicle accounts: Margaret as mother and queen, as informed and forceful negotiator in international politics, and as military commander. Again the version that made fewest cuts to the scene as a whole was the BBC, with no reduction in Margaret's part. But Hands 1977 cut 20 of her lines, ESC 28, Noble 1988 19, and Mitchell 1994 12. When Margaret asks Lewis for aid, she refers to specific political developments to support her case:

> And if thou fail us, all our hope is done.
> Scotland hath will to help, but cannot help.
> Our people and our peers are both misled,
> Our treasure seized, our soldiers put to flight,
> And (as thou seest) ourselves in heavy plight. (33–7)

By eliminating such details the basis of Margaret's appeal in the remaining lines shifts from informed practical argument – in traditional terms, male reasoning – to personalized but impotent complaint – a genre more often associated with female speakers, and exemplified by Queen Elizabeth's stoical passion in 4.4. While Margaret's emotional distress at this moment can be properly implied by the actor's performance when Shakespeare's lines are retained, it remains balanced by their factual content.

From a different perspective in the case of Mitchell 1994, which like Howell's BBC version did not cut this passage, the speech's capacity to Margaret's verbal authority was diminished by the fact that the opening 45 lines of dialogue between her and Lewis were spoken in French (using Victor Hugo's translation) during the first few months of the production. For an English-speaking audience this put Margaret at a rhetorical disadvantage with Warwick when he entered speaking English at line 44. (Comparable rhetorical disabling afflicts Katherine in *Henry V*.) By foregrounding Margaret's French origins, this staging reminded spectators of her continuing foreign status: that since Part Two she has been an unruly Frenchwoman meddling in English politics who has failed by Part Three to become naturalized. Even after Mitchell's production reverted to English, the actress playing Margaret spoke with a fairly strong French accent throughout the performance. In short, this verbal mannerism – reminiscent of but different from Peggy Ashcroft's less obtrusive and gradually diminishing French burr – worked against the text's representation of Margaret as a serious political player, and seemed to make her merely a vehicle for pathos, closer to stock Elizabethan dramatic types such as the lamenting Hecuba.

One final instance of the tendency of these productions to stress qualities corresponding with traditional female weaknesses occurred at lines 236–7, in a speech in which King Lewis addresses both Warwick and Margaret after all three have agreed to join forces against Edward:

> Warwick
> Thou and Oxford, with five thousand men,
> Shall cross the seas and bid false Edward battle;
> And as occasion serves, this noble queen
> And prince shall follow with a fresh supply. (234–7)

Lewis makes it clear that Warwick and Margaret are co-commanders, each leading separate forces. And this, as we have seen, corresponds with the action Shakespeare dramatizes in Act 5, when the one fights at Barnet and the other at Tewkesbury. Hands 1977, ESC, and Mitchell 1994 eliminated the lines in which Lewis refers to Margaret, thus creating the impression that Warwick is sole commander of the Lancastrian forces. By extension, therefore, when Margaret reappears in 5.4, she seems to have assumed command by default, or to be again strongly seized by personal ambition.

By retaining these lines, however, BBC and Noble 1988 preserved a greater sense that she is articulating shared motivations and displaying signs of an evolving inner self.

The several ways in which these productions narrowed Part Three's fully scripted spectrum represented a step backwards to a neo-chronicle portrayal of Margaret. This occurred in spite of fashionable Thatcherian (or in the case of Mitchell 1994, anti-war) updatings, which may have amounted to no more than what Alan Sinfield has called 'mannerisms of radical relevance'.[25] In a social context of increased political polarization, Shakespeare's ambivalences were perhaps judged to be irrelevant or unsound. Yet as I have tried to suggest, the cuts made by these productions worked against opening up Shakespeare's text to plural interpretation or wider cultural debate. Instead they tended to flatten the unruly amalgam of social and historical roles suggested by Shakespeare's text into gender and genre stereotypes.[26] And their cuts eliminated potentially affective or empowering moments of dramatic reversal or emotional contradiction which are arguably more truly subversive than spuriously liberating 'radical critique' founded on textual manipulation or erasure. To varying degrees Margaret tended to be tamed as a disruptive public figure, and Shakespeare recuperated for a regressive gender discourse. In the same way that the Yorks make Margaret a scapegoat for the civil war to divert attention away from their own culpabilities, the Thatcherizing of Margaret represented self-affirming revenge directed at Tory government policies. Yet it also led to an inadvertent rehabilitation of patriarchal values, while ironically betraying the actual impotence of the political left.[27] These paradoxes likewise seemed a telling instance of what H.R. Coursen has described as one of the dangers of making Shakespeare too much our contemporary: a loss of perspective from which representations of past moments can be seen in properly historicized contexts which serve to sharpen awareness of our own, often different, values and positions.[28]

Collectively, these productions also represented a loss of ground won by Ashcroft's 1963 performance and the critical revisionism it helped to inspire. I have been using Ashcroft as a touchstone for the multifaceted Margaret suggested by Shakespeare's full text. But of course Hall and Barton's production, even though many found it revelatory, was by no means definitive in this or any other regard since it too rewrote the original plays substantially – a move which Barton himself admitted was indefensible in principle.[29] If this reminds us of anything, it is that even when we feel we are getting close to the 'real' or 'authentic' Shakespeare, it is always a discursive representation of particular ideological and textual interventions. What I wish to measure these productions against, therefore, is not an idealized or transcendent interpretation of Margaret's role, but what might be called underachieved Shakespeare, materially traceable to lost verbal terrain and missed transgressive opportunities. In the performances which followed Ashcroft's, while there was ample display of Margaret's moral and mental deterioration, there was little scope to develop the uncomfortable brand of female integrity latent in many of excised lines discussed here, let alone any old-fashioned sense of tragic grandeur. While the latter dimension has undoubtedly become more difficult to capture within the context of post-Second World War interpretations of Shakespeare's histories and tragedies, and may even be deemed to be now properly absent, these productions raise questions about whether such readings can be sustained without a significant distortion of the destabilising directions in which Shakespeare takes Margaret in *Henry VI Part Three*.

Notes

[1] For example: Irene Dash, *Wooing, Wedding, and Power* (New York: Columbia Univ. Press, 1981), Ch. 7; Marilyn L. Williamson, '"When Men Are Rul'd by Women": Shakespeare's First Tetralogy', *Shakespeare Studies,* 19 (1987), 41–59; Robert Potter, 'The Rediscovery of Queen Margaret: "The Wars of the Roses", 1963', *New Theatre Quarterly*, 14 (1988), 105–19. Isabel Armstrong, 'Thatcher's Shakespeare?', *Textual Practice*, 3 (1989), 1–14; Phyllis Rackin, *Stages of History* (Ithaca: Cornell University Press, 1990); Jean E. Howard and Phyllis Rackin, *Engendering a Nation* (London and New York: Routledge, 1997), 20–30, 43–99.

[2] Privately to Sarah Lyons, 'Shakespeare's Margaret of Anjou: "Oure Queene Margarete to signifie"', unpublished MA dissertation, The Shakespeare Institute, University of Birmingham, 1990, 63, n. 60.

[3] The most important earlier productions of *Henry VI* were: Barry Jackson and Douglas Seale, Birmingham Repertory Theatre, 1951–3; Robert Atkins, The Old Vic, 1923; Frank Benson, Shakespeare Memorial Theatre, 1906; Richard Duke of York, Edmund Kean and J.H. Merivale, Drury Lane, 1817. The fullest discussion I am aware of is S.M. Kay, 'A Stage History of William Shakespeare's *Henry VI* Trilogy', unpublished MA dissertation, The Shakespeare Institute, University of Birmingham, 1980.

[4] Homer Swander, 'The Rediscovery of Henry VI', *Shakespeare Quarterly*, 29 (1978), 146–63; G.K. Hunter, 'The Royal Shakespeare Company Plays *Henry VI*', *Renaissance Drama*, 9 (1978), 91–108; Michael Bogdanov and Michael Pennington, *The English Shakespeare*

Company *The Story of 'The Wars of the Roses' 1986–1989* (London: Nick Hern Books, 1990); Lois Potter, 'Recycling the Early Histories: "The Wars of the Roses" and "The Plantagenets"', *Shakespeare Survey*, 43 (1991), 171–81; Robert Shaughnessy, *Representing Shakespeare: England, History, and the RSC* (New York and London: Harvester Wheatsheaf, 1994).

[5] The original promptbook scripts for all these productions, except the BBC, were inspected at The Theatre Museum Library, London. The BBC edition based upon the Alexander text was published in 1983 (London: British Broadcasting Corporation). Otherwise quotations are taken from *Henry VI Parts Two and Three*, eds Robert K. Turner and George Walton Williams (Baltimore: Penguin Books, 1967).

[6] Shaughnessy, 82.

[7] John Barton and Peter Hall, *The Wars of the Roses* (London: British Broadcasting Corporation, 1970).

[8] Barton and Hall, xviii–xix.

[9] Herbert Blau, 'Ideology and Performance', *Theatre Journal*, 35 (1983), 448.

[10] Peggy Ashcroft, '*King Henry VI Parts 1, 2 and 3*', *Introductions to Shakespeare*, ed. Charles Ede (London: Michael Joseph, 1977), 22.

[11] Edward I. Berry, *Patterns of Decay: Shakespeare's Early Histories* (Charlottesville: Univ. of Virginia Press, 1975), 53–74; Howard and Rackin, 84.

[12] Howard and Rackin, 85.

[13] Paul Taylor, *The Independent* (12 August 1994).

[14] Howard and Rackin, 97.

[15] *The Times* (13 July 1977); *Financial Times* (13 July 1977). Also John Barber, *The Daily Telegraph* (15 July 1977); Robert Cushman, *The Observer* (17 July 1977); Bernard Levin, *The Sunday Times* (17 July 1988).

[16] *The Times* (15 July 1977).

[17] Anthony B. Dawson, 'Performance and Participation: Desdemona, Foucault, and the Actor's Body', *Shakespeare, Theory, Performance*, ed. James C. Bulman (London and New York: Routledge, 1966), 29–45.

[18] Antonia Fraser, *Boadicea's Chariot The Warrior Queens* (London: Weidenfeld and Nicolson, 1988), 314–15.

[19] Elizabeth S.C. Brandow, 'History, Royal or English: A Study of the Royal Shakespeare Company's *The Plantagenets* and The English Shakespeare Company's *The Wars of the Roses*', unpublished MA dissertation, The Shakespeare Institute, University of Birmingham, 1989, 38.

[20] Allen Robertson, *Time Out* (26 August 1988); Christopher Edwards, *The Spectator* (5 November 1988).
[21] Paul Taylor, *The Independent* (24 August 1988). Also Michael Coveney, *Financial Times* (24 August 1988); Michael Ratcliffe, *The Observer* (30 October 1988). Michael Billington, alluding to the Thatcherian suggestiveness of Downie's performance, remarked that a 'ravening, unchecked ambition for power is a danger that is permanently relevant' (*The Guardian*, 24 August 1988).
[22] Dash, 207; Fraser, 7.
[23] Eugene M. Waith, 'Heywood's Women Worthies', *Concepts of the Hero in the Middle Ages and the Renaissance* (Albany: State University Press of New York, 1975), pp. 222–38; also Celeste Turner Wright, 'The Elizabethan Female Worthies', *Studies in Philology*, 43 (1946), 628–43.
[24] Hunter, 93.
[25] Alan Sinfield, 'Royal Shakespeare: Theatre and the Making of Ideology', *Political Shakespeare New Essays in Cultural Materialism*, eds Jonathan Dollimore and Alan Sinfield (Manchester: Manchester Univ. Press, 1985), 171.
[26] A point made by Kate McLuskie in 'Unruly women and dancing dogs: literature and history in renaissance drama', conference paper read at SCAENA: Shakespeare in Performance, Cambridge, 1997.
[27] Robert Shaughnessy made this observation during the SCAENA seminar at which an earlier version of this paper was presented.
[28] *Shakespeare in Production: Whose History?* (Athens: Ohio University Press, 1996), 136–71.
[29] Barton and Hall, xv.

CHAPTER 20

The Disappearing Queen: Looking for Isabel in *Henry V*

Diana E. Henderson

The French Queen Consort does not appear until Act 5 in Shakespeare's playtext of *Henry V*, and then she speaks less than thirty lines. Like the Duke of Burgundy, she arrives in time to participate in the peace accords designed to end the bloodshed produced by King Henry's campaign for the French throne, the war between England and France that constitutes the play's central action. Both the Queen's belatedness and brevity have no doubt contributed to the relative dearth of attention accorded her ambiguous remarks and dramatic function. Even critical discussions that focus on the play's gendered anxieties regarding the Salic law (the bar to inheritance through the female line that blocks Henry's claim to the French throne), or on the role of Princess Katherine, or the feminized representation of France, either ignore Queen Isabel or mention a few of her words in passing.[1] Nor have twentieth-century directors often been kinder. Why include a character who arrives so late and says so little?

Some influential contemporary productions do not. The many people whose knowledge of *Henry V* comes filtered through Kenneth Branagh's 1989 film quite literally cannot remember Isabel at all; following the precedent of the Royal Shakespeare Company's directors Terry Hands and Adrian Noble (the latter of whom directed the stage production starring Branagh which helped launch the idea of the film), Branagh removes the Queen completely. His screenplay cuts her first substantial speech and gives her final words, a prayer for peace, to no-one other than himself.[2] Branagh not only reenacts the English conquest by giving the French queen's words to the English king but thereby caps his film's systematic presentation of himself as a beneficent 'star of England', asserting his stature as actor/director by focusing relentlessly on Henry. The film tends to equate *Henry V* with Henry V, collapsing the play's multiple perspectives into a study of a single psyche or vantage. In this moment, as in his other conscious choices to reconceive the filmic technique and thematic emphases of his theatrical ancestor Laurence Olivier, Branagh outdoes the self-aggrandizing bravado of his Oedipal model.[3] Yet this victory comes at a cost: putting Isabel back in the picture clarifies Shakespeare's delicate balancing act at the end of *Henry V*.

Olivier's film at least retains the queen's role, though making her a remarkably pliant accomplice to Henry. In the final scene, Queen Isabel (Janet Burnell) follows the English king's instructions as willingly as an actress attending to her director. When he asks whether she will 'Go with the princes' to help settle the terms of the peace treaty, he simultaneously prompts her with a tiny nod of his head; the offered alternative, that she 'stay here with us' (5.2.91), is accompanied by an equally understated negative shake which she acknowledges. Thus Olivier creates a visual joke out of her (that is, his) decision to contribute 'a woman's voice' (5.2.93) to the state negotiations, a joke that confirms his control and domesticates her political boldness.

Yet like her fellow latecomer Burgundy, Queen Isabel does speak out, in the interests of conquered France and peace. Capturing this dimension of her role, and therefore more challenging to Henry's authority and charm, was the English Shakespeare Company's *Henry V* directed by Michael Bogdanov and released on videotape in 1990. Like the New York Shakespeare Festival's production in Central Park during the summer of 1996, the ESC had an actress (June Watson) double Mistress Quickly and Queen Isabel, calling greater attention in performance to that actress and thus to Isabel's role in the negotiations that temporarily end a state of war between France and England.[4] Having altered Shakespeare's text to include the Dauphin Louis in the final scene, Bogdanov makes Isabel's willingness to leave Princess Katherine with Henry into a provocation driving the French prince offstage in anger. After the wooing scene, when the Dauphin again disrupts the marital accord, Isabel repairs the awkwardness by using both speech and physical action to reunite an offended, sulking Henry with the princess.

But the performance that led me to reconsider Isabel's presence as a structurally powerful figure was the most unconventional of all, the Company of Women's 1994 all-female production. In it, a physically dominating African-American actress, Diane Beckett, doubled the parts of two suffering survivors, Pistol and the Queen. During the final scene, Beckett wore an African-influenced robe, evoking the fate of other colonized peoples. Her appearance reinforced this production's predominantly critical view of Henry. Clutching her fearful daughter even as she offered her in marriage to the callous conqueror, this Isabel embodied a counterimage of noble lamentation challenging Henry's crowning moment of imperial triumph.[5] Whether or not one endorsed the interpretation, one could hardly return to Branagh's film without noticing the Queen's absence. It is Isabel's potential to provide a different perspective on Henry's actions that is often erased by directors and scholars alike, in the process simplifying the gendered political dynamics of the play's conclusion.

As we shall see, the lines Shakespeare assigns to Isabel contain implicit challenges, with the potential to qualify the comedic conclusion towards which Henry and the play otherwise aspire. The extent to which productions acknowledge her importance often epitomizes or at least correlates with their treatment of gender and nationhood as complex issues throughout the play. My performance examples demonstrate the variety of ways in which Shakespeare's representation of Isabel has been adapted, sometimes to address subsequent history and other times to abet the personal or artistic agenda of the production's director. They also prompt analogous questions regarding Shakespeare's own representation of the queen: to what extent did the playwright alter his textual sources, why, and what is at stake historically in his inclusion of Isabel? While an earlier play, the *Famous Victories of Henry the Fifth* (1586) provided some material for Shakespeare's concluding act, such as Henry's 'Englishing' of the French princess Katherine into his 'Kate', Isabel did not appear there.[6] It was to the chronicle historians Hall and Holinshed rather than to the stage, then, that Shakespeare turned when deciding to reanimate the figure of the French queen. In so doing he changed and chose his material, not only condensing the events represented in Act 5 but also allowing two nearly antithetical interpretations of them.

Reading Shakespeare's text alongside its historical sources will highlight the play's uneasiness in resolving problems of gendered power, in ways prefiguring (and constituitive of) the tensions revealed by comparing contemporary performance of *Henry V* with the Elizabethan playscript. Such doubled reading confirms *Henry V* as a text involved in both ideological complication and simplification of the woman's part. That doubleness is too often discounted in subsequent performance and scholarly history. And if ever there were a queen to prompt discussion of doubleness and even duplicity, it is the figure here represented, variously known as Isabel, Isabella, Elizabeth or Isabeau de Bavière.[7]

In the first speech of Shakespeare's French queen, Isabella seems not so much to supplement the ceremonial welcome between King Henry of England and King Charles of France as to challenge it, refusing to ignore (as the men have just done in their greetings) the violent history that has led to the meeting:

> So happy be the issue, brother England,
> Of this good day and of this gracious meeting,

> As we are now glad to behold your eyes –
> Your eyes which hitherto have borne in them,
> Against the French that met them in their bent,
> The fatal balls of murdering basilisks.
> The venom of such looks we fairly hope
> Have lost their quality, and that this day
> Shall change all griefs and quarrels into love. (5.2.12–20)

Isabel's view of Henry's eyes prompts a swerve in the rhetoric away from polite formality to the language of war and mythology, culminating in the punning invocation of basilisks. Among the sixteenth-century meanings of 'basilisk', the first listed in the *OED* is the 'fabulous reptile' whose 'hissing drove away all other serpents' and whose 'breath, and even its look, was fatal'; Gary Taylor notes further that its eyes were believed to project rather than receive light.[8] By a common sixteenth-century transference, using the names of venomous reptiles as slang for ordnance, the word also came to signify a large cannon which threw shot of about 200 pounds weight – perhaps the sort imagined battering the walls of Harfleur in Act 3. Thus Isabel's recollection of the 'fatal balls of murdering basilisks' is a layered reminiscence of Henry's violent deeds and intent, in terms that extend his own figurative language from earlier in the play. Her speech confirms that Henry's threats have indeed transformed the Dauphin's gift of tennis balls into 'gunstones' to make mothers weep; moreover, that the sun always associated with this English king has risen, though it remains questionable whether his fatal look carries the sort of 'glory' that Henry had declared would 'dazzle all the eyes of France, / Yea strike the Dauphin blind to look on us' (1.2.278–9). The truly dazzled, Isabel reminds us, are the dead. Along with Burgundy's extended lamentation for a feminized, conquered French landscape, Isabel's lines expose the false dichotomy in Henry's initial speech, when he stated that 'France being ours we'll bend it to our awe, / Or break it all to pieces' (1.2.24–5). He has instead bent it precisely *by* breaking it, collapsing the primarily linguistic distinction between conquest and destruction.

The prominence or absence of Isabel's first speech correlates with the comparative emphasis several screen productions place upon Henry's opening lines and his general attitude towards the war: the greater Henry's internal ambivalence, the less need or opportunity for other characters to confront him. In his first scene, Branagh reinforces Henry's cognizance and concern about the risks to a more glorious idea of conquest by delivering the second half of the sentence cited above as if it were his private reservation. No wonder then that this director deflects attention from Burgundy's speech about France through a flashback series of

English faces (Henry's private losses) and entirely erases the figure and these words of Isabel. What matters in his film is not the material fate of female France so much as the cost to the conscience of the king. By contrast, in the often pedestrian Time-Life/BBC television production, David Gwillim begins by stating out loud the two seeming alternatives of bending or breaking France as he addresses an approving court. This choice, perhaps more consonant with the play's military tenor, is less overtly concerned with rendering Henry's actions palatable to a late twentieth-century audience sceptical about the glories of war. It also accords better with the historical accounts of Henry's remarkably brutal actions during the sieges of Harfleur and Rouen, as on other occasions during his French campaigns. Here too a primly haughty Isabel speaks out. Olivier's choices hover somewhere between. The metatheatricality of the opening scene, played as if at the Globe Theatre in 1600, makes Henry's oratorical flourish overtly performative; the concluding scenes begin to move back from the realism of Agincourt and a meditative Henry to a playful world, muting the seriousness of Isabel's criticism. Prefaced by her jabbing her daft husband to prompt his brief speech and followed by the visual comedy with Henry mentioned earlier, Olivier's Isabel speaks her harshest lines but is comically framed.

The French Queen's first speech borders on an overt challenge to Henry's actions and authority; the cutting of all or part of it in nineteenth-century stage productions celebrating the English king further reinforces this perception. Whereas John P. Kemble's 1806 edition gives the full speech (cutting her second speech instead), William Charles Macready's promptbook for the Covent Garden production of 1815, using Kemble's edition, crosses out the three lines most frankly recalling Henry's warfare ('Your eyes which hitherto have borne in them, / ... The fatal balls of murdering basilisks'). His was a powerful precedent: Charles Kean's 1859 production made the same cut. Additionally, Kean's desire to have his wife participate in his final revival as manager led him to make the Chorus into Clio, the Muse of History, further erasing the gendered associations of women with an effeminized, conquered France (whereas in Shakespeare's text, even Nell Quickly – the only English female in the play – dies of 'a malady of France' (5.1.76)). Other productions keep the basilisk speech but place it later in the sequence, substituting it for the text's 'post-wooing' lines of Isabel. Thus Charles Calvert's 1872–5 production split 5.2 into two parts surrounding the cudgelling of Pistol by Fluellen; the Queen's first speech now becomes her last, initiating a scene within the cathedral at which Katherine and Henry are about to wed. Her most challenging lines thus come after the treaty negotiations when the marital solution is a *fait accompli*, her words denuded of their potential to block or resist Henry's idea of a happy ending. Here too the producer's wife played the Chorus, this time as a rather lofty version of Rumor. Anthony Brennan observes that 'Women continued to play the Chorus in the 1920s and 1930s, Sybil Thorndike strutting about in a brisk performance'.[9] Again, the performance choices mute the gendered pattern associating England with victorious masculinity conquering an effeminate and female France.[10]

The issues raised by Isabel's first speech are all the more suggestive given the conventional gendering of fatal looks, dating back to Medusa's killing gaze.[11] In the first act, Henry had taken on the position of dazzling blinder; his assertion echoes Marlowe's *Tamburlaine*, where another underestimated young man transforms himself into an epic figure of military terror and verbal mastery. Katherine Eggert rightly associates Henry's self-presentation with the phallic power of England (29); yet it is also true that in Shakespeare's plays, the paralyzing gaze is often associated with women as 'anti-historians' (as Phyllis Rackin terms them), women who disrupt the male narrative of action.[12] Isabel's explicit naming of the basilisk and her attribution of that killing look to Henry inverts the dominant paradigm, exposing its gendering as reliant on the speaker's perspective and power.

In theorizing Shakespeare's women as anti-historians, Rackin draws on Laura Mulvey's application of Freud to discuss the dominant paradigms of the gaze in classic Hollywood cinema. Viewed in the context of such feminist readings of the filmic gaze, the taming of Isabel's own potentially disruptive presence in films of *Henry V* becomes all the more intriguing. Isabel complicates the conventional gendering of that film paradigm as well, in that her words (rather than her sight or image) carry the disruptive force: attributing the basilisk look to Henry, she exposes the location of the actual destroyer in historical narratives of war, the one who threatens the living bodies of the French. Because Isabel's words are resistant yet elegantly framed, echoing Henry though phrased more critically, she cannot easily be presented as monstrous nor dismissed as irrational.[13] Moreover, as a maternal yet potent female, the words cannot be decoded as sexual invitations or foreplay, nor do they encourage visual framing of her as an object of desire. Thus both her words and position defy the paradigm of the woman's part in classic Hollywood film. Perhaps this helps explain why she is so thoroughly domesticated by Olivier and erased by Branagh; certainly in both films the fetishized position of woman-as-image falls to Katherine.

Between her two major speeches, Isabel has two brief comments crucial to the political matters at hand. First she volunteers to join the treaty negotiations, observing: 'Haply a woman's voice may do some good / When articles too nicely urged be stood on'. She then sanctions Henry's request that Katherine stay to be wooed ('She hath good leave'). Although in Olivier's version the first comment may seem merely a pretext allowing the second, it signals both Isabella's unusual position of power and provides a throughline for her part, linking her dismay at Henry's destructiveness with her willingness to adopt him as her surrogate son: she wishes peace and an end to conflict above all, above sovereignty and nationhood. In this, she embodies one conventional female position as peacemaker, yet also challenges the men's power politics and the marginalization of her role within the emergent political domain of nation-states.[14]

Her participation here recalls the play's political as well as its military starting point: the (il)legitimacy of the Salic Law. Perhaps it is another jab at the gap between French rhetoric and practice, or just the neatest illustration of the importance of maternity in claiming the throne. Either way, having Isabel appear only in the scene of diplomacy endorsing Henry's claim to the French throne, after the English have 'proven' their claim on the battlefield, bookends the play's concern with the lawfulness of inheritance through the female line. As we shall see, the historical queen's role in legitimating Henry was even more remarkable than in Shakespeare's play; but even here, she is structurally crucial in validating Henry as one who does not simply batter the weaker nation/sex into submission. Indeed, in theory he is not only marrying the French princess but also upholding his grandfather Edward III's claim to inherit through his mother, an earlier French princess who married an English king. As Henry thus undoes the Salic Law's prohibition on such inheritance, the cooperation of the French females is symbolically essential. Were he resisted – that is, if Katherine and her mother were to continue seeing him as 'de *ennemi* of France', as the Dauphin surely does – Henry would only be one more male empowered by force (5.2.166). By replacing the Dauphin with his mother in the final reconciliation scene, Shakespeare achieves in the public domain what Henry's wooing accomplishes in the more intimate scene with Katherine: he enlists the females as collaborators with the charismatic Englishman, as if Henry were the chivalric champion of their rights, their means of access to sovereign power through acknowledgement of their reproductive power.

When she returns after Katherine and Henry's private interview, Isabel adopts a more conciliatory tone, befitting this meeting designed to ratify a peace treaty. She marks a shift from French grieving to the (desperate) hope that the marriage contained among the treaty's conditions will prevent further violence:

> God, the best maker of marriages,
> Combine your hearts in one, your realms in one.
> As man and wife, being two, are one in love,
> So be there 'twixt your kingdoms such a spousal
> That never may ill office or fell jealousy,
> Which troubles oft the bed of blessèd marriage,
> Thrust in between the paction of these kingdoms
> To make divorce of their incorporate league;
> That English may as French, French Englishmen,
> Receive each other, God speak this 'Amen'.
> ALL. Amen. (5.2.344–54)

Structurally, Isabel's prayer can contribute to a comedic, even utopian, sense of a happy ending, as if to endorse Henry's assertion that God fought for the English at Agincourt, that the spirit of Richard II and internal English dissension have been laid to rest by the King's rhetoric and military exploits, and that he and his 'Kate' can indeed create a crusader to unite western Europe, if not universalize Christendom. Of course, the epilogue will soon remind those not familiar with the basics of English history (or with the popular *Henry VI* plays Shakespeare had penned nearly a decade earlier) that the hopes expressed in this prayer will promptly come to nothing.

Moreover, close reading again reveals a negative turn within the Queen's rhetoric. Like the intrusion of the basilisks earlier, like the many fearful possibilities to be forestalled by the fairies' speeches at the conclusion of *A Midsummer Night's Dream*, nearly half of Isabel's prayer attempts to ward off evil: the jealousy, ill office, and consequent divorce that threaten to wreck this tenuous vision. God must indeed help if this marriage is to enclose France within England as neatly as does her penultimate line's chiasmus. As the discovered treason plot, thievery and verbal battles amongst the soldiers of various 'nations' fighting for Henry have attested, even 'England' is far from an easily 'incorporate[d] league'; Katherine's bawdy English lesson and Henry's quite brief excursus into another tongue comically recall the distances to be overcome – and at whose cost. It is of course the 'foreigner' who must eventually compromise or submit, not the Englishman.[15]

Thus an actress's emphasis in performing the Queen's second speech can legitimately range from ritual celebration to plaintiveness, from a happy merger of domestic and international relations to a recognition that each 'incorporate league' is vulnerable to all the ills that flesh is heir to. Those in the audience familiar with the history will know that Henry's own flesh dies soon after he produces an heir, and the Hundred Years War will eventually be won by the very Dauphin Charles whom Isabel is displacing through this alliance with the English monarch. The ESC's choice to keep the earlier Dauphin Louis alive and onstage until this speech reinforces the political significance and humiliation for France that the marriage constitutes and Isabel's prayer attempts to transcend; his angry exit prefigures the vexed history to come.[16] The Company of Women's emphasis on Henry's callousness and roughness in the prior 'wooing' scene adds a haunting quality to the Queen's desperate plea that violence will not trouble the marriage bed or the kingdoms; the ugliness associated with masculine power throughout shows no signs of abatement. But in most productions that allow the Queen her place and her lines, the dominant effect is still to create a moment of harmony and order, the mother's blessing providing an emotional and theoretical endorsement for what the English have already achieved.

Branagh's 'usurpation' of Isabella's final lines might seem a conscious sign of the play's own ironies in subduing the feminine, were it not that the previous wooing is so clearly played as romantic comedy. Moreover, his conclusion confirms Henry as having indeed come of age through his own suffering and sacrifice. Samuel Crowl observes: 'Henry's French expedition began with the conviction that he inherited his rights there by claiming from the female, and now he completes his multiple mergers by uttering his own dream of union and assimilation; Branagh's Henry and Kate are seen here not only as the makers of manners but as the creators of powerful political symbols as well'.[17] No doubt this aptly captures much of Branagh's intent, though it sidesteps even those subordinated gestures at complexity that the film's ending contains: Katherine's public muteness (Emma Thompson silently looking down, sombre and glassy-eyed as she becomes a symbol of France in the final pose) and the weary concessions and nearly tragic consciousness of Paul Scofield as the war-haunted, shamed French king. It also glosses over the play's crucial concern with the difference between 'claiming from' and removing or usurping power, pushing euphemism to the limits in seeing Henry as one who desires 'assimilation' through 'mergers'. For Henry has quite literally 'gotten' the girl and taken the woman's part as 'his own dream' without giving away a whit of his wit or masculine authority. The French Queen's erasure is complete.

The partial shift in tone between Isabel's first and second speeches may result not only from the structural demands of Shakespeare's formally comedic conclusion, but also from his merging of two historical meetings, a year apart. At the first in Meulan, Isabeau de Bavière led the French party in an attempt to negotiate a peace treaty with England. Those negotiations failed, whereas a year later at Troyes, deaths and factional fighting among the French shifted the balance of power and led to Henry's success. A look at these historical events reveals how much artistic craft was required to make *Henry V* end peacefully.

In fact, the historical situation adapted in Act 5 was far more contentious than the play represents, and Isabeau was a major participant in the wrangling as well as the peacemaking. What Shakespeare omits of her history reveals the extent of her threat to his form of gendered resolution, which requires what one might call her 'domestication' or 'pacification'. Gary Taylor notes in passing that 'the transformation of Isabel from the dissolute and treacherous figure of history into the moderate, gracious, dignified queen of 5.2 helps to summon up the social world of peace, love, and civilization which the play has until then excluded'.[18] While, as we have seen, interpretive choices may vary regarding Shakespeare's figure, many historians concur with Taylor's condemnation of the Queen. As in the case of the play's representation, though, we may be wary about such quick conclusions.

After Agincourt and a first round of diplomacy, there was stalemate and division among French for two years until, in Peter Saccio's words, 'Charles's queen, the self-indulgent, licentious, and flighty Isabel of Bavaria, altered the balance of affairs'.[19] Not only did she declare herself the regent for her mentally errant husband, but she aligned herself with Jean Sans Peur, Duke of Burgundy, in opposition to the Dauphin's party (the Armagnacs), and won the support of Paris. But Isabel did not simply up and leave the Armagnacs due to fickle giddiness, as this and other accounts imply. She had in fact been imprisoned, and robbed of her wealth through the agency of the Constable Armagnac and her son Charles, the Dauphin who succeeded Louis and Jean upon their deaths. The Armagnac party also had arranged the murder of her lover. Knowing her son's alliances, it becomes less surprising that it was Isabeau, along with Burgundy and without the King, who led her preferred child, the princess Katherine, to the meeting where Henry first kissed the princess. A year later, after the murder of Jean Sans Peur by the Armagnacs, it was Isabeau and the new Duke of Burgundy who initiated the Treaty of Troyes. There, Hall reports, Henry 'went to visit the King, the Queen, and the Lady Katherine ... where was a joyous meeting, honorable receiving and a loving embracing on both parties ...'.[20] More remarkable was the consequence for the Dauphin Charles: he was disinherited. '(Isabel herself declared him a bastard, borne by her to an unnamed lover.)'.[21] This scandalous renunciation provided the rationale for the treaty conditions making Henry the son of Charles and Isabel and the heir to France. Suddenly it was a wise Dauphin who knew his own father.

Shakespeare omits this most unmaternal – and, to the French, infamous – action by Isabeau.[22] His queen recalls the earlier Dauphin's jest when she mentions those 'fatal balls' that have 'mock[ed] mothers from their sons', yet her estrangement and mockery of her own sons is removed. Moreover, she is the only mother Shakespeare includes in his play, and her final speech blessing the marriage of her daughter emphasizes the importance of maternity in perpetuating a royal line. Her historical antecedent was far less benign. The chroniclers' Isabeau, in fact, more closely resembles those fearsome, wanton, warrior women who haunted Shakespeare's imagination in the *Henry VI* tetralogy, the earlier plays to which the epilogue of *Henry V* returns in sadness. By giving his Isabel two differently toned speeches before and after the wooing scene between Katherine and Henry, Shakespeare appears to finesse the problem of Henry's needing the endorsement of a woman who at Troyes became his official mother, yet whose actions challenged not only male prerogative in the public realm but also a son's faith in the maternal bond that undergirded the English assault on Salic law.

The more one explores the historical sources in relation to Shakespeare's choice to include Isabel, the murkier the relationships involving maternity and powerful women appear. I will only gesture at some of these briefly.[23] Isabel carries with her a subtext of fear of the female that extends beyond her own representation; she recalls by name the earlier queen Isabella (1292–1358), Edward II's wife and Edward III's mother, who was the historical source for Henry's claim to the French throne, a figure excised from earlier speeches in the play directly concerning that inheritance. As Alan Sinfield and Katherine Eggert have noted, Shakespeare's Archbishop of Canterbury – who seems to name everyone he possibly can when recounting the genealogy of the Salic law itself – does not mention her. Nor does any other character rousing Henry to remember his family line refer to that crucial French queen Isabel. This is all the more notable given that Hall's chronicle had the Archbishop assert the connection directly.

This inheritance through the female was always Henry's 'capital demand'; it was not Princess Katherine, as he disingenuously declares in Shakespeare's last act. When the French offered money and that princess, he rejected the offer, instead wanting the princess and the inheritance. But the maternal figure providing the basis for that inheritance is erased from Shakespeare's play, leaving only a (superficially) less daunting namesake. For theatregoers familiar with Marlowe's *Edward II*, one reason might be obvious: after suffering from Edward's neglect, that 'source Isabel' became Mortimer's lover and her husband's nemesis, as if to confirm that a potentially sinister wanton hid within even the most patient Griselda (this is starkly represented in Derek Jarman's film adaptation of *Edward II*. In Marlowe's play, Isabella's son Edward III sends her to the Tower, and Shakespeare's play which so lauds the memory of that Edward and his son the Black Prince as a mythic source for military conquest similarly banishes the elder Isabel from history. Nevertheless, by bringing a less fearsome version of a French queen consort named Isabel into his concluding scene, he suggests that the spectre is not entirely forgotten, though it may be thoroughly domesticated and marginalized.

One might also add to this list of royal Isabels Isabeau de Bavière's own daughter. Remembering her during Act 5 of *Henry V* would increase the audience's anxiety and scepticism, which Shakespeare's epilogue will arouse soon enough to temper the apparently comedic conclusion. For this Isabel had been the child-wife of Richard II: another instance of a French princess being used as a bargaining chip in English-French state relations, and another failure. Indeed, England's refusal to return her dower money after Richard's deposition and murder initiated a protracted dispute between the countries.

Still one more shadowy female informs the appearance of Shakespeare's Isabel; she is Joan of Navarre (1370?–1437), the other Queen mother to Henry. Reading the second tetralogy, one would neither suspect Henry IV of having a living wife nor Henry V of having a mother, even a stepmother. Yet such a woman not only lived but was the person left in power when Henry V began his French campaign. While Act 1, scene 2 of *Henry V* includes discussion of the kingdom's safety from Scottish invasion should Henry go abroad, it is again the Archbishop who counters such fears by citing the number of men left in England whose 'hardiness and policy' will defend them; he makes no mention of women. The chronicler Hall once more serves as a reminder that historical events transpired differently, and that Shakespeare knew it: 'the King ... leaving behind him for governor of the realm the Queen, his mother-in-law [i.e., stepmother], departed to the town of Southampton ...'[24] Queen Joan of Navarre was yet another powerful woman who attracted controversy and mistrust. After being suspected of treason she was replaced by the Duke of Bedford,[25] who later accused her of witchcraft and had her confined. Again, only obliquely does the play reflect on the historical problems involving the precarious political situation of queens – crucial because of their reproductive power and often through their agency as consorts or relatives; yet distrusted, feared and in France officially barred from sovereignty. In this instance, a foreign queen mother stands in while the potentially more threatening figure of a corrupted English queen mother is deleted. To have lost both one's parents, in Henry V's case, seems far from an act of carelessness.

Shakespeare's inclusion of a domesticated version of Isabel, then, can be read in two quite antithetical ways. She can be regarded as an addition that complicates the play's narrative trajectory toward subjugation of the female and France through her important role as a public negotiator and a frank commentator on Henry's triumph, carrying with her the historical traces of other powerful, even threatening women. Her eventual alliance with Henry dramatizes his acknowledgement of the legal importance of maternity in claims of sovereignty. Conversely she can be seen as a carefully tamed version of women's place in history demonstrating the shaping power of a masculine English voice, be it Henry's or Shakespeare's, and – to the extent we hear a voice onstage that can be called female at all – one that has been thoroughly coopted by the conqueror in the service of a peaceful rather than violent traffic in women. Isabel's earlier lines are crucial to the former view, whereas emphasis on Shakespeare's alternations from the chronicles and her second major speech tend to support the latter view, one more consistent with recent readings of women's place in the play as a whole. Either way, her participation is structurally crucial to the formally comedic resolution, and she provides further opportunities for complexity in performance.

Isabel ultimately confirms what Henry wants: a place for the maternal figure as an abettor of an English son's inheritance. Yet given the history of Henry VI's reign, Isabel's prayer that the royal union will bring peace resounds as a pathetic pipedream, even before the Epilogue confirms its failure to come true. And the Queen's very presence in a public scene of diplomacy challenges the gendered ideology she abets, as she tells Henry, 'Haply a woman's voice may do some good' (5.2.93). If one removes that voice, as many influential productions have, and most scholarship still does, the gendered complexity that Shakespeare only partially resurrected from the historical chronicles for the stage is lost once more, and the process of domestication in the service of empire-building – be the empire English, masculinist, or theatrical – becomes all too complete.

Notes

[1] Notable discussions of the woman's part in *Henry V* include Katherine Eggert, 'Nostalgia and the Not Yet Late Queen: Refusing Female Rule in *Henry V*', *ELH* 61.3 (1994), 523–50; Juliet Fleming, '*The French Garden*: An Introduction to Women's French', *ELH* 56 (1989), 19–51; Lisa Hopkins, 'Fluellen's Name', *Shakespeare Studies* 24 (1996), 148–55; Jean E. Howard and Phyllis Rackin, *Engendering a Nation: A Feminist Account of Shakespeare's English Histories* (New York:

Routledge, 1997); Laurie E. Maguire, '"Household Kates": Chez Petruchio, Percy and Plantagenet', in *Gloriana's Face: Women, Public and Private, in the English Renaissance*, eds S.P. Cerasano and Marion Wynne-Davies (Detroit: Wayne State University Press, 1992), 129–65; Karen Newman, *Fashioning Femininity and English Renaissance Drama* (Chicago: University of Chicago Press, 1991); Phyllis Rackin, *Stages of History: Shakespeare's English Chronicles* (Ithaca: Cornell University Press, 1990); Alan Sinfield, *Faultlines: Cultural Materialism and the Politics of Dissident Reading* (Berkeley: University California Press, 1992); and Lance Wilcox, 'Katherine of France as Victim and Bride', *Shakespeare Studies* 17 (1985), 61–76. Taylor briefly calls attention to some of the salient aspects of the queen's appearance; all line references refer to his edition of the play (Gary Taylor, ed., William Shakespeare *Henry V* (Oxford: Clarendon Press, 1982)). Other essential work on the play, without particular attention to Isabel, includes Joel B. Altman, '"Vile Participation": The Amplification of Violence in the Theatre of *Henry V*', *Shakespeare Quarterly* 42.1 (1991), 1–32; T.W. Craik, ed., William Shakespeare *King Henry V* (New York: Routledge, 1995); Peter S. Donaldson, 'Taking on Shakespeare: Kenneth Branagh's *Henry V*'. *Shakespeare Quarterly* 42.1 (1991), 60–71; Peter Erickson, *Patriarchal Structures in Shakespeare's Drama* (Berkeley: University of California Press, 1985); Barbara Hodgdon, *The End Crowns All: Closure and Contradiction in Shakespeare's History* (Princeton: Princeton University Press, 1991); Claire McEachern, '*Henry V* and the Paradox of the Body Politic', in *Materialist Shakespeare: A History*, ed. Ivo Kamps (New York: Verso, 1995), 292–319; and Christopher Pye, *The Regal Phantasm: Shakespeare and the Politics of Spectacle* (New York: Routledge, 1990).

2   Keneth Branagh, *Henry V by William Shakespeare: A Screen Adaptation by Kenneth Branagh* (London: Chatto and Windus, 1989) does not comment on this change in his published screenplay. Samuel Crowl, *Shakespeare Observed: Studies in Performance on Stage and Screen* (Athens: Ohio University Press, 1992), 173 and 190, acknowledging a debt to Eggert, notes that Isabel's part is frequently cut, the last speech 'often assigned to the king [of France] as his blessing'; this was true of the RSC's 1975 production (dir. Terry Hands) starring Alan Howard. The part was also cut from the 1989 Stratford Ontario production.

3   See Donaldson's nuanced comparison of Branagh's film with Olivier's; my reading of Isabel also supplements his sense of Olivier's greater ease in mastering the feminine/woman (less threatening than

the agonistic male), whereas Branagh shows more sensitivity for the defeated father. For a polemical reading of Branagh's film as a betrayal of the ideological challenge in Noble's production, see Chris Fitter, 'A Tale of Two Branaghs: *Henry V*, Ideology, and the Mekong Agincourt', in Ivo Kamps, ed., *Shakespeare Left and Right* (New York: Routledge, 1991), 259–75, who argues that, unlike Elizabethan apron staging, the film's framed rectangle and the modern proscenium stage 'invite "tyranny" of directorial control of meaning' (272). Scholars and practitioners in both media have challenged such monolithic formal arguments, and I wish to distinguish my remarks above from this formalist critique.

[4] The 1996 New York production (dir. Douglas Hughes) had Kathleen Chalfont in the double role, and also had the Dauphin stride off during the final negotiations. See below for more on the way the Dauphin's disruption reintroduces into Shakespeare's play an actual rupture between the historical Isabel and her son – though the Dauphin in question was Charles, not Louis.

[5] Diane Beckett also played Ely in the production (dir. Maureen Shea). While much of the Company's promotional material stresses the liberal feminist agenda of simply gaining access to more opportunities for playing Shakespeare and cultivating women's voices, this production went much further in its gendered critique of the masculine military 'heroism'.

[6] The *Famous Victories* (1586) may be the first English history play: see Seymour M. Pitcher, *The Case for Shakespeare's Authorship of 'The Famous Victories', with the complete text of the anonymous play* (New York: State University of New York, 1961) and Richard Helgerson, *Forms of Nationhood: The Elizabethan Writing of England* (Chicago: University of Chicago Press, 1992), 203. On this 'Englishing', see Newman and Fleming; Maguire rightly stresses the pattern of Shakespeare's use of the name 'Kate', though in this case there was the direct precedent of the *Famous Victories*. Hodgdon's work on how female spectators must 'play(K)ate' patriarchal strictures to enjoy watching *The Taming of the Shrew* seems relevant here, with an equally valid pun on the domestic(K)ation of the royal French women. Isabel does not appear in the 1600 'bad Quarto' of Shakespeare's play.

[7] Her name appears in the First Folio stage directions as Queen Isabel. I take advantage of her multiple naming to distinguish this Shakespearean character from the historical Isabeau.

[8] Taylor, 266, note to 5.2.17.

[9] Anthony Brennan, *Henry V* (New York: Twayne, 1992), xxiii.

10   By contrast, the presentation of dancing girls in the French camp in some nineteenth-century productions extended the association between France and the feminine (and 'Gallic looseness of morals', wrily notes Brennan, xxiv). Information on nineteenth-century productions is drawn from *Shakespeare and the Stage*, Series One: Prompt Books from the Folger Shakespeare Library (Washington, DC: Harvester Microform, 1985). Brennan notes that Lewis Waller, Bridges-Adams and Robert Atkins all used female Choruses during the first part of the twentieth century, though by the 1930s some dressed as men (see Brennan xix–xxiv). The 1996 New York production distributed the Chorus lines among many cast members, some of the richest passages going to female speakers; while the need to enrich the roles for actresses (especially in a play where they speak less than five per cent of the lines) often provides incentive, in these cases it is worth recognizing that they constitute a significant act of adaptation – comparable to the much-discussed shift from boy actors to actresses.

11   Craik's edition, which favours a positive reading of the King, has a single mention of Isabel here; noting these lines, he quickly concludes that she 'hopes that now quarrels are to be changed into love – a hope which he echoes' (63).

12   Eggert, 29 and see Rackin. Notable examples of such women include Margaret and La Pucelle in the *Henry VI* tetralogy.

13   Of course many (including Mulvey herself) have critiqued Mulvey's 1975 discussion of the male gaze. Nevertheless, the outlines of her argument remain a starting point for much work on the gaze and inform Rackin's work; each critic provides useful generalizations worth troubling through specific cases such as this.

14   Speaking in a more local sense about these lines as reminders that Henry made Katherine a 'capital demand', Gary Taylor reaches a similar conclusion about their general import; when cut, he remarks, it 'makes the wooing seem innocent of political overtones' (315). I am arguing that Isabel's lines also glance at the larger questions of gender and politics that structure the play as a whole, of which the 'wooing' is but one (crucial) manifestation.

15   On those scenes, see especially Maguire, Fleming and Newman. Brennan reads the language scene more simply as 'charming', but goes on to note a parallelism between Henry's wooing and Pistol's stumbling French on the battlefield: 'Henry's struggle with French reminds us that England's gain and Pistol's individual profit have something in common – the demand for submission to irresistible mastery' (59–60, 91).

16 The Dauphin Louis' death provides the obvious explanation for his absence from Shakespeare's treaty scene – although the Branagh film and the ESC and 1996 New York productions all allow him extratextual and anachronistic life until the end. See Rackin on the implications of dramatizing history. Here Shakespeare simultaneously resurrects the 'person' now dead as the 'star of England', yet in doing so only through an actor's impersonation makes recognition of the gaps between performance and history all the more poignant. The differences between the Chorus's laudatory comments and the events as represented provide further ground for doubt about the recoverability of the past (and for some interpreters even cynicism about the very notion of military heroism).

17 Crowl, 173.

18 Taylor, 32.

19 Peter Saccio, *Shakespeare's English Kings: History, Chronicle, and Drama* (New York: Oxford University Press, 1977), 85.

20 Quoted in Pitcher, 225.

21 Saccio, 87.

22 Space does not allow a full consideration here of Shakespeare's exact familiarity with these historical events, but the disinheritance of Charles was clearly known, as well the subsequent French villification of Isabeau as dissolute and treacherous. The French soon repudiated the Treaty of Troyes as a national shame. Isabeau even served rhetorically as a negative cause for the rise of Jeanne d'Arc: betrayed by its foreign-born, wanton queen – so the argument went – France required cleansing and salvation by a virginal Frenchwoman. Of course Shakespeare mocks this vision of 'La Pucelle' in his *Henry VI, Part I*.

23 I discuss these figures, as well as the historical evidence and accounts concerning Isabeau de Bavière, more fully in a longer essay based on this paper.

24 Hall, f. HV, xi, recto, quoted in Pitcher, 215.

25 Pitcher, 228; also see Raphael Holinshed, *Holinshed's Chronicles*, eds R.S. Wallace and Alma Hansen (Westport, Connecticut: Greenwood Press, 1978) [rpt of Clarendon Press edn, 1917], 1168b, 1198a.

Index

acting, early modern, 178–87
Adams, William, 131
Admiral's Men, 162
Agnew, Christophe, 163, 170
Alchemist, The, 306, 307
Aleksandrinskii Theatre, 299
All's Well that Ends Well, 206
Althusser, Louis, 127
Andreini, Giambattista, 181
antiquarianism, 142–3
Antony and Cleopatra, 23, 138
Armin, Robert, 193, 204, 207
Armstrong, Craig, 268
Arnold, Matthew, 137
Arraignment of Lewde, idle, froward, and unconstant women, The, 281–3
As You Like It, 110
Ashcroft, Peggy, 319, 324–5, 326, 329, 334–6

Bachmetev, Y.P., 299
Bakhtin, Mikhail, 163, 194
Balakrishnan, Sadanam, 83, 84
Bandmann, Maurice E., 56
Bandmann Company, 56
Bandmann-Palmer, Millicent, 123
Banks, 196–7
Bann, Stephen, 142–3
Barba, Eugenio, 73
Barber, C.L., 194
Barnam Vana (*Macbeth*), 74, 77–83, 85–6
Barrett, Wilson, 54
Barthes, Roland, 285
Bartholomew Fair, 306, 307
Barton, Anne, 170
Barton, John, 319–20, 323, 324–5, 335
Bassermann, Albert, 99
Baudelaire, Charles, 166
Baudrillard, Jean, 7–8, 17
Beckett, Diane, 340

Beier, A.L., 150
Bellow, Kyrle, 54
Bells, The, 202
Bengali theatres, 75
Benjamin, Walter, 164–5, 166
Benthall, Michael, 112, 116, 119
Berlin Staadstheater, 91–6, 100
Bernhardt, Sarah, 123
Bhanumati Chittavilas, 75
Bhavabutti's Uttar Ram Charitam, 75
Blackfriars, 162, 305
Bland, Harriet, 296–8, 300
Bloom, Claire, 112
Bloom, Leopold, 123
Bogdanov, Michael, 322–3, 326–34, 340
Borchert, Wolfgang, 105
Boston Theatre, 296–7
Boyd, Michael, 261–74
Bradbrook, Muriel, 191–2, 200
Branagh, Kenneth, 23, 31, 32, 110, 149, 156, 242, 247, 255, 339–40, 342, 344
Braudel, Fernand, 228
Brecht, Bertolt, 95, 96, 98, 103, 104–5, 132, 197
Bridewell, 150
British Broadcasting Corporation (BBC), 322–3, 327–8, 331–5, 343
British Museum, 143
Broken Heart, The, 261–74
Brook, Peter, 73, 86, 347
Brown, Ivor, 113
Brown, John Russell, 286–7
Brown-Potter, Mrs, 54
Bruce, Lenny, 197–8
Bruckner, Ferdinand, 97–8
Buddism, 44, 80
Bungei Kyokai (Literary Arts Association), 56–7, 64
Burckhardt, Jacob, 217, 225–6
Burgtheater, Vienna, 100
Burnell, Jane, 340

Burton, Richard, 112, 116, 119
Butler, Judith, 35–6
Butter, Nathaniel, 305
Buzacott, Martin, 194–5, 200

Calcutta Theatre, Bengal, 74–5
Calvert, Charles, 343
Canterbury Tales, The, 311
Cantona, Eric, 198
Carlisle, Carol, 297
Carlyle, Thomas, 140
carnival, 195, 205
carnivalesque, 3
Case is Altered, The, 172
Catholic Europe, 216–28
Caux, Robert, 124, 125
Caverley, Walter, 293
Cawley, Arthur, 294
Cecchini, Pier Maria, 180–1
Celebrated Eton Boy, The, 141
Chapel Children, 162, 170
Charles I, 305, 306
Charles II, 123
Chaucer, Geoffrey, 311
Chekhov, Anton, 57, 63
Chettle, Henry, 192
children's theatre, 122, 167
Chinese opera, 132
Christian humanist plays, 102–3, 105
Christian-Moslem opposition, 215–16, 220
Churchill, Winston, 97
clowns, 193–4, 203–4, 207
Cohen, Erik, 3, 10, 12
Cole, J.W., 143
Collinson, Patrick, 207
colonialism, 78
colonization, 73–5
Comedians, 197–8
Comédie Française, 57
Commedia dell'Arte, 177–90, 316
Commendation of Cockes and Cock-fighting, 202
Company of Women, 340, 347
Constantinople, capture of, 216–17, 228
Conversations with Drummond, 307
Cooke, Alexander, 130
Coriolan, 125
Coriolanus, 138
Coryate, Thomas, 178

Course of Lectures on Dramatic Art and Literature, A, 297–8
Covent Garden, 141, 343
Craig, Gordon, 129–30
Crauford, Russell, 54
cultural tourism, 3–20, 73
Cushman, Charlotte Saunders, 123
Cynthia's Revels, 162, 167–72
Cyprus, Turkish capture of, 221–4

Dalmatov, Vasilii Panteleimonovich, 298–300
Damon and Pythias, 60
Dartmoor village pantomime, 203
Davenant, William, 123, 255
Dawson, Anthony B., 127–30
decolonization, 76, 87
Dekker, Thomas, 166, 167
Dell'Arte Rappresentativa, 177
Derrida, Jacques, 35–6
Deutsches Theater, 91–2
Devereux, Robert, 196–7
Devil is an Ass, The, 306, 309, 313–14
Devil's General, The, 105
Die Rassen, 97–8
Dignam, Mark, 115
Disneyland, 8, 10–11, 12, 14
Doctor Faustus, 83
Doi, Shunyo, 62, 63
Don Carlos, 94
Downie, Penny, 330
Dryden, John, 306
Dublin Gate Theatre, 110
Düsseldorf Manifesto against Directorial Licence, 105

Edward II, 349–50
Edward IV, 324, 330
1 Edward IV, 167
Edwards, Gale, 275–91
Elizabeth I, 201, 205, 218–20, 225, 227
Elizabethan clowning, 193, 204
Elizabethan theatre, 77, 78–9, 113, 132, 161–76, 178, 204
Elsinore, 109–19
Elsinore, 121–35
Emery, Winifred, 242
Engel, Erich, 94–5
English Stage Company (ESC), 322–3, 326–34, 340, 347

Epicoene, 306
Essex, Earl of, 196–7
ethnicity, 212
Every Man in His Humour, 182–4, 308
Every Man Out of His Humour, 162, 167, 168, 170, 184–7
Ex Machina, 122, 129–30
Exemplary Lives and Memorable Acts of Nine of the Most Worthy Women of the World, 331
Eyre, Richard, 121

Famous Victories of Henry V, The, 195, 201–4, 341
fashion, 161–76
Fatal Extravagance, The, 295
Faucit, Helen, 298
Fehling, Jürgen, 92–6, 103
festivals, cultural, 4–6
Field, Nathan, 130
Fields, W.C., 203
Fillion, Carl, 124, 130, 132
First Part of the Contention, The, 333
flâneur, 164–9
fool, 193, 207
Fool's Revenge, The, 60
Ford, John, 261–74
Fortune, 167
Foucault, Michel, 127
1453 narrative, 217–28
Frye, Northrop, 206
Fugger News Letter, 279

Gade, Svend, 123
Gaity Theatre, Yokohama, 55, 57, 61–3
Gaity Theatres, 56
Garzoni, Tommaso, 178–9
Gauleiter, Hessian, 97
German theatre, 89–108
gender, 35–49 *passim*, 121–135 *passim*, 337–53 *passim*
Gielgud, John, 111–15, 118
Gill, Alexander, 305
Gillies, John, 213
Ginsberg, Ernst, 100
Gleichschaltung, 89
globalization, 7, 121
Globe (Shakespeare's), 113, 167, 204, 207, 294, 343
Globe (Wanamaker's), 9–17, 122

Gnedich, Petr Petrovich, 299–300
Godolphin, Francis, 295
Goebbels, Josef, 26, 90, 91–2, 93, 97, 99
Goffe, Robert, 130
Göring, Hermann, 91–2, 93, 99
Gorki, Maxim, 57, 64
Gothic revival, 140–42
Great Exhibition of 1851, 141
Greenaway, Peter, 26
Greenblatt, Stephen, 226–7
Griffiths, Trevor, 197
Groucho Marxists, 203
Gründgens, Gustaf, 91–2, 100–101, 103, 104–5, 110, 114
Guilpin, Everard, 165
Gull's Hornbook, 167
Gurr, Andrew, 13, 156
Guthrie, Tyrone, 4, 5, 111, 114, 115, 118
Gwillim, David, 343
Gymnasium Theatre, Kobe, 55

Hall, Edward, 325, 341, 349–50
Hall, Peter, 319–20, 323, 324
Halprin, Anna and Lawrence, 129
Hamlet, 23, 27, 28, 31, 57, 58, 59–60, 61–2, 63, 64, 109–19, 121–35, 242, 247, 306
Hamlet: The Drama of Vengeance, 123
Hands, Terry, 322–3, 327–34, 339
hannya mask, 44
Hartung, Gustav, 96–7
Harvey, Gabriel, 207, 247
Hawkes, Terence, 247
Hazlitt, C. Carew, 200
Hegt, M.J.B. Noordhoek, 55
Heinz, Wolfgang, 100
Henriad, 151
1 Henry IV, 99, 153, 298
2 Henry IV, 149–54
Henry V, 13, 14, 23, 32, 122, 138, 139, 149, 151–7, 334, 339–55
1 Henry VI, 324, 326, 329, 330, 333, 347
2 Henry VI, 324, 326, 327, 329, 330, 333, 347
3 Henry VI, 319–38, 347
Henry VIII, 218
Henry VIII, 139
Her Majesty's Theatre, Sydney, 59
Her Majesty's Opera House, Brisbane, 60

360 INDEX

heritage, 7–13, 17
Heywood, Thomas, 295, 331
Hill, Aaron, 295
Hilpert, Heinz, 91–2, 103, 104
Hindu Theatre, 75
Hinman, Charles, 244–5
Hinkel, Hans, 90–91
Hirschfeld, Kurt, 96–7, 100
Histriomastix, 168
Hitler, Adolph, 97, 99
Holinshed, Raphael, 325, 341
Holland, Peter, 269
Holloway Company, 54
Holy Alliance, 219–20, 222–3, 225, 228
Hopkins, Lisa, 262
Horwitz, Kurt, 100
Howell, Jane, 322–3, 327–8, 331–5
Hugo, Victor, 166
humour plays, 177–90
Hunt, Hugh, 111, 119
Hunter-Watts, Frediswyde, 56

Ibsen, Henrik, 56, 57, 63, 64
Ichikawa, Sadanji, 56–7
Importance of Being Earnest, The, 57
indigenization, 73–88
interculturalism, 73–88
Irving, Henry, 53, 202, 241
Isabeau de Bavière, 341, 347–51
Isabella, Edward II's wife, 349
Izzard, Eddie, 122

Jack Drum, 172
Jest-Book genre, 200
Jiyu Gekijo (Free Theatre), 57
Jacobi, Derek, 110
James I, 167–8, 220–22, 225, 307
Janet Waldorf Company, 56
Jarmen, Derek, 350
Jenks, Chris, 164–5
Jew of Malta, The, 215
Jigs, 193, 203, 207–8
Joan of Navarre, 350
Jones, Emrys, 221–3, 227
Jones, Inigo, 305, 307, 310
Jonson, Ben, 162–3, 177–90, 305–17; see also individual titles
Julius Caesar, 58, 60, 61, 75, 94–6, 99

Kabuki, 43, 44, 56, 63, 77, 130–31

Karanth, B.V., 78, 79
Karaoke Shakespeare, 16
Kashin, P.A., 298
Kathakali *Lear*, 83, 86
Kathakali *Othello*, 74, 77–8, 83–6
Kaut-Howson, Helena, 122
Kawakami, Otojiro, 64
Kean, Charles, 138–43, 297, 343
Kemble, John P., 343
Kempe, Will, 109, 193, 203, 204, 207
Kesavan, Kalamandalam, 83
Kind Heart's Dream, 192
King John, 99, 139
King Lear, 35–49, 83, 122
King's Men, 221, 293–4, 306
Kitamura, Tokoku, 62–3
Knapp, Alain, 129
Kolomin, A.P., 299
Korner, Fritz, 103, 104
Kronborg Castle, 109–19
Kugel, Aleksandr Rafailovich, 300
Kulturbund deutscher Juden (Cultural Association of German Jews), 90–1
Kurosawa, Akira, 35, 37–46, 80

Lamb, Charles, 64, 65, 141
Landestheater Darmstadt, 96
Langhoff, Wolfgang, 100
Last Judgement, The, 284, 289
Lavery, Bryony, 122
Law Against Lovers, The, 255
Lebedeff's Theatre, 75
Leicester, Earl of, 196
Leigh, Vivien, 111
Lensky, P.D., 299
Lepage, Robert, 121–35
Lepanto, battle of, 219–28
Lepanto, 221, 225
Laud, Archbishop, 305
Lessard, Jacques, 129
Lessing, Gotthold, 102
Levant Company, 225
Lincoln Inn Fields, 295
Lindtberg, 99, 100
Literary and Artistic Club Theatre, St Petersburg, 298–300
Looking for Richard, 23, 30–31
Loncraine, Richard, 17, 23
Love's Triumph through Callipolis, 307
Luhrmann, Baz, 17, 23, 24–6,

Lusty Juventus, 151
Lyceum Company, 53

Macbeth, 23, 58, 61, 62, 74, 77–83, 97, 139
MacCannell, Dean, 10, 13
Macready, William Charles, 298, 343
Magdelene College, Cambridge, 191–2
Magnetick Lady, The, 305–17
Mahabharat, 78, 81–2
Maid's Tragedy, The, 14
Man Outside, The, 105
Mann, Erika, 91
Markham, Mary, 285
Marlowe, Christopher, 344, 349–50
Marprelate Tracts, 207–8
Marriott, Alice, 123
Marston, John, 168, 170, 172
Marx, Karl, 163, 164
Marx Brothers, 203
Measure for Measure, 27, 97, 104, 255–6
Mehmet III, 218
Merchant of Venice, The, 57, 58, 61–2, 75, 138, 326
Merleau-Ponty, Maurice, 127–8
Merry Wives of Windsor, The, 151
Middleton, Thomas, 154, 294
Midsummer Night's Dream, A, 23, 31–2, 91, 121, 125, 138, 140, 346
Mid-Victorian Stage, 137–45
Midwinter's Tale, A, 23, 27–8
Miln, George Crichton, 53, 58–65
Miln, Louise Jordan, 61
Miln Company, 53–72
Minakuchi, Biyo, 62, 63
Minetti, Bernhard, 93, 95
Mirren, Helen, 329–30
Mitchell, Joseph, 295
Mitchell, Katie, 322–3, 326–35
Mnouchkine, Ariane, 73, 86
modern (-ity, -ize, etc.), 3–4, 7, 10, 13, 15–17, 73
Morecambe, Eric 202–3
More Light, 122
Mother Courage, 98
Motley, 113, 115
Much Ado About Nothing, 23, 91, 99, 110, 241–60
  editors, 245–7, 249, 253, 255
  Folio text, 241

Quarto text, 241, 244–6, 255, 258
  productions listed, 257
Mulvey, Lara, 344
Murad III, 218
Mussolini, Benito, 99
Mystery of Hamlet, The, 123

Nagasaki Public Hall and Theatre, 55
Nashe, Thomas, 202–3, 207, 247
Nathan the Wise, 102
National Open-air Stage, Denmark, 109–10, 117
nationalism, British, 138, 140–42
Natyashastra, 85–6
Nazis, 26, 89–108
Needles and Opium, 124
Neumark, Hans, 92
New Inn, The, 305
New Playhouse, Bengal, 74
Newmark, John, 92
Nicoll, Allardyce, 295
Nielson, Asta, 123
Nietzsche, Friedrich, 137
Noble, Adrian, 23, 31–2, 322–3, 326–33, 335, 339
Noh, 36, 38, 43, 44, 131–2
Nunn, Trevor, 6, 23, 29–30

Ode to Himself, 305
Olivier, Laurence, 97, 111, 114, 118, 339–40, 343, 344–5
Old Vic Company, 109, 111–12, 115–17
On the Advantage and Disadvantage of History, 137
onnagata, 36
Opera House, Melbourne, 60
Orgel, Stephen, 130
Osanai, Kaoru, 56–7
Othello, 23, 58, 61, 74, 78, 83–6, 91, 99, 122–3, 211–38
Otto, Teo, 100
Ottoman Empire, 212, 216–20, 225
Oxford Playhouse, 110

Pacino, Al, 23, 30–31
Parker, Patricia, 226
Parsi theatre, 76
Parvati, 85
Paryla, Karl, 100
Pater, Walter, 139–40

patriarchy, 40–42, 45–6, 164, 283
Pavlov, Mrs, 299
Peking Opera, 122
Pennington, Michael, 322–3, 326–34
Pericles, 294
Perrucci, Andrea, 177–82
Phénoménologie de la Perception, 127–8
Philip II, 220, 227
Philocothonista, 295
Piscator, Erwin, 96, 103, 104–5
Pit, Barbican, 275–6, 279–81
Plantagenets, The, 322, 330
Playhouse, The, Bengal, 74
playhouses, first in London, 193
Plummer, Christopher, 110
Poel, William, 4, 17
Poetaster, 307
post-colonial cultures, 73–4
postmodern (-ism, -ity, etc.), 7, 13–15, 17, 24, 73
post-poststructuralist, 127
Princess's Theatre, London, 138–41
Prodigal, The, 295
Professor Mannheim, 97
Prospero's Books, 23, 26
Protestant England, 215–28
Puritans, 197
Puritanism, 193, 207–8

Queen's Men, 202

racial stereotypes, 213
Rackin, Phyllis, 344
Ramayana, 78, 81–2
Ran, 35, 37–46
Reading University, 316
Red Bull, 276, 290
Redgrave, Michael, 111–12, 115, 119
Reformation, 215, 217, 220
Reinhardt, Max, 4, 89, 91
Renaissance Theatre Company, 110, 243, 247, 249
Restoration Comedy, 306
Return from Parnasus, 161–2, 172
2 Return from Parnasus, 161–2
Rich, Penelope, 285
Richard II, 4, 122, 139–40, 142–3
Richard III, 17, 23, 58, 60, 61, 92–4, 99, 206, 253, 319, 328
Richelieu, 60

Rieser, Ferdinand, 96–101
Ring, Herman, Tom, 284, 289
Rise of the Common Player, The, 191
Romeo and Juliet, 17, 23–6, 58, 61, 64
Rose, 167
Rosencrantz and Guildenstern are Dead, 23, 28–9
Rotha, Wanda, 115
Rowell, Kenneth, 116
Royal National Theatre of Great Britain, 121
Royal Shakespeare Company (RSC), 5, 6, 8, 15, 122, 243, 246, 261–91, 306, 319–36, 339
Royal Theatre, Copenhagen, 109, 110
Ruskin, John, 144
rustic clown, 193–4
Rylance, Mark, 12–14, 122

Saba Tavern, 199
Said, Edward, 214–15
St John's College, Cambridge, 161
Salome, 56, 57
Sandbach Boys Comprehensive, 122
Sansrit drama, 75, 78
Savage, Lily, 122
scenari, 177
Schall, Henz, 123
Schechter, Joel, 203
Schlegel, Friedrich, 297–8
Schiller, Friedrich, 94
Scofield, Paul, 347
Scourge of Villainie, The, 170
Second Mrs Tanqueray, The, 56
serpent, 42–4
Seven Streams of the River Ota, The, 129
Shakespeare, William, *passim*; see also individual play titles
  apocrypha, 294, 297
  editors, 297–8
  festivals, 5–6, 76
  on film, 17, 23–49
  in Germany, 26, 89–108
  in India, 73–88
  in Japan, 35–49, 53–72
Shakespeare Birthplace, 11, 16
Shakespeare Memorial Theatre (SMT), 5
Shakespearean Medievalism, 137–45
Shaw, Fiona, 122
Shaw, George Bernard, 241–2, 256

Shepherd, Simon, 219
Shiva, 85
Shoemaker's Holiday, The, 167
Siddons, Sarah, 123
Singer, Kurt, 90
Sisson, C.J., 75–6, 77
Society of Antiquaries, 143
Spain, 217, 219, 221–3, 225
Spanish Armada, 223
Staatliches Schauspielhaus, Berlin, 110
Stauffenberg, Claus von, 94
Steckel, Leonhard, 99
Stewart, Patrick, 123
Stoppard, Tom, 23, 28–9
Storozhenko, N., 298
Stratford, Connecticut, 5
Stratford, Ontario, 4, 15
Stratford-upon-Avon, 5, 6, 16, 247, 249, 257
Sunbank, Mr, 199–200
Sussex, Earl of, 200
Suvorin, A., 299
Swetnam, Joseph, 281–3
Swetnam the Woman Hater, 283, 290
Swinburne, Charles Algernon, 294

Tadashi, Suzuki, 35, 36–7
Tagore, Prasanna Kumar, 75
Tale of Lear, The, 35, 36–7
Tales From Shakespeare, 64
Tamburlaine, 215, 344
Taming of the Shrew, The, 91, 99
Tarlton, Richard, 191–210
Tarlton's Jests, 192–3, 195–7, 199–201, 205, 206
Tarlton's jiz, 202–8
Taylor, Gary, 227, 342, 348
Teikoku Gekijo (Imperial Theatre), 62
Tempest, The, 23, 83, 247
Terry, Ellen, 241
Thacker, David, 27
Thatcher, Mrs, 325, 330
Theaterstadt Berlin, 89–96
Théâtre Repère, Quebec, 129
Thomson, Emma, 347
Thorndike, Sybil, 344
Threlfall, David, 110
Throne of Blood, The, 80
touring companies, 53–72
Troilus and Cressida, 99–100

Trösch, Robert, 100
True Tragedy of Richard Duke of York, The, 333
Tsubouchi, Shoyo, 53, 56–8, 60, 62–4
Turks, representations of, 213–14
Turkish expectations (of Jacobean audience), 211–38
Twelfth Night, 23, 29–30, 91, 206
Two Gentlemen of Verona, 13, 205

Varneke, B.V., 300
Vaughan, Virginia Mason, 214
Vice, 193–5
Victoria, Queen, 141
Victorian medievalism, 137–45
Victorian theatre, 137–45
Viertel, Berthold, 104
Vinci, 124
Vining, Edmund, 123
Volpone, 306, 307, 314

Wanamaker, Sam, 10–13, 15, 17
Wälterlin, Oskar, 97–101
War of the Theatres, 162, 168, 170, 307
Wars of the Roses, The (RSC), 319–20, 324–5
Wars of the Roses, The (ESC), 322
Warner, Deborah, 122
Watson, Jane, 330, 340
Weaver, Richard, 151
Webster, John, 275–91
Wedekind, Frank, 57
Weimann, Robert, 192–4, 201
West, Mae, 203
Westminster School, 309
White Devil, The, 275–91
Wilde, Oscar, 195
Wiles, David, 193–4, 203, 204
Wilhelm Tell, 94
Wilkie, Allan, 56, 62
Williams, Kenneth, 203
Winter's Tale, The, 32, 91, 138, 140
Wise, Ernie, 202
Wolf, Friedrich, 97–8
Womak, Peter, 163

Yakshagana *Macbeth*, 74, 77–83
Yorkshire Tragedy, A, 293–303
Young Vic, 122
Your Five Gallants, 154

Zaionchkovskaya, N.D., 298
Zuckmayer, Carl, 102, 105

Zurich Schauspielhaus, 96–101

For Product Safety Concerns and Information please contact our EU representative GPSR@taylorandfrancis.com
Taylor & Francis Verlag GmbH, Kaufingerstraße 24, 80331 München, Germany

www.ingramcontent.com/pod-product-compliance
Lightning Source LLC
Chambersburg PA
CBHW071232290426
44108CB00013B/1388